Predictive Analytics using R

ISBN 978-1-312-84101-7

Published by Lulu, Inc. All Rights Reserved

Acknowledgements

The author would like to thank colleagues Adam Wright, Adam Miller, Matt Santoni. Working with them over the past two years has validated the concepts presented herein.

A special thanks to Dr. Bob Simmonds, who mentored me as a senior operations research analyst.

Contents

xvii

Preface

This book is about predictive analytics. Yet, each chapter could easily be handled by an entire volume of its own. So one might think of this a survey of predictive models, both statistical and machine learning. We define predictive model as a statistical model or machine learning model used to predict future behavior based on past behavior.

This was a three year project that started just before I ventured away from DoD modeling and simulation. Hoping to transition to private industry, I began to look at way in which my modeling experience would be a good fit. I had taught statistical modeling and machine learning (e.g., neural networks) for years, but I had not applied these on the scale of "Big Data". I have now done so, many times over—often dealing with data sets containing 2000+ variables and 20 million observations (records).

In order to use this book, one should have a basic understanding of mathematical statistics (statistical inference, models, tests, etc.)—this is an advanced book. Some theoretical foundations are laid out (perhaps subtlety) but not proven, but references are provided for additional coverage. Every chapter culminates in an example using R. R is a free software environment for statistical computing and graphics. It compiles and runs on a wide variety of UNIX platforms, Windows and MacOS. To download R, please choose your preferred CRAN mirror at http://www.r-project.org/. An introduction to R is also available at http://cran.r-project.org/doc/manuals/r-release/R-intro.html.

The book is organized so that statistical models are presented first (hopefully in a logical order), followed by machine learning models, and then applications: uplift modeling and time series. One could use this a textbook with problem solving in R—but there are no "by-hand" exercises.

This book is self-published and print-on-demand. I do not use an editor in order to keep the retail cost near production cost. The best discount is provided by the publisher, Lulu.com. If you find errors as you read, please feel free to contact me at jeff@sumulation-educators.com.

More Books by the Author

Discrete Event Simulation using ExtendSim 8. Copyright © 2010 by Jeffrey S. Strickland. Lulu.com. ISBN 978-0-557-72821-3

Fundamentals of Combat Modeling. Copyright © 2010 by Jeffrey S. Strickland. Lulu.com. ISBN 978-1-257-00583-3

Missile Flight Simulation - Surface-to-Air Missiles. Copyright © 2010 by Jeffrey S. Strickland. Lulu.com. ISBN 978-0-557-88553-4

Systems Engineering Processes and Practice. Copyright © 2010 by Jeffrey S. Strickland. Lulu.com. ISBN 978-1-257-09273-4

Mathematical Modeling of Warfare and Combat Phenomenon. Copyright © 2011 by Jeffrey S. Strickland. Lulu.com. ISBN 978-1-4583-9255-8

Simulation Conceptual Modeling. Copyright © 2011 by Jeffrey S. Strickland. Lulu.com. ISBN 978-1-105-18162-7.

Men of Manhattan: Creators of the Nuclear Age. Copyright © 2011 by Jeffrey S. Strickland. Lulu.com. ISBN 978-1-257-76188-3

Quantum Phaith. Copyright © 2011 by Jeffrey S. Strickland. Lulu.com. ISBN 978-1-257-64561-9

Using Math to Defeat the Enemy: Combat Modeling for Simulation. Copyright © 2011 by Jeffrey S. Strickland. Lulu.com. 978-1-257-83225-5

Albert Einstein: "Nobody expected me to lay golden eggs". Copyright © 2011 by Jeffrey S. Strickland. Lulu.com. ISBN 978-1-257-86014-2.

Knights of the Cross. Copyright © 2012 by Jeffrey S. Strickland. Lulu.com. ISBN 978-1-105-35162-4.

Introduction to Crime Analysis and Mapping. Copyright © 2013 by Jeffrey S. Strickland. Lulu.com. ISBN 978-1-312-19311-6.

1. Predictive analytics

Predictive analytics—sometimes used synonymously with predictive modeling—encompasses a variety of statistical techniques from modeling, machine learning, and data mining that analyze current and historical facts to make predictions about future, or otherwise unknown, events (Nyce, 2007) (Eckerson, 2007).

In business, predictive models exploit patterns found in historical and transactional data to identify risks and opportunities. Models capture relationships among many factors to allow assessment of risk or potential associated with a particular set of conditions, guiding decision making for candidate transactions.

Predictive analytics is used in actuarial science (Conz, 2008), marketing (Fletcher, 2011), financial services (Korn, 2011), insurance, telecommunications (Barkin, 2011), retail (Das & Vidyashankar, 2006), travel (McDonald, 2010), healthcare (Stevenson, 2011), pharmaceuticals (McKay, 2009) and other fields.

One of the most well-known applications is credit scoring (Nyce, 2007), which is used throughout financial services. Scoring models process a customer's credit history, loan application, customer data, etc., in order to rank-order individuals by their likelihood of making future credit payments on time. A well-known example is the FICO® Score.

Where does predictive analytics lie in the world of business analytics?

Business Analytics

Business analytics (BA) refers to the skills, technologies, practices for continuous iterative exploration and investigation of past business performance to gain insight and drive business planning. Business analytics makes extensive use of statistical analysis, including descriptive and predictive modeling, and fact-based management to drive decision making. In recent years, prescriptive modeling has also taken a role in BA. It is therefore closely related to management science and operations research. Business analytics can answer questions like why is this happening, what if these trends continue, what will happen next (that is, predict), what is the best that can happen (that is, optimize).

Types

Business analytics is comprised of descriptive, predictive and prescriptive analytics, these are generally understood to be descriptive modeling, predictive modeling, and prescriptive modeling..

Descriptive analytics

Descriptive models quantify relationships in data in a way that is often used to classify customers or prospects into groups. Unlike predictive models that focus on predicting a single customer behavior (such as credit risk), descriptive models identify many different relationships between customers or products. Descriptive analytics provides simple summaries about the sample audience and about the observations that have been made. Such summaries may be either quantitative, i.e. summary statistics, or visual, i.e. simple-to-understand graphs. These summaries may either form the basis of the initial description of the data as part of a more extensive statistical analysis, or they may be sufficient in and of themselves for a particular investigation.

Predictive analytics

Predictive analytics encompasses a variety of statistical techniques from modeling, machine learning, and data mining that analyze current and historical facts to make predictions about future, or otherwise unknown, events. Predictive models are models of the relation between the specific performance of a unit in a sample and one or more known attributes or features of the unit. The objective of the model is to assess the likelihood that a similar unit in a different sample will exhibit the specific performance. This category encompasses models that are in many areas, such as marketing, where they seek out subtle data patterns to answer questions about customer performance, such as fraud detection models.

Prescriptive analytics

Prescriptive analytics not only anticipates what will happen and when it will happen, but also why it will happen. Further, prescriptive analytics suggests decision options on how to take advantage of a future opportunity or mitigate a future risk and shows the implication of each decision option. Prescriptive analytics can continually take in new data to re-predict and re-prescribe, thus automatically improving prediction accuracy and prescribing better decision options. Prescriptive analytics ingests hybrid data, a combination of structured (numbers, categories) and unstructured data (videos, images, sounds, texts), and business rules to predict what lies ahead and to prescribe how to take advantage of this predicted future without compromising other priorities

Applications

Although predictive analytics can be put to use in many applications, I list a few here:

- Analytical customer relationship management (CRM)
- Clinical decision support systems
- Collection analytics
- Cross-sell
- Customer retention
- Direct marketing
- Fraud detection
- Portfolio, product or economy-level prediction
- Risk management
- Underwriting

Definition

Predictive analytics is an area of data mining that deals with extracting information from data and using it to predict trends and behavior patterns. Often the unknown event of interest is in the future, but predictive analytics can be applied to any type of unknown whether it be in the past, present or future. For example, identifying suspects after a crime has been committed, or credit card fraud as it occurs (Strickland J. , 2013). The core of predictive analytics relies on capturing relationships between explanatory variables and the predicted variables from past occurrences, and exploiting them to predict the unknown outcome. It is important to note, however, that the accuracy and usability of results will depend greatly on the level of data analysis and the quality of assumptions.

Not Statistics

Predictive analytics uses statistical methods, but also machine learning algorithms, and heuristics. Though statistical methods are important, the Analytics professional cannot always follow the "rules of statistics to the letter." Instead, the analyst often implements what I call "modeler judgment". Unlike the statistician, the analytics professional—akin to the operations research analyst—must understand the system, business, or enterprise where the problem lies, and in the context of the business processes, rules, operating procedures, budget, and so on, make judgments about the analytical solution subject to various constraints. This requires a certain degree of creativity, and lends itself to being both a science and an art, For example, a pure statistical model, say a logistic regression, may determine that the response is explained by 30 independent variables with a significance of 0.05. However, the analytics professional knows that 10 of the variables cannot be used subject to legal constraints imposed for say a bank product. Moreover, the analytics modeler is aware that variables with many degrees of freedom can lead to overfitting the model. Thus, in their final analysis they develop a good model with 12 explanatory variables using modeler judgment. The regression got them near to a solution, and their intuition carried them to the end.

Types

Generally, the term predictive analytics is used to mean predictive modeling, "scoring" data with predictive models, and forecasting. However, people are increasingly using the term to refer to related analytical disciplines, such as descriptive modeling and decision modeling or optimization. These disciplines also involve rigorous data analysis, and are widely used in business for segmentation and decision making, but have different purposes and the statistical techniques underlying them vary.

Predictive models

Predictive models are models of the relation between the specific performance of a unit in a sample and one or more known attributes or features of the unit. The objective of the model is to assess the likelihood that a similar unit in a different sample will exhibit the specific performance. This category encompasses models that are in many areas, such as marketing, where they seek out subtle data patterns to answer questions about customer performance, such as fraud detection models. Predictive models often perform calculations during live transactions, for example, to evaluate the risk or opportunity of a given customer or transaction, in order to guide a decision. With advancements in computing speed, individual agent modeling systems have become capable of simulating human behavior or reactions to given stimuli or scenarios.

The available sample units with known attributes and known performances is referred to as the "training sample." The units in other sample, with known attributes but un-known performances, are referred to as "out of [training] sample" units. The out of sample bear no chronological relation to the training sample units. For example, the training sample may consists of literary attributes of writings by Victorian authors, with known attribution, and the out-of sample unit may be newly found writing with unknown authorship; a predictive model may aid the attribution of the unknown author. Another example is given by analysis of blood splatter in simulated crime scenes in which the out-of sample unit is the actual blood splatter pattern from a crime scene. The out of sample unit may be from the same time as the training units, from a previous time, or from a future time.

Descriptive models

Descriptive models quantify relationships in data in a way that is often used to classify customers or prospects into groups. Unlike predictive models that focus on predicting a single customer behavior (such as credit risk), descriptive models identify many different relationships between customers or products. Descriptive models do not rank-order customers by their likelihood of taking a particular action the way predictive models do. Instead, descriptive models can be used, for example, to categorize customers by their product preferences and life stage. Descriptive modeling tools can be utilized to develop further models that can simulate large number of individualized agents and make predictions.

Decision models

Decision models describe the relationship between all the elements of a decision—the known data (including results of predictive models), the decision, and the forecast results of the decision—in order to predict the results of decisions involving many variables. These models can be used in optimization, maximizing certain outcomes while minimizing others. Decision models are generally used to develop decision logic or a set of business rules that will produce the desired action for every customer or circumstance.

Applications

Although predictive analytics can be put to use in many applications, we outline a few examples where predictive analytics has shown positive impact in recent years.

Analytical customer relationship management (CRM)

Analytical Customer Relationship Management is a frequent commercial application of Predictive Analysis. Methods of predictive analysis are applied to customer data to pursue CRM objectives, which involve constructing a holistic view of the customer no matter where their information resides in the company or the department involved. CRM uses predictive analysis in applications for marketing campaigns, sales, and customer services to name a few. These tools are required in order for a company to posture and focus their efforts effectively across the breadth of their customer base. They must analyze and understand the products in demand or have the potential for high demand, predict customers' buying habits in order to promote relevant products at multiple touch points, and proactively identify and mitigate issues that have the potential to lose customers or reduce their ability to gain new ones. Analytical Customer Relationship Management can be applied throughout the customer lifecycle (acquisition, relationship growth, retention, and win-back). Several of the application areas described below (direct marketing, cross-sell, customer retention) are part of Customer Relationship Managements.

Clinical decision support systems

Experts use predictive analysis in health care primarily to determine which patients are at risk of developing certain conditions, like diabetes, asthma, heart disease, and other lifetime illnesses. Additionally, sophisticated clinical decision support systems incorporate predictive analytics to support medical decision making at the point of care. A working definition has been proposed by Robert Hayward of the Centre for Health Evidence: "Clinical Decision Support Systems link health observations with health knowledge to influence health choices by clinicians for improved health care." (Hayward, 2004)

Collection analytics

Every portfolio has a set of delinquent customers who do not make their payments on time. The financial institution has to undertake collection activities on these customers to recover the amounts due. A lot of collection resources are wasted on customers who are difficult or impossible to recover. Predictive analytics can help optimize the allocation of collection resources by identifying the most effective collection agencies, contact strategies, legal actions and other strategies to each customer, thus significantly increasing recovery at the same time reducing collection costs.

Cross-sell

Often corporate organizations collect and maintain abundant data (e.g. customer records, sale transactions) as exploiting hidden relationships in the data can provide a competitive advantage. For an organization that offers multiple products, predictive analytics can help analyze customers' spending, usage and other behavior, leading to efficient cross sales, or selling additional products to current customers. This directly leads to higher profitability per customer and stronger customer relationships.

Customer retention

With the number of competing services available, businesses need to focus efforts on maintaining continuous consumer satisfaction, rewarding consumer loyalty and minimizing customer attrition. Businesses tend to respond to customer attrition on a reactive basis, acting only after the customer has initiated the process to terminate service. At this stage, the chance of changing the customer's decision is almost impossible. Proper application of predictive analytics can lead to a more proactive retention strategy. By a frequent examination of a customer's past service usage, service performance, spending and other behavior patterns, predictive models can determine the likelihood of a customer terminating service sometime soon (Barkin, 2011). An intervention with lucrative offers can increase the chance of retaining the customer. Silent attrition, the behavior of a customer to slowly but steadily reduce usage, is another problem that many companies face. Predictive analytics can also predict this behavior, so that the company can take proper actions to increase customer activity.

Direct marketing

When marketing consumer products and services, there is the challenge of keeping up with competing products and consumer behavior. Apart from identifying prospects, predictive analytics can also help to identify

8

the most effective combination of product versions, marketing material, communication channels and timing that should be used to target a given consumer. The goal of predictive analytics is typically to lower the cost per order or cost per action.

Fraud detection

Fraud is a big problem for many businesses and can be of various types: inaccurate credit applications, fraudulent transactions (both offline and online), identity thefts and false insurance claims. These problems plague firms of all sizes in many industries. Some examples of likely victims are credit card issuers, insurance companies (Schiff, 2012), retail merchants, manufacturers, business-to-business suppliers and even services providers. A predictive model can help weed out the "bads" and reduce a business's exposure to fraud.

Predictive modeling can also be used to identify high-risk fraud candidates in business or the public sector. Mark Nigrini developed a risk-scoring method to identify audit targets. He describes the use of this approach to detect fraud in the franchisee sales reports of an international fast-food chain. Each location is scored using 10 predictors. The 10 scores are then weighted to give one final overall risk score for each location. The same scoring approach was also used to identify high-risk check kiting accounts, potentially fraudulent travel agents, and questionable vendors. A reasonably complex model was used to identify fraudulent monthly reports submitted by divisional controllers (Nigrini, 2011).

The Internal Revenue Service (IRS) of the United States also uses predictive analytics to mine tax returns and identify tax fraud (Schiff, 2012).

Recent advancements in technology have also introduced predictive behavior analysis for web fraud detection. This type of solution utilizes heuristics in order to study normal web user behavior and detect anomalies indicating fraud attempts.

9

Portfolio, product or economy-level prediction

Often the focus of analysis is not the consumer but the product, portfolio, firm, industry or even the economy. For example, a retailer might be interested in predicting store-level demand for inventory management purposes. Or the Federal Reserve Board might be interested in predicting the unemployment rate for the next year. These types of problems can be addressed by predictive analytics using time series techniques (see Chapter 18). They can also be addressed via machine learning approaches which transform the original time series into a feature vector space, where the learning algorithm finds patterns that have predictive power.

Risk management

When employing risk management techniques, the results are always to predict and benefit from a future scenario. The Capital asset pricing model (CAM-P) and Probabilistic Risk Assessment (PRA) examples of approaches that can extend from project to market, and from near to long term. CAP-M (Chong, Jin, & Phillips, 2013) "predicts" the best portfolio to maximize return. PRA, when combined with mini-Delphi Techniques and statistical approaches, yields accurate forecasts (Parry, 1996). @Risk is an Excel add-in used for modeling and simulating risks (Strickland, 2005). Underwriting (see below) and other business approaches identify risk management as a predictive method.

Underwriting

Many businesses have to account for risk exposure due to their different services and determine the cost needed to cover the risk. For example, auto insurance providers need to accurately determine the amount of premium to charge to cover each automobile and driver. A financial company needs to assess a borrower's potential and ability to pay before granting a loan. For a health insurance provider, predictive analytics can analyze a few years of past medical claims data, as well as lab, pharmacy and other records where available, to predict how expensive an enrollee is likely to be in the future. Predictive analytics can help underwrite these quantities by predicting the chances of illness, default, bankruptcy, etc. Predictive analytics can streamline the process of customer acquisition by predicting the future risk behavior of a customer using application level data. Predictive analytics in the form of credit scores have reduced the amount of time it takes for loan approvals, especially in the mortgage market where lending decisions are now made in a matter of hours rather than days or even weeks. Proper predictive analytics can lead to proper pricing decisions, which can help mitigate future risk of default.

Technology and big data influences

Big data is a collection of data sets that are so large and complex that they become awkward to work with using traditional database management tools. The volume, variety and velocity of big data have introduced challenges across the board for capture, storage, search, sharing, analysis, and visualization. Examples of big data sources include web logs, RFID and sensor data, social networks, Internet search indexing, call detail records, military surveillance, and complex data in astronomic, biogeochemical, genomics, and atmospheric sciences. Thanks to technological advances in computer hardware—faster CPUs, cheaper memory, and MPP architectures—and new technologies such as Hadoop, MapReduce, and in-database and text analytics for processing big data, it is now feasible to collect, analyze, and mine massive amounts of structured and unstructured data for new insights (Conz, 2008). Today, exploring big data and using predictive analytics is within reach of more organizations than ever before and new methods that are capable for handling such datasets are proposed (Ben-Gal I. Dana A., 2014).

Analytical Techniques

The approaches and techniques used to conduct predictive analytics can broadly be grouped into regression techniques and machine learning techniques.

Regression techniques

Regression models are the mainstay of predictive analytics. The focus lies on establishing a mathematical equation as a model to represent the interactions between the different variables in consideration. Depending on the situation, there is a wide variety of models that can be applied while performing predictive analytics. Some of them are briefly discussed below.

Linear regression model

The linear regression model analyzes the relationship between the response or dependent variable and a set of independent or predictor variables. This relationship is expressed as an equation that predicts the response variable as a linear function of the parameters. These parameters are adjusted so that a measure of fit is optimized. Much of the effort in model fitting is focused on minimizing the size of the residual, as well as ensuring that it is randomly distributed with respect to the model predictions (Draper & Smith, 1998).

The goal of regression is to select the parameters of the model so as to minimize the sum of the squared residuals. This is referred to as ordinary least squares (OLS) estimation and results in best linear unbiased estimates (BLUE) of the parameters if and only if the Gauss-Markov assumptions are satisfied (Hayashi, 2000).

Once the model has been estimated we would be interested to know if the predictor variables belong in the model – i.e. is the estimate of each variable's contribution reliable? To do this we can check the statistical significance of the model's coefficients which can be measured using the t-statistic. This amounts to testing whether the coefficient is significantly different from zero. How well the model predicts the dependent variable based on the value of the independent variables can be assessed by using the R^2 statistic. It measures predictive power of the model, i.e., the proportion of the total variation in the dependent variable that is "explained" (accounted for) by variation in the independent variables.

Discrete choice models

Multivariate regression (above) is generally used when the response variable is continuous and has an unbounded range (Greene, 2011). Often the response variable may not be continuous but rather discrete. While mathematically it is feasible to apply multivariate regression to discrete ordered dependent variables, some of the assumptions behind the theory of multivariate linear regression no longer hold, and there are other techniques such as discrete choice models which are better suited for this type of analysis. If the dependent variable is discrete, some of those superior methods are logistic regression, multinomial logit and probit models. Logistic regression and probit models are used when the dependent variable is binary.

Logistic regression

For more details on this topic, see Chapter 12, Logistic Regression.

In a classification setting, assigning outcome probabilities to observations can be achieved through the use of a logistic model, which is basically a method which transforms information about the binary dependent variable into an unbounded continuous variable and estimates a regular multivariate model (Hosmer & Lemeshow, 2000).

The Wald and likelihood-ratio test are used to test the statistical significance of each coefficient b in the model (analogous to the t-tests used in OLS regression; see Chapter 8). A test assessing the goodness-of-fit of a classification model is the "percentage correctly predicted".

Multinomial logistic regression

An extension of the binary logit model to cases where the dependent variable has more than 2 categories is the multinomial logit model. In such cases collapsing the data into two categories might not make good sense or may lead to loss in the richness of the data. The multinomial logit model is the appropriate technique in these cases, especially when the dependent variable categories are not ordered (for examples colors like red, blue, green). Some authors have extended multinomial regression to include feature selection/importance methods such as

13

Random multinomial logit.

Probit regression
Probit models offer an alternative to logistic regression for modeling categorical dependent variables. Even though the outcomes tend to be similar, the underlying distributions are different. Probit models are popular in social sciences like economics (Bliss, 1934).

A good way to understand the key difference between probit and logit models is to assume that there is a latent variable z. We do not observe z but instead observe y which takes the value 0 or 1. In the logit model we assume that y follows a logistic distribution. In the probit model we assume that y follows a standard normal distribution. Note that in social sciences (e.g. economics), probit is often used to model situations where the observed variable y is continuous but takes values between 0 and 1.

Logit versus probit
The Probit model has been around longer than the logit model (Bishop, 2006). They behave similarly, except that the logistic distribution tends to be slightly flatter tailed. One of the reasons the logit model was formulated was that the probit model was computationally difficult due to the requirement of numerically calculating integrals. Modern computing however has made this computation fairly simple. The coefficients obtained from the logit and probit model are fairly close. However, the odds ratio is easier to interpret in the logit model (Hosmer & Lemeshow, 2000).

Practical reasons for choosing the probit model over the logistic model would be:

- There is a strong belief that the underlying distribution is normal
- The actual event is not a binary outcome (e.g., bankruptcy status) but a proportion (e.g., proportion of population at different debt levels).

Time series models
Time series models are used for predicting or forecasting the future

behavior of variables. These models account for the fact that data points taken over time may have an internal structure (such as autocorrelation, trend or seasonal variation) that should be accounted for. As a result standard regression techniques cannot be applied to time series data and methodology has been developed to decompose the trend, seasonal and cyclical component of the series. Modeling the dynamic path of a variable can improve forecasts since the predictable component of the series can be projected into the future (Imdadullah, 2014).

Time series models estimate difference equations containing stochastic components. Two commonly used forms of these models are autoregressive models (AR) and moving average (MA) models. The Box-Jenkins methodology (1976) developed by George Box and G.M. Jenkins combines the AR and MA models to produce the ARMA (autoregressive moving average) model which is the cornerstone of stationary time series analysis (Box & Jenkins, 1976). ARIMA (autoregressive integrated moving average models) on the other hand are used to describe non-stationary time series. Box and Jenkins suggest differencing a non-stationary time series to obtain a stationary series to which an ARMA model can be applied. Non stationary time series have a pronounced trend and do not have a constant long-run mean or variance.

Box and Jenkins proposed a three stage methodology which includes: model identification, estimation and validation. The identification stage involves identifying if the series is stationary or not and the presence of seasonality by examining plots of the series, autocorrelation and partial autocorrelation functions. In the estimation stage, models are estimated using non-linear time series or maximum likelihood estimation procedures. Finally the validation stage involves diagnostic checking such as plotting the residuals to detect outliers and evidence of model fit (Box & Jenkins, 1976).

In recent years, time series models have become more sophisticated and attempt to model conditional heteroskedasticity with models such as ARCH (autoregressive conditional heteroskedasticity) and GARCH (generalized autoregressive conditional heteroskedasticity) models frequently used for financial time series. In addition time series models are also used to understand inter-relationships among economic variables represented by systems of equations using VAR (vector autoregression) and structural VAR models.

Survival or duration analysis

Survival analysis is another name for time-to-event analysis. These techniques were primarily developed in the medical and biological sciences, but they are also widely used in the social sciences like economics, as well as in engineering (reliability and failure time analysis) (Singh & Mukhopadhyay, 2011).

Censoring and non-normality, which are characteristic of survival data, generate difficulty when trying to analyze the data using conventional statistical models such as multiple linear regression. The normal distribution, being a symmetric distribution, takes positive as well as negative values, but duration by its very nature cannot be negative and therefore normality cannot be assumed when dealing with duration/survival data. Hence the normality assumption of regression models is violated.

The assumption is that if the data were not censored it would be representative of the population of interest. In survival analysis, censored observations arise whenever the dependent variable of interest represents the time to a terminal event, and the duration of the study is limited in time.

An important concept in survival analysis is the hazard rate, defined as the probability that the event will occur at time t conditional on surviving until time t. Another concept related to the hazard rate is the survival function which can be defined as the probability of surviving to time t.

Most models try to model the hazard rate by choosing the underlying distribution depending on the shape of the hazard function. A distribution whose hazard function slopes upward is said to have positive duration dependence, a decreasing hazard shows negative duration dependence whereas constant hazard is a process with no memory usually characterized by the exponential distribution. Some of the distributional choices in survival models are: F, gamma, Weibull, log normal, inverse normal, exponential, etc. All these distributions are for a non-negative random variable.

Duration models can be parametric, non-parametric or semi-parametric. Some of the models commonly used are Kaplan-Meier and Cox proportional hazard model (nonparametric) (Kaplan & Meier, 1958).

Classification and regression trees
Hierarchical Optimal Discriminant Analysis (HODA), (also called classification tree analysis) is a generalization of Optimal Discriminant Analysis that may be used to identify the statistical model that has maximum accuracy for predicting the value of a categorical dependent variable for a dataset consisting of categorical and continuous variables (Yarnold & Soltysik, 2004). The output of HODA is a non-orthogonal tree that combines categorical variables and cut points for continuous variables that yields maximum predictive accuracy, an assessment of the exact Type I error rate, and an evaluation of potential cross-generalizability of the statistical model. Hierarchical Optimal Discriminant analysis may be thought of as a generalization of Fisher's linear discriminant analysis. Optimal discriminant analysis is an alternative to ANOVA (analysis of variance) and regression analysis, which attempt to express one dependent variable as a linear combination of other features or measurements. However, ANOVA and regression analysis give a dependent variable that is a numerical variable, while hierarchical optimal discriminant analysis gives a dependent variable that is a class variable.

Classification and regression trees (CART) is a non-parametric decision tree learning technique that produces either classification or regression trees, depending on whether the dependent variable is categorical or numeric, respectively (Rokach & Maimon, 2008).

Decision trees are formed by a collection of rules based on variables in the modeling data set:

- Rules based on variables' values are selected to get the best split to differentiate observations based on the dependent variable
- Once a rule is selected and splits a node into two, the same process is applied to each "child" node (i.e. it is a recursive procedure)
- Splitting stops when CART detects no further gain can be made, or some pre-set stopping rules are met. (Alternatively, the data are split as much as possible and then the tree is later pruned.)

Each branch of the tree ends in a terminal node. Each observation falls into one and exactly one terminal node, and each terminal node is uniquely defined by a set of rules.

A very popular method for predictive analytics is Leo Breiman's Random forests (Breiman L. , Random Forests, 2001) or derived versions of this technique like Random multinomial logit (Prinzie, 2008).

Multivariate adaptive regression splines
Multivariate adaptive regression splines (MARS) is a non-parametric technique that builds flexible models by fitting piecewise linear regressions (Friedman, 1991).

An important concept associated with regression splines is that of a knot. Knot is where one local regression model gives way to another and thus is the point of intersection between two splines.

In multivariate and adaptive regression splines, basis functions are the tool used for generalizing the search for knots. Basis functions are a set of functions used to represent the information contained in one or more variables. MARS model almost always creates the basis functions in pairs.

Multivariate and adaptive regression spline approach deliberately over-fits the model and then prunes to get to the optimal model. The algorithm is computationally very intensive and in practice we are required to specify an upper limit on the number of basis functions.

Machine learning techniques

Machine learning, a branch of artificial intelligence, was originally employed to develop techniques to enable computers to learn. Today, since it includes a number of advanced statistical methods for regression and classification, it finds application in a wide variety of fields including medical diagnostics, credit card fraud detection, face and speech recognition and analysis of the stock market. In certain applications it is sufficient to directly predict the dependent variable without focusing on the underlying relationships between variables. In other cases, the underlying relationships can be very complex and the mathematical form of the dependencies unknown. For such cases, machine learning techniques emulate human cognition and learn from training examples to predict future events.

A brief discussion of some of these methods used commonly for predictive analytics is provided below. A detailed study of machine learning can be found in Mitchell's *Machine Learning* (Mitchell, 1997).

Neural networks
Neural networks are nonlinear sophisticated modeling techniques that are able to model complex functions (Rosenblatt, 1958). They can be applied to problems of prediction, classification or control in a wide spectrum of fields such as finance, cognitive psychology/neuroscience, medicine, engineering, and physics.

Neural networks are used when the exact nature of the relationship between inputs and output is not known. A key feature of neural networks is that they learn the relationship between inputs and output through training. There are three types of training in neural networks used by different networks, supervised and unsupervised training, reinforcement learning, with supervised being the most common one.

Some examples of neural network training techniques are back propagation, quick propagation, conjugate gradient descent, projection

19

operator, Delta-Bar-Delta etc. Some unsupervised network architectures are multilayer perceptrons (Freund & Schapire, 1999), Kohonen networks (Kohonen & Honkela, 2007), Hopfield networks (Hopfield, 2007), etc.

Multilayer Perceptron (MLP)
The Multilayer Perceptron (MLP) consists of an input and an output layer with one or more hidden layers of nonlinearly-activating nodes or sigmoid nodes. This is determined by the weight vector and it is necessary to adjust the weights of the network. The back-propagation employs gradient fall to minimize the squared error between the network output values and desired values for those outputs. The weights adjusted by an iterative process of repetitive present of attributes. Small changes in the weight to get the desired values are done by the process called training the net and is done by the training set (learning rule) (Riedmiller, 2010).

Radial basis functions
A radial basis function (RBF) is a function which has built into it a distance criterion with respect to a center. Such functions can be used very efficiently for interpolation and for smoothing of data. Radial basis functions have been applied in the area of neural networks where they are used as a replacement for the sigmoidal transfer function. Such networks have 3 layers, the input layer, the hidden layer with the RBF non-linearity and a linear output layer. The most popular choice for the non-linearity is the Gaussian. RBF networks have the advantage of not being locked into local minima as do the feedforward networks such as the multilayer perceptron (Łukaszyk, 2004).

Support vector machines
Support Vector Machines (SVM) are used to detect and exploit complex patterns in data by clustering, classifying and ranking the data (Cortes & Vapnik, 1995). They are learning machines that are used to perform binary classifications and regression estimations. They commonly use kernel based methods to apply linear classification techniques to non-linear classification problems. There are a number of types of SVM such

as linear, polynomial, sigmoid etc.

Naïve Bayes
Naïve Bayes based on Bayes conditional probability rule is used for performing classification tasks. Naïve Bayes assumes the predictors are statistically independent which makes it an effective classification tool that is easy to interpret. It is best employed when faced with the problem of 'curse of dimensionality' i.e. when the number of predictors is very high (Rennie, Shih, Teevan, & Karger, 2003).

k-nearest neighbors
The nearest neighbor algorithm k-NN belongs to the class of pattern recognition statistical methods (Altman, 1992). The method does not impose *a priori* any assumptions about the distribution from which the modeling sample is drawn. It involves a training set with both positive and negative values. A new sample is classified by calculating the distance to the nearest neighboring training case. The sign of that point will determine the classification of the sample. In the k-nearest neighbor classifier, the k nearest points are considered and the sign of the majority is used to classify the sample. The performance of the k-NN algorithm is influenced by three main factors: (1) the distance measure used to locate the nearest neighbors; (2) the decision rule used to derive a classification from the k-nearest neighbors; and (3) the number of neighbors used to classify the new sample. It can be proved that, unlike other methods, this method is universally asymptotically convergent, i.e.: as the size of the training set increases, if the observations are independent and identically distributed (i.i.d.), regardless of the distribution from which the sample is drawn, the predicted class will converge to the class assignment that minimizes misclassification error (Devroye, Györfi, & Lugosi, 1996).

Geospatial predictive modeling
Conceptually, geospatial predictive modeling is rooted in the principle that the occurrences of events being modeled are limited in distribution. Occurrences of events are neither uniform nor random in distribution – there are spatial environment factors (infrastructure, sociocultural,

topographic, etc.) that constrain and influence where the locations of events occur. Geospatial predictive modeling attempts to describe those constraints and influences by spatially correlating occurrences of historical geospatial locations with environmental factors that represent those constraints and influences. Geospatial predictive modeling is a process for analyzing events through a geographic filter in order to make statements of likelihood for event occurrence or emergence.

Tools

Historically, using predictive analytics tools—as well as understanding the results they delivered—required advanced skills. However, modern predictive analytics tools are no longer restricted to IT specialists. As more organizations adopt predictive analytics into decision-making processes and integrate it into their operations, they are creating a shift in the market toward business users as the primary consumers of the information. Business users want tools they can use on their own. Vendors are responding by creating new software that removes the mathematical complexity, provides user-friendly graphic interfaces and/or builds in short cuts that can, for example, recognize the kind of data available and suggest an appropriate predictive model (Halper, 2011). Predictive analytics tools have become sophisticated enough to adequately present and dissect data problems, so that any data-savvy information worker can utilize them to analyze data and retrieve meaningful, useful results (Eckerson, 2007). For example, modern tools present findings using simple charts, graphs, and scores that indicate the likelihood of possible outcomes (MacLennan, 2012).

There are numerous tools available in the marketplace that help with the execution of predictive analytics. These range from those that need very little user sophistication to those that are designed for the expert practitioner. The difference between these tools is often in the level of customization and heavy data lifting allowed.

Notable open source predictive analytic tools include:

- scikit-learn

- KNIME
- OpenNN
- Orange
- R
- RapidMiner
- Weka
- GNU Octave
- Apache Mahout

Notable commercial predictive analytic tools include:

- Alpine Data Labs
- BIRT Analytics
- Angoss KnowledgeSTUDIO
- IBM SPSS Statistics and IBM SPSS Modeler
- KXEN Modeler
- Mathematica
- MATLAB
- Minitab
- Oracle Data Mining (ODM)
- Pervasive
- Predixion Software
- Revolution Analytics
- SAP
- SAS and SAS Enterprise Miner
- STATA
- STATISTICA
- TIBCO

PMML

In an attempt to provide a standard language for expressing predictive models, the Predictive Model Markup Language (PMML) has been proposed. Such an XML-based language provides a way for the different tools to define predictive models and to share these between PMML compliant applications. PMML 4.0 was released in June, 2009.

Criticism

There are plenty of skeptics when it comes to computers and algorithms abilities to predict the future, including Gary King, a professor from Harvard University and the director of the Institute for Quantitative Social Science. People are influenced by their environment in innumerable ways. Trying to understand what people will do next assumes that all the influential variables can be known and measured accurately. "People's environments change even more quickly than they themselves do. Everything from the weather to their relationship with their mother can change the way people think and act. All of those variables are unpredictable. How they will impact a person is even less predictable. If put in the exact same situation tomorrow, they may make a completely different decision. This means that a statistical prediction is only valid in sterile laboratory conditions, which suddenly isn't as useful as it seemed before." (King, 2014)

2. Predictive modeling

Predictive modeling is the process by which a model is created or chosen to try to best predict the probability of an outcome (Geisser, 1993). In many cases the model is chosen on the basis of detection theory to try to guess the probability of an outcome given a set amount of input data, for example, given an email determining how likely that it is spam. Models can use one or more classifiers in trying to determine the probability of a set of data belonging to another set, say spam or 'ham'.

There are three types of predictive models marketers should know about, but I will only talk about the first one in this article:

- Propensity models (predictions)
- Clustering models (segments)
- Collaborative filtering (recommendations)

Propensity models are what most people think of when they hear "predictive analytics". Propensity models make predictions about a customer's future behavior. With propensity models you can anticipate a customers' future behavior. However, keep in mind that even propensity models are abstractions and do not necessarily predict absolute true behavior. wewill go through six examples of propensity models to explain the concept.

Propensity Models

Model 1: Predicted customer lifetime value

CLV (Customer Lifetime Value) is a prediction of all the value a business will derive from their entire relationship with a customer. The Pareto Principle states that, for many events, roughly 80% of the effects come from 20% of the causes. When applied to e-commerce, this means that 80% of your revenue can be attributed to 20% of your customers. While the exact percentages may not be 80/20, it is still the case that some customers are worth a whole lot more than others, and identifying your

"All-Star" customers can be extremely valuable to your business. Algorithms can predict how much a customer will spend with you long before customers themselves realizes this.

At the moment a customer makes their first purchase you may know a lot more than just their initial transaction record: you may have email and web engagement data for example, as well as demographic and geographic information. By comparing a customer to many others who came before them, you can predict with a high degree of accuracy their future lifetime value. This information is extremely valuable as it allows you to make value based marketing decisions. For example, it makes sense to invest more in those acquisition channels and campaigns that produce customers with the highest predicted lifetime value.

Model 2: Predicted share of wallet

Predicted share of wallet refers to the amount of the customer's total spending that a business captures in the products and services that it offers. Increasing the share of a customer's wallet a company receives is often a cheaper way of boosting revenue than increasing market share. For example if a customer spends $100 with you on groceries, is this 10% or 90% of their grocery spending for a given year? Knowing this allows you to see where future revenue potential is within your existing customer base and to design campaigns to capture this revenue.

Model 3: Propensity to engage

A propensity to engage model predicts the likelihood that a person will engage in some activity, like unethical behavior or post purchases. For example, a propensity to engage model can predict how likely it is that a customer will click on your email links. Armed with this information you can decide not to send an email to a certain "low likelihood to click" segment.

Model 4: Propensity to unsubscribe

A propensity to unsubscribe model tells you which customers not to touch: if there are high value customers you are at risk of losing to unsubscribe, you need to find other ways to reaching out to them that are not by email. For example, you can predict how likely it is that a customer will unsubscribe from your email list at any given point in time. Armed with this information you can optimize email frequency. For "high likelihood to unsubscribe" segments, you should decrease send frequency; whereas for "low likelihood to unsubscribe" segments, you can increase email send frequency. You could also decide to use different channels (like direct mail or LinkedIn) to reach out to "high likelihood to unsubscribe" customers.

Model 5: Propensity to buy

The propensity to buy model tells you which customers are ready to make their purchase, so you can find who to target. Moreover, once you know who is ready and who is not helps you provide the right aggression in your offer. Those that are likely to buy won't need high discounts (You can stop cannibalizing your margin) while customers who are not likely to buy may need a more aggressive offer, thereby bringing you incremental revenue.

For example, a "propensity to buy a new vehicle" model built with only data the automotive manufacturer has in their database can be used to predict percent of sales. By incorporating demographic and lifestyle data from third parties, the accuracy of that model can be improved. That is, if the first model predicts 50% sales in the top five deciles (there are ten deciles), then the latter could improve the result to 70% in the top five deciles.

Model 6: Propensity to churn

Companies often rely on customer service agents to "save" customers who call to say they are taking their business elsewhere. But by this time, it is often too late to save the relationship. The propensity to churn model tells you which active customers are at risk, so you know which high value, at risk customers to put on your watch list and reach out.

Armed with this information, you may be able to save those customers with preemptive marketing programs designed to retain them.

Often propensity models can be combined to make campaign decisions. For example, you may want to do an aggressive customer win back campaign for customers who have both a high likelihood to unsubscribe and a high predicted lifetime value.

Cluster Models

Clustering is the predictive analytics term for customer segmentation. Clustering, like classification, is used to segment the data. Unlike classification, clustering models segment data into groups that were not previously defined. Cluster analysis itself is not one specific algorithm, but the general task to be solved. It can be achieved by various algorithms that differ significantly in their notion of what constitutes a cluster and how to efficiently find them.

With clustering you let the algorithms, rather than the marketers, create customer segments. Think of clustering as auto-segmentation. Algorithms are able to segment customers based on many more variables than a human being ever could. It's not unusual for two clusters to be different on 30 customer dimensions or more. In this article I will talk about three different types of predictive clustering models.

Model 7: Behavioral clustering

Behavioral clustering informs you how people behave while purchasing. Do they use the web site or the call center? Are they discount addicts? How frequently do they buy? How much do they spend? How much time will go buy before they purchase again? This algorithm helps set the right tone while contacting the customer. For instance, customers that buy frequently but with low sized orders might react well to offers like 'Earn double rewards points when you spend $100 or more.

	Murder	Assault	UrbanPop	Rape	classif
Alabama	13.2	236	58	21.2	1
Alaska	10.0	263	48	44.5	1
Arizona	8.1	294	80	31.0	1
Arkansas	8.8	190	50	19.5	2
California	9.0	276	91	40.6	1
Colorado	7.9	204	78	38.7	1
Connecticut	3.3	110	77	11.1	2
Delaware	5.9	238	72	15.8	2
Florida	15.4	335	80	31.9	1
Georgia	17.4	211	60	25.8	1

Behavioral clustering can also informs us on other behaviors, such as crime and is used in performing crime analysis. In the example below there are three crime clusters (only the top ten are shown in the table):

Graphically, the clusters appear as follow:

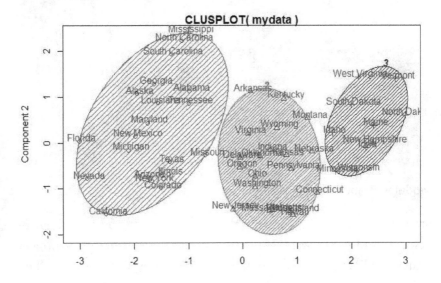

Cluster plot created in R Studio

Model 8: Product based clustering (also called category based clustering)

Product based clustering algorithms discover what different groupings of products people buy from. See the example below of a category (or product) based segment or cluster. You can see people in one customer

29

segment ONLY buy Pinot Noir, whereas those in another customer segment buy different types of Varietal products, such as Champagne, Chardonnay, Pinot Grigio and Prosecco – but never Cabernet Sauvignon, Malbec or Espumante. This is useful information when deciding which product offers or email content to send to each of these customer segments.

Offer #	Offer date	Product	Minimum	Discount	Origin	Past Peak	1	2	3	4
1	January	Malbec	72	56	France	FALSE	0	0	4	6
2	January	Pinot Noir	72	17	France	FALSE	4	0	4	2
3	February	Espumante	144	32	Oregon	TRUE	0	0	2	4
4	February	Champagne	72	48	France	TRUE	0	0	7	5
5	February	Cabernet Sa	144	44	New Zealar	TRUE	0	0	2	2
6	March	Prosecco	144	86	Chile	FALSE	0	0	5	7
7	March	Prosecco	6	40	Australia	TRUE	0	12	4	3
8	March	Espumante	6	45	South Afric	FALSE	0	11	6	3
9	April	Chardonnay	144	57	Chile	FALSE	0	0	7	8
10	April	Prosecco	72	52	California	FALSE	0	0	5	2
11	May	Champagne	72	85	France	FALSE	0	0	7	6
12	May	Prosecco	72	83	Australia	FALSE	0	0	3	2
13	May	Merlot	6	43	Chile	FALSE	0	6	0	0
14	June	Merlot	72	64	Chile	FALSE	0	0	5	4
15	June	Cabernet Sa	144	19	Italy	FALSE	0	0	2	4
16	June	Merlot	72	88	California	FALSE	0	0	5	0
17	July	Pinot Noir	12	47	Germany	FALSE	7	0	0	0
18	July	Espumante	6	50	Oregon	FALSE	0	11	2	1
19	July	Champagne	12	66	Germany	FALSE	0	0	2	3
20	August	Cabernet Sa	72	82	Italy	FALSE	0	0	4	2
21	August	Champagne	12	50	California	FALSE	0	0	2	2
22	August	Champagne	72	63	France	FALSE	0	0	0	21
23	September	Chardonnay	144	39	South Afric	FALSE	0	0	3	2
24	September	Pinot Noir	6	34	Italy	FALSE	12	0	0	0
25	October	Cabernet Sa	72	59	Oregon	TRUE	0	0	3	3
26	October	Pinot Noir	144	83	Australia	FALSE	8	0	5	2
27	October	Champagne	72	88	New Zealar	FALSE	0	0	6	3
28	November	Cabernet Sa	12	56	France	TRUE	0	0	4	2
29	November	Pinot Grigic	6	87	France	FALSE	0	15	2	0
30	December	Malbec	6	54	France	FALSE	0	16	2	4
31	December	Champagne	72	89	France	FALSE	0	0	10	7
32	December	Cabernet Sa	72	45	Germany	TRUE	0	0	3	1

Model 9: Brand based clustering

Brand-based clustering, on the other hand, focuses on the brand of items customers purchase. Marketers can use this information to project what other brands those customers are likely to buy. Customers are then ordered according to Nike, Adidas, Under Armour, etc. Now you know what specific brands to pitch to certain customers. When a brand releases new products – you know who is likely to be interested.

Conclusion

Predictive analytics models are great, but they are ultimately useless unless you can actually tie them to your day-to-day marketing campaigns. This leads me to the first rule of predictive analytics:

"Always make sure that your predictive analytics platform is directly integrated with your marketing execution systems such as your email service provider, web site, call center or Point of Sell (POS) system."

It is better to start with just one model that you use in day-to-day marketing campaigns than to have 10 models without the data being actionable in the hands of marketers.

Presenting and Using the Results of a Predictive Model

Predictive models can either be used directly to estimate a response (output) given a defined set of characteristics (input), or indirectly to drive the choice of decision rules (Steyerberg, 2010).

Depending on the methodology employed for the prediction, it is often possible to derive a formula that may be used in a spreadsheet software. This has some advantages for end users or decision makers, the main one being familiarity with the software itself, hence a lower barrier to adoption.

Nomograms are useful graphical representation of a predictive model. As in spreadsheet software, their use depends on the methodology chosen. The advantage of nomograms is the immediacy of computing predictions without the aid of a computer.

Point estimates tables are one of the simplest form to represent a predictive tool. Here combination of characteristics of interests can either be represented via a table or a graph and the associated prediction read off the y-axis or the table itself.

Tree based methods (e.g. CART, survival trees) provide one of the most graphically intuitive ways to present predictions. However, their usage is limited to those methods that use this type of modeling approach which can have several drawbacks (Breiman L. , 1996). Trees can also be employed to represent decision rules graphically.

Score charts are graphical tabular or graphical tools to represent either predictions or decision rules.

A new class of modern tools are represented by web based applications. For example, *Shiny* is a web based tool developed by *Rstudio*, an *R* IDE (integrated development environment). With a *Shiny* app, a modeler has the advantage to represent any which way he or she chooses to represent the predictive model while allowing the user some control. A user can choose a combination of characteristics of interest via sliders or input boxes and results can be generated, from graphs to confidence intervals to tables and various statistics of interests. However, these tools often require a server installation of *Rstudio*.

Applications

Uplift Modeling

Uplift Modeling (see Chapter 17) is a technique for modeling the change in probability caused by an action. Typically this is a marketing action such as an offer to buy a product, to use a product more or to re-sign a contract. For example in a retention campaign you wish to predict the change in probability that a customer will remain a customer if they are contacted. A model of the change in probability allows the retention campaign to be targeted at those customers on whom the change in probability will be beneficial. This allows the retention program to avoid triggering unnecessary churn or customer attrition without wasting money contacting people who would act anyway.

Archaeology

Predictive modeling in archaeology gets its foundations from Gordon Willey's mid-fifties work in the Virú Valley of Peru (Willey, 1953). Complete, intensive surveys were performed then covariability between cultural remains and natural features such as slope, and vegetation were determined. Development of quantitative methods and a greater availability of applicable data led to growth of the discipline in the 1960s and by the late 1980s, substantial progress had been made by major land managers worldwide.

Generally, predictive modeling in archaeology is establishing statistically valid causal or covariable relationships between natural proxies such as soil types, elevation, slope, vegetation, proximity to water, geology, geomorphology, etc., and the presence of archaeological features. Through analysis of these quantifiable attributes from land that has undergone archaeological survey, sometimes the "archaeological sensitivity" of unsurveyed areas can be anticipated based on the natural proxies in those areas. Large land managers in the United States, such as the Bureau of Land Management (BLM), the Department of Defense (DOD) (Altschul, Sebastian, & Heidelberg, 2004), and numerous highway and parks agencies, have successfully employed this strategy. By using predictive modeling in their cultural resource management plans, they are capable of making more informed decisions when planning for activities that have the potential to require ground disturbance and subsequently affect archaeological sites.

Customer relationship management

Predictive modeling is used extensively in analytical customer relationship management and data mining to produce customer-level models that describe the likelihood that a customer will take a particular action. The actions are usually sales, marketing and customer retention related.

For example, a large consumer organization such as a mobile telecommunications operator will have a set of predictive models for product cross-sell, product deep-sell and churn. It is also now more common for such an organization to have a model of "savability" using an uplift model. This predicts the likelihood that a customer can be saved at the end of a contract period (the change in churn probability) as opposed to the standard churn prediction model.

Auto insurance

Predictive Modeling is utilized in vehicle insurance to assign risk of incidents to policy holders from information obtained from policy holders. This is extensively employed in usage-based insurance solutions where predictive models utilize telemetry based data to build a model of predictive risk for claim likelihood. Black-box auto insurance predictive models utilize GPS or accelerometer sensor input only. Some models include a wide range of predictive input beyond basic telemetry including advanced driving behavior, independent crash records, road history, and user profiles to provide improved risk models.

Health care

In 2009 Parkland Health & Hospital System began analyzing electronic medical records in order to use predictive modeling to help identify patients at high risk of readmission. Initially the hospital focused on patients with congestive heart failure, but the program has expanded to include patients with diabetes, acute myocardial infarction, and pneumonia.

Notable failures of predictive modeling

Although not widely discussed by the mainstream predictive modeling community, predictive modeling is a methodology that has been widely used in the financial industry in the past and some of the spectacular failures have contributed to the financial crisis of 2008. These failures exemplify the danger of relying blindly on models that are essentially backforward looking in nature. The following examples are by no mean a complete list:

1) Bond rating. S&P, Moody's and Fitch quantify the probability of default of bonds with discrete variables called rating. The rating can take on discrete values from AAA down to D. The rating is a predictor of the risk of default based on a variety of variables associated with the borrower and macro-economic data that are drawn from historicals. The rating agencies failed spectacularly with their ratings on the 600 billion USD mortgage backed CDO market. Almost the entire AAA sector (and the super-AAA sector, a new rating the rating agencies provided to represent super safe investment) of the CDO market defaulted or severely downgraded during 2008, many of which obtained their ratings less than just a year ago.

2) Statistical models that attempt to predict equity market prices based on historical data. So far, no such model is considered to consistently make correct predictions over the long term. One particularly memorable failure is that of Long Term Capital Management, a fund that hired highly qualified analysts, including a Nobel Prize winner in economics, to develop a sophisticated statistical model that predicted the price spreads between different securities. The models produced impressive profits until a spectacular debacle that caused the then Federal Reserve chairman Alan Greenspan to step in to broker a rescue plan by the Wall Street broker dealers in order to prevent a meltdown of the bond market.

Possible fundamental limitations of predictive model based on data fitting

1) History cannot always predict future: using relations derived from historical data to predict the future implicitly assumes there are certain steady-state conditions or constants in the complex system. This is almost always wrong when the system involves people.

2) The issue of unknown unknowns: in all data collection, the collector first defines the set of variables for which data is collected. However, no matter how extensive the collector considers his selection of the variables, there is always the possibility of new variables that have not been considered or even defined, yet critical to the outcome.

3) Self-defeat of an algorithm: after an algorithm becomes an accepted standard of measurement, it can be taken advantage of by people who understand the algorithm and have the incentive to fool or manipulate the outcome. This is what happened to the CDO rating. The CDO dealers actively fulfilled the rating agencies input to reach an AAA or super-AAA on the CDO they are issuing by cleverly manipulating variables that were "unknown" to the rating agencies' "sophisticated" models.

Software

Throughout the main chapters (3-16) we will give examples of software packages that have the functionality to perform the modeling discussed in a chapter. The "main" software packages are discussed here, due to the expanse of functionality. Software packages built specifically for a functionality, like Support Vector Machines, will be addressed further in the chapters. We will not address software for Uplift models and Time Series models, since they are applications of methods discussed in the main chapters.

Open Source

DAP – GNU Dap is a statistics and graphics program, that performs data management, analysis, and graphical visualization tasks which are commonly required in statistical consulting practice. Dap was written to be a free replacement for SAS, but users are assumed to have a basic familiarity with the C programming language in order to permit greater flexibility. Unlike R it has been designed to be used on large data sets.

KNIME – GNU KNIME, the Konstanz Information Miner, is an open source data analytics, reporting and integration platform. KNIME integrates various components for machine learning and data mining through its modular data pipelining concept. A graphical user interface allows assembly of nodes for data preprocessing (ETL: Extraction, Transformation, Loading), for modeling and data analysis and visualization.

Octave – GNU Octave is a high-level programming language, primarily intended for numerical computations. It provides a command-line interface for solving linear and nonlinear problems numerically, and for performing other numerical experiments using a language that is mostly compatible with MATLAB. WE have used Octave extensively for predictive modeling.

Orange – GNU Orange is a component-based data mining and machine learning software suite, featuring a visual programming front-end for explorative data analysis and visualization, and Python bindings and libraries for scripting. It includes a set of components for data preprocessing, feature scoring and filtering, modeling, model evaluation, and exploration techniques. It is implemented in C++ and Python.

PNL (Probabilistic Networks Library) – is a tool for working with graphical models, supporting directed and undirected models, discrete and continuous variables, various inference and learning algorithms.

R – GNU R is an open source software environment for statistical computing. It uses "packages", which are loaded with commands in a console, to provide modeling functionality. As mentioned, all the computer examples in the book are implementations of R packages. The R language is widely used among statisticians and data miners for developing statistical software and data analysis. R is an implementation of the S programming language. We have used R extensively for predictive modeling, using fairly large data sets, but not greater than 900,000 records.

scikit-learn – GNU scikit-learn (formerly scikits.learn) is an open source machine learning library for the Python programming language. It features various classification, regression and clustering algorithms including support vector machines, logistic regression, naive Bayes, random forests, gradient boosting, k-means and DBSCAN, and is designed to interoperate with the Python numerical and scientific libraries NumPy and SciPy.

Weka – GNU Weka (Waikato Environment for Knowledge Analysis) is a popular suite of machine learning software written in Java, developed at the University of Waikato, New Zealand. Weka is free software available under the GNU General Public License.

Commercial

Analytica – by Lumina Decision Systems, is an influence diagram-based, visual environment for creating and analyzing probabilistic models.

IBM SPSS Modeler – is a data mining and text analytics software application built by IBM. It is used to build predictive models and conduct other analytic tasks. It has a visual interface which allows users to leverage statistical and data mining algorithms without programming. We will refer to it later as SPSS Modeler.

MATLAB – (matrix laboratory) is a multi-paradigm numerical computing environment and fourth-generation programming language. Developed by MathWorks, MATLAB allows matrix manipulations, plotting of functions and data, implementation of algorithms, creation of user interfaces, and interfacing with programs written in other languages, including C, C++, Java, and Fortran. An additional package, **Simulink**, adds graphical multi-domain simulation and Model-Based Design for dynamic and embedded systems. We have used MATLAB and Simulink extensively for predictive modeling.

RapidMiner – is a software platform developed by the company of the same name that provides an integrated environment for machine learning, data mining, text mining, predictive analytics and business analytics.

SAS Enterprise Miner – SAS (Statistical Analysis System) is a software suite developed by SAS Institute for advanced analytics, business intelligence, data management, and predictive analytics. Enterprise Miner, as the name suggests, is the SAS data mining and modeling tool.

STATISTICA – is a statistics and analytics software package developed by StatSoft. STATISTICA provides data analysis, data management, statistics, data mining, and data visualization procedures.

Introduction to R

This introduction serves as background material for our examples with R. The only hardware requirement for is a PC with the latest free open source R software installed. R has extensive documentation and active online community support. It is the perfect environment to get started in predictive modeling.

Installation. R can be downloaded from one of the mirror sites in http://cran.r-project.org/mirrors.html. You should pick your nearest location.

Using External Data. R offers plenty of options for loading external data, including Excel, Minitab and SPSS files.

R Session. After R is started, there is a console awaiting for input. At the prompt (>), you can enter numbers and perform calculations.

```
> 1 + 2
[1] 3
```

Variable Assignment. We assign values to variables with the assignment operator "=". Just typing the variable by itself at the prompt will print out the value. We should note that another form of assignment operator "<-" is also in use.

```
> x = 1
> x
[1] 1
```

Functions. R functions are invoked by its name, then followed by the parenthesis, and zero or more arguments. The following apply the function c to combine three numeric values into a vector.

```
> c(1, 2, 3)
[1] 1 2 3
```

Comments. All text after the pound sign "#" within the same line is considered a comment.

```
> 1 + 1      # this is a comment
[1] 2
```

Extension Package. Sometimes we need additional functionality beyond those offered by the core R library. In order to install an extension package, you should invoke the install.packages function at the prompt and follow the instruction.

```
> install.packages()
```

Getting Help. R provides extensive documentation. For example, entering ?c or help(c) at the prompt gives documentation of the function c in R.

```
> help(c)
```

If you are not sure about the name of the function you are looking for, you can perform a fuzzy search with the apropos function.

```
> apropos("nova")
[1] "anova"                "anova.glm"
    ....
```

Finally, there is an R specific Internet search engine at http://www.rseek.org for more assistance.

3. Modeling Techniques

There are many ways to construct the models that we just discussed. Propensity models are often constructed using statistical techniques and machine learning. Cluster models may also use statistical techniques, but may also employ heuristic algorithms.

Statistical Modeling

Nearly any regression model (linear, logistic, general linear model (GLM), robust regression, etc.) can be used for prediction purposes. We will cover all of these in the chapters to follow. In particular, logistic regression is a very popular modeling technique for propensity models with a binary (e.g., Yes or No) response (dependent) variable.

Broadly speaking, there are two classes of predictive models: parametric and non-parametric. A third class, semi-parametric models, includes features of both. Parametric models make "specific assumptions with regard to one or more of the population parameters that characterize the underlying distribution(s)" (Sheskin, 2011), while non-parametric regressions make fewer assumptions than their parametric counterparts. These models fall under the class of statistical models (Marascuilo, 1977).

A statistical model is a formalization of relationships between variables in the form of mathematical equations. A statistical model describes how one or more random variables are related to one or more other variables. The model is statistical as the variables are not deterministically but stochastically related. In mathematical terms, a statistical model is frequently thought of as a pair (Y, P) where Y is the set of possible observations and P the set of possible probability distributions on Y. It is assumed that there is a distinct element of P which generates the observed data. Statistical inference enables us to make statements about which element(s) of this set are likely to be the true one.

Most statistical tests can be described in the form of a statistical model. For example, the Student's t-test for comparing the means of two groups can be formulated as seeing if an estimated parameter in the model is different from 0. Another similarity between tests and models is that there are assumptions involved. Error is assumed to be normally distributed in most models.

Formal definition

A statistical model is a collection of probability distribution functions or probability density functions (collectively referred to as distributions for brevity). A parametric model is a collection of distributions, each of which is indexed by a unique finite-dimensional parameter: $P\{P_0 : \theta \in \Theta\}$, where θ is a parameter and $\Theta \subseteq R^d$ is the feasible region of parameters, which is a subset of d-dimensional Euclidean space. A statistical model may be used to describe the set of distributions from which one assumes that a particular data set is sampled. For example, if one assumes that data arise from a univariate Gaussian distribution, then one has assumed a Gaussian model

$$\mathcal{P} = \left\{ \mathbb{P}(x; \mu, \sigma) = \frac{1}{\sqrt{2\pi}\sigma} \exp\left\{-\frac{1}{2\sigma^2}(x - \mu)^2\right\} : \mu \in \mathbb{R}, \sigma > 0 \right\}.$$

A non-parametric model is a set of probability distributions with infinite dimensional parameters, and might be written as $\mathcal{P} = \{$all distributions$\}$. A semi-parametric model also has infinite dimensional parameters, but is not dense in the space of distributions. For example, a mixture of Gaussians with one Gaussian at each data point is dense in the space of distributions. Formally, if d is the dimension of the parameter, and n is the number of samples, if $d \to \infty$ as $n \to \infty$ and $d/n \to 0$ as $n \to \infty$, then the model is semi-parametric.

Model comparison

Models can be compared to each other. This can either be done when you have performed an exploratory data analysis or a confirmatory data analysis. In an exploratory analysis, you formulate all models you can think of, and see which describes your data best. In a confirmatory analysis you test which of your models you have described before the data was collected fits the data best, or test if your only model fits the data. In linear regression analysis you can compare the amount of variance explained by the independent variables, R^2, across the different models. In general, you can compare models that are nested by using a Likelihood-ratio test. Nested models are models that can be obtained by restricting a parameter in a more complex model to be zero.

An example

Height and age are probabilistically distributed over humans. They are stochastically related; when you know that a person is of age 10, this influences the chance of this person being 6 feet tall. You could formalize this relationship in a linear regression model of the following form: $\text{height}_i = b_0 + b_1 \text{age}_i + \varepsilon_i$, where b_0 is the intercept, b_1 is a parameter that age is multiplied by to get a prediction of height, ε is the error term, and i is the subject. This means that height starts at some value, there is a minimum height when someone is born, and it is predicted by age to some amount. This prediction is not perfect as error is included in the model. This error contains variance that stems from sex and other variables. When sex is included in the model, the error term will become smaller, as you will have a better idea of the chance that a particular 16-year-old is 6 feet tall when you know this 16-year-old is a girl. The model would become $\text{height}_i = b_0 + b_1 \text{age}_i + b_2 \text{sex}_i + \varepsilon_i$, where the variable sex is dichotomous. This model would presumably have a higher R^2. The first model is nested in the second model: the first model is obtained from the second when b_2 is restricted to zero.

Classification

According to the number of the endogenous variables and the number of equations, models can be classified as complete models (the number of equations equal to the number of endogenous variables) and incomplete models. Some other statistical models are the general linear

43

model (restricted to continuous dependent variables), the generalized linear model (for example, logistic regression), the multilevel model, and the structural equation model.

Machine Learning

Machine learning is a scientific discipline that explores the construction and study of algorithms that can learn from data (Kovahi & Provost, 1998). Such algorithms operate by building a model based on inputs (Bishop, Pattern Recognition and Machine Learning, 2006) and using them to make predictions or decisions, rather than following only explicitly programmed instructions.

Machine learning can be considered a subfield of computer science and statistics. It has strong ties to artificial intelligence and optimization, which deliver methods, theory and application domains to the field. Machine learning is employed in a range of computing tasks where designing and programming explicit, rule-based algorithms is infeasible. Example applications include spam filtering, optical character recognition (OCR) (Wernick, Yang, Brankov, Yourganov, & Strother, 2010), search engines and computer vision. Machine learning is sometimes conflated with data mining (Mannila, 1996), although that focuses more on exploratory data analysis (Friedman, Data Mining and Statistics: What's the connection?, 1998). Machine learning and pattern recognition "can be viewed as two facets of the same field." (Bishop, Pattern Recognition and Machine Learning, 2006)

Types of problems/tasks

Machine learning tasks are typically classified into three broad categories, depending on the nature of the learning "signal" or "feedback" available to a learning system. These are (Russell & Norvig, 2003):

Supervised learning. The computer is presented with example inputs and their desired outputs, given by a "teacher", and the goal is to learn a general rule that maps inputs to outputs.

Unsupervised learning. Here, no labels are given to the learning algorithm, leaving it on its own to find structure in its input. Unsupervised learning can be a goal in itself (discovering hidden patterns in data) or a means towards an end.

Reinforcement learning. In this instance, a computer program interacts with a dynamic environment in which it must perform a certain goal (such as driving a vehicle), without a teacher explicitly telling it whether it has come close to its goal or not. Another example is learning to play a game by playing against an opponent (Bishop, Pattern Recognition and Machine Learning, 2006).

Between supervised and unsupervised learning is semi-supervised learning, where the teacher gives an incomplete training signal: a training set with some (often many) of the target outputs missing. Transduction is a special case of this principle where the entire set of problem instances is known at learning time, except that part of the targets are missing.

Among other categories of machine learning problems, learning to learn learns its own inductive bias based on previous experience. Developmental learning, elaborated for robot learning, generates its own sequences (also called curriculum) of learning situations to cumulatively acquire repertoires of novel skills through autonomous self-exploration and social interaction with human teachers, and using guidance mechanisms such as active learning, maturation, motor synergies, and imitation.

Another categorization of machine learning tasks arises when one considers the desired output of a machine-learned system (Bishop, Pattern Recognition and Machine Learning, 2006):

- In **classification**, inputs are divided into two or more classes, and the learner must produce a model that assigns unseen inputs to one (or multi-label classification) or more of these classes. This is typically tackled in a supervised way. Spam filtering is an example of classification, where the inputs are email (or other) messages and the classes are "spam" and "not spam".

- In **regression**, also a supervised problem, the outputs are continuous rather than discrete.
- In **clustering**, a set of inputs is to be divided into groups. Unlike in classification, the groups are not known beforehand, making this typically an unsupervised task.
- **Density estimation** finds the distribution of inputs in some space.
- **Dimensionality reduction** simplifies inputs by mapping them into a lower-dimensional space. Topic modeling is a related problem, where a program is given a list of human language documents and is tasked to find out which documents cover similar topics.

Approaches

There are numerous approaches to machine learning. We discuss several of these in the chapters to follow. To these we will devote less narrative here. And describe those not in the book in more detail.

Decision tree learning
Decision tree learning uses a decision tree as a predictive model, which maps observations about an item to conclusions about the item's target value.

Association rule learning
Association rule learning is a method for discovering interesting relations between variables in large databases.

Artificial neural networks
An artificial neural network (ANN) learning algorithm, usually called "neural network" (NN), is a learning algorithm that is inspired by the structure and functional aspects of biological neural networks. Computations are structured in terms of an interconnected group of artificial neurons, processing information using a connectionist approach to computation. Modern neural networks are non-linear statistical data modeling tools. They are usually used to model complex relationships between inputs and outputs, to find patterns in data, or to

capture the statistical structure in an unknown joint probability distribution between observed variables.

Support vector machines
Support vector machines (SVMs) are a set of related supervised learning methods used for classification and regression. Given a set of training examples, each marked as belonging to one of two categories, an SVM training algorithm builds a model that predicts whether a new example falls into one category or the other.

Clustering
Cluster analysis is the assignment of a set of observations into subsets (called clusters) so that observations within the same cluster are similar according to some predesignated criterion or criteria, while observations drawn from different clusters are dissimilar. Different clustering techniques make different assumptions on the structure of the data, often defined by some similarity metric and evaluated for example by internal compactness (similarity between members of the same cluster) and separation between different clusters. Other methods are based on estimated density and graph connectivity. Clustering is a method of unsupervised learning, and a common technique for statistical data analysis.

Bayesian networks
A Bayesian network, belief network or directed acyclic graphical model is a probabilistic graphical model that represents a set of random variables and their conditional independencies via a directed acyclic graph (DAG). For example, a Bayesian network could represent the probabilistic relationships between diseases and symptoms. Given symptoms, the network can be used to compute the probabilities of the presence of various diseases. Efficient algorithms exist that perform inference and learning.

Inductive logic programming
Inductive logic programming (ILP) is an approach to rule learning using logic programming as a uniform representation for input examples,

47

background knowledge, and hypotheses. Given an encoding of the known background knowledge and a set of examples represented as a logical database of facts, an ILP system will derive a hypothesized logic program that entails all positive and no negative examples. Inductive programming is a related field that considers any kind of programming languages for representing hypotheses (and not only logic programming), such as functional programs.

Reinforcement learning

Reinforcement learning is concerned with how an agent ought to take actions in an environment so as to maximize some notion of long-term reward. Reinforcement learning algorithms attempt to find a policy that maps states of the world to the actions the agent ought to take in those states. Reinforcement learning differs from the supervised learning problem in that correct input/output pairs are never presented, nor sub-optimal actions explicitly corrected.

Representation learning

Several learning algorithms, mostly unsupervised learning algorithms, aim at discovering better representations of the inputs provided during training. Classical examples include principal components analysis and cluster analysis. Representation learning algorithms often attempt to preserve the information in their input but transform it in a way that makes it useful, often as a pre-processing step before performing classification or predictions, allowing to reconstruct the inputs coming from the unknown data generating distribution, while not being necessarily faithful for configurations that are implausible under that distribution.

Manifold learning algorithms attempt to do so under the constraint that the learned representation is low-dimensional. Sparse coding algorithms attempt to do so under the constraint that the learned representation is sparse (has many zeros). Multilinear subspace learning algorithms aim to learn low-dimensional representations directly from tensor representations for multidimensional data, without reshaping them into (high-dimensional) vectors (Lu, Plataniotis, & Venetsanopoulos, 2011).

Deep learning algorithms discover multiple levels of representation, or a hierarchy of features, with higher-level, more abstract features defined in terms of (or generating) lower-level features. It has been argued that an intelligent machine is one that learns a representation that disentangles the underlying factors of variation that explain the observed data (Bengio, 2009).

Similarity and metric learning
In this problem, the learning machine is given pairs of examples that are considered similar and pairs of less similar objects. It then needs to learn a similarity function (or a distance metric function) that can predict if new objects are similar. It is sometimes used in Recommendation systems.

Sparse dictionary learning
In this method, a datum is represented as a linear combination of basis functions, and the coefficients are assumed to be sparse. Let x be a d-dimensional datum, D be a d by n matrix, where each column of D represents a basis function. r is the coefficient to represent x using D. Mathematically, sparse dictionary learning means the following $x \approx Dr$ where r is sparse. Generally speaking, n is assumed to be larger than d to allow the freedom for a sparse representation.

Learning a dictionary along with sparse representations is strongly NP-hard and also difficult to solve approximately (Tillmann, 2015). A popular heuristic method for sparse dictionary learning is K-SVD.

Sparse dictionary learning has been applied in several contexts. In classification, the problem is to determine which classes a previously unseen datum belongs to. Suppose a dictionary for each class has already been built. Then a new datum is associated with the class such that it's best sparsely represented by the corresponding dictionary. Sparse dictionary learning has also been applied in image de-noising. The key idea is that a clean image path can be sparsely represented by an image dictionary, but the noise cannot (Aharon, Elad, & Bruckstein, 2006).

Genetic algorithms

A genetic algorithm (GA) is a search heuristic that mimics the process of natural selection, and uses methods such as mutation and crossover to generate new genotype in the hope of finding good solutions to a given problem. In machine learning, genetic algorithms found some uses in the 1980s and 1990s (Goldberg & Holland, 1988).

Applications

- Applications for machine learning include:
- Machine perception
- Computer vision, including object recognition
- Natural language processing
- Syntactic pattern recognition
- Search engines
- Medical diagnosis
- Bioinformatics
- Brain-machine interfaces
- Cheminformatics
- Detecting credit card fraud
- Stock market analysis
- Sequence mining
- Speech and handwriting recognition
- Game playing
- Adaptive websites
- Computational advertising
- Computational finance
- Structural health monitoring
- Sentiment analysis (or opinion mining)
- Affective computing
- Information retrieval
- Recommender systems
- Optimization and Metaheuristic

In 2006, the online movie company Netflix held the first "Netflix Prize" competition to find a program to better predict user preferences and improve the accuracy on its existing Cinematch movie recommendation algorithm by at least 10%. A joint team made up of researchers from AT&T Labs-Research in collaboration with the teams Big Chaos and Pragmatic Theory built an ensemble model to win the Grand Prize in 2009 for $1 million.

In 2010 The Wall Street Journal wrote about a money management firm Rebellion Research's use of machine learning to predict economic movements, the article talks about Rebellion Research's prediction of the financial crisis and economic recovery.

In 2014 it has been reported that a machine learning algorithm has been applied in Art History to study fine art paintings, and that it may have revealed previously unrecognized influences between artists.

52

4. Empirical Bayes method

Empirical Bayes methods are procedures for statistical inference in which the prior distribution is estimated from the data. This approach stands in contrast to standard Bayesian methods, for which the prior distribution is fixed before any data are observed. Despite this difference in perspective, empirical Bayes may be viewed as an approximation to a fully Bayesian treatment of a hierarchical model wherein the parameters at the highest level of the hierarchy are set to their most likely values, instead of being integrated out. Empirical Bayes, also known as maximum marginal likelihood (Bishop, Neural networks for pattern recognition, 2005), represents one approach for setting hyperparameters.

Introduction

Empirical Bayes methods can be seen as an approximation to a fully Bayesian treatment of a hierarchical Bayes model.

In, for example, a two-stage hierarchical Bayes model, observed data $y = \{y_1, y_2, \dots, y_N\}$ are assumed to be generated from an unobserved set of parameters $\theta = \{\theta_1, \theta_2, \dots, \theta_n\}$ according to a probability distribution. In turn, the parameters θ can be considered samples drawn from a population characterized by hyperparameters η according to a probability distribution $p(\theta|\eta)$. In the hierarchical Bayes model, though not in the empirical Bayes approximation, the hyperparameters η are considered to be drawn from an unparameterized distribution $p(\theta|\eta)$.

Information about a particular quantity of interest θ_i therefore comes not only from the properties of those data which directly depend on it, but also from the properties of the population of parameters θ as a whole, inferred from the data as a whole, summarized by the hyperparameters η.

Using Bayes' theorem,

$$p(\theta|y) = \frac{p(y|\theta)p(\theta)}{p(y)} = \frac{p(y|\theta)p}{p(y)} \int p(\theta|\eta)p(\eta)d\eta.$$

In general, this integral will not be tractable analytically and must be evaluated by numerical methods. Stochastic approximations using, e.g., Markov Chain Monte Carlo sampling or deterministic approximations such as quadrature are common.

Alternatively, the expression can be written as

$$p(\theta|y) = \int p(\theta|\eta, y)p(\eta|y)d\eta = \int \frac{p(y|\theta)p(\theta|\eta)}{p(y|\eta)} p(\eta|y)d\eta,$$

and the term in the integral can in turn be expressed as

$$p(\eta|y) = \int p(\eta|\theta)p(\theta|y)d\theta.$$

These suggest an iterative scheme, qualitatively similar in structure to a Gibbs sampler, to evolve successively improved approximations to $p(\theta|y)$ and $p(\eta|y)$. First, we calculate an initial approximation to $p(\theta|y)$ ignoring the η dependence completely; then we calculate an approximation to $p(\eta|y)$ based upon the initial approximate distribution of $p(\theta|y)$; then we use this $p(\eta|y)$ to update the approximation for $p(\theta|y)$; then we update $p(\eta|y)$; and so on.

When the true distribution $p(\eta|y)$ is sharply peaked, the integral determining $p(\theta|y)$ may not be changed much by replacing the probability distribution over η with a point estimate η^* representing the distribution's peak (or, alternatively, its mean),

$$p(\theta|y) \approx \frac{p(y|\theta)p(\theta|\eta^*)}{p(y|\eta^*)}$$

With this approximation, the above iterative scheme becomes the EM algorithm.

The term "Empirical Bayes" can cover a wide variety of methods, but most can be regarded as an early truncation of either the above scheme or something quite like it. Point estimates, rather than the whole distribution, are typically used for the parameter(s) η. The estimates for η^* are typically made from the first approximation to $p(\theta|y)$ without subsequent refinement. These estimates for η^* are usually made without considering an appropriate prior distribution for η.

Point estimation

Robbins method: non-parametric empirical Bayes (NPEB)

Robbins (Robbins, 1956) considered a case of sampling from a compound distribution, where probability for each y_i (conditional on θ_i) is specified by a Poisson distribution,

$$p(y_i|\theta_i) = \frac{\theta_i^{y_i} e^{-\theta_i}}{y_i!},$$

while the prior is unspecified except that it is also i.i.d. from an unknown distribution, with cumulative distribution function $G(\theta)$. Compound sampling arises in a variety of statistical estimation problems, such as accident rates and clinical trials. We simply seek a point prediction of θ_i given all the observed data. Because the prior is unspecified, we seek to do this without knowledge of G (Carlin & Louis, 2000).

Under mean squared error loss (SEL), the conditional expectation $E(\theta_i|Y_i)$ is a reasonable quantity to use for prediction (Nikulin, 2001). For the Poisson compound sampling model, this quantity is

$$E(\theta_i|y_i) = \frac{\int (\theta^{y+1} e^{-\theta}/y_i!) dG(\theta)}{\int (\theta^y e^{-\theta}/y_i!) dG(\theta)}.$$

This can be simplified by multiplying the expression by $(y_i + 1/y_i + 1)$, yielding

$$E(\theta_i|y_i) = \frac{(y_i + 1)p_G(y_i + 1)}{p_G(y_i)},$$

where p_G is the marginal distribution obtained by integrating out θ over G (Wald, 1971).

To take advantage of this, Robbins (Robbins, 1956) suggested estimating the marginals with their empirical frequencies, yielding the fully non-parametric estimate as:

$$E(\theta_i|y_i) = (y_i + 1)\frac{\#\{Y_j = y_i + 1\}}{\#\{Y_j = y_i\}},$$

where # denotes "number of" (Good, 1953).

Example - Accident rates

Suppose each customer of an insurance company has an "accident rate" θ and is insured against accidents; the probability distribution of θ is the underlying distribution, and is unknown. The number of accidents suffered by each customer in a specified time period has a Poisson distribution with expected value equal to the particular customer's accident rate. The actual number of accidents experienced by a customer is the observable quantity. A crude way to estimate the underlying probability distribution of the accident rate θ is to estimate the proportion of members of the whole population suffering $0, 1, 2, 3, \ldots$ accidents during the specified time period as the corresponding proportion in the observed random sample. Having done so, we then desire to predict the accident rate of each customer in the sample. As above, one may use the conditional expected value of the accident rate θ given the observed number of accidents during the baseline period. Thus, if a customer suffers six accidents during the baseline period, that customer's estimated accident rate is

7 × [the proportion of the sample who suffered 7 accidents] / [the proportion of the sample who suffered 6 accidents].

Note that if the proportion of people suffering k accidents is a decreasing function of k, the customer's predicted accident rate will often be lower than their observed number of accidents. This shrinkage effect is typical of empirical Bayes analyses.

Parametric empirical Bayes

If the likelihood and its prior take on simple parametric forms (such as 1- or 2-dimensional likelihood functions with simple conjugate priors), then the empirical Bayes problem is only to estimate the marginal $m(y|\eta)$ and the hyperparameters η using the complete set of empirical measurements. For example, one common approach, called parametric empirical Bayes point estimation, is to approximate the marginal using the maximum likelihood estimate (MLE), or a Moments expansion, which allows one to express the hyperparameters η in terms of the empirical mean and variance. This simplified marginal allows one to plug in the empirical averages into a point estimate for the prior θ. The resulting equation for the prior θ is greatly simplified, as shown below.

There are several common parametric empirical Bayes models, including the Poisson–gamma model (below), the Beta-binomial model, the Gaussian–Gaussian model, the Dirichlet-multinomial model (Johnson, Kotz, & Kemp, 1992), as well specific models for Bayesian linear regression (see below) and Bayesian multivariate linear regression. More advanced approaches include hierarchical Bayes models and Bayesian mixture models.

Poisson–gamma model

For example, in the example above, let the likelihood be a Poisson distribution, and let the prior now be specified by the conjugate prior, which is a gamma distribution $(G(\alpha, \beta))$ (where $\eta = (\alpha, \beta)$):

$$p(\theta|\alpha, \beta) = \frac{\theta^{\alpha-1}e^{-\theta/\beta}}{\beta^{\alpha}\Gamma(\alpha)}, \text{ for } \theta > 0, \alpha > 0, \beta > 0.$$

It is straightforward to show the posterior is also a gamma distribution. Write

$$p(\theta|y) \propto p(y|\theta)p(\theta|\alpha,\beta),$$

where the marginal distribution has been omitted since it does not depend explicitly on θ. Expanding terms which do depend on θ gives the posterior as:

$$p(\theta|y) \propto \left(\theta^y e^{-\theta}\right)\left(\theta^{\alpha-1}e^{-\theta/\beta}\right) = \theta^{y+\alpha-1}e^{-\theta(1+1/\beta)}.$$

So the posterior density is also a gamma distribution $G(\alpha',\beta')$, where $\alpha' = y + \alpha$, and $\beta' = (1+1/\beta)^{-1}$. Also notice that the marginal is simply the integral of the posterior over all Θ, which turns out to be a negative binomial distribution.

To apply empirical Bayes, we will approximate the marginal using the maximum likelihood estimate (MLE). However, since the posterior is a gamma distribution, the MLE of the marginal turns out to be just the mean of the posterior, which is the point estimate $E(\theta|y)$ we need. Recalling that the mean μ of a gamma distribution $G(\alpha',\beta')$ is simply $\alpha'\beta'$, we have

$$E(\theta|y) = \alpha'\beta' = \frac{\bar{y}+\alpha}{1+1/\beta} = \frac{\beta}{1+\beta}\bar{y} + \frac{1}{1+\beta}(\alpha\beta).$$

To obtain the values of α and β, empirical Bayes prescribes estimating mean $\alpha\beta$ and variance $\alpha\beta^2$ using the complete set of empirical data.

The resulting point estimate $E(\theta|y)$ is therefore like a weighted average of the sample mean $\bar{y}$ and the prior mean $\mu = \alpha\beta$. This turns out to be a general feature of empirical Bayes; the point estimates for the prior (i.e., mean) will look like a weighted averages of the sample estimate and the prior estimate (likewise for estimates of the variance).

Bayesian Linear Regression

Bayesian linear regression is an approach to linear regression in which the statistical analysis is undertaken within the context of Bayesian inference. When the regression model has errors that have a normal distribution, and if a particular form of prior distribution is assumed, explicit results are available for the posterior probability distributions of the model's parameters.

Consider a standard linear regression problem, in which for $i = 1, \ldots, n$. We specify the conditional distribution of y_i given a $k \times 1$ predictor vector x_i:

$$y_i = X_i^T \beta + \varepsilon_i,$$

where β is a $k \times 1$ vector, and the ε_i are independent and identical normally distributed random variables:

$$\varepsilon_i \sim N(\mu, \sigma^2).$$

This corresponds to the following likelihood function:

$$p(y|X, \beta, \sigma^2) \propto (\sigma^2)^{-n/2} \exp\left(-\frac{1}{2\sigma^2}(y - X\beta)^T(y - X\beta)\right).$$

The ordinary least squares solution is to estimate the coefficient vector using the Moore-Penrose pseudoinverse (Penrose, 1955) (Ben-Israel & Greville, 2003):

$$\hat{\beta} = (X^T X)^{-1} X^T y,$$

Where X is the $n \times k$ design matrix, each row of which is a predictor vector X_i^T; and y is the column n-vector $[y_1 \cdots y_n]^T$.

This is a "frequentist" approach (Neyman, 1937), and it assumes that there are enough measurements to say something meaningful about β. In the Bayesian approach, the data are supplemented with additional information in the form of a prior probability distribution. The prior belief about the parameters is combined with the data's likelihood function according to Bayes theorem to yield the posterior belief about the parameters β and σ. The prior can take different functional forms depending on the domain and the information that is available *a priori*.

Software

Several software packages are available that perform Empirical Bayes, including the Open Source software R with the limma package. Tos start the package in R, one simply enters the following in the R console at the prompt

```
>
source("http://bioconductor.org/biocLite.R")biocLite("limma
").
```

Commercial software includes MATLAB, SAS and SPSS.

Example Using R

Model Selection in Bayesian Linear Regression

Consider data generated by $y_i = b_1 x_i + b_3 x_i^3 + \varepsilon_i$, and suppose we wish to fit a polynomial of degree 3 to the data. There are then 4 regression coefficients, namely, the intercept and the three coefficients of the power of x. This yields $2^4 = 16$ models possible models for the data. Let $b_1 = 8$ and $b_3 = -0.5$ so that the data looks like this in R:

```
> rm(list=ls())
> x=runif(200,-10,10)
> a=c(18,0,-0.5,0)
> Y=a[1]*x^1+a[2]*x^2+a[3]*x^3+a[4]
> Y=Y+rnorm(length(Y),0,5)
> plot(x,Y)
```

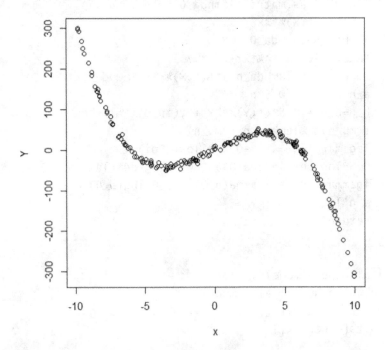

The code to generate the data and calculate the log marginal likelihood for the different models appears below.

```
> p=4
> X=cbind(x,x^2,x^3,1)
> tf <- c(TRUE, FALSE)
> models <- expand.grid(replicate(p,tf,simplify=FALSE))
> names(models) <- NULL
> models=as.matrix(models)
> models=models[-dim(models)[1],]

> a_0=100
> b_0=0.5
> mu_0=rep(0,p)
> lambda_0=diag(p)

> lml <- function(model){
+       n=length(Y)
+       Y=as.matrix(Y)
+       X=as.matrix(X[,model])
+       mu_0=as.matrix(mu_0[model])
```

61

```
+       lambda_0=as.matrix(lambda_0[model,model])
+          XtX=t(X)%*%X
+       lambda_n=lambda_0 + XtX
+       BMLE=solve(XtX)%*%t(X)%*%Y
+       mu_n=solve(lambda_n)%*%(t(X)%*%Y+lambda_0%*%mu_0)
+       a_n = a_0 + 0.5*n
+       b_n=b_0 + 0.5*(t(Y)%*%Y + t(mu_0)%*%lambda_0%*%mu_0 -
+       t(mu_n)%*%lambda_n%*%mu_n)
+       log_mar_lik  <-  -0.5*n*log(2*pi) +
+       0.5*log(det(lambda_0)) - 0.5*log(det(lambda_n)) +
+       lgamma(a_n) - lgamma(a_0) + a_0*log(b_0) -
+       a_n*log(b_n)
+       return(mle)
+       }

> lml.all=apply(models,1,lml)
> results=cbind(lml.all, models)
> order=sort(results[,1],index=TRUE,decreasing=TRUE)
> results[order$ix,]
```

Model Evaluation

The models are listed in order of descending log marginal likelihood below:

	lml	x	x^2	x^3	c
[1,]	-1339.085	1	0	1	0
[2,]	-1341.611	1	0	1	1
[3,]	-1345.397	1	1	1	0
[4,]	-1347.116	1	1	1	1
[5,]	-2188.934	0	0	1	0
[6,]	-2190.195	0	0	1	1
[7,]	-2194.238	0	1	1	0
[8,]	-2196.109	0	1	1	1
[9,]	-2393.395	1	0	0	0
[10,]	-2395.309	1	0	0	1
[11,]	-2399.188	1	1	0	0
[12,]	-2401.248	1	1	0	1
[13,]	-2477.084	0	0	0	1
[14,]	-2480.784	0	1	0	0
[15,]	-2483.047	0	1	0	1

```
> BMLE
            [,1]
x  18.241814068
    0.008942083
   -0.502597759
   -0.398375650
```

The model with the highest log marginal likelihood is the model which includes x and x^3 only, for which the MLE of the regression coefficients are 18.241814068 and -0.502597759 for x and x^3 respectively. Compare this to how the data was generated.

5. Naïve Bayes classifier

In machine learning, Naïve Bayes classifiers are a family of simple probabilistic classifiers based on applying Bayes' theorem with strong (naive) independence assumptions between the features.

Naïve Bayes is a popular (baseline) method for text categorization, the problem of judging documents as belonging to one category or the other (such as spam or legitimate, sports or politics, etc.) with word frequencies as the features. With appropriate preprocessing, it is competitive in this domain with more advanced methods including support vector machines (Rennie, Shih, Teevan, & Karger, 2003).

Training Naïve Bayes can be done by evaluating an approximation algorithm in closed form in linear time, rather than by expensive iterative approximation.

Introduction

In simple terms, a Naïve Bayes classifier assumes that the value of a particular feature is unrelated to the presence or absence of any other feature, given the class variable. For example, a fruit may be considered to be an apple if it is red, round, and about 3" in diameter. A Naïve Bayes classifier considers each of these features to contribute independently to the probability that this fruit is an apple, regardless of the presence or absence of the other features.

For some types of probability models, Naïve Bayes classifiers can be trained very efficiently in a supervised learning setting. In many practical applications, parameter estimation for Naïve Bayes models uses the method of maximum likelihood; in other words, one can work with the Naïve Bayes model without accepting Bayesian probability or using any Bayesian methods.

Despite their naive design and apparently oversimplified assumptions,

Naïve Bayes classifiers have worked quite well in many complex real-world situations. In 2004, an analysis of the Bayesian classification problem showed that there are sound theoretical reasons for the apparently implausible efficacy of Naïve Bayes classifiers (Zhang, 2004). Still, a comprehensive comparison with other classification algorithms in 2006 showed that Bayes classification is outperformed by other approaches, such as boosted trees or random forests (Caruana & Niculescu-Mizil, 2006).

An advantage of Naïve Bayes is that it only requires a small amount of training data to estimate the parameters (means and variances of the variables) necessary for classification. Because independent variables are assumed, only the variances of the variables for each class need to be determined and not the entire covariance matrix.

Probabilistic model

Abstractly, the probability model for a classifier is a conditional model

$$p(C|F_1, \dots, F_n)$$

over a dependent class variable C with a small number of outcomes or classes, conditional on several feature variables F_1 through F_n. The problem is that if the number of features n is large or if a feature can take on a large number of values, then basing such a model on probability tables is infeasible. We therefore reformulate the model to make it more tractable.

Using Bayes' theorem, this can be written

$$p(C|F_1, \dots, F_n) = \frac{p(C)p(F_1, \dots, F_n|C)}{p(F_1, \dots, F_n)}.$$

In plain English, using Bayesian Probability terminology, the above equation can be written as

$$\text{posterior} = \frac{\text{prior} \times \text{likelihood}}{\text{evidence}}.$$

In practice, there is interest only in the numerator of that fraction, because the denominator does not depend on C and the values of the features F_i are given, so that the denominator is effectively constant. The numerator is equivalent to the joint probability model

$$p(C|F_1, \dots, F_n),$$

which can be rewritten as follows, using the chain rule for repeated applications of the definition of conditional probability:

$$
\begin{aligned}
p(C|F_1, \dots, F_n) &= p(C)p(F_1, \dots, F_n|C) \\
&= p(C)p(F_1|C)p(F_2, \dots, F_n|C, F_1) \\
&= p(C)p(F_1|C)p(F_2|C, F_1)p(F_3, \dots, F_n|C, F_1, F_2) \\
&= p(C)p(F_1|C)p(F_2|C, F_1)p(F_3|C, F_1, F_2) \\
&\quad p(F_4, \dots, F_n|C, F_1, F_2, F_3) \\
&= p(C)p(F_1|C)p(F_2|C, F_1) \dots p(F_n|C, F_1, F_2, F_3, \dots, F_n)
\end{aligned}
$$

Now the "naïve" conditional independence assumptions come into play: assume that each feature F_i is conditionally independent of every other feature F_j for $i \neq j$ given the category C. This means that

$$
\begin{aligned}
p(F_i|C, F_j) &= p(F_i|C) \\
p(F_i|C, F_j, F_k) &= p(F_i|C) \\
p(F_i|C, F_j, F_k, F_l) &= p(F_i|C)
\end{aligned}
$$

and so on, for $i \neq j, k, l$. Thus, the joint model can be expressed as

$$
\begin{aligned}
p(C|F_1, \dots, F_n) &\propto p(C, F_1, \dots, F_n) \\
&\propto p(C)p(F_1|C)p(F_2|C)p(F_3|C) \cdots \\
&\propto p(C) \prod_{i-1}^{n} p(F_i|C).
\end{aligned}
$$

This means that under the above independence assumptions, the conditional distribution over the class variable C is:

$$p(C|F_1, \dots, F_n) = \frac{1}{Z} p(C) \prod_{i-1}^{n} p(F_i|C),$$

where the evidence $Z = p(F_1, \dots, F_n)$ is a scaling factor dependent only on $F_1, \dots, F_n$, that is, a constant if the values of the feature variables are known (Rish, 2001).

Constructing a classifier from the probability model

The discussion so far has derived the independent feature model, that is, the Naïve Bayes probability model. The Naïve Bayes classifier combines this model with a decision rule. One common rule is to pick the hypothesis that is most probable; this is known as the maximum *a posteriori* or MAP decision rule. The corresponding classifier, a Bayes classifier, is the function classify defined as follows:

$$\text{classify}(f_1, \dots, f_n) = \underset{c}{\operatorname{argmax}} \, p(C = c) \prod_{i=1}^{n} p(F_i = f_i|C = c)$$

Parameter estimation and event models

All model parameters (i.e., class priors and feature probability distributions) can be approximated with relative frequencies from the training set. These are maximum likelihood estimates of the probabilities. A class' prior may be calculated by assuming equiprobable classes (i.e., $priors = 1 / (number\ of\ classes)$), or by calculating an estimate for the class probability from the training set (i.e., $(prior\ for\ a\ given\ class) = (number\ of\ samples\ in\ the\ class) / (total\ number\ of\ samples)$). To estimate the parameters for a feature's distribution, we must assume a distribution or generate nonparametric models for the features from the training set (John & Langley, 1995).

The assumptions on distributions of features are called the event model of the Naïve Bayes classifier. For discrete features like the ones encountered in document classification (include spam filtering), multinomial and Bernoulli distributions are popular. These assumptions lead to two distinct models, which are often confused (McCallum & Nigam, 1998) (Metsis, Androutsopoulos, & Paliouras, 2006).

Gaussian Naïve Bayes

When dealing with continuous data, a typical assumption is that the continuous values associated with each class are distributed according to a Gaussian distribution. For example, suppose the training data contain a continuous attribute, x. We first segment the data by the class, and then compute the mean and variance of x in each class. Let μ_c be the mean of the values in   associated with class c, and let σ_c^2 be the variance of the values in associated with class c. Then, the probability density of some value given a class, $P(x = v|c)$, can be computed by plugging v into the equation for a Normal distribution parameterized by μ_c and μ_c. That is,

$$P(x = v|c) = \frac{1}{\sqrt{2\pi\sigma_c^2}} e^{-\frac{(v-\mu_c)^2}{2\sigma_c^2}}$$

Another common technique for handling continuous values is to use binning to discretize the feature values, to obtain a new set of Bernoulli-distributed features. In general, the distribution method is a better choice if there is a small amount of training data, or if the precise distribution of the data is known. The discretization method tends to do better if there is a large amount of training data because it will learn to fit the distribution of the data. Since Naïve Bayes is typically used when a large amount of data is available (as more computationally expensive models can generally achieve better accuracy), the discretization method is generally preferred over the distribution method.

Multinomial Naïve Bayes

With a multinomial event model, samples (feature vectors) represent the frequencies with which certain events have been generated by a multinomial $(p_1, \ldots, p_n)$ where p_i is the probability that event i occurs (or k such multinomials in the multiclass case). This is the event model typically used for document classification; the feature values are then term frequencies, generated by a multinomial that produces some number of words ("bag of words" assumption, where word order is ignored). The likelihood of observing a feature vector (histogram) F is given by

$$p(F|C) = \frac{(\sum_i F_i)!}{\prod_i F_i!} \prod_i p_i^{F_i}$$

The multinomial Naïve Bayes classifier becomes a linear classifier when expressed in log-space:

$$\log p(C|F) = \log \left(p(C) \prod_{i=1}^{n} p(F_i|C) \right)$$

$$= \log p(C) + \sum_{i=1}^{n} \log p(F_i|C)$$

$$= b + w_C^T F$$

Where $b = \log p(C)$ and $w_{c_i} = \log p(F_i|C)$.

If a given class and feature value never occur together in the training data, then the frequency-based probability estimate will be zero. This is problematic because it will wipe out all information in the other probabilities when they are multiplied. Therefore, it is often desirable to incorporate a small-sample correction, called pseudo-count, in all probability estimates such that no probability is ever set to be exactly zero. This way of regularizing Naïve Bayes is called Additive smoothing when the pseudo-count is one, and Lidstone smoothing in the general case.

Rennie et al. (Rennie, Lawrence, Teevan, & Karger, 2003) discuss problems with the multinomial assumption in the context of document classification and possible ways to alleviate those problems, including the use of *tf–idf* weights instead of raw term frequencies and document length normalization, to produce a Naïve Bayes classifier that is competitive with support vector machines.

Bernoulli Naïve Bayes

In the multivariate Bernoulli event model, features are independent Booleans (binary variables) describing inputs. This model is also popular for document classification tasks, where binary term occurrence features are used rather than term frequencies. If F_i is a Boolean expressing the occurrence or absence of the i-th term from the vocabulary, then the likelihood of a document given a class C is given by

$$p(F_1, \ldots, F_n | C) = \prod_{i=1}^{n} [F_i p(w_i | C) + (1 - F_i)(1 - p(w_i | C))]$$

where $p(w_i | C)$ is the probability of class C generating the term w_i. This event model is especially popular for classifying short texts. It has the benefit of explicitly modeling the absence of terms. Note that a Naïve Bayes classifier with a Bernoulli event model is not the same as a multinomial NB classifier with frequency counts truncated to one.

Discussion

Despite the fact that the far-reaching independence assumptions are often inaccurate, the Naïve Bayes classifier has several properties that make it surprisingly useful in practice. In particular, the decoupling of the class conditional feature distributions means that each distribution can be independently estimated as a one-dimensional distribution. This helps alleviate problems stemming from the curse of dimensionality, such as the need for data sets that scale exponentially with the number of features. While Naïve Bayes often fails to produce a good estimate for the correct class probabilities, this may not be a requirement for many applications. For example, the Naïve Bayes classifier will make the correct MAP decision rule classification so long as the correct class is more probable than any other class. This is true regardless of whether the probability estimate is slightly, or even grossly inaccurate. In this manner, the overall classifier can be robust enough to ignore serious deficiencies in its underlying naive probability model. Other reasons for the observed success of the Naïve Bayes classifier are discussed in the literature cited below.

Examples

Sex classification

Problem: classify whether a given person is a male or a female based on the measured features. The features include height, weight, and foot size.

Training

Example training set below.

sex	height	weight (lbs)	foot
male	6	180	12
male	5.92	190	11
male	5.58	170	12
male	5.92	165	10
female	5	100	6
female	5.5	150	8
female	5.42	130	7
female	5.75	150	9

The classifier created from the training set using a Gaussian distribution assumption would be (given variances are sample variances):

sex	mean (height)	variance (height)	mean (weight)	variance (weight)	Mean (foot size)	Variance (foot size)
male	5.8550	3.50e-02	176.25	1.23e+02	11.25	9.16e-01
female	5.4175	9.72e-02	132.50	5.58e+02	7.50	1.66e+00

Let's say we have equiprobable classes so $P(\text{male}) = P(\text{female}) =$

72

0.5. This prior probability distribution might be based on our knowledge of frequencies in the larger population, or on frequency in the training set.

Testing

Below is a sample to be classified as a male or female.

sex	height	weight	foot
sample	6	130	8

We wish to determine which posterior is greater, male or female. For the classification as male the posterior is given by

$$posterior(\text{male})$$
$$= \frac{P(\text{male})p(\text{height}|\text{male})p(\text{weight}|\text{male})p(\text{foot size}|\text{male})}{evidence}$$

For the classification as female the posterior is given by

$$posterior(\text{female})$$
$$= \frac{P(\text{female})p(\text{height}|\text{female})p(\text{weight}|\text{female})p(\text{foot size}|\text{female})}{evidence}$$

The evidence (also termed normalizing constant) may be calculated:

$$evidence$$
$$= P(\text{male})p(\text{height}|\text{male})p(\text{weight}|\text{male})p(\text{foot size}|\text{male})$$
$$+ P(\text{female})p(\text{height}|\text{female})p(\text{weight}|\text{female})p(\text{foot size}|\text{female})$$

However, given the sample the evidence is a constant and thus scales both posteriors equally. It therefore does not affect classification and can be ignored. We now determine the probability distribution for the sex of the sample.

$$P(\text{male}) = 0.5$$

$$p(\text{height}|\text{male}) = \frac{1}{\sqrt{2\pi\sigma^2}} \exp\left(\frac{-(6-\mu)^2}{2\sigma^3}\right)$$

where $\mu = 5.855$ and $\sigma^2 = 3.5033 \cdot 10^{-2}$ are the parameters of normal distribution which have been previously determined from the training set. Note that a value greater than 1 is OK here—it is a probability density rather than a probability, because height is a continuous variable.

$p(\text{weight}|\text{male}) = 5.9881 \cdot 10^{-6}$

$p(\text{foot size}|\text{male}) = 1.3112 \cdot 10^{-3}$

posterior numerator (male)=their product $= 6.1984 \cdot 10^{-9}$

$P(\text{female}) = 0.5$

$p(\text{height}|\text{female}) = 2.2346 \cdot 10^{-1}$

$p(\text{weight}|\text{female}) = 1.6789 \cdot 10^{-2}$

$p(\text{foot size}|\text{female}) = 2.8669 \cdot 10^{-3}$

posterior numerator (female)=their product $= 5.3378 \cdot 10^{-4}$

Since posterior numerator is greater in the female case, we predict the sample is female.

Document classification

Here is a worked example of Naïve Bayesian classification to the document classification problem. Consider the problem of classifying documents by their content, for example into spam and non-spam e-mails. Imagine that documents are drawn from a number of classes of documents which can be modelled as sets of words where the (independent) probability that the i-th word of a given document occurs in a document from class C can be written as

$$p(w_i|C)$$

(For this treatment, we simplify things further by assuming that words are randomly distributed in the document—that is, words are not dependent on the length of the document, position within the document with relation to other words, or other document-context.)

Then the probability that a given document D contains all of the words w_i, given a class C, is

$$p(D|C) = \prod_i p(w_i|C)$$

The question that we desire to answer is: "what is the probability that a given document D belongs to a given class C?" In other words, what is $p(C|D)$? Now by definition

$$p(D|C) = \frac{p(D \cap C)}{p(C)}$$

and

$$p(C|D) = \frac{p(D \cap C)}{p(D)}$$

Bayes' theorem manipulates these into a statement of probability in terms of likelihood.

$$p(C|D) = \frac{p(C)}{p(C)} p(D|C)$$

Assume for the moment that there are only two mutually exclusive classes, S and $\neg S$ (e.g. spam and not spam), such that every element (email) is in either one or the other;

$$p(D|S) = \prod_i p(w_i|S)$$

And

$$p(D|\neg S) = \prod_i p(w_i|\neg S)$$

Using the Bayesian result above, we can write:

$$p(S|D) = \frac{p(S)}{p(D)} \prod_i p(w_i|S)$$

$$p(\neg S|D) = \frac{p(\neg S)}{p(D)} \prod_i p(w_i|\neg S)$$

Dividing one by the other gives:

$$\frac{p(S|D)}{p(\neg S|D)} = \frac{p(S) \prod_i p(w_i|S)}{p(\neg S) \prod_i p(w_i|\neg S)}$$

Which can be re-factored as:

$$\frac{p(S|D)}{p(\neg S|D)} = \frac{p(S)}{p(\neg S)} \prod_i \frac{p(w_i|S)}{p(w_i|\neg S)}$$

Thus, the probability ratio $p(S|D)/p(\neg S|D)$ can be expressed in terms of a series of likelihood ratios. The actual probability $p(S|D)$ can be easily computed from $\log(p(S|D)/p(\neg S|D))$ based on the observation that $p(S|D) + p(\neg S|D) = 1$.

Taking the logarithm of all these ratios, we have:

$$\ln \frac{p(S|D)}{p(\neg S|D)} = \ln \frac{p(S)}{p(\neg S)} = \sum_i \ln \frac{p(w_i|S)}{p(w_i|\neg S)}$$

(This technique of "log-likelihood ratios" is a common technique in statistics. In the case of two mutually exclusive alternatives (such as this example), the conversion of a log-likelihood ratio to a probability takes the form of a sigmoid curve: see logit for details.)

Finally, the document can be classified as follows. It is spam if $p(S|D) >$

$p(\neg S|D)$ (i.e., $\ln \frac{p(S|D)}{p(\neg S|D)} > 0$), otherwise it is not spam (Kibriya, Frank, Pfahringer, & Holmes, 2008).

Software

Open Source software packages include PNL and R. Software packages that are specifically designed for this function include:

- **Bayesian belief network software** – from J. Cheng, includes:
  o BN PowerConstructor: An efficient system for learning BN structures and parameters from data;
  o BN PowerPredictor: A data mining program for data modeling/classification/prediction.
- **Bayesian Network tools in Java** (BNJ) – is an open-source suite of Java tools for probabilistic learning and reasoning (Kansas State University KDD Lab)
- **GeNIe** – is a decision modeling environment implementing influence diagrams and Bayesian networks.
- **JNCC2** (Naive Credal Classifier 2) – is an extension of Naive Bayes towards imprecise probabilities; it is designed to return robust classification, even on small and/or incomplete data sets.

Commercial software packages include:

- **AgenaRisk** – by Ajena, is a visual tool, combining Bayesian networks and statistical simulation.
- **BayesiaLab** – by, Bayesia is a complete set of Bayesian network tools, including supervised and unsupervised learning, and analysis toolbox.
- **BNet** – by Charles River Analytics, includes BNet.Builder for rapidly creating Belief Networks, entering information, and getting results and BNet.EngineKit for incorporating Belief Network Technology in your applications.
- **Flint** – by Logic Programming Associates, combines bayesian networks, certainty factors and fuzzy logic within a logic

programming rules-based environment.

- **Netica** – by NORSYS, is Bayesian network development software provides Bayesian network tools.
- **PrecisionTree** – by Paslisade (makers of @Risk), is an add-in for Microsoft Excel for building decision trees and influence diagrams directly in the spreadsheet

Example Using R

The Iris dataset is pre-installed in R, since it is in the standard `datasets` package. To access its documentation, click on 'Packages' at the top-level of the R documentation, then on 'datasets' and then on 'iris'. As explained, there are 150 data points and 5 variables. Each data point concerns a particular iris flower and gives 4 measurements of the flower: `Sepal.Length`, `Sepal.Width`, `Petal.Length` and `Petal.Width` together with the flower's Species. The goal is to build a classifier that predicts species from the 4 measurements, so species is the class variable.

To get the `iris` dataset into your R session, do:

```
> data(iris)
```

at the R prompt. As always, it makes sense to **look at the data**. The following R command (from the Wikibook) does a nice job of this.

```
> pairs(iris[1:4],main="Iris Data
+     (red=setosa,green=versicolor,blue=virginica)", pch=21,
+       bg=c("red","green3","blue")[unclass(iris$Species)])
```

The 'pairs' command creates a scatterplot. Each dot is a data point and its position is determined by the values that data point has for a pair of variables. The class determines the color of the data point. From the plot note that setosa irises have smaller petals than the other two species.

Iris Data (red=setosa,green=versicolor,blue=virginica)

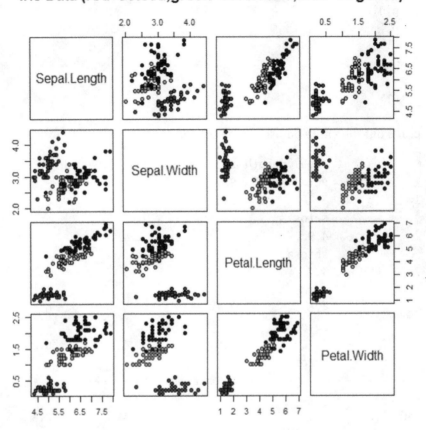

Typing:

```
> summary(iris)
```

provides a summary of the data.

```
Sepal.Length Sepal.Width  Petal.Length Petal.Width
Min.   :4.300Min.    :2.000Min.    :1.000Min.    :0.100
1st Qu.:5.1001st Qu.:2.8001st Qu.:1.6001st Qu.:0.300
Median :5.800Median :3.000Median :4.350Median :1.300
Mean   :5.843Mean    :3.057Mean    :3.758Mean    :1.199
3rd Qu.:6.4003rd Qu.:3.3003rd Qu.:5.1003rd Qu.:1.800
Max.   :7.900Max.    :4.400Max.    :6.900Max.    :2.500
Species
```

```
setosa     :50
versicolor:50
virginica :50
```

Typing:

```
> iris
```

prints out the entire dataset to the screen.

	Sepal.Length	Sepal.Width	Petal.Length	
	Petal.Width	Species		
1	5.1	3.5	1.4	0.2
	setosa			
2	4.9	3	1.4	0.2
	setosa			
3	4.7	3.2	1.3	0.2
	setosa			
4	4.6	3.1	1.5	0.2
	setosa			
5	5	3.6	1.4	0.2
	setosa			

```
-----------------------------Data omitted-------------------
-------
```

149	6.2	3.4	5.4	2.3
	virginica			
150	5.9	3	5.1	1.8
	virginica			

Constructing a Naïve Bayes classifier
We will use the e1071 R package to build a Naïve Bayes classifier. Firstly you need to download the package (since it is not pre-installed here). Do:

```
> install.packages("e1071")
```

Choose a mirror in US from the menu that will appear. You will be prompted to create a personal R library (say yes) since you don't have permission to put e1071 in the standard directory for R packages.

To (1) load e1071 into your workspace (2) build a Naïve Bayes classifier and (3) make some predictions **on the training data**, do:

```
> library(e1071)
> classifier<-naiveBayes(iris[,1:4], iris[,5])
> table(predict(classifier, iris[,-5]), iris[,5],
+      dnn=list('predicted','actual'))
```

As you should see the classifier does a pretty good job of classifying. Why is this not surprising?

```
predicted     setosa versicolor virginica
  setosa          50          0         0
  versicolor       0         47         3
  virginica        0          3        47
```

To see what's going on 'behind-the-scenes', first do:

```
> classifier$apriori
```

This gives the class distribution in the data: the **prior** distribution of the classes. (*'A priori'* is Latin for 'from before'.)

```
iris[, 5]
    setosa versicolor   virginica
      50         50          50
```

Since the predictor variables here are all continuous, the Naïve Bayes classifier generates three Gaussian (Normal) distributions for each predictor variable: one for each value of the class variable Species. If you type:

```
> classifier$tables$Petal.Length
```

You will see the mean (first column) and standard deviation (second column) for the 3 class-dependent Gaussian distributions:

```
            Petal.Length
iris[, 5]      [,1]       [,2]
  setosa      1.462  0.1736640
```

```
versicolor 4.260 0.4699110
virginica  5.552 0.5518947
```

You can plot these 3 distributions against each other with the following three R commands:

```
> plot(function(x) dnorm(x, 1.462, 0.1736640), 0, 8,
+     col="red", main="Petal length distribution for the 3
+     different species")
> curve(dnorm(x, 4.260, 0.4699110), add=TRUE, col="blue")
> curve(dnorm(x, 5.552, 0.5518947), add=TRUE, col="green")
```

Note that setosa irises (the red curve) tend to have smaller petals (mean value = 1.462) and there is less variation in petal length (standard deviation is only 0.1736640).

Petal length distribution for the 3 different species

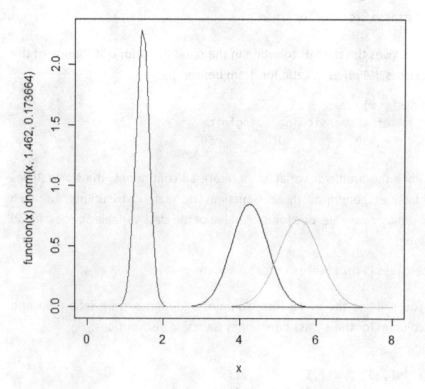

Understanding Naïve Bayes

In the previous example you were given a recipe which allowed you to construct a Naïve Bayes classifier. This was for a case where we had continuous predictor variables. In this question you have to work out what the parameters of a Naïve Bayes model should be for some discrete data.

The dataset in question is called HairEyeColor and has three variables: Sex, Eye and Hair, giving values for these 3 variables for each of 592 students from the University of Delaware. First have a look at the numbers:

```
> HairEyeColor

, , Sex = Male

        Eye
Hair     Brown Blue Hazel Green
   Black    32   11    10     3
   Brown    53   50    25    15
   Red      10   10     7     7
   Blond     3   30     5     8

, , Sex = Female

        Eye
Hair     Brown Blue Hazel Green
   Black    36    9     5     2
   Brown    66   34    29    14
   Red      16    7     7     7
   Blond     4   64     5     8
```

You can also plot it as a 'mosaic' plot which uses rectangles to represent the numbers in the data:

```
> mosaicplot(HairEyeColor)
```

Your job here is to compute the parameters for a Naïve Bayes classifier which attempts to predict Sex from the other two variables. The parameters should be estimated using maximum likelihood. To save you the tedium of manual counting, here's how to use margin.table to get the counts you need:

```
> margin.table(HairEyeColor,3)

Sex
  Male Female
   279    313
```

HairEyeColor

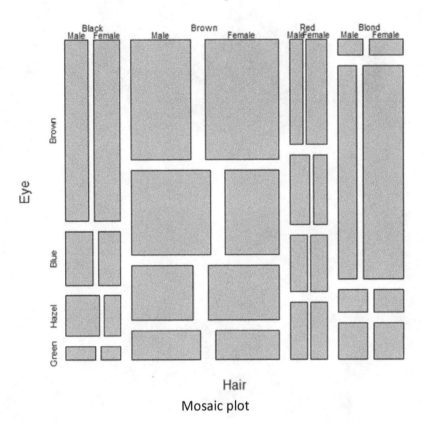

Mosaic plot

```
> margin.table(HairEyeColor,c(1,3))
```

```
       Sex
Hair    Male Female
  Black   56     52
  Brown  143    143
  Red     34     37
  Blond   46     81
```

Note that Sex is variable 3, and Hair is variable 1. Once you think you have the correct parameters speak to me or one of the demonstrators to see if you have it right. (Or if you can manage it, construct the Naïve Bayes model using the naiveBayes function and yank out the parameters from the model. Read the documentation to do this.)

6.   Decision tree learning

Decision tree learning uses a decision tree as a predictive model which maps observations about an item to conclusions about the item's target value. It is one of the predictive modeling approaches used in statistics, data mining and machine learning. More descriptive names for such tree models are classification trees or regression trees. In these tree structures, leaves represent class labels and branches represent conjunctions of features that lead to those class labels.

In decision analysis, a decision tree can be used to visually and explicitly represent decisions and decision making. In data mining, a decision tree describes data but not decisions; rather the resulting classification tree can be an input for decision making. This chapter deals with decision trees in data mining.

General

Decision tree learning is a method commonly used in data mining (Rokach & Maimon, 2008). The goal is to create a model that predicts the value of a target variable based on several input variables. An example is shown on the right. Each interior node corresponds to one of the input variables; there are edges to children for each of the possible values of that input variable. Each leaf represents a value of the target variable given the values of the input variables represented by the path from the root to the leaf.

A decision tree is a simple representation for classifying examples. Decision tree learning is one of the most successful techniques for supervised classification learning. For this section, assume that all of the features have finite discrete domains, and there is a single target feature called the classification. Each element of the domain of the classification is called a class. A decision tree or a classification tree is a tree in which each internal (non-leaf) node is labeled with an input feature. The arcs coming from a node labeled with a feature are labeled with each of the possible values of the feature. Each leaf of the tree is labeled with a class or a probability distribution over the classes.

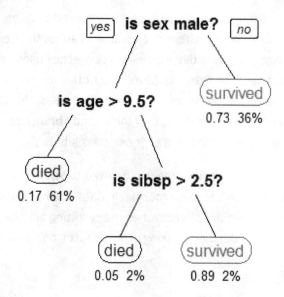

A tree showing survival of passengers on the Titanic ("sibsp" is the number of spouses or siblings aboard). The figures under the leaves show the probability of survival and the percentage of observations in the leaf.

A tree can be "learned" by splitting the source set into subsets based on an attribute value test. This process is repeated on each derived subset in a recursive manner called recursive partitioning. The recursion is completed when the subset at a node has all the same value of the target variable, or when splitting no longer adds value to the predictions. This process of top-down induction of decision trees ($TDIDT$) (Quinlan, 1986) is an example of a "greedy" algorithm, and it is by far the most common strategy for learning decision trees from data.

In data mining, decision trees can be described also as the combination of mathematical and computational techniques to aid the description, categorization and generalization of a given set of data.

Data comes in records of the form:

$$(x, Y) = (x_1, x_2, x_3, \dots, x_k, Y).$$

The dependent variable, Y, is the target variable that we are trying to understand, classify or generalize. The vector x is composed of the input variables, x_1, x_2, x_3, etc., that are used for that task.

Types

Decision trees used in data mining are of two main types:

- Classification tree analysis is when the predicted outcome is the class to which the data belongs.
- Regression tree analysis is when the predicted outcome can be considered a real number (e.g. the price of a house, or a patient's length of stay in a hospital).

The term **Classification And Regression Tree** (CART) analysis is an umbrella term used to refer to both of the above procedures, first introduced by Breiman et al. (Breiman, Friedman, Olshen, & Stone, 1984). Trees used for regression and trees used for classification have some similarities—but also some differences, such as the procedure used to determine where to split.

Some techniques, often called ensemble methods, construct more than one decision tree:

- Bagging decision trees, an early ensemble method, builds multiple decision trees by repeatedly resampling training data with replacement, and voting the trees for a consensus prediction (Breiman L. , Bagging predictors, 1996).
- A Random Forest classifier uses a number of decision trees, in order to improve the classification rate.
- Boosted Trees can be used for regression-type and classification-type problems (Friedman, Stochastic Gradient Boosting, 1999) (Hastie, Tibshirani, & Friedman, The elements of

statistical learning : Data mining, inference, and prediction, 2001).

- Rotation forest, in which every decision tree is trained by first applying principal component analysis (PCA) on a random subset of the input features (Rodriguez, Kuncheva, & Alonso, 2006).

Decision tree learning is the construction of a decision tree from class-labeled training tuples. A decision tree is a flow-chart-like structure, where each internal (non-leaf) node denotes a test on an attribute, each branch represents the outcome of a test, and each leaf (or terminal) node holds a class label. The topmost node in a tree is the root node.

There are many specific decision-tree algorithms. Notable ones include:

- ID3 (Iterative Dichotomiser 3)
- C4.5 (successor of ID3)
- CART (Classification And Regression Tree)
- CHAID (CHi-squared Automatic Interaction Detector). Performs multi-level splits when computing classification trees (Kass, 1980).
- MARS: extends decision trees to handle numerical data better.
- Conditional Inference Trees. Statistics-based approach that uses non-parametric tests as splitting criteria, corrected for multiple testing to avoid overfitting. This approach results in unbiased predictor selection and does not require pruning (Hothorn, Hornik, & Zeileis, 2006).

ID3 and CART were invented independently at around same time (between 1970-1980), yet follow a similar approach for learning decision tree from training tuples.

Metrics

Algorithms for constructing decision trees usually work top-down, by choosing a variable at each step that best splits the set of items (Rokach & Maimon, Top-down induction of decision trees classifiers-a survey, 2005). Different algorithms use different metrics for measuring "best".

These generally measure the homogeneity of the target variable within the subsets. Some examples are given below. These metrics are applied to each candidate subset, and the resulting values are combined (e.g., averaged) to provide a measure of the quality of the split.

Gini impurity

Used by the CART (classification and regression tree) algorithm, Gini impurity is a measure of how often a randomly chosen element from the set would be incorrectly labeled, if it were randomly labeled according to the distribution of labels in the subset. Gini impurity can be computed by summing the probability of each item being chosen times the probability of a mistake in categorizing that item. It reaches its minimum (zero) when all cases in the node fall into a single target category. This should not be confused with Gini coefficient.

To compute Gini impurity for a set of items, suppose i takes on values in $\{1, 2, \ldots, m\}$, and let f_i be the fraction of items labeled with value i in the set.

$$I_G(f) = \sum_{i=1}^{m} f_i(1 - f_i) = \sum_{i=1}^{m} (f_i - f_i^2) = \sum_{i=1}^{m} f_i - \sum_{i=1}^{m} f_i^2 = 1 - \sum_{i=1}^{m} f_i^2$$

Information gain

In information theory and machine learning, information gain is a synonym for Kullback–Leibler divergence. However, in the context of decision trees, the term is sometimes used synonymously with mutual information, which is the expectation value of the Kullback–Leibler divergence of a conditional probability distribution.

In particular, the information gain about a random variable X obtained from an observation that a random variable A takes the value $A = a$ is the Kullback-Leibler divergence $D_{KL}(p(x|a)||p(x|I))$ of the prior distribution $p(x|I)$ for x from the posterior distribution $p(x|a)$ for x given a.

The expected value of the information gain is the mutual information $I(X; A)$ of X and A, i.e., the reduction in the entropy of X achieved by learning the state of the random variable A.

In machine learning, this concept can be used to define a preferred sequence of attributes to investigate to most rapidly narrow down the state of X. Such a sequence (which depends on the outcome of the investigation of previous attributes at each stage) is called a decision tree. Usually an attribute with high mutual information should be preferred to other attributes.

General definition

In general terms, the expected information gain is the change in information entropy H from a prior state to a state that takes some information as given:

$$IG(T, a) = H(T) - H(T|a).$$

Formal Definition

Let T denote a set of training examples, each of the form $(x, y) = (x_1, x_2, x_3, \ldots, x_k, y)$ where $x_a \in vals(a)$ is the value of the ath attribute of example x and y is the corresponding class label. The information gain for an attribute a is defined in terms of entropy $H(\ )$ as follows:

$$IG(T, a) = H(T) - \sum_{v \in vals(a)} \frac{|\{x \in T | x_a = v\}|}{|T|} \cdot H(\{x \in T | x_a = v\}).$$

The mutual information is equal to the total entropy for an attribute if for each of the attribute values a unique classification can be made for the result attribute. In this case, the relative entropies subtracted from the total entropy are 0.

Drawbacks

Although information gain is usually a good measure for deciding the relevance of an attribute, it is not perfect. A notable problem occurs when information gain is applied to attributes that can take on a large number of distinct values. For example, suppose that one is building a decision tree for some data describing the customers of a business. Information gain is often used to decide which of the attributes are the most relevant, so they can be tested near the root of the tree. One of the input attributes might be the customer's credit card number. This attribute has a high mutual information, because it uniquely identifies each customer, but we do not want to include it in the decision tree: deciding how to treat a customer based on their credit card number is unlikely to generalize to customers we haven't seen before (overfitting).

Information gain ratio is sometimes used instead. This biases the decision tree against considering attributes with a large number of distinct values. However, attributes with very low information values then appeared to receive an unfair advantage. In addition, methods such as permutation tests have been proposed to correct the bias (Deng, Runger, & Tuv, 2011).

Decision tree advantages

Amongst other data mining methods, decision trees have various advantages:

- Simple to understand and interpret. People are able to understand decision tree models after a brief explanation.
- Requires little data preparation. Other techniques often require data normalization, dummy variables need to be created and blank values to be removed.
- Able to handle both numerical and categorical data. Other techniques are usually specialized in analyzing datasets that have only one type of variable. (For example, relation rules can be used only with nominal variables while neural networks can be used only with numerical variables.)
- Uses a white box model. If a given situation is observable in a model the explanation for the condition is easily explained by Boolean logic. (An example of a black box model is an artificial neural network since the explanation for the results is difficult to understand.)

- Possible to validate a model using statistical tests. That makes it possible to account for the reliability of the model.
- Robust. Performs well even if its assumptions are somewhat violated by the true model from which the data were generated.
- Performs well with large datasets. Large amounts of data can be analyzed using standard computing resources in reasonable time.

Limitations

- The problem of learning an optimal decision tree is known to be NP-complete under several aspects of optimality and even for simple concepts (Hyafil & Rivest, 1976). Consequently, practical decision-tree learning algorithms are based on heuristics such as the greedy algorithm where locally-optimal decisions are made at each node. Such algorithms cannot guarantee to return the globally-optimal decision tree. To reduce the greedy effect of local-optimality some methods such as the dual information distance (DID) tree were proposed (I., A., N., & Singer, 2014).
- Decision-tree learners can create over-complex trees that do not generalize well from the training data. (This is known as overfitting (Bramer, 2007).) Mechanisms such as pruning are necessary to avoid this problem (with the exception of some algorithms such as the Conditional Inference approach, which does not require pruning (Strobl, Malley, & Tutz, 2009) (Hothorn, Hornik, & Zeileis, 2006)).
- There are concepts that are hard to learn because decision trees do not express them easily, such as XOR, parity or multiplexer problems. In such cases, the decision tree becomes prohibitively large. Approaches to solve the problem involve either changing the representation of the problem domain (known as propositionalization) (Horváth & Yamamoto, 2003) or using learning algorithms based on more expressive representations (such as statistical relational learning or inductive logic programming).
- For data including categorical variables with different numbers of levels, information gain in decision trees is biased in favor of those attributes with more levels (Deng, Runger, & Tuv, 2011). However,

the issue of biased predictor selection is avoided by the Conditional Inference approach.

Extensions

Decision graphs

In a decision tree, all paths from the root node to the leaf node proceed by way of conjunction, or AND. In a decision graph, it is possible to use disjunctions (ORs) to join two more paths together using Minimum message length (MML) (Tan & Dowe, 2004). Decision graphs have been further extended to allow for previously unstated new attributes to be learnt dynamically and used at different places within the graph. The more general coding scheme results in better predictive accuracy and log-loss probabilistic scoring. In general, decision graphs infer models with fewer leaves than decision trees.

Alternative search methods

Evolutionary algorithms have been used to avoid local optimal decisions and search the decision tree space with little a *priori* bias (Papagelis, 2001) (Barros, Basgalupp, Carvalho, & Freitas, 2011).

It is also possible for a tree to be sampled using MCMC in a Bayesian paradigm (Chipman, George, & McCulloch, 1998).

The tree can be searched for in a bottom-up fashion (Barros, Cerri, Jaskowiak, & Carvalho, 2011).

Software

Many data mining software packages provide implementations of one or more decision tree algorithms. Open Source software packages for decision tree modeling include KNIME, Orange, R, scikit-learn, and Weka.

Commercial packages include RapidMiner, SAS Enterprise Miner, and SPSS Modeler. CART, by Salford Systems, is the licensed proprietary code of the original CART authors.

Examples Using R

Classification Tree example

Let's use the data frame kyphosis to predict a type of deformation (kyphosis) after surgery, from age in months (Age), number of vertebrae involved (Number), and the highest vertebrae operated on (Start).

In R, call the rpart library. Recursive partitioning for classification, regression and survival trees. An implementation of most of the functionality of the 1984 book by Breiman, Friedman, Olshen and Stone (Breiman, Friedman, Olshen, & Stone, 1984).

```
# Classification Tree with rpart
> library(rpart)
```

We will not grow the tree with the fit() and rpart functions.

```
 # grow tree
> fit <- rpart(Kyphosis ~ Age + Number + Start,
+          method="class", data=kyphosis)
```

where kyphosis is the response, with variables Age, Number, and Start. Class in the method and kyphosis is the data set. Next, we display the results.

```
> printcp(fit) # display the results

Classification tree:
rpart(formula = Kyphosis~Age + Number + Start, data =
kyphosis,
    method = "class")

Variables actually used in tree construction:
[1] Age    Start

Root node error: 17/81 = 0.20988

n= 81

        CP nsplit rel error xerror     xstd
```

96

```
1 0.176471        0    1.00000 1.0000 0.21559
2 0.019608        1    0.82353 1.2353 0.23200
3 0.010000        4    0.76471 1.2941 0.23548
```

Now, we plot the tree to visualize the cross validation results.

```
> plotcp(fit) # visualize cross-validation results
```

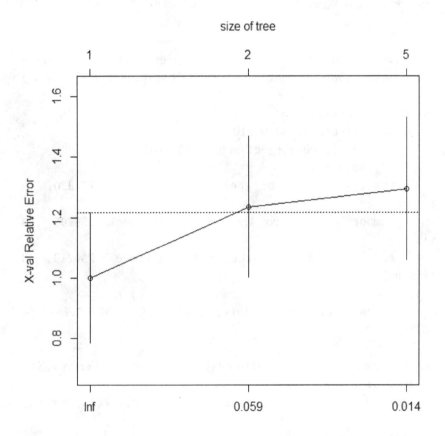

Next, we display a summary of the model.

```
> summary(fit) # detailed summary of splits
```

```
Call:
rpart(formula = Kyphosis ~ Age + Number + Start, data =
kyphosis,
    method = "class")
  n= 81
```

```
        CP nsplit rel error   xerror      xstd
1 0.17647059      0 1.0000000 1.000000 0.2155872
2 0.01960784      1 0.8235294 1.117647 0.2243268
3 0.01000000      4 0.7647059 1.117647 0.2243268


Variable importance
  Start    Age Number
    64      24     12


Node number 1: 81 observations,    complexity param=0.1764706
  predicted class=absent    expected loss=0.2098765  P(node)
=1
    class counts:     64     17
  probabilities: 0.790 0.210
  left son=2 (62 obs) right son=3 (19 obs)
  Primary splits:
    Start   < 8.5   to the right, improve=6.762330, (0
missing)
    Number < 5.5   to the left,  improve=2.866795, (0
missing)
    Age     < 39.5 to the left,  improve=2.250212, (0
missing)
  Surrogate splits:
    Number < 6.5  to the left,  agree=0.802, adj=0.158, (0
split)


Node   number  2:  62  observations,              complexity
param=0.01960784
  predicted class=absent   expected loss=0.09677419  P(node)
=0.7654321
    class counts:     56     6
  probabilities: 0.903 0.097
  left son=4 (29 obs) right son=5 (33 obs)
  Primary splits:
    Start   < 14.5 to the right, improve=1.0205280, (0
missing)
    Age     < 55   to the left,  improve=0.6848635, (0
missing)
    Number < 4.5   to the left,  improve=0.2975332, (0
```

missing)
  Surrogate splits:
      Number < 3.5 to the left, agree=0.645, adj=0.241, (0
split)
      Age   < 16   to the left, agree=0.597, adj=0.138, (0
split)

Node number 3: 19 observations
  predicted class=present expected loss=0.4210526 P(node)
=0.2345679
      class counts: 8   11
    probabilities: 0.421 0.579

Node number 4: 29 observations
  predicted class=absent   expected loss=0   P(node)
=0.3580247
      class counts: 29   0
    probabilities: 1.000 0.000

Node number 5: 33 observations,   complexity
param=0.01960784
  predicted class=absent   expected loss=0.1818182 P(node)
=0.4074074
      class counts: 27   6
    probabilities: 0.818 0.182
  left son=10 (12 obs) right son=11 (21 obs)
  Primary splits:
      Age   < 55   to the left,   improve=1.2467530, (0
missing)
      Start   < 12.5 to the right, improve=0.2887701, (0
missing)
      Number < 3.5   to the right, improve=0.1753247, (0
missing)
  Surrogate splits:
      Start < 9.5 to the left, agree=0.758, adj=0.333, (0
split)
      Number < 5.5 to the right, agree=0.697, adj=0.167, (0
split)

Node number 10: 12 observations

99

    predicted   class=absent   expected   loss=0   P(node)
=0.1481481
     class counts: 12   0
     probabilities: 1.000 0.000

Node   number   11:   21   observations,   complexity
param=0.01960784
    predicted class=absent   expected loss=0.2857143 P(node)
=0.2592593
     class counts: 15   6
     probabilities: 0.714 0.286
    left son=22 (14 obs) right son=23 (7 obs)
    Primary splits:
        Age   < 111   to the right, improve=1.71428600, (0
missing)
        Start   < 12.5 to the right, improve=0.79365080, (0
missing)
        Number < 4.5   to the left, improve=0.07142857, (0
missing)

Node number 22: 14 observations
    predicted class=absent   expected loss=0.1428571 P(node)
=0.1728395
     class counts: 12   2
     probabilities: 0.857 0.143

Node number 23: 7 observations
    predicted class=present expected loss=0.4285714 P(node)
=0.08641975
     class counts: 3   4
     probabilities: 0.429 0.571

We will now display a "rough" plot of the classification tree.

```
 # plot tree
> plot(fit, uniform=TRUE,
+      main="Classification Tree for Kyphosis")
> text(fit, use.n=TRUE, all=TRUE, cex=.8)
```

Classification Tree for Kyphosis

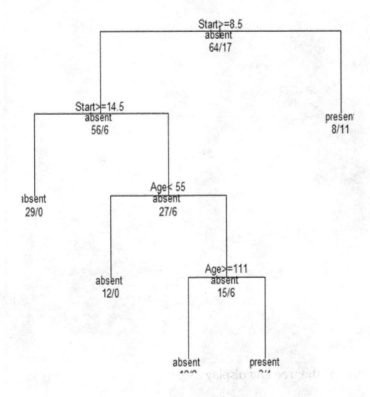

Now, we display a more refined plot of the tree.

```
# create attractive postscript plot of tree
> post(fit, file = "c:/tree.ps",
+       title = "Classification Tree for Kyphosis")
```

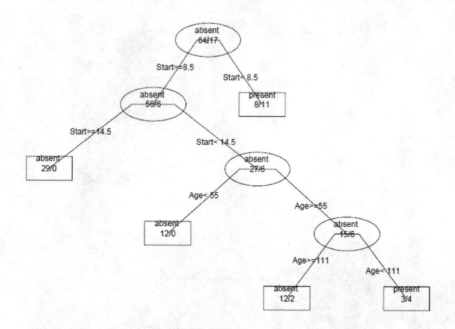

We now "prune" the tree and display its plot.

```
# prune the tree
> Pfit <- prune(fit,cp=   fit$cptable [which.min(
+       fit$cptable[,"xerror"]),"CP"])

 # plot the pruned tree
> plot(pfit, uniform=TRUE,
+       main="Pruned Classification Tree for Kyphosis")
> text(pfit, use.n=TRUE, all=TRUE, cex=.8)
> post(pfit, file = "c:/ptree.ps",
+       title = "Pruned Classification Tree for Kyphosis")
```

Pruned Classification Tree for Kyphosis

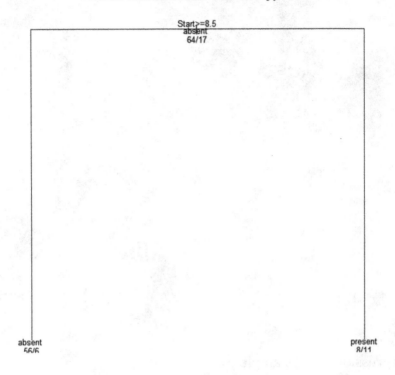

Start>=8.5
absent
64/17

absent
56/6

present
8/11

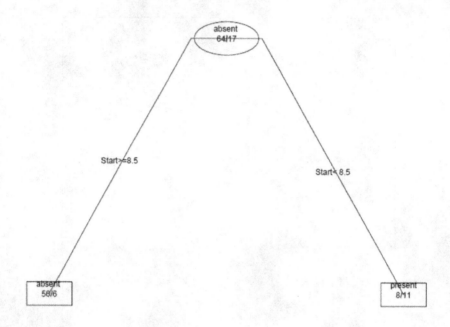

Regression Tree example

In this example we will predict car mileage from price, country, reliability, and car type. The data frame is `cu.summary`. We will only show the R inputs and plots here.

```
# Regression Tree Example
> library(rpart)

 # grow tree
> fit <- rpart(Mileage~Price + Country + Reliability +
+      Type, method="anova", data=cu.summary)

> printcp(fit) # display the results
> plotcp(fit) # visualize cross-validation results
> summary(fit) # detailed summary of splits

 # create additional plots
> par(mfrow=c(1,2)) # two plots on one page
```

104

```
> rsq.rpart(fit) # visualize cross-validation results

 # plot tree
> plot(fit, uniform=TRUE,
+       main="Regression Tree for Mileage ")
> text(fit, use.n=TRUE, all=TRUE, cex=.8)

 # create attractive postcript plot of tree
> post(fit, file = "c:/tree2.ps",
+       title = "Regression Tree for Mileage ")
```

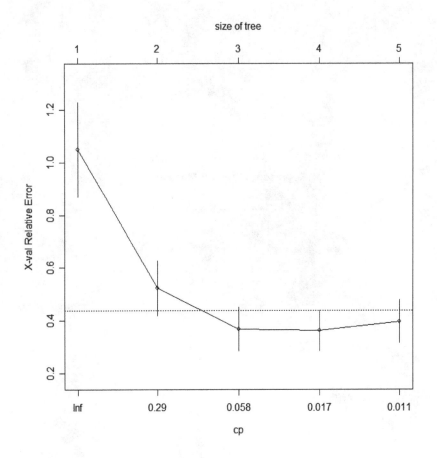

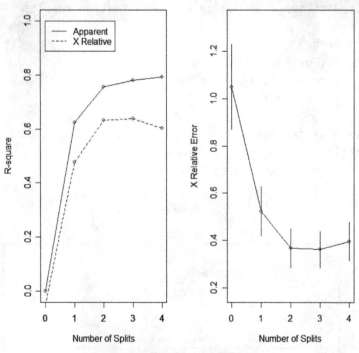

Regression Tree for Mileage

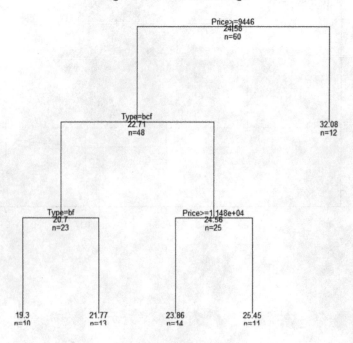

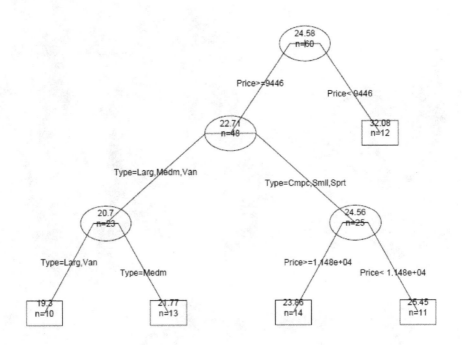

Regression Tree for Mileage

```
# prune the tree
> pfit<- prune(fit, cp=0.01160389) # from cptable

 # plot the pruned tree
> plot(pfit, uniform=TRUE,
+       main="Pruned Regression Tree for Mileage")
> text(pfit, use.n=TRUE, all=TRUE, cex=.8)
> post(pfit, file = "c:/ptree2.ps",
+       title = "Pruned Regression Tree for Mileage")
```

It turns out that this produces the same tree as the original.

7.   Random forests

Random forests are an ensemble learning method for classification (and regression) that operate by constructing a multitude of decision trees at training time and outputting the class that is the mode of the classes output by individual trees. The algorithm for inducing a random forest was developed by Leo Breiman (Breiman L. , Random Forests, 2001) and Adele Cutler (Liaw, 2012), and "Random Forests" is their trademark. The term came from random decision forests that was first proposed by Tin Kam Ho of Bell Labs in 1995. The method combines Breiman's "bagging" idea and the random selection of features, introduced independently by Ho (Ho T. , 1995) (Ho T. , 1998) and Amit and Geman (Amit & Geman, 1997) in order to construct a collection of decision trees with controlled variance.

The selection of a random subset of features is an example of the random subspace method, which, in Ho's formulation, is a way to implement classification proposed by Eugene Kleinberg (Kleinberg, 1996).

History

The early development of random forests was influenced by the work of Amit and Geman (Amit & Geman, 1997) which introduced the idea of searching over a random subset of the available decisions when splitting a node, in the context of growing a single tree. The idea of random subspace selection from Ho (Ho T. , 1998) was also influential in the design of random forests. In this method a forest of trees is grown, and variation among the trees is introduced by projecting the training data into a randomly chosen subspace before fitting each tree. Finally, the idea of randomized node optimization, where the decision at each node is selected by a randomized procedure, rather than a deterministic optimization was first introduced by Dietterich (Dietterich T. , 2000).

The introduction of random forests proper was first made in a paper by Leo Breiman (Breiman L. , Random Forests, 2001). This paper describes a method of building a forest of uncorrelated trees using a CART like procedure, combined with randomized node optimization and bagging. In addition, this paper combines several ingredients, some previously known and some novel, which form the basis of the modern practice of random forests, in particular:

1. Using out-of-bag error as an estimate of the generalization error.

2. Measuring variable importance through permutation.

The report also offers the first theoretical result for random forests in the form of a bound on the generalization error which depends on the strength of the trees in the forest and their correlation.

More recently several major advances in this area have come from Microsoft Research (Criminisi, Shotton, & Konukoglu, 2011), which incorporate and extend the earlier work from Breiman.

Algorithm

The training algorithm for random forests applies the general technique of bootstrap aggregating (see Bootstrap aggregating), or bagging, to tree learners. Given a training set $X = x_1, ..., x_n$ with responses $Y = y_1$ through y_n, bagging repeatedly selects a bootstrap sample of the training set and fits trees to these samples:

For $b = 1$ through B:

1. Sample, with replacement, n training examples from X, Y; call these X_b, Y_b .

2. Train a decision or regression tree f_b on X_b, Y_b.

After training, predictions for unseen samples x' can be made by averaging the predictions from all the individual regression trees on x':

$$\hat{f} = \frac{1}{B} \sum_{b=1}^{B} \hat{f}_b(x'),$$

or by taking the majority vote in the case of decision trees.

In the above algorithm, B is a free parameter. Typically, a few hundred to several thousand trees are used, depending on the size and nature of the training set. Increasing the number of trees tends to decrease the variance of the model, without increasing the bias. As a result, the training and test error tend to level off after some number of trees have been fit. An optimal number of trees B can be found using cross-validation, or by observing the out-of-bag error: the mean prediction error on each training sample x_i, using only the trees that did not have x_i in their bootstrap sample (James, Witten, Hastie, & Tibshirani, 2013).

Bootstrap aggregating

Bootstrap aggregating, also called bagging, is a machine learning ensemble meta-algorithm designed to improve the stability and accuracy of machine learning algorithms used in statistical classification and regression. It also reduces variance and helps to avoid overfitting. Although it is usually applied to decision tree methods, it can be used with any type of method. Bagging is a special case of the model averaging approach.

Description of the technique

Given a standard training set D of size n, bagging generates m new training sets D_i, each of size n', by sampling from D uniformly and with replacement. By sampling with replacement, some observations may be repeated in each. If $n' = n$, then for large n the set is expected to have the fraction $(1 - 1/e)$ ($\approx 63.2\%$) of the unique examples of D, the rest being duplicates (Aslam, Popa, & Rivest, 2007). This kind of sample is known as a bootstrap sample. The m models are fitted using the above m bootstrap samples and combined by averaging the output (for regression) or voting (for classification). Bagging leads to "improvements for unstable procedures" (Breiman L. , Random Forests, 2001), which include, for example, neural nets, classification and regression trees, and subset selection in linear regression (Breiman L. , 1996). An interesting application of bagging showing improvement in preimage learning is provided here (Sahu, Runger, & Apley, 2011) (Shinde, Sahu, Apley, & Runger, 2014). On the other hand, it can mildly degrade the performance of stable methods such as K-nearest neighbors (Breiman, 1996).

Example: Ozone data

To illustrate the basic principles of bagging, below is an analysis on the relationship between ozone and temperature (data from Rousseeuw and Leroy (Rousseeuw & Leroy, 2003), available at classic data sets, analysis done in R).

The relationship between temperature and ozone in this data set is apparently non-linear, based on the scatter plot. To mathematically describe this relationship, LOESS smoothers (with span 0.5) are used. Instead of building a single smoother from the complete data set, 100 bootstrap samples of the data were drawn. Each sample is different from the original data set, yet resembles it in distribution and variability. For each bootstrap sample, a LOESS smoother was fit. Predictions from these 100 smoothers were then made across the range of the data. The first 10 predicted smooth fits appear as grey lines in the figure below. The lines are clearly very wiggly and they overfit the data - a result of the span being too low.

But taking the average of 100 smoothers, each fitted to a subset of the original data set, we arrive at one bagged predictor (red line). Clearly, the mean is more stable and there is less overfit.

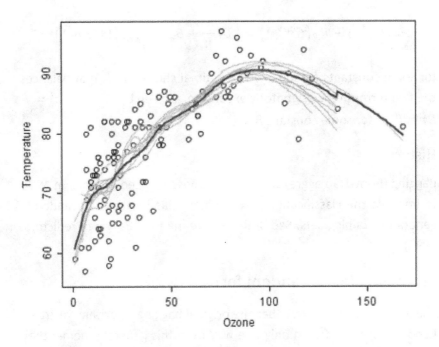

Bagging for nearest neighbor classifiers

It is well known that the risk of a 1 nearest neighbor (1NN) classifier is at most twice the risk of the Bayes classifier, but there are no guarantees that this classifier will be consistent. By careful choice of the size of the resamples, bagging can lead to substantial improvements of the performance of the 1NN classifier. By taking a large number of resamples of the data of size n', the bagged nearest neighbor classifier will be consistent provided $n' \to \infty$ diverges but $n'/n \to 0$ as the sample size $n \to \infty$.

Under infinite simulation, the bagged nearest neighbor classifier can be viewed as a weighted nearest neighbor classifier. Suppose that the feature space is d dimensional and denote by $C_{n,n'}^{bnn}$ the bagged nearest neighbor classifier based on a training set of size n, with resamples of size n'. In the infinite sampling case, under certain regularity conditions on the class distributions, the excess risk has the following asymptotic

113

expansion

$$\mathcal{R}_\mathcal{R}(C_{n,n'}^{bnn}) - \mathcal{R}_\mathcal{R}(C^{bayes}) = \left(B_1\frac{n'}{n} + B_2\frac{1}{(n')^{4/d}}\right)\{1 + o(1)\},$$

for some constants B_1 and B_2. The optimal choice of n', that balances the two terms in the asymptotic expansion, is given by $n' = Bn^{d/(d+4)}$ for some constant B.

History

Bagging (Bootstrap aggregating) was proposed by Leo Breiman in 1994 to improve the classification by combining classifications of randomly generated training sets. See Breiman (Breiman L. , Bagging Predictors, 1994).

From bagging to random forests

The above procedure describes the original bagging algorithm for trees. Random forests differ in only one way from this general scheme: they use a modified tree learning algorithm that selects, at each candidate split in the learning process, a random subset of the features. The reason for doing this is the correlation of the trees in an ordinary bootstrap sample: if one or a few features are very strong predictors for the response variable (target output), these features will be selected in many of the B trees, causing them to become correlated.

Typically, for a dataset with p features, $\sqrt{p}$ features are used in each split.

Random subspace method

Random subspace method (or attribute bagging (Bryll, 2003)) is an ensemble classifier that consists of several classifiers and outputs the class based on the outputs of these individual classifiers. Random subspace method is a generalization of the random forest algorithm (Ho T. , 1998). Whereas random forests are composed of decision trees, a random subspace classifier can be composed from any underlying classifiers. Random subspace method has been used for linear classifiers (Skurichina, 2002), support vector machines (Tao, 2006), nearest neighbors (Tremblay, 2004) and other types of classifiers. This method is also applicable to one-class classifiers.

The algorithm is an attractive choice for classification problems where the number of features is much larger than the number of training objects, such as fMRI data or gene expression data (Kuncheva, Rodríguez, Plumpton, Linden, & Johnston, 2010).

Algorithm

The ensemble classifier is constructed using the following algorithm:

1. Let the number of training objects be N and the number of features in the training data be D.

2. Choose L to be the number of individual classifiers in the ensemble.

3. For each individual classifier, l, Choose $d_l (d_l < D)$ to be the number of input variables for l. It is common to have only one value of d_l for all the individual classifiers

4. For each individual classifier, l, create a training set by choosing d_l features from D without replacement and train the classifier.

5. For classifying a new object, combine the outputs of the L individual classifiers by majority voting or by combining the posterior probabilities.

Relationship to Nearest Neighbors

Given a set of training data

$$\mathcal{D}_n = \{(X_i, Y_i)\}_{i=1}^n$$

a weighted neighborhood scheme makes a prediction for a query point X, by computing

115

$$\hat{Y} = \sum_{i=1}^{n} W_i(X) Y_i,$$

for some set of non-negative weights $\{W_i(X)\}_{i=1}^{n}$ which sum to 1. The set of points X_i where $W_i(X) > 0$ are called the neighbors of X. A common example of a weighted neighborhood scheme is the k-NN algorithm which sets $W_i(X) = 1/k$ if X_i is among the k closest points to X in $\mathcal{D}_n$ and 0 otherwise.

Random forests with constant leaf predictors can be interpreted as a weighted neighborhood scheme in the following way. Given a forest of M trees, the prediction that the m-th tree makes for X can be written as

$$T_m(X) = \sum_{i=1}^{n} W_{im}(X) Y_i,$$

where $W_{im}(X)$ is equal to $1/k_m$ if X and X_i are in the same leaf in the m-th tree and 0 otherwise, and k_m is the number of training data which fall in the same leaf as X in the m-th tree. The prediction of the whole forest is

$$F(X) = \sum_{i=1}^{n} T_m(X) = \frac{1}{M} \sum_{m=1}^{M} \sum_{i=1}^{n} W_{im}(X) Y_i = \sum_{i=1}^{n} \left(\frac{1}{M} \sum_{m=1}^{M} W_{im}(X) \right) Y_i,$$

which shows that the random forest prediction is a weighted average of the Y_i's, with weights

$$W_i(X) = \frac{1}{M} \sum_{m=1}^{M} W_{im}(X).$$

The neighbors of X in this interpretation are the points X_i which fall in the same leaf as X in at least one tree of the forest. In this way, the neighborhood of X depends in a complex way on the structure of the trees, and thus on the structure of the training set.

This connection was first described by Lin and Jeon in a technical report from 2001 where they show that the shape of the neighborhood used by a random forest adapts to the local importance of each feature (Lin & Jeon, 2001).

Variable importance

Random forests can be used to rank the importance of variables in a regression or classification problem in a natural way. The following technique was described in Breiman's original paper (Breiman L. , Random Forests, 2001) and is implemented in the R package *randomForest* (Liaw, 2012).

The first step in measuring the variable importance in a data set $\mathcal{D}_n = \{(X_i, Y_i)\}_{i=1}^{n}$ is to fit a random forest to the data. During the fitting process the out-of-bag error for each data point is recorded and averaged over the forest (errors on an independent test set can be substituted if bagging is not used during training).

To measure the importance of the j-th feature after training, the values of the j-th feature are permuted among the training data and the out-of-bag error is again computed on this perturbed data set. The importance score for the j-th feature is computed by averaging the difference in out-of-bag error before and after the permutation over all trees. The score is normalized by the standard deviation of these differences.

Features which produce large values for this score are ranked as more important than features which produce small values.

This method of determining variable importance has some drawbacks. For data including categorical variables with different number of levels, random forests are biased in favor of those attributes with more levels. Methods such as partial permutations can be used to solve the problem (Deng, Runger, & Tuv, 2011) (Altmann, Tolosi, Sander, & Lengauer, 2010). If the data contain groups of correlated features of similar relevance for the output, then smaller groups are favored over larger groups (Tolosi & Lengauer, 2011).

Variants

Instead of decision trees, linear models have been proposed and evaluated as base estimators in random forests, in particular multinomial logistic regression and Naïve Bayes classifiers (Prinzie & Van den Poel, 2008).

Software

Open Source software package that have random forest functionality include R, and one specifically designed for this purpose:

- **R** – GNU R has several packages that perform random forest. Specifically, `cforest()` from library "`party`" or `randomForest()` from library "`randomForest`".
- **Random Forest™** - GNU Random Forests(tm) is a trademark of Leo Breiman and Adele Cutler. Runs can be set up with no knowledge of FORTRAN 77. The user is required only to set the right zero-one switches and give names to input and output files. This is done at the start of the program. It is licensed exclusively to Salford Systems for the commercial release of the software (see below). Their trademarks also include RF™, RandomForests™, RandomForest™ and Random Forest™.

Commercial software package that have random forest functionality include SPSS Modeler, and two specifically designed for this purpose:

- **Random Forests** – by Salford Systems, is a bagging tool that apply methods applied after the trees are grown and include new technology for identifying clusters or segments in data as well as new methods for ranking the importance of variables.
- **RapidMiner** – is a software platform developed by the company of the same name that provides an integrated environment for machine learning, data mining, text mining, predictive analytics and business analytics. It performs random forest.

Example Using R

Description

randomForest implements Breiman's random forest algorithm (based on Breiman and Cutler's original Fortran code) for classification and regression in R. It can also be used in unsupervised mode for assessing proximities among data points.

We use the Forensic Glass data set was used in Chapter 12 of MASS4 (Venables and Ripley, 2002) to show how random forests work:

```
> library(randomForest)
> library(MASS)
> data(fgl)
> set.seed(17)
> fgl.rf <- randomForest(type ~ ., data = fgl,
+      mtry = 2, importance = TRUE,
+      do.trace = 100)
ntree       OOB      1      2      3      4      5      6
  100:   21.50% 14.29% 21.05% 64.71% 30.77% 11.11% 13.79%
  200:   19.63% 11.43% 21.05% 58.82% 23.08% 11.11% 13.79%
  300:   19.16% 11.43% 19.74% 58.82% 23.08% 11.11% 13.79%
  400:   18.69% 10.00% 18.42% 64.71% 23.08% 11.11% 13.79%
  500:   18.69% 10.00% 18.42% 64.71% 23.08% 11.11% 13.79%
> print(fgl.rf)
Call:
 randomForest(formula = type ~ ., data = fgl, mtry = 2,
+            importance = TRUE,       do.trace = 100)
               Type of random forest: classification
                     Number of trees: 500
No. of variables tried at each split: 2

        OOB estimate of error rate: 18.69%
Confusion matrix:
      WinF WinNF Veh Con Tabl Head class.error
WinF    63     6   1   0    0    0   0.1000000
WinNF   10    62   1   1    2    0   0.1842105
Veh      9     2   6   0    0    0   0.6470588
Con      0     2   0  10    0    1   0.2307692
```

119

| Tabl | 0 | 1 | 0 | 0 | 8 | 0 | 0.1111111 |
| Head | 1 | 3 | 0 | 0 | 0 | 25 | 0.1379310 |

Model Comparison

We can compare random forests with support vector machines by doing ten repetitions of 10-fold cross-validation, using the errorest functions in the **ipred** package:

```
> library(ipred)
> set.seed(131)
> error.RF <- numeric(10)
> for(i in 1:10) error.RF[i] <-
+       errorest(type ~ ., data = fgl,
+       model = randomForest, mtry = 2)$error
> summary(error.RF)
Min. 1st Qu. Median Mean 3rd Qu. Max.
0.1869 0.1974 0.2009 0.2009 0.2044 0.2103
> library(e1071)
> set.seed(563)
> error.SVM <- numeric(10)
> for (i in 1:10) error.SVM[i] <-
+       errorest(type ~ ., data = fgl,
+       model = svm, cost = 10, gamma = 1.5)$error
> summary(error.SVM)
   Min. 1st Qu.  Median   Mean 3rd Qu.   Max.
 0.1822  0.1974  0.2079  0.2051  0.2138  0.2290
```

We see that the random forest compares quite favorably with SVM. We have found that the variable importance measures produced by random forests can sometimes be useful for model reduction (e.g., use the "important" variables to build simpler, more readily interpretable models). Figure 1 shows the variable importance of the Forensic Glass data set, based on the fgl.rf object created above. Roughly, it is created by

```
> par(mfrow = c(2, 2))
> for (i in 1:4)
+       plot(sort(fgl.rf$importance[,i], dec = TRUE),
```

```
+        type = "h", main = paste("Measure", i))
```

We can see that measure 1 most clearly differentiates the variables. If we run random forest again dropping Na, K, and Fe from the model, the error rate remains below 20%.

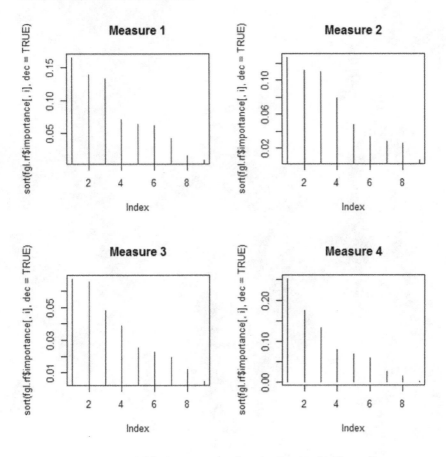

Figure 1: Variable importance for the Forensic Glass data.

8. Multivariate adaptive regression splines

Multivariate adaptive regression splines (MARS) is a form of regression analysis introduced by Jerome H. Friedman in 1991 (Friedman, Multivariate Adaptive Regression Splines, 1991). It is a non-parametric regression technique and can be seen as an extension of linear models that automatically models non-linearities and interactions between variables.

The term "MARS" is trademarked and licensed to Salford Systems. In order to avoid trademark infringements, many open source implementations of MARS are called "Earth" (Milborrow, Multivariate Adaptive Regression Spline Models, 2011) (Milborrow, 2014).

The basics

This section introduces MARS using a few examples. We start with a set of data: a matrix of input variables x, and a vector of the observed responses **y**, with a response for each row in x. For example, the data could be:

x	y
10.5	16.4
10.7	18.8
10.8	19.7
...	...
20.6	77.0

Here there is only one independent variable, so the x matrix is just a single column. Given these measurements, we would like to build a model which predicts the expected y for a given x.

A linear model for the above data is

$$\hat{y} = -37 + 5.1x.$$

The hat on the $\hat{y}$ indicates that $\hat{y}$ is estimated from the data. The figure on the right shows a plot of this function: a line giving the predicted $\hat{y}$ versus x, with the original values of y shown as red dots. The data at the extremes of x indicates that the relationship between y and x may be non-linear (look at the red dots relative to the regression line at low and high values of x).

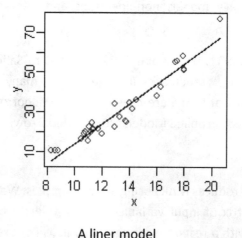

A liner model

We thus turn to MARS to automatically build a model taking into account non-linearities. MARS software constructs a model from the given x and y as follows

$$\hat{y} = 25 + 6.1 \, max(0, x - 13) - 3.1 \, max(0, 13 - x).$$

The figure on the right shows a plot of this function: the predicted $\hat{y}$ versus x, with the original values of y once again shown as red dots. The predicted response is now a better fit to the original y values.

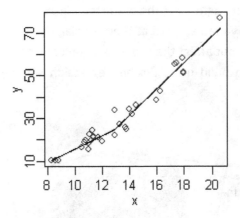

A simple MARS model of the same data

MARS has automatically produced a kink in the predicted y to take into account non-linearity. The kink is produced by *hinge functions*. The hinge functions are the expressions starting with (where $max(a, b)$ is a if $a > b$, else b). Hinge functions are described in more detail below.

In this simple example, we can easily see from the plot that y has a non-linear relationship with x (and might perhaps guess that y varies with the square of x). However, in general there will be multiple independent variables, and the relationship between y and these variables will be unclear and not easily visible by plotting. We can use MARS to discover that non-linear relationship.

An example MARS expression with multiple variables is

$$Ozone = 5.2$$
$$+0.93 \max(0, temp - 58)$$
$$-0.64 \max(0, temp - 68)$$
$$-0.046 \max(0, 234 - ibt)$$
$$-0.016 \, max(0, wind - 7) max(0, 200 - vis).$$

This expression models air pollution (the ozone level) as a function of the temperature and a few other variables. Note that the last term in the formula (on the last line) incorporates an interaction between *wind* and *vis*.

125

The figure on the right plots the predicted *ozone* as *wind* and *vis* vary, with the other variables fixed at their median values. The figure shows that wind does not affect the ozone level unless visibility is low. We see that MARS can build quite flexible regression surfaces by combining hinge functions.

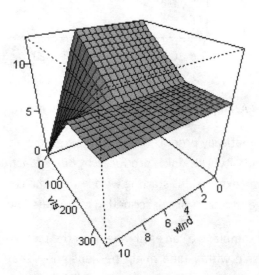

Variable interaction in a MARS model

To obtain the above expression, the MARS model building procedure automatically selects which variables to use (some variables are important, others not), the positions of the kinks in the hinge functions, and how the hinge functions are combined.

The MARS model

MARS builds models of the form

$$\hat{f}(x) = \sum_{i=1}^{k} c_i B_i(x).$$

The model is a weighted sum of basis functions $B_i(x)$. Each c_i is a constant coefficient. For example, each line in the formula for ozone above is one basis function multiplied by its coefficient.

Each basis function $B_i(x)$ takes one of the following three forms:

1) a constant 1. There is just one such term, the intercept. In the ozone formula above, the intercept term is 5.2.

2) a hinge function. A hinge function has the form $max(0, x - const)$ or $max(0, const - x)$. MARS automatically selects variables and values of those variables for knots of the hinge functions. Examples of such basis functions can be seen in the middle three lines of the ozone formula.

3) a product of two or more hinge functions. These basis function can model interaction between two or more variables. An example is the last line of the ozone formula.

Hinge functions

Hinge functions are a key part of MARS models. A hinge function takes the form

$$max(0, x - c),$$

or

$$max(0, c - x),$$

where is c a constant, called the knot. The figure below shows a mirrored pair of hinge functions with a knot at 3.1.

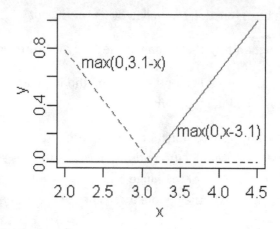

A mirrored pair of hinge functions with a knot at $x = 3.1$

A hinge function is zero for part of its range, so can be used to partition the data into disjoint regions, each of which can be treated independently. Thus for example a mirrored pair of hinge functions in the expression

$$6.1 \, max(0, x - 13) - 3.1 \, max(0, 13 - x)$$

creates the piecewise linear graph shown for the simple MARS model in the previous section.

One might assume that only piecewise linear functions can be formed from hinge functions, but hinge functions can be multiplied together to form non-linear functions.

Hinge functions are also called hockey stick functions. Instead of the max notation used in this article, hinge functions are often represented by $[\pm(x_i - c)]_+$ where means $[.]_+$ take the positive part.

The model building process

MARS builds a model in two phases: the forward and the backward pass. This two stage approach is the same as that used by recursive partitioning trees.

128

The forward pass

MARS starts with a model which consists of just the intercept term (which is the mean of the response values). MARS then repeatedly adds basis function in pairs to the model. At each step it finds the pair of basis functions that gives the maximum reduction in sum-of-squares residual error (it is a greedy algorithm). The two basis functions in the pair are identical except that a different side of a mirrored hinge function is used for each function. Each new basis function consists of a term already in the model (which could perhaps be the intercept i.e. a constant 1) multiplied by a new hinge function. A hinge function is defined by a variable and a knot, so to add a new basis function, MARS must search over all combinations of the following:

1) existing terms (called parent terms in this context)

2) all variables (to select one for the new basis function)

3) all values of each variable (for the knot of the new hinge function).

This process of adding terms continues until the change in residual error is too small to continue or until the maximum number of terms is reached. The maximum number of terms is specified by the user before model building starts.

The search at each step is done in a brute force fashion, but a key aspect of MARS is that because of the nature of hinge functions the search can be done relatively quickly using a fast least-squares update technique. Actually, the search is not quite brute force. The search can be sped up with a heuristic that reduces the number of parent terms to consider at each step ("Fast MARS" (Friedman, Fast MARS, 1993)).

The backward pass

The forward pass usually builds an overfit model. (An overfit model has a good fit to the data used to build the model but will not generalize well to new data.) To build a model with better generalization ability, the backward pass prunes the model. It removes terms one by one, deleting the least effective term at each step until it finds the best submodel. Model subsets are compared using the GCV criterion described below.

The backward pass has an advantage over the forward pass: at any step it can choose any term to delete, whereas the forward pass at each step can only see the next pair of terms.

The forward pass adds terms in pairs, but the backward pass typically discards one side of the pair and so terms are often not seen in pairs in the final model. A paired hinge can be seen in the equation for $\hat{y}$ in the first MARS example above; there are no complete pairs retained in the ozone example.

Generalized cross validation (GCV)

The backward pass uses generalized cross validation (GCV) to compare the performance of model subsets in order to choose the best subset: lower values of GCV are better. The GCV is a form of regularization: it trades off goodness-of-fit against model complexity.

(We want to estimate how well a model performs on new data, not on the training data. Such new data is usually not available at the time of model building, so instead we use GCV to estimate what performance would be on new data. The raw residual sum-of-squares (RSS) on the training data is inadequate for comparing models, because the RSS always increases as MARS terms are dropped. In other words, if the RSS were used to compare models, the backward pass would always choose the largest model—but the largest model typically does not have the best generalization performance.)

The formula for the GCV is

$$GCV = \frac{RSS}{N \cdot \left(1 - \frac{EffectiveNumberOfParameters}{N}\right)^2},$$

where RSS is the residual sum-of-squares measured on the training data and N is the number of observations (the number of rows in the x

matrix).

The *EffectiveNumberOfParameters* is defined in the MARS context as

$$EffectiveNumberOfParameters$$
$$= NumberOfMarsTerms + Penalty$$
$$\times \frac{(NumberOfMarsTerms - 1)}{2},$$

where *Penalty* is about 2 or 3 (the MARS software allows the user to preset *Penalty*).

Note that $(NumberOfMarsTerms - 1)/2$ is the number of hinge-function knots, so the formula penalizes the addition of knots. Thus the GCV formula adjusts (i.e. increases) the training *RSS* to take into account the flexibility of the model. We penalize flexibility because models that are too flexible will model the specific realization of noise in the data instead of just the systematic structure of the data.

Generalized Cross Validation is so named because it uses a formula to approximate the error that would be determined by leave-one-out validation. It is just an approximation but works well in practice. GCVs were introduced by Craven and Wahba and extended by Friedman for MARS.

Constraints

One constraint has already been mentioned: the user can specify the maximum number of terms in the forward pass. A further constraint can be placed on the forward pass by specifying a maximum allowable degree of interaction.

Typically only one or two degrees of interaction are allowed, but higher degrees can be used when the data warrants it. The maximum degree of interaction in the first MARS example above is one (i.e. no interactions or an *additive model*); in the ozone example it is two.

131

Other constraints on the forward pass are possible. For example, the user can specify that interactions are allowed only for certain input variables. Such constraints could make sense because of knowledge of the process that generated the data.

Pros and cons

No regression modeling technique is best for all situations. The guidelines below are intended to give an idea of the pros and cons of MARS, but there will be exceptions to the guidelines. It is useful to compare MARS to recursive partitioning and this is done below. (Recursive partitioning is also commonly called regression trees, decision trees, or CART; see the recursive partitioning article for details).

- MARS models are more flexible than linear regression models.
- MARS models are simple to understand and interpret. Compare the equation for ozone concentration above to, say, the innards of a trained neural network or a random forest.
- MARS can handle both continuous and categorical data (Friedman, Estimating Functions of Mixed Ordinal and Categorical Variables Using Adaptive Splines, 1993). MARS tends to be better than recursive partitioning for numeric data because hinges are more appropriate for numeric variables than the piecewise constant segmentation used by recursive partitioning.
- Building MARS models often requires little or no data preparation. The hinge functions automatically partition the input data, so the effect of outliers is contained. In this respect MARS is similar to recursive partitioning which also partitions the data into disjoint regions, although using a different method. (Nevertheless, as with most statistical modeling techniques, known outliers should be considered for removal before training a MARS model.)
- MARS (like recursive partitioning) does automatic variable selection (meaning it includes important variables in the model and excludes unimportant ones). However, bear in mind that variable selection is not a clean problem and there is usually some arbitrariness in the selection, especially in the presence of collinearity and 'concurvity'.

- MARS models tend to have a good bias-variance trade-off. The models are flexible enough to model non-linearity and variable interactions (thus MARS models have fairly low bias), yet the constrained form of MARS basis functions prevents too much flexibility (thus MARS models have fairly low variance).

- MARS is suitable for handling fairly large datasets. It is a routine matter to build a MARS model from an input matrix with, say, 100 predictors and 105 observations. Such a model can be built in about a minute on a 1 GHz machine, assuming the maximum degree of interaction of MARS terms is limited to one (i.e. additive terms only). A degree two model with the same data on the same 1 GHz machine takes longer—about 12 minutes. Be aware that these times are highly data dependent. Recursive partitioning is much faster than MARS.

- With MARS models, as with any non-parametric regression, parameter confidence intervals and other checks on the model cannot be calculated directly (unlike linear regression models). Cross-validation and related techniques must be used for validating the model instead.

- MARS models do not give as good fits as boosted trees, but can be built much more quickly and are more interpretable. (An 'interpretable' model is in a form that makes it clear what the effect of each predictor is.)

- The earth, mda, and polspline implementations do not allow missing values in predictors, but free implementations of regression trees (such as rpart and party) do allow missing values using a technique called surrogate splits.

- MARS models can make predictions quickly. The prediction function simply has to evaluate the MARS model formula. Compare that to making a prediction with say a Support Vector Machine, where every variable has to be multiplied by the corresponding element of every support vector. That can be a slow process if there are many variables and many support vectors.

Software

Open Source software package that have MARS functionality include:

- **R** – GNU R has several R packages fit MARS-type models:

  - `earth` function in the `earth` (Milborrow, Multivariate Adaptive Regression Spline Models, 2011) package
  - `mars` function in the `mda` (Leisch, Hornik, & Ripley, 2013) package
  - `polymars` function in the `polspline` package (Kooperberg, 2013). Not Friedman's MARS.
- Matlab code:
  - ARESLab: Adaptive Regression Splines toolbox for Matlab (Jekabsons, 2011)
- Python
  - Earth - Multivariate adaptive regression splines (Milborrow, Earth - Multivariate adaptive regression splines , 2011)
  - py-earth (Rudy, 2013)

Commercial software package that have MARS functionality include:

- **MARS** (MARS - Multivariate Adaptive Regression Splines , n.d.) from Salford Systems. Based on Friedman's implementation (Friedman, Multivariate Adaptive Regression Splines, 1991).
- **MARSSpines** from StatSoft (Multivariate Adaptive Regression Splines (MARSplines), n.d.)
- **STATISTICA** Data Miner from StatSoft (STATISTICA Data Miner , 2012)
- ADAPTIVEREG from SAS (The ADAPTIVEREG Procedure, n.d.).

Example Using R

This exercise uses multivariate adaptive regression splines (MARS) to develop an additive model allowing the estimation of body fat for men. The body fat data was sourced from the "fat" dataset contained in the R library "faraway". The R library "mda" was used as open-source implementation of MARS. The outcome variable was "siri", which represents a gold standard body fat measurement using the Siri underwater technique. Fourteen feature variables were considered during model development. These variables included age, weight, height, adiposity index, and the circumference measurements of various limbs and body areas such as the abdomen, biceps, and hip.

Setting up the Model

We first load the required libraries, and perform some basic data management.

```
### Instructions
# Download the faraway library which has the 'fat' dataset
# Develop an additive model that allows estimation of body
# fat for men using only a scale and a measuring tape.
# Your model should predict %bodyfat according to the Siri
# method.
# Do not use the Brozek %bodyfat, density or fat free
# weight as predictors.

> library(faraway) # Functions and datasets for books by
                    # Julian Faraway
> library(mda) # Mixture and flexible discriminant analysis


### ---- Dataset 'fat' ----
> data(fat)  # Percentage of Body Fat and Body Measurements
### Description:
# Age, weight, height, and 10 body circumference
# measurements are recorded for 252 men. Each
# manâs percentage of body fat was accurately estimated by
# an underwater weighing technique.
### Format:
```

```
# A data frame with 252 observations on the following 18
# variables.
# brozek   Percent body fat using Brozekâs equation,   #
457/Density - 414.2
# siri     Percent body fat using Siriâs equation,
# 495/Density - 450
# density Density (gm/$cm^3$)
# age      Age (yrs)
# weight   Weight (lbs)
# height   Height (inches)
# adipos   Adiposity index = Weight/Height$^2$ (kg/$m^2$)
# free     Fat Free Weight = (1 - fraction of body fat) *
# Weight, using Brozekâ™s formula (lbs)
# neck     Neck circumference (cm)
# chest    Chest circumference (cm)
# abdom    Abdomen circumference (cm) at the umbilicus and
# level with the iliac crest
# hip      Hip circumference (cm)
# thigh    Thigh circumference (cm)
# knee     Knee circumference (cm)
# ankle    Ankle circumference (cm)
# biceps   Extended biceps circumference (cm)
# forearm Forearm circumference (cm)
# wrist    Wrist circumference (cm) distal to the styloid
# processes
### Outcome variable of interest: siri


# ---- remove unwanted variables ----
> df <- fat[c(-1, -3, -8)] # Remove Brozek measurement,
+             density, and fat free weight
> head(df)
```

	siri age	weight	height	
	adipos	neck	chest	abdom
1	12.3 23	154.25	67.75	23.7
	36.2	93.1	85.2	
2	6.1 22	173.25	72.25	23.4
	38.5	93.6	83	
3	25.3 22	154	66.25	24.7
	34	95.8	87.9	

4	10.4	26	184.75	72.25	24.9
	37.4		101.8	86.4	
5	28.7	24	184.25	71.25	25.6
	34.4		97.3	100	
6	20.9	24	210.25	74.75	26.5
	39		104.5	94.4	

	hip	thigh	knee	ankle
	biceps	forearm	wrist	
1	94.5	59	37.3	21.9
	32	27.4	17.1	
2	98.7	58.7	37.3	23.4
	30.5	28.9	18.2	
3	99.2	59.6	38.9	24
	28.8	25.2	16.6	
4	101.2	60.1	37.3	22.8
	32.4	29.4	18.2	
5	101.9	63.2	42.2	24
	32.2	27.7	17.7	
6	107.8	66	42	25.6
	35.7	30.6	18.8	

Next, we use the default parameters for MARS. Specifically, an additive model was desired, which calls for degree to be one. We also wanted to enable pruning; thus, prune = T.

Model Generation

```
# ---- apply mars to fat dataset ----
# default choice is only additive (first order) predictors
# and chooses the
# model size using a GCV criterion.  The basis functions
# can be
# used as predictors in a linear regression model
> fatfit <- mars(df[, -1], # matrix containing the
>                          # independent variables
+         df[, 1], # vector containing the response variable
+         degree = 1, # default: 1 -- no interaction terms
+         prune = T) # default: TRUE -- backward-selection-
>                    # like pruning
> summary(lm(df[,1] ~ fatfit$x-1))
```

```
Call:
lm(formula = df[, 1] ~ fatfit$x - 1)

Residuals:
     Min       1Q    Median       3Q       Max
-12.7595   -2.5925   -0.0623    2.5263   10.9438

Coefficients:
             Estimate Std. Error t value Pr(>|t|)
fatfit$x1    14.80796    1.26879  11.671  < 2e-16 ***
fatfit$x2    -0.10716    0.03394  -3.158  0.00179 **
fatfit$x3     2.84378    0.58813   4.835 2.38e-06 ***
fatfit$x4    -1.26743    0.46615  -2.719  0.00703 **
fatfit$x5    -0.43375    0.15061  -2.880  0.00434 **
fatfit$x6     1.81931    0.76495   2.378  0.01817 *
fatfit$x7    -0.08755    0.02843  -3.079  0.00232 **
fatfit$x8    -1.50179    0.27705  -5.421 1.45e-07 ***
fatfit$x9     1.15735    0.09021  12.830  < 2e-16 ***
fatfit$x10   -0.57252    0.14433  -3.967 9.62e-05 ***
fatfit$x11    0.65233    0.27658   2.359  0.01915 *
fatfit$x12   -1.94923    0.64968  -3.000  0.00298 **
---
Signif. codes:  0 '***' 0.001 '**' 0.01 '*' 0.05 '.' 0.1 '
' 1

Residual standard error: 3.922 on 240 degrees of freedom
Multiple R-squared:  0.9664,    Adjusted R-squared:  0.9648
F-statistic: 575.9 on 12 and 240 DF,  p-value: < 2.2e-16

> fatfit$gcv
[1] 17.74072

> sum(fatfit$res^2)
[1] 3691.83 # fit is good in terms of R2
```

With the default parameters, we note that MARS has generated a model with twelve basis functions, with a generalized cross-validation (GCV) error of 17.74072 and a total sum of squared residuals (SSR) of 3691.83.

These basis functions can be tabulated.

```
# ---- Visualize the cut points
> cuts <- fatfit$cuts[fatfit$selected.terms, ]
> dimnames(cuts) <- list(NULL, names(df[-1]))
# dimnames must be a list
> cuts
```

	age	weight	height	
	adipos	neck	chest	abdom
[1,]	0	0	0	0
	0	0	0	
[2,]	0	166.75	0	0
	0	0	0	
[3,]	0	0	0	0
	0	0	0	
[4,]	0	0	0	0
	0	0	0	
[5,]	0	0	0	0
	0	0	0	
[6,]	0	0	0	0
	37	0	0	
[7,]	57	0	0	0
	0	0	0	
[8,]	0	0	0	0
	0	0	0	
[9,]	0	0	0	0
	0	0	83.3	
[10,]	0	0	0	0
	0	0	94.1	
[11,]	0	0	0	25
	0	0	0	
[12,]	0	0	0	0
	35.6	0	0	

	hip	thigh	knee	ankle
	biceps	forearm	wrist	
[1,]	0	0	0	0
	0	0	0	
[2,]	0	0	0	0
	0	0	0	
[3,]	0	0	0	0

```
                 0              0           18.5
[4,]             0              0              0              0
              35.7              0              0
[5,]             0              0              0              0
              35.7              0              0
[6,]             0              0              0              0
                 0              0              0
[7,]             0              0              0              0
                 0              0              0
[8,]             0           54.7              0              0
                 0              0              0
[9,]             0              0              0              0
                 0              0              0
[10,]            0              0              0              0
                 0              0              0
[11,]            0              0              0              0
                 0              0              0
[12,]            0              0              0              0
                 0              0              0
```

```
> factor <- fatfit$factor[fatfit$selected.terms, ]
dimnames(factor) <- list(NULL, names(df[-1])) # dimnames
must be a list
factor
```

```
               age         weight         height
            adipos           neck          chest          abdom
[1,]             0              0              0              0
                 0              0              0
[2,]             0              1              0              0
                 0              0              0
[3,]             0              0              0              0
                 0              0              0
[4,]             0              0              0              0
                 0              0              0
[5,]             0              0              0              0
                 0              0              0
[6,]             0              0              0              0
                 1              0              0
[7,]            -1              0              0              0
                 0              0              0
```

```
[8,]         0              0              0              0
             0              0              0
[9,]         0              0              0              0
             0              0              1
[10,]        0              0              0              0
             0              0              1
[11,]        0              0              0              1
             0              0              0
[12,]        0              0              0              0
             1              0              0
             hip            thigh          knee           ankle
             biceps         forearm        wrist
[1,]         0              0              0              0
             0              0              0
[2,]         0              0              0              0
             0              0              0
[3,]         0              0              0              0
             0              0              -1
[4,]         0              0              0              0
             1              0              0
[5,]         0              0              0              0
             -1             0              0
[6,]         0              0              0              0
             0              0              0
[7,]         0              0              0              0
             0              0              0
[8,]         0              -1             0              0
             0              0              0
[9,]         0              0              0              0
             0              0              0
[10,]        0              0              0              0
             0              0              0
[11,]        0              0              0              0
             0              0              0
[12,]        0              0              0              0
             0              0              0
```

This gives us the model:

siri = 14.69871   1 ***

```
    - 0.10716 * [166.75 - weight]   2 **
    + 2.84378 * [wrist - 18.5]      3 ***
    - 1.26743 * [35.7 - biceps]     4 **
    - 0.43375 * [35.7 - biceps]     5 **
    + 1.81931 * [necck -37]         6 *
    - 0.08755 * [57 - age]          7 **
    - 1.50179 * [54.7 - thigh]      8 ***
    + 1.15735 * [abdom - 83.3]      9 ***
    - 0.57252 * [abdom - 94.1]     10 ***
    + 0.65233 * [adips - 25 ]      11 *
    - 1.94923 * [neck - 35.6]      12 ***
```

These basis functions can also be plotted, individually.

```
> par(mfrow = c(3, 5),    # c(nrows, ncols)
+    mar = c(2, 2, 2, 2), # margin: bottom-left-top-right
+    pty = "s")
> for (i in 2:15) {
+ j <- i - 1} # adjust index for matrices below

# Next is a 252x14 double matrix
>  xp <- matrix(sapply(df[2:15], mean),
+              nrow(df),
+              ncol(df) - 1,
+              byrow = TRUE);
>  colnames(xp) <- names(df[2:15])
>  xr <- sapply(df, range);    # 2x15 double matrix
>  xp[, j] <- seq(xr[1, i],    # minimum of variable i
+              xr[2, i],    # maximum of variable i
+              len = nrow(df));
>  xf <- predict(fatfit, xp);
>  plot(xp[, j], xf,
+       xlab = names(df)[i],
+       ylab = "",
+       ylim = c(0, 50),
+       type = "l");
```

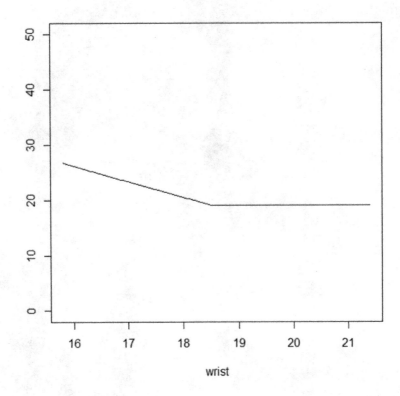

wrist

9. Clustering Models

Cluster analysis or clustering is the task of grouping a set of objects in such a way that objects in the same group (called a cluster) are more similar (in some sense or another) to each other than to those in other groups (clusters). It is a main task of exploratory data mining, and a common technique for statistical data analysis, used in many fields, including machine learning, pattern recognition, image analysis, information retrieval, and bioinformatics.

Cluster analysis itself is not one specific algorithm, but the general task to be solved. It can be achieved by various algorithms that differ significantly in their notion of what constitutes a cluster and how to efficiently find them. Popular notions of clusters include groups with small distances among the cluster members, dense areas of the data space, intervals or particular statistical distributions. Clustering can therefore be formulated as a multi-objective optimization problem. The appropriate clustering algorithm and parameter settings (including values such as the distance function to use, a density threshold or the number of expected clusters) depend on the individual data set and intended use of the results. Cluster analysis as such is not an automatic task, but an iterative process of knowledge discovery or interactive multi-objective optimization that involves trial and failure. It will often be necessary to modify data preprocessing and model parameters until the result achieves the desired properties.

Besides the term clustering, there are a number of terms with similar meanings, including automatic classification, numerical taxonomy, botryology (from Greek βότρυς "grape") and typological analysis. The subtle differences are often in the usage of the results: while in data mining, the resulting groups are the matter of interest, in automatic classification the resulting discriminative power is of interest. This often leads to misunderstandings between researchers coming from the fields of data mining and machine learning, since they use the same terms and often the same algorithms, but have different goals.

Cluster analysis was originated in anthropology by Driver and Kroeber in 1932 and introduced to psychology by Zubin in 1938 and Robert Tryon in 1939 (Bailey K. , 1994) (Tryon, 1939) and famously used by Cattell beginning in 1943 (Cattell, 1943) for trait theory classification in personality psychology.

Definition

According to Vladimir Estivill-Castro, the notion of a "cluster" cannot be precisely defined, which is one of the reasons why there are so many clustering algorithms (Estivill-Castro, 2002). There is a common denominator: a group of data objects. However, different researchers employ different cluster models, and for each of these cluster models again different algorithms can be given. The notion of a cluster, as found by different algorithms, varies significantly in its properties. Understanding these "cluster models" is key to understanding the differences between the various algorithms. Typical cluster models include:

Connectivity models: for example hierarchical clustering builds models based on distance connectivity.

Centroid models: for example the k-means algorithm represents each cluster by a single mean vector.

Distribution models: clusters are modeled using statistical distributions, such as multivariate normal distributions used by the Expectation-maximization algorithm.

Density models: for example DBSCAN and OPTICS defines clusters as connected dense regions in the data space.

Subspace models: in Biclustering (also known as Co-clustering or two-mode-clustering), clusters are modeled with both cluster members and relevant attributes.

Group models: some algorithms do not provide a refined model for their results and just provide the grouping information.

Graph-based models: a clique, i.e., a subset of nodes in a graph such that every two nodes in the subset are connected by an edge can be considered as a prototypical form of cluster. Relaxations of the complete connectivity requirement (a fraction of the edges can be missing) are known as quasi-cliques.

A "clustering" is essentially a set of such clusters, usually containing all objects in the data set. Additionally, it may specify the relationship of the clusters to each other, for example a hierarchy of clusters embedded in each other. Clusterings can be roughly distinguished as:

- hard clustering: each object belongs to a cluster or not
- soft clustering (also: fuzzy clustering): each object belongs to each cluster to a certain degree (e.g. a likelihood of belonging to the cluster)

There are also finer distinctions possible, for example:

- strict partitioning clustering: here each object belongs to exactly one cluster
- strict partitioning clustering with outliers: objects can also belong to no cluster, and are considered outliers.
- overlapping clustering (also: alternative clustering, multi-view clustering): while usually a hard clustering, objects may belong to more than one cluster.
- hierarchical clustering: objects that belong to a child cluster also belong to the parent cluster
- subspace clustering: while an overlapping clustering, within a uniquely defined subspace, clusters are not expected to overlap.

Algorithms

Clustering algorithms can be categorized based on their cluster model, as listed above. The following overview will only list the most prominent examples of clustering algorithms, as there are possibly over 100 published clustering algorithms. Not all provide models for their clusters and can thus not easily be categorized. An overview of algorithms explained in Wikipedia can be found in the list of statistics algorithms.

There is no objectively "correct" clustering algorithm, but as it was noted, "clustering is in the eye of the beholder." (Estivill-Castro, 2002) The most appropriate clustering algorithm for a particular problem often needs to be chosen experimentally, unless there is a mathematical reason to prefer one cluster model over another. It should be noted that an algorithm that is designed for one kind of model has no chance on a data set that contains a radically different kind of model. For example, k-means cannot find non-convex clusters (Estivill-Castro, 2002).

Connectivity based clustering (hierarchical clustering)

Connectivity based clustering, also known as hierarchical clustering, is based on the core idea of objects being more related to nearby objects than to objects farther away. These algorithms connect "objects" to form "clusters" based on their distance. A cluster can be described largely by the maximum distance needed to connect parts of the cluster. At different distances, different clusters will form, which can be represented using a dendrogram, which explains where the common name "hierarchical clustering" comes from: these algorithms do not provide a single partitioning of the data set, but instead provide an extensive hierarchy of clusters that merge with each other at certain distances. In a dendrogram, the y-axis marks the distance at which the clusters merge, while the objects are placed along the x-axis such that the clusters don't mix.

Strategies for hierarchical clustering generally fall into two types:

Agglomerative: This is a "bottom up" approach: each observation starts in its own cluster, and pairs of clusters are merged as one moves up the hierarchy.

Divisive: This is a "top down" approach: all observations start in one cluster, and splits are performed recursively as one moves down the hierarchy.

Connectivity based clustering is a whole family of methods that differ by the way distances are computed. Apart from the usual choice of distance functions, the user also needs to decide on the linkage criterion (since a cluster consists of multiple objects, there are multiple candidates to compute the distance to) to use. Popular choices are known as single-linkage clustering (the minimum of object distances), complete linkage clustering (the maximum of object distances) or UPGMA ("Unweighted Pair Group Method with Arithmetic Mean", also known as average linkage clustering). Furthermore, hierarchical clustering can be agglomerative (starting with single elements and aggregating them into clusters) or divisive (starting with the complete data set and dividing it into partitions).

Metric

The choice of an appropriate metric will influence the shape of the clusters, as some elements may be close to one another according to one distance and farther away according to another. For example, in a 2-dimensional space, the distance between the point (1,0) and the origin (0,0) is always 1 according to the usual norms, but the distance between the point (1,1) and the origin (0,0) can be 2 under Manhattan distance, $\sqrt{2}$ under Euclidean distance, or 1 under maximum distance.

Some commonly used metrics for hierarchical clustering are (The DISTANCE Procedure: Proximity Measures):

Names	Formula
Euclidean distance	$\|a - b\|_2 = \sqrt{\sum_i (a_i - b_i)^2}$
Squared Euclidean distance	$\|a - b\|_2^2 = \sum_i (a_i - b_i)^2$

Manhattan distance	$\|a - b\|_1 = \sum_i \|a_i - b_i\|$
maximum distance	$\|a - b\|_\infty = \max_i \|a_i - b_i\|$
Mahalanobis distance	$\sqrt{(a - b)^T S^{-1}(a - b)}$ where S is the Covariance matrix

For text or other non-numeric data, metrics such as the Hamming distance or Levenshtein distance are often used. A review of cluster analysis in health psychology research found that the most common distance measure in published studies in that research area is the Euclidean distance or the squared Euclidean distance

Linkage criteria

The linkage criterion determines the distance between sets of observations as a function of the pairwise distances between observations.

Some commonly used linkage criteria between two sets of observations A and B are (The CLUSTER Procedure: Clustering Methods):

Names	Formula
Maximum or complete linkage clustering	$\max\{d(a, b): a \in A, b \in B\}$
Minimum or single-linkage clustering	$\min\{d(a, b): a \in A, b \in B\}$
Mean or average linkage clustering, or UPGMA	$\frac{1}{\|A\|\|B\|}\sum_{a \in A}\sum_{b \in B} d(a, b)$
Centroid linkage clustering, or UPGMC	$\|c_s - c_t\|$ where c_s and c_t are the centroids of clusters s and t, respectively.

Minimum energy clustering	$$\frac{2}{nm}\sum_{i,j=1}^{n,m}\|a_i - b_j\|_2 - \frac{1}{n^2}\sum_{i,j=1}^{n}\|a_i - a_j\|_2$$ $$-\frac{1}{m^2}\sum_{i,j=1}^{m}\|b_i - b_j\|_2$$

where d is the chosen metric. Other linkage criteria include:

- The sum of all intra-cluster variance.
- The decrease in variance for the cluster being merged (Ward's criterion) (Ward, 1963).
- The probability that candidate clusters spawn from the same distribution function (V-linkage).
- The product of in-degree and out-degree on a k-nearest-neighbor graph (graph degree linkage) (Zhang e. a., October 7–13, 2012).
- The increment of some cluster descriptor (i.e., a quantity defined for measuring the quality of a cluster) after merging two clusters (Zhang e. a., Agglomerative clustering via maximum incremental path integral, 2013).

These methods will not produce a unique partitioning of the data set, but a hierarchy from which the user still needs to choose appropriate clusters. They are not very robust towards outliers, which will either show up as additional clusters or even cause other clusters to merge (known as "chaining phenomenon", in particular with single-linkage clustering). In the general case, the complexity is $\mathcal{O}(n^3)$, which makes them too slow for large data sets. For some special cases, optimal efficient methods (of complexity $\mathcal{O}(n^2)$) are known: SLINK (Sibson, 1973) for single-linkage and CLINK (Defays, 1977) for complete-linkage clustering. In the data mining community these methods are recognized as a theoretical foundation of cluster analysis, but often considered obsolete. They did however provide inspiration for many later methods such as density based clustering.

Examples Using R

The 'cluster' package provides several useful functions for clustering analysis. We will use one here called 'agnes', which performs agglomerative hierarchical clustering of a dataset. The dataset we will use, 'votes.repub' is included in the package.

```
## First load the package.
> library(cluster)
> data(votes.repub)
> agn1 <- agnes(votes.repub, metric = "manhattan",
+               stand = TRUE)
agn1
Call: agnes(x = votes.repub, metric = "manhattan", stand =
TRUE)
Agglomerative coefficient:  0.7977555
Order of objects:
 [1] Alabama         Georgia        Arkansas       Louisiana
Mississippi    South Carolina
 [7] Alaska          Vermont        Arizona        Montana
Nevada         Colorado
[13] Idaho           Wyoming        Utah           California
Oregon         Washington
[19] Minnesota       Connecticut    New York       New Jersey
Illinois       Ohio
[25] Indiana         Michigan       Pennsylvania   New
Hampshire  Wisconsin       Delaware
[31] Kentucky        Maryland       Missouri       New Mexico
West Virginia  Iowa
[37] South Dakota    North Dakota   Kansas         Nebraska
Maine          Massachusetts
[43] Rhode Island    Florida        North Carolina Tennessee
Virginia       Oklahoma
[49] Hawaii          Texas
Height (summary):
   Min. 1st Qu.  Median    Mean 3rd Qu.     Max.
  8.382  12.800  18.530  23.120  28.410  87.460

Available components:
[1] "order"     "height"    "ac"        "merge"      "diss"
"call"      "method"    "order.lab"
[9] "data"

> plot(agn1)
```

Banner of agnes(x = votes.repub, metric = "manhattan", stand = TRUI

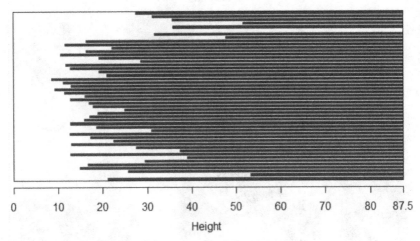

Agglomerative Coefficient = 0.8

Dendrogram of agnes(x = votes.repub, metric = "manhattan", stand = TRUE

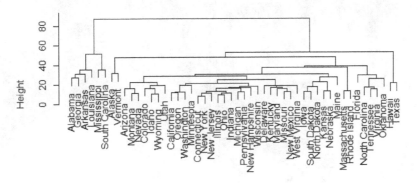

votes.repub
Agglomerative Coefficient = 0.8

```
> op <- par(mfrow=c(2,2))
> agn2 <- agnes(daisy(votes.repub), diss = TRUE,
+             method = "complete")
> plot(agn2)
## alpha = 0.625 ==> beta = -1/4 is "recommended" by some
```

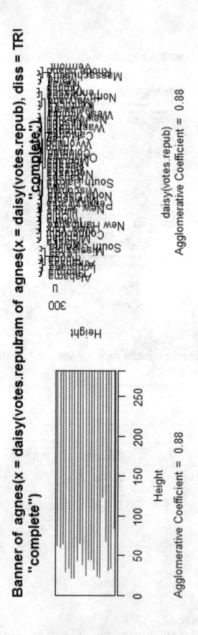

Banner of agnes(x = daisy(votes.repub), diss = TRI "complete")

daisy(votes.repub)
Agglomerative Coefficient = 0.88

Height

Height

Agglomerative Coefficient = 0.88

```
> agnS <- agnes(votes.repub, method = "flexible",
+               par.meth = 0.625)
> plot(agnS)
```

154

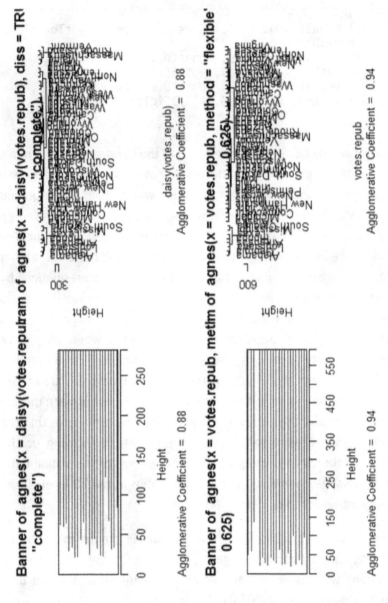

```
par(op)
## "show" equivalence of three "flexible" special cases
> d.vr <- daisy(votes.repub)
> a.wgt <- agnes(d.vr, method = "weighted")
> a.sing <- agnes(d.vr, method = "single")
> a.comp <- agnes(d.vr, method = "complete")
> iC <- -(6:7) # not using 'call' and 'method' for
+              comparisons
```

```
> stopifnot(
+       all.equal(a.wgt [iC], agnes(d.vr, method="flexible",
+       par.method = 0.5)[iC]) ,
+       all.equal(a.sing[iC], agnes(d.vr, method="flex",
+       par.method= c(.5,.5,0, -.5))[iC]),
+       all.equal(a.comp[iC], agnes(d.vr, method="flex",
+       par.method= c(.5,.5,0, +.5))[iC]))
```

If you choose any height along the y-axis of the dendrogram, and move across the dendrogram counting the number of lines that you cross, each line represents a group that was identified when objects were joined together into clusters. The observations in that group are represented by the branches of the dendrogram that spread out below the line. For example, if we look at a height of 60, and move across the x-axis at that height, we'll cross two lines. That defines a two-cluster solution; by following the line down through all its branches, we can see the names of the states that are included in these two clusters. Since the y-axis represents how close together observations were when they were merged into clusters, clusters whose branches are very close together (in terms of the heights at which they were merged) probably aren't very reliable. But if there is a big difference along the y-axis between the last merged cluster and the currently merged one, which indicates that the clusters formed are probably doing a good job in showing us the structure of the data. Looking at the dendrogram for the voting data, there are (maybe not clearly) five distinct groups at the 20-level; at the 0-level there seems to be nine distinct groups.

For this data set, it looks like either five or six groups might be an interesting place to start investigating. This is not to imply that looking at solutions with more clusters would be meaningless, but the data seems to suggest that five or six clusters might be a good start. For a problem of this size, we can see the names of the states, so we could start interpreting the results immediately from the dendrogram, but when there are larger numbers of observations, this won't be possible.

Exploring the dendrogram structure

```
> (d2 <- as.dendrogram(agn2)) # two main branches
'dendrogram' with 2 branches and 50 members total, at
height 281.9508

> d2[[1]] # the first branch
'dendrogram' with 2 branches and 8 members total, at height
116.7048

> d2[[2]] # the 2nd one { 8 + 42 = 50 }
'dendrogram' with 2 branches and 42 members total, at
height 178.4119

> d2[[1]][[1]]# first sub-branch of branch 1 .. and shorter
form
'dendrogram' with 2 branches and 6 members total, at height
72.92212

> identical(d2[[c(1,1)]], d2[[1]][[1]])
[1] TRUE
```

a "textual picture" of the dendrogram :
```
str(d2)
```

```
--[dendrogram w/ 2 branches and 50 members at h = 282]
  |--[dendrogram w/ 2 branches and 8 members at h = 117]
  |  |--[dendrogram w/ 2 branches and 6 members at h = 72.9]
  |  |  |--[dendrogram w/ 2 branches and 3 members at h = 60.9]
  |  |  |  |--[dendrogram w/ 2 branches and 2 members at h = 48.2]
  |  |  |  |  |--leaf "Alabama"
  |  |  |  |  |--leaf "Georgia"
  |  |  |  |--leaf "Louisiana"
  |  |  |--[dendrogram w/ 2 branches and 3 members at h = 58.8]
  |  |  |  |--[dendrogram w/ 2 branches and 2 members at h = 56.1]
  |  |  |  |  |--leaf "Arkansas"
  |  |  |  |  |--leaf "Florida"
  |  |  |  |--leaf "Texas"
  |  |--[dendrogram w/ 2 branches and 2 members at h = 63.1]
  |  |  |--leaf "Mississippi"
  |  |  |--leaf "South Carolina"
  |--[dendrogram w/ 2 branches and 42 members at h = 178]
  |  |--[dendrogram w/ 2 branches and 37 members at h = 121]
  |  |  |--[dendrogram w/ 2 branches and 31 members at h = 80.5]
  |  |  |  |--[dendrogram w/ 2 branches and 17 members at h = 64.5]
  |  |  |  |  |--[dendrogram w/ 2 branches and 13 members at h = 56.4]
  |  |  |  |  |  |--[dendrogram w/ 2 branches and 10 members at h = 47.2]
  |  |  |  |  |  |  |--[dendrogram w/ 2 branches and 2 members at h = 28.1]
  |  |  |  |  |  |  |  |--leaf "Alaska"
  |  |  |  |  |  |  |  |--leaf "Michigan"
  |  |  |  |  |  |  |--[dendrogram w/ 2 branches and 8 members at h = 39.2]
  |  |  |  |  |  |  |  |--[dendrogram w/ 2 branches and 5 members at h = 36.8]
  |  |  |  |  |  |  |  |  |--[dendrogram w/ 2 branches and 3 members at h = 32.9]
  |  |  |  |  |  |  |  |  |  |--[dendrogram w/ 2 branches and 2 members at h = 19.4]
  |  |  |  |  |  |  |  |  |  |  |--leaf "Connecticut"
  |  |  |  |  |  |  |  |  |  |  |--leaf "New York"
  |  |  |  |  |  |  |  |  |  |--leaf "New Hampshire"
  |  |  |  |  |  |  |  |  |--[dendrogram w/ 2 branches and 2 members at h = 20.2]
  |  |  |  |  |  |  |  |  |  |--leaf "Indiana"
  |  |  |  |  |  |  |  |  |  |--leaf "Ohio"
  |  |  |  |  |  |  |  |--[dendrogram w/ 2 branches and 3 members at h = 25.3]
  |  |  |  |  |  |  |  |  |--[dendrogram w/ 2 branches and 2 members at h = 20.9]
  |  |  |  |  |  |  |  |  |  |--leaf "Illinois"
  |  |  |  |  |  |  |  |  |  |--leaf "New Jersey"
  |  |  |  |  |  |  |  |  |--leaf "Pennsylvania"
  |  |  |  |  |  |--[dendrogram w/ 2 branches and 3 members at h = 42.2]
  |  |  |  |  |  |  |--leaf "Minnesota"
  |  |  |  |  |  |  |--[dendrogram w/ 2 branches and 2 members at h = 33.7]
  |  |  |  |  |  |  |  |--leaf "North Dakota"
  |  |  |  |  |  |  |  |--leaf "Wisconsin"
  |  |  |  |  |--[dendrogram w/ 2 branches and 4 members at h = 37.5]
  |  |  |  |  |  |--[dendrogram w/ 2 branches and 2 members at h = 26.2]
  |  |  |  |  |  |  |--leaf "Iowa"
  |  |  |  |  |  |  |--leaf "South Dakota"
  |  |  |  |  |  |--[dendrogram w/ 2 branches and 2 members at h = 25.9]
  |  |  |  |  |  |  |--leaf "Kansas"
  |  |  |  |  |  |  |--leaf "Nebraska"
  |  |  |  |--[dendrogram w/ 2 branches and 14 members at h = 70.5]
  |  |  |  |  |--[dendrogram w/ 2 branches and 8 members at h = 48]
  |  |  |  |  |  |--[dendrogram w/ 2 branches and 4 members at h = 43.4]
  |  |  |  |  |  |  |--[dendrogram w/ 2 branches and 3 members at h = 27.8]
  |  |  |  |  |  |  |  |--[dendrogram w/ 2 branches and 2 members at h = 23.4]
  |  |  |  |  |  |  |  |  |--leaf "Arizona"
  |  |  |  |  |  |  |  |  |--leaf "Nevada"
  |  |  |  |  |  |  |  |--leaf "Montana"
  |  |  |  |  |  |  |--leaf "Oklahoma"
  |  |  |  |  |  |--[dendrogram w/ 2 branches and 4 members at h = 43.7]
  |  |  |  |  |  |  |--leaf "Colorado"
  |  |  |  |  |  |  |--[dendrogram w/ 2 branches and 3 members at h = 31.2]
  |  |  |  |  |  |  |  |--[dendrogram w/ 2 branches and 2 members at h = 17.2]
  |  |  |  |  |  |  |  |  |--leaf "Idaho"
  |  |  |  |  |  |  |  |  |--leaf "Wyoming"
  |  |  |  |  |  |  |  |--leaf "Utah"
  |  |  |  |  |--[dendrogram w/ 2 branches and 6 members at h = 54.3]
  |  |  |  |  |  |--[dendrogram w/ 2 branches and 3 members at h = 33.2]
  |  |  |  |  |  |  |--leaf "California"
  |  |  |  |  |  |  |--[dendrogram w/ 2 branches and 2 members at h = 22.2]
  |  |  |  |  |  |  |  |--leaf "Oregon"
  |  |  |  |  |  |  |  |--leaf "Washington"
  |  |  |  |  |  |--[dendrogram w/ 2 branches and 3 members at h = 35.1]
  |  |  |  |  |  |  |--[dendrogram w/ 2 branches and 2 members at h = 21.1]
  |  |  |  |  |  |  |  |--leaf "Missouri"
  |  |  |  |  |  |  |  |--leaf "New Mexico"
  |  |  |  |  |  |  |--leaf "West Virginia"
  |  |--[dendrogram w/ 2 branches and 6 members at h = 66.8]
  |  |  |--[dendrogram w/ 2 branches and 3 members at h = 43.4]
  |  |  |  |--leaf "Delaware"
  |  |  |  |--[dendrogram w/ 2 branches and 2 members at h = 33.5]
  |  |  |  |  |--leaf "Kentucky"
  |  |  |  |  |--leaf "Maryland"
  |  |  |--[dendrogram w/ 2 branches and 3 members at h = 30.2]
  |  |  |  |--[dendrogram w/ 2 branches and 2 members at h = 29.5]
  |  |  |  |  |--leaf "North Carolina"
  |  |  |  |  |--leaf "Tennessee"
  |  |  |  |--leaf "Virginia"
```

158

```
`--[dendrogram w/ 2 branches and 5 members at h = 83.1]
  |--[dendrogram w/ 2 branches and 4 members at h = 55.4]
  | |--[dendrogram w/ 2 branches and 2 members at h = 32.8]
  | | |--leaf "Hawaii"
  | | `--leaf "Maine"
  | `--[dendrogram w/ 2 branches and 2 members at h = 22.6]
  |   |--leaf "Massachusetts"
  |   `--leaf "Rhode Island"
  `--leaf "Vermont"
```

Now, we need to interpret the results of this analysis. From the dendrogram we can see some logical clustering at the 0-level. For instance, California, Oregon and Washington are clustered together as we would expect. Also, at the 40-level Georgia, Alabama, Mississippi, Arkansas, South Carolina and Louisiana are grouped together. What other clusters make sense?

The next

```
plot(agnes(agriculture), ask = TRUE)
> data(animals)
> aa.a <- agnes(animals) # default method = "average"
> aa.ga <- agnes(animals, method = "gaverage")
> op <- par(mfcol=1:2, mgp=c(1.5, 0.6, 0),
+              mar=c(.1+ > c(4,3,2,1)),cex.main=0.8)
> plot(aa.a, which.plot = 2)
```

Dendrogram of agnes(x = animals)

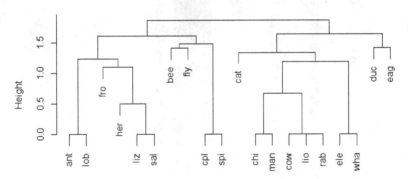

animals
Agglomerative Coefficient = 0.77

```
plot(agnes(agriculture), ask = TRUE)
```

159

```
Make a plot selection (or 0 to exit):

1: plot  All
2: plot  Banner
3: plot  Clustering Tree

Selection:
Enter an item from the menu, or 0 to exit
Selection: 2
```

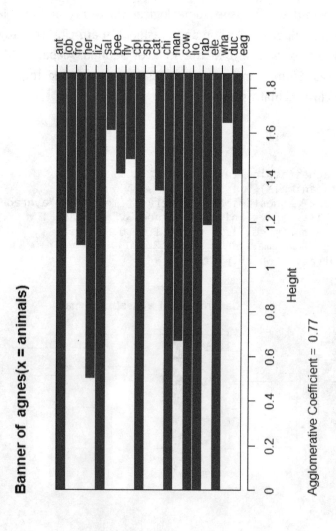

```
> plot(aa.ga, which.plot = 2)
```

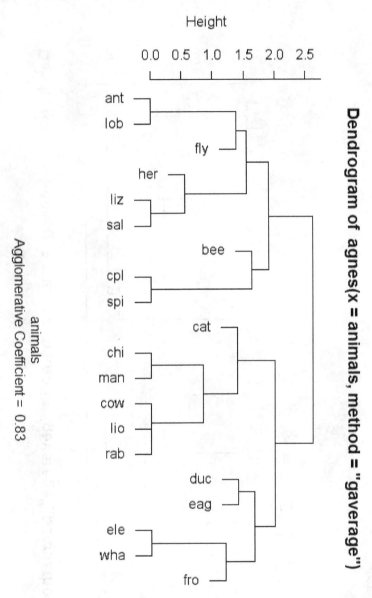

```
> par(op)
## Show how "gaverage" is a "generalized average":
> aa.ga.0 <- agnes(animals, method = "gaverage",
+                  par.method = 0)
> stopifnot(all.equal(aa.ga.0[iC], aa.a[iC]))
```

> plot(aa.ga.0, which.plot=2) plot(aa.ga.0, which.plot=2)

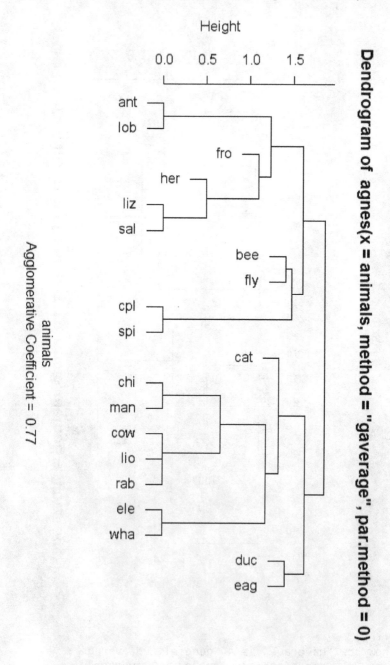

We next introduce another popular clustering technique, k-means. The format of the k-means function in R is $kmeans(x, centers)$ where x is a numeric dataset (matrix or data frame) and centers is the number of clusters to extract. The function returns the cluster memberships, centroids, sums of squares (within, between, total), and cluster sizes.

K-means cluster analysis starts with k randomly chosen centroids, a different solution can be obtained each time the function is invoked. Use the `set.seed()` function to guarantee that the results are reproducible. Additionally, this clustering approach can be sensitive to the initial selection of centroids. The kmeans() function has an `nstart` option that attempts multiple initial configurations and reports on the best one. For example, adding `nstart=25` will generate 25 initial configurations. This approach is often recommended.

Unlike hierarchical clustering, k-means clustering requires that the number of clusters to extract be specified in advance. Here, a dataset containing 13 chemical measurements on 178 Italian wine samples is analyzed. The data originally come from the UCI Machine Learning Repository (http://www.ics.uci.edu/~mlearn/MLRepository.html) but we will access it via the rattle package.

```
> library(rattle)
> data(wine)
> head(wine)
```

	Type	Alcohol	Malic	Ash	Alcalinity	Magnesium	Phenols	Flavanoids
1	1	14.23	1.71	2.43	15.6	127	2.80	3.06
2	1	13.20	1.78	2.14	11.2	100	2.65	2.76
3	1	13.16	2.36	2.67	18.6	101	2.80	3.24
4	1	14.37	1.95	2.50	16.8	113	3.85	3.49
5	1	13.24	2.59	2.87	21.0	118	2.80	2.69
6	1	14.20	1.76	2.45	15.2	112	3.27	3.39

It looks like the variables are measured on different scales, so we will likely want to standardize the data before proceeding. The 'scale' function will do this. Additionally, a plot of the total within-groups sums of squares against the number of clusters in a k-means solution can be helpful. A bend in the graph can suggest the appropriate number of clusters. The graph can be produced by the following function. We also use the NbClust package here. NbClust package provides 30 indices for determining the number of clusters and proposes to user the best clustering scheme from the different results obtained by varying all combinations of number of clusters, distance measures, and clustering methods.

```
> df <- scale(wine)
> wssplot(df)
```

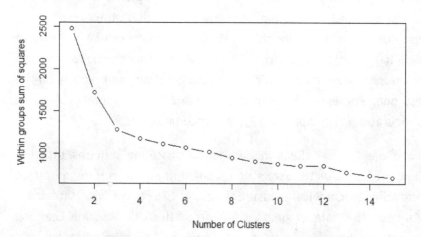

```
> Library(NbClust)
> set.seed(1234)
> nc <- NbClust(df, min.nc=2, max.nc=15, method="kmeans")
*** : The Hubert index is a graphical method of determining
the number of clusters.
          In the plot of Hubert index, we seek a significant
          knee that corresponds to a significant increase of
          the value of the measure i.e. the significant peak
          in Hubert index second differences plot.

*** : The D index is a graphical method of determining the
number of clusters.
          In the plot of D index, we seek a significant knee
          (the significant peak in Dindex second differences
          plot) that corresponds to a significant increase of
          the value of the measure.

All 178 observations were used.

*******************************************************************
* Among all indices:
* 4 proposed 2 as the best number of clusters
* 16 proposed 3 as the best number of clusters
* 1 proposed 11 as the best number of clusters
```

* 2 proposed 15 as the best number of clusters

***** Conclusion *****

* According to the majority rule, the best number of clusters is 3

****

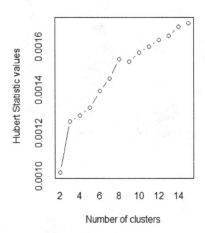

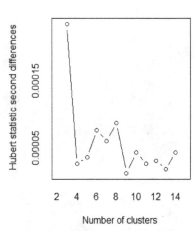

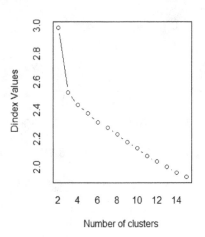

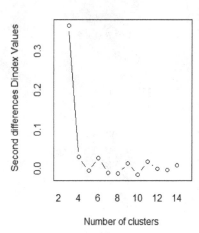

```
> table(nc$Best.n[1,])
```

 0 1 2 3 11 15

```
  2  1  4 16  1  2
> barplot(table(nc$Best.n[1,]),
+        xlab="Numer of Clusters", ylab="Number of Criteria",
+        main="Number of Clusters Chosen by 26 Criteria")
```

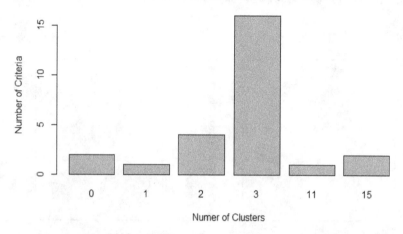

Number of Clusters Chosen by 26 Criteria

```
> set.seed(1234)
> fit.km <- kmeans(df, 3, nstart=25)

> fit.km$size
[1] 61 68 49

> fit.km$centers

               v1          v2          v3          v4          v5
v6          v7          v8
1 -1.16822514  0.8756272 -0.3037196  0.3180446 -0.6626544
0.56329925  0.87403990  0.94098462
2  0.07973544 -0.9195318 -0.3778231 -0.4643776  0.1750133 -
0.46892793 -0.07372644  0.04416309
3  1.34366784  0.1860184  0.9024258  0.2485092  0.5820616 -
0.05049296 -0.98577624 -1.23271740
               v9         v10         v11         v12         v13
v14
1 -0.583942581  0.58014642  0.1667181  0.4823674  0.7648958
1.1550888
2  0.008736157  0.01821349 -0.8598525  0.4233092  0.2490794
-0.7630972
3  0.714825281 -0.74749896  0.9857177 -1.1879477 -1.2978785
-0.3789756
```

166

```
> aggregate(wine[-1], by=list(cluster=fit.km$cluster),
mean)

    cluster         V2          V3        V4        V5          V6
V7          V8          V9        V10       V11
1         1 13.71148 1.997049 2.453770 17.28197 107.78689
2.842131 2.9691803 0.2891803 1.922951 5.444590
2         2 12.25412 1.914265 2.239118 20.07941  93.04412
2.248971 2.0733824 0.3629412 1.601324 3.064706
3         3 13.15163 3.344490 2.434694 21.43878  99.02041
1.678163 0.7979592 0.4508163 1.163061 7.343265
          V12       V13        V14
1 1.0677049 3.154754 1110.6393
2 1.0542059 2.788529  506.5882
3 0.6859184 1.690204  627.5510
```

Two additional cluster plot may be useful in your analysis.

```
> clusplot(wine, fit.km$cluster, color=TRUE, shade=TRUE,
+            labels=2, lines=0)
```

CLUSPLOT(wine)

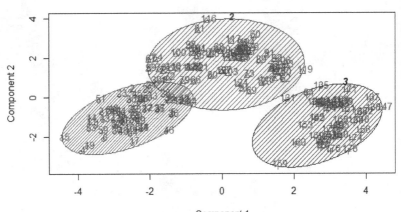

Component 1
These two components explain 57.38 % of the point variability.

167

```
> plotcluster(wine, fit.km$cluster)
```

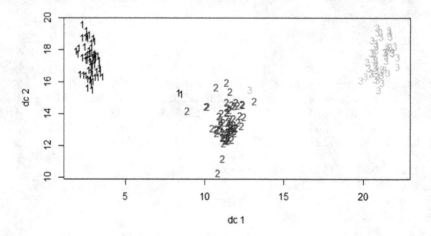

10. Ordinary least squares

In statistics, ordinary least squares (OLS) or linear least squares is a method for estimating the unknown parameters in a linear regression model. This method minimizes the sum of squared vertical distances between the observed responses in the dataset and the responses predicted by the linear approximation. The resulting estimator can be expressed by a simple formula, especially in the case of a single regressor on the right-hand side.

The OLS estimator is consistent when the regressors are exogenous and there is no perfect multicollinearity, and optimal in the class of linear unbiased estimators when the errors are homoscedastic and serially uncorrelated. Under these conditions, the method of OLS provides minimum-variance mean-unbiased estimation when the errors have finite variances. Under the additional assumption that the errors be normally distributed, OLS is the maximum likelihood estimator. OLS is used in economics (econometrics), political science and electrical engineering (control theory and signal processing), among many areas of application.

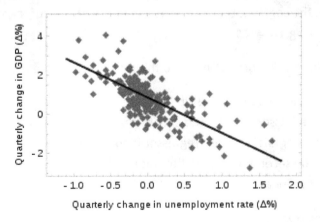

Okun's law in macroeconomics states that in an economy the GDP growth should depend linearly on the changes in the unemployment rate. Here the ordinary least squares method is used to construct the regression line describing this law.

Linear model

Suppose the data consists of n observations $\{y_i, x_i\}_{i=1}^n$. Each observation includes a scalar response y_i and a vector of p predictors (or regressors) x_i. In a linear regression model the response variable is a linear function of the regressors:

$$y_i = x_i'\beta + \varepsilon_i,$$

where β is a $p \times 1$ vector of unknown parameters; ε_i 's are unobserved scalar random variables (errors) which account for the discrepancy between the actually observed responses y_i and the "predicted outcomes" $x_i'\beta$; and x' denotes matrix transpose, so that $x'\beta$ is the dot product between the vectors x and β. This model can also be written in matrix notation as

$$y = X\beta + \varepsilon,$$

where y and ε are $n \times 1$ vectors, and X is an $n \times p$ matrix of regressors, which is also sometimes called the *design matrix*.

As a rule, the constant term is always included in the set of regressors X, say, by taking $x_{i1} = 11$ for all $i = 1, ..., n$.

The coefficient β_1 corresponding to this regressor is called the *intercept*.

There may be some relationship between the regressors. For instance, the third regressor may be the square of the second regressor. In this case (assuming that the first regressor is constant) we have a quadratic model in the second regressor. But this is still considered a linear model because it is linear in the βs.

Assumptions

There are several different frameworks in which the linear regression model can be cast in order to make the OLS technique applicable. Each of these settings produces the same formulas and same results. The only difference is the interpretation and the assumptions which have to be imposed in order for the method to give meaningful results. The choice of the applicable framework depends mostly on the nature of data in hand, and on the inference task which has to be performed.

One of the lines of difference in interpretation is whether to treat the regressors as random variables, or as predefined constants. In the first case (random design) the regressors x_i are random and sampled together with the y_i 's from some population, as in an observational study. This approach allows for more natural study of the asymptotic properties of the estimators. In the other interpretation (fixed design), the regressors X are treated as known constants set by a design, and y is sampled conditionally on the values of X as in an experiment. For practical purposes, this distinction is often unimportant, since estimation and inference is carried out while conditioning on X. All results stated in this article are within the random design framework.

The primary assumption of OLS is that there is zero or negligible errors in the independent variable, since this method only attempts to minimize the mean squared error in the dependent variable.

Classical linear regression model

The classical model focuses on the "finite sample" estimation and inference, meaning that the number of observations n is fixed. This contrasts with the other approaches, which study the asymptotic behavior of OLS, and in which the number of observations is allowed to grow to infinity.

- **Correct specification**. The linear functional form is correctly specified.
- **Strict exogeneity**. The errors in the regression should have conditional mean zero (Hayashi, 2000):

$$E[\varepsilon|X] = 0.$$

171

The immediate consequence of the exogeneity assumption is that the errors have mean zero: $E[\varepsilon] = 0$, and that the regressors are uncorrelated with the errors: $E[X'\varepsilon] = 0$.

The exogeneity assumption is critical for the OLS theory. If it holds then the regressor variables are called *exogenous* (Hayashi, 2000). If it doesn't, then those regressors that are correlated with the error term are called endogenous, and then the OLS estimates become invalid. In such case the method of instrumental variables may be used to carry out inference.

- **No linear dependence**. The regressors in X must all be linearly independent. Mathematically it means that the matrix X must have full column rank almost surely (Hayashi, 2000):

$$Pr[\text{rank}(X) = p] = 1$$

Usually, it is also assumed that the regressors have finite moments up to at least second. In such case the matrix $Q_{xx} = E[X'X/n]$ will be finite and positive semi-definite. When this assumption is violated the regressors are called linearly dependent or perfectly multicollinear. In such case the value of the regression coefficient β cannot be learned, although prediction of y values is still possible for new values of the regressors that lie in the same linearly dependent subspace.

- **Spherical errors**:

$$Var[\varepsilon|X] = \sigma^2 I_n$$

where I_n is an $n \times n$ identity matrix, and σ^2 is a parameter which determines the variance of each observation. This σ^2 is considered a nuisance parameter in the model, although usually it is also estimated. If this assumption is violated then the OLS estimates are still valid, but no longer efficient. It is customary to split this assumption into two parts:

- **Homoscedasticity**: $E[\varepsilon_i^2|X] = \sigma^2$, which means that the error term has the same variance σ^2 in each i observation. When this requirement is violated this is called heteroscedasticity, in such case a more efficient estimator would be weighted least squares. If the errors have infinite variance then the OLS estimates will also have infinite variance (although by the law of large numbers they will nonetheless tend toward the true values so long as the errors have zero mean). In this case, robust estimation techniques are recommended.

- **Nonautocorrelation**: the errors are uncorrelated between observations: $E[\varepsilon_i \varepsilon_j|X] = 0$ for $i \neq j$. This assumption may be violated in the context of time series data, panel data, cluster samples, hierarchical data, repeated measures data, longitudinal data, and other data with dependencies. In such cases generalized least squares provides a better alternative than the OLS.

- **Normality**. It is sometimes additionally assumed that the errors have normal distribution conditional on the regressors (Hayashi, 2000):

$$\varepsilon|X \sim \mathcal{N}(0, \sigma^2 I_n).$$

This assumption is not needed for the validity of the OLS method, although certain additional finite-sample properties can be established in case when it does (especially in the area of hypotheses testing). Also when the errors are normal, the OLS estimator is equivalent to the maximum likelihood estimator (MLE), and therefore it is asymptotically efficient in the class of all regular estimators.

Independent and identically distributed

In some applications, especially with cross-sectional data, an additional assumption is imposed — that all observations are independent and identically distributed (iid). This means that all observations are taken from a random sample which makes all the assumptions listed earlier simpler and easier to interpret. Also this framework allows one to state asymptotic results (as the sample size $n \to \infty$), which are understood as a theoretical possibility of fetching new independent observations from the data generating process. The list of assumptions in this case is:

- iid observations: (x_i, y_i) is independent from, and has the same distribution as, (x_j, y_j) for all $i \neq j$;
- no perfect multicollinearity: $Q_{xx} = E[x_i x_i']$ is a positive-definite matrix;
- exogeneity: $E[\varepsilon_i | x_i] = 0$
- homoscedasticity: $Var[\varepsilon_i | x_i] = \sigma^2$

Time series model

- The stochastic process $\{x_i, y_i\}$ is stationary and ergodic;
- The regressors are predetermined: $E[x_i \varepsilon_i] = 0$ for all $i = 1, \dots, n$;
- The $p \times p$ matrix $Q_{xx} = E[x_i x_j']$ is of full rank, and hence positive-definite;
- $\{x_i \varepsilon_i\}$ is a martingale difference sequence, with a finite matrix of second moments $Q_{xx\varepsilon^2} = E[\varepsilon_i^2 x_i x_j']$

Estimation

Suppose b is a "candidate" value for the parameter β. The quantity $y_i - x_i'b$ is called the residual for the i-th observation, it measures the vertical distance between the data point (x_i, y_i) and the hyperplane $y = x'b$, and thus assesses the degree of fit between the actual data and the model. The sum of squared residuals (SSR) (also called the error sum of squares (ESS) or residual sum of squares (RSS)) (Hayashi, 2000) is a measure of the overall model fit:

$$S(b) = \sum_{i=1}^{n} (y_i - x_i'b)^2 = (y - Xb)^T (y - Xb),$$

where T denotes the matrix transpose. The value of b which minimizes this sum is called the OLS estimator for β. The function $S(b)$ is quadratic in b with positive-definite Hessian, and therefore this function possesses a unique global minimum at $b = \hat{\beta}$, which can be given by the explicit formula (Hayashi, 2000):

$$\hat{\beta} = \arg\min_{b \in \mathbb{R}^p} S(b) = \left(\frac{1}{n}\sum_{i=1}^{n} x_i x_i'\right)^{-1} \cdot \frac{1}{n}\sum_{i=1}^{n} x_i y_i$$

or equivalently in matrix form,

$$\hat{\beta} = (X^T X)^{-1} X^T y.$$

After we have estimated β, the fitted values (or predicted values) from the regression will be

$$\hat{y} = X\hat{\beta} = Py,$$

where $P = X(X^T X)^{-1} X^T$ is the projection matrix onto the space spanned by the columns of X. This matrix P is also sometimes called the hat matrix because it "puts a hat" onto the variable y. Another matrix, closely related to P is the annihilator matrix $M = I_n - P$, this is a projection matrix onto the space orthogonal to X. Both matrices P and M are symmetric and idempotent (meaning that $P^2 = P$), and relate to the data matrix X via identities $PX = X$ and $MX = 0$ (Hayashi, 2000).

Matrix M creates the residuals from the regression:

$$\hat{\varepsilon} = y - X\hat{\beta} = My = M\varepsilon$$

Using these residuals we can estimate the value of σ^2:

$$s^2 = \frac{\hat{\varepsilon}'\hat{\varepsilon}}{n-p} = \frac{y'My}{n-p} = \frac{S(\hat{\beta})}{n-p}, \qquad \hat{\sigma}^2 = \frac{n-p}{n}s^2$$

The numerator, $n - p$, is the statistical degrees of freedom. The first quantity, s^2, is the OLS estimate for σ^2, whereas the second, $\hat{\sigma}^2$, is the MLE estimate for σ^2. The two estimators are quite similar in large samples; the first one is always unbiased, while the second is biased but minimizes the mean squared error of the estimator. In practice s^2 is used more often, since it is more convenient for the hypothesis testing. The square root of s^2 is called the standard error of the regression (SER), or standard error of the equation (SEE).

It is common to assess the goodness-of-fit of the OLS regression by comparing how much the initial variation in the sample can be reduced by regressing onto X. The coefficient of determination R^2 is defined as a ratio of "explained" variance to the "total" variance of the dependent variable y (Hayashi, 2000):

$$R^2 = \frac{\Sigma(\hat{y}_i - \bar{y})^2}{\Sigma(y_i - \bar{y})^2} = \frac{y'P'LPy}{y'Ly} = 1 - \frac{y'My}{y'Ly} = 1 - \frac{SSR}{TSS}$$

where TSS is the total sum of squares for the dependent variable, $L = I_n - \mathbf{1}\mathbf{1}'/n$, and $\mathbf{1}$ is an $n \times 1$ vector of ones. (L is a "centering matrix" which is equivalent to regression on a constant; it simply subtracts the mean from a variable.)

In order for R^2 to be meaningful, the matrix X of data on regressors must contain a column vector of ones to represent the constant whose coefficient is the regression intercept. In that case, R^2 will always be a number between 0 and 1, with values close to 1 indicating a good degree of fit.

Simple regression model

If the data matrix X contains only two variables: a constant, and a scalar regressor x_i, then this is called the "simple regression model" (Hayashi, 2000). This case is often considered in the beginner statistics classes, as it provides much simpler formulas even suitable for manual calculation. The vectors of parameters in such model is 2-dimensional, and is commonly denoted as (α, β):

$$y_i = \alpha + \beta x_i + \varepsilon_i.$$

The least squares estimates in this case are given by simple formulas

$$\hat{\beta} = \frac{\sum x_i y_i - \frac{1}{n}\sum x_i \sum y_i}{\sum x_i^2 - \frac{1}{n}(\sum x_i)^2} = \frac{\text{Cov}[x, y]}{\text{Var}[x]}, \hat{\alpha} = \bar{y} - \hat{\beta}\bar{x}$$

Alternative derivations

In the previous section the least squares estimator $\hat{\beta}$ was obtained as a value that minimizes the sum of squared residuals of the model. However it is also possible to derive the same estimator from other approaches. In all cases the formula for OLS estimator remains the same: $\hat{\beta} = (X'X)^{-1}X'y$, the only difference is in how we interpret this result.

Geometric approach

For mathematicians, OLS is an approximate solution to an overdetermined system of linear equations $X\beta \approx y$, where β is the unknown. Assuming the system cannot be solved exactly (the number of equations n is much larger than the number of unknowns p), we are looking for a solution that could provide the smallest discrepancy between the right- and left- hand sides. In other words, we are looking for the solution that satisfies

$$\hat{\beta} = \arg\min_{\beta} \|y - X\beta\|$$

where $\|\cdot\|$ is the standard L^2 norm in the n-dimensional Euclidean space R^n. The predicted quantity $X\beta$ is just a certain linear combination of the vectors of regressors. Thus, the residual vector $y - X\beta$ will have the smallest length when y is projected orthogonally onto the linear subspace spanned by the columns of X. The OLS estimator in this case can be interpreted as the coefficients of vector decomposition of $\hat{y} = Py$ along the basis of X.

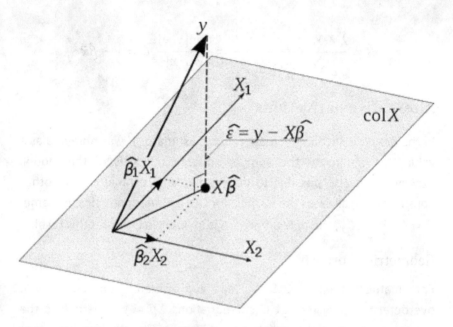

OLS estimation can be viewed as a projection onto the linear space spanned by the regressors.

Another way of looking at it is to consider the regression line to be a weighted average of the lines passing through the combination of any two points in the dataset (Akbarzadeh, 2013). Although this way of calculation is more computationally expensive, it provides a better intuition on OLS.

Maximum likelihood

The OLS estimator is identical to the maximum likelihood estimator (MLE) under the normality assumption for the error terms (Hayashi, 2000). This normality assumption has historical importance, as it provided the basis for the early work in linear regression analysis by Yule and Pearson. From the properties of MLE, we can infer that the OLS estimator is asymptotically efficient (in the sense of attaining the Cramér-Rao bound for variance) if the normality assumption is satisfied (Hayashi, 2000).

Generalized method of moments

In iid case the OLS estimator can also be viewed as a GMM estimator arising from the moment conditions

$$E[x_i(y_i - x_i'\beta)] = 0.$$

These moment conditions state that the regressors should be uncorrelated with the errors. Since x_i is a p-vector, the number of moment conditions is equal to the dimension of the parameter vector β, and thus the system is exactly identified. This is the so-called classical GMM case, when the estimator does not depend on the choice of the weighting matrix.

Note that the original strict exogeneity assumption $E[\varepsilon_i|x] = 0$ implies a far richer set of moment conditions than stated above. In particular, this assumption implies that for any vector-function f, the moment condition $E[f(x_i) \cdot \varepsilon_i] = 0$ will hold. However it can be shown using the Gauss–Markov theorem that the optimal choice of function f is to take $f(x) = x$, which results in the moment equation posted above.

Finite sample properties

First of all, under the strict exogeneity assumption the OLS estimators $\hat{\beta}$ and s^2 are unbiased, meaning that their expected values coincide with the true values of the parameters (Hayashi, 2000):

$$E[\hat{\beta}|X] = \beta, \qquad E[s^2|X] = \sigma^2.$$

If the strict exogeneity does not hold (as is the case with many time series models, where exogeneity is assumed only with respect to the past shocks but not the future ones), then these estimators will be biased in finite samples.

The variance-covariance matrix of $\hat{\beta}$ is equal to (Hayashi, 2000)

$$\text{Var}[\hat{\beta}|X] = \sigma^2(X'X)^{-1}.$$

In particular, the standard error of each coefficient $\hat{\beta}_j$ is equal to square root of the j-th diagonal element of this matrix. The estimate of this standard error is obtained by replacing the unknown quantity σ^2 with its estimate s^2.

Thus,

$$\widehat{se}(\hat{\beta}_j) = \sqrt{s^2(X'X)^{-1}_{jj}}$$

It can also be easily shown that the estimator is $\hat{\beta}$ uncorrelated with the residuals from the model (Hayashi, 2000):

$$\text{Cov}[\hat{\beta}, \hat{\varepsilon}|X] = 0.$$

The Gauss–Markov theorem states that under the spherical errors assumption (that is, the errors should be uncorrelated and homoscedastic) the estimator is efficient in the class of linear unbiased estimators. This is called the **best linear unbiased estimator** (BLUE). Efficiency should be understood as if we were to find some other estimator $\tilde{\beta}$ which would be linear in y and unbiased, then (Hayashi, 2000)

$$\text{Var}[\tilde{\beta}|X] - \text{Var}[\hat{\beta}|X]$$

in the sense that this is a nonnegative-definite matrix. This theorem establishes optimality only in the class of linear unbiased estimators, which is quite restrictive. Depending on the distribution of the error terms ε, other, non-linear estimators may provide better results than OLS.

Assuming normality

The properties listed so far are all valid regardless of the underlying distribution of the error terms. However if you are willing to assume that the normality assumption holds (that is, that $\varepsilon \sim N(0, \sigma^2 I_n)$), then additional properties of the OLS estimators can be stated.

The estimator $\hat{\beta}$ is normally distributed, with mean and variance as given before (Amemiya, 1985):

$$\hat{\beta} \sim \mathcal{N}(\beta, \sigma^2 (X'X)^{-1})$$

This estimator reaches the Cramér–Rao bound for the model, and thus is optimal in the class of all unbiased estimators. Note that unlike the Gauss–Markov theorem, this result establishes optimality among both linear and non-linear estimators, but only in the case of normally distributed error terms.

The estimator s^2 will be proportional to the chi-squared distribution (Amemiya, 1985):

$$s^2 \sim \frac{\sigma^2}{n-p} \cdot \chi^2_{n-p}$$

The variance of this estimator is equal to $2\sigma^4/(n-p)$, which does not attain the Cramér–Rao bound of $2\sigma^4/n$. However it was shown that there are no unbiased estimators of σ^2 with variance smaller than that of the estimator s^2 (Rao, 1973). If we are willing to allow biased estimators, and consider the class of estimators that are proportional to the sum of squared residuals (SSR) of the model, then the best (in the sense of the mean squared error) estimator in this class will be $\tilde{\sigma}2 = SSR/(n-p+2)$, which even beats the Cramér–Rao bound in case when there is only one regressor ($p = 1$) (Amemiya, 1985).

Moreover, the $\hat{\beta}$ estimators and s^2 are independent (Amemiya, 1985), the fact which comes in useful when constructing the t- and F-tests for the regression.

Influential observations

As was mentioned before, the estimator $\hat{\beta}$ is linear in y, meaning that it represents a linear combination of the dependent variables y_i's. The weights in this linear combination are functions of the regressors X, and generally are unequal. The observations with high weights are called influential because they have a more pronounced effect on the value of the estimator.

To analyze which observations are influential we remove a specific j-th observation and consider how much the estimated quantities are going to change (similarly to the jackknife method). It can be shown that the change in the OLS estimator for β will be equal to (Davidson & Mackinnon, 1993)

$$\hat{\beta}^{(j)} - \hat{\beta} = -\frac{1}{1 - h_j}(X'X)^{-1}x_j'\varepsilon_j,$$

where $h = x_j(X'X)^{-1}x_j$ is the j-th diagonal element of the hat matrix P, and x_j is the vector of regressors corresponding to the j-th observation. Similarly, the change in the predicted value for j-th observation resulting from omitting that observation from the dataset will be equal to (Davidson & Mackinnon, 1993)

$$\hat{y}_j^{(j)} - \hat{y}_j = x_j'\hat{\beta}^{(j)} - x_j'\hat{\beta} = -\frac{h_j}{1 - h_j}\hat{\varepsilon}_j$$

From the properties of the hat matrix, $0 \le h_j \le 1$, and they sum up to p, so that on average $h_j \approx p/n$. These quantities h_j are called the leverages, **and observations with high h_j's — leverage points** (Davidson & Mackinnon, 1993). Usually the observations with high leverage ought to be scrutinized more carefully, in case they are erroneous, or outliers, or in some other way atypical of the rest of the dataset.

Partitioned regression

Sometimes the variables and corresponding parameters in the regression can be logically split into two groups, so that the regression takes form

$$y = X_1\beta_1 + X_2\beta_2 + \varepsilon,$$

where X_1 and X_2 have dimensions $n \times p$, $n \times p$, and β_1, β_2 are $p \times 1$ and $p \times 1$ vectors, with $p_1 + p_2 = p$.

The Frisch–Waugh–Lovell theorem states that in this regression the residuals $\hat{\varepsilon}$ and the OLS estimate $\hat{\beta}_2$ will be numerically identical to the residuals and the OLS estimate for β_2 in the following regression (Davidson & Mackinnon, 1993):

$$M_1 y = M_1 X_2 \beta_2 + \eta,$$

where M_1 is the annihilator matrix for regressors X_1 .

The theorem can be used to establish a number of theoretical results. For example, having a regression with a constant and another regressor is equivalent to subtracting the means from the dependent variable and the regressor and then running the regression for the demeaned variables but without the constant term.

Constrained estimation

Suppose it is known that the coefficients in the regression satisfy a system of linear equations

$$H_0 : Q'\beta = c$$

where Q is a $p \times q$ matrix of full rank, and c is a $q \times 1$ vector of known constants, where $q < p$. In this case least squares estimation is equivalent to minimizing the sum of squared residuals of the model subject to the constraint H_0 .The **constrained least squares** (CLS) estimator can be given by an explicit formula (Amemiya, 1985):

$$\hat{\beta}^c = \hat{\beta} - (X'X)^{-1} Q (Q'(X'X)^{-1}Q)^{-1} \left(Q'\hat{\beta} - c \right)$$

This expression for the constrained estimator is valid as long as the matrix $X'X$ is invertible. It was assumed from the beginning of this article that this matrix is of full rank, and it was noted that when the rank condition fails, β will not be identifiable. However it may happen that adding the restriction H_0 makes β identifiable, in which case one would like to find the formula for the estimator. The estimator is equal to (Amemiya, 1985)

$$\hat{\beta}^c = R(R'X'XR)^{-1}R'X'y + \left(I_p - R(R'X'XR)^{-1}R'X'X\right)Q(Q'Q)^{-1}c,$$

where R is a $p \times (p - q)$ matrix such that the matrix $[QR]$ is non-singular, and $R'Q = 0$. Such a matrix can always be found, although generally it is not unique. The second formula coincides with the first in case when $X'X$ is invertible (Amemiya, 1985).

Large sample properties

The least squares estimators are point estimates of the linear regression model parameters β. However, generally we also want to know how close those estimates might be to the true values of parameters. In other words, we want to construct the interval estimates.

Since we haven't made any assumption about the distribution of error term ε_i, it is impossible to infer the distribution of the estimators $\hat{\beta}$ and $\hat{\sigma}^2$. Nevertheless, we can apply the law of large numbers and central limit theorem to derive their asymptotic properties as sample size n goes to infinity. While the sample size is necessarily finite, it is customary to assume that n is "large enough" so that the true distribution of the OLS estimator is close to its asymptotic limit, and the former may be approximately replaced by the latter.

We can show that under the model assumptions, the least squares estimator for β is consistent (that is $\hat{\beta}$ converges in probability to β) and asymptotically normal:

$$\sqrt{n}(\hat{\beta} - \beta) \xrightarrow{d} \mathcal{N}(0, \sigma^2 Q_{xx}^{-1}),$$

where $Q_{xx} = X'X$.

Using this asymptotic distribution, approximate two-sided confidence intervals for the j-th component of the vector $\hat{\beta}$ can be constructed as at the $1 - \alpha$ confidence level,

$$\beta_j \in \left[\hat{\beta}_j \pm q_{1-\alpha/2}^{\mathcal{N}(0,1)} \sqrt{\frac{1}{n} \hat{\sigma}^2 [Q_{xx}^{-1}]_{jj}} \right]$$

where q denotes the quantile function of standard normal distribution, and $[\cdot]_{jj}$ is the j-th diagonal element of a matrix.

Similarly, the least squares estimator for σ^2 is also consistent and asymptotically normal (provided that the fourth moment of ε_i exists) with limiting distribution

$$\sqrt{n}(\hat{\sigma}^2 - \sigma^2) \xrightarrow{d} \mathcal{N}\left(0, E[\varepsilon_i^4] - \sigma^4\right).$$

These asymptotic distributions can be used for prediction, testing hypotheses, constructing other estimators, etc. As an example consider the problem of prediction. Suppose x_0 is some point within the domain of distribution of the regressors, and one wants to know what the response variable would have been at that point. The mean response is the quantity $y_0 = x_0'\beta$, whereas the predicted response is $\hat{y}_0 = x_0'\hat{\beta}$. Clearly the predicted response is a random variable, its distribution can be derived from that of   :

$$\sqrt{n}(\hat{y}_0 - y_0) \xrightarrow{d} \mathcal{N}(0, \sigma^2 x_0' Q_{xx}^{-1} x_0),$$

which allows construct confidence intervals for mean response y_0 to be constructed:

$$y_0 \in \left[x_0'\hat{\beta} \pm q_{1-\alpha/2}^{\mathcal{N}(0,1)} \sqrt{\frac{1}{n} \hat{\sigma}^2 x_0' Q_{xx}^{-1} x_0} \right]$$

at the $1 - \alpha$ confidence level.

Example with real data

This example exhibits the common mistake of ignoring the condition of having zero error in the dependent variable.

The following data set gives average heights and weights for American women aged 30–39 (source: The World Almanac and Book of Facts, 1975).

n	1	2	3	4	5	6	7	8
Height (m):	1.47	1.50	1.52	1.55	1.57	1.60	1.63	1.65
Weight (kg):	52.21	53.12	54.48	55.84	57.20	58.57	59.93	61.29

n	9	10	11	12	13	14	15
Height (m):	1.68	1.70	1.73	1.75	1.78	1.80	1.83
Weight (kg):	63.11	64.47	66.28	68.10	69.92	72.19	74.46

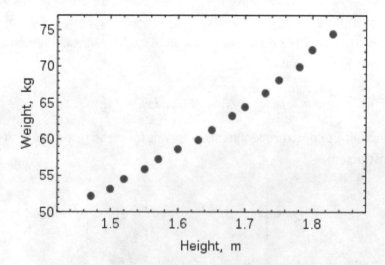

Scatterplot of the data; the relationship is slightly curved but close to linear.

When only one dependent variable is being modeled, a scatterplot will suggest the form and strength of the relationship between the dependent variable and regressors. It might also reveal outliers, heteroscedasticity, and other aspects of the data that may complicate the interpretation of a fitted regression model. The scatterplot suggests that the relationship is strong and can be approximated as a quadratic function. OLS can handle non-linear relationships by introducing the regressor $HEIGHT^2$. The regression model then becomes a multiple linear model:

$$w_i = \beta_1 + \beta_2 h_i + \beta_e h_i^2 + \varepsilon_i.$$

The output from most popular statistical packages will look similar to this:

Method: Least Squares Dependent variable: WEIGHT				
Included observations: 15				
Variable	Coefficient	Std. Error	t-statistic	p-value
β	128.8128	16.3083	7.8986	0.0000
h	−143.1620	19.8332	−7.2183	0.0000
h^2	61.9603	6.0084	10.3122	0.0000
R^2	0.9989	S.E. of regression		0.2516
Adjusted R^2	0.9987	Model sum-of-sq		692.61
Log-likelihood	1.0890	Residual sum-of-sq		0.7595
Durbin–Watson stats.	2.1013	Total sum-of-sq		693.37
Akaike criterion	0.2548	F-statistic		5471.2
Schwarz criterion	0.3964	p-value (F-stat)		0.0000

In this table:

- The Coefficient column gives the least squares estimates of parameters β_j
- The Std. errors column shows standard errors of each coefficient

estimate: $\left(\frac{1}{n}\hat{\sigma}^2[Q_{xx}^{-1}]_{jj}\right)^{1/2}$

- The t-statistic and p-value columns are testing whether any of the coefficients might be equal to zero. The t-statistic is calculated simply as $t = \hat{\beta}_j/\hat{\sigma}_j$. If the errors ε follow a normal distribution, t follows a Student-t distribution. Under weaker conditions, t is asymptotically normal. Large values of t indicate that the null hypothesis can be rejected and that the corresponding coefficient is not zero. The second column, p-value, expresses the results of the hypothesis test as a significance level. Conventionally, p-values smaller than 0.05 are taken as evidence that the population coefficient is nonzero.

- R-squaredR^2 is the coefficient of determination indicating goodness-of-fit of the regression. This statistic will be equal to one if fit is perfect, and to zero when regressors X have no explanatory power whatsoever. This is a biased estimate of the population R-squared, and will never decrease if additional regressors are added, even if they are irrelevant.

- Adjusted R-squaredR^2 is a slightly modified version of R^2, designed to penalize for the excess number of regressors which do not add to the explanatory power of the regression. This statistic is always smaller than R^2R^2, can decrease as new regressors are added, and even be negative for poorly fitting models:

$$\bar{R}^2 = 1 - \frac{n-1}{n-p}(1 - R^2)$$

- Log-likelihood is calculated under the assumption that errors follow normal distribution. Even though the assumption is not very reasonable, this statistic may still find its use in conducting LR tests.

- Durbin–Watson statistic tests whether there is any evidence of serial correlation between the residuals. As a rule of thumb, the value smaller than 2 will be an evidence of positive correlation.

- Akaike information criterion and Schwarz criterion are both used for model selection. Generally when comparing two alternative models, smaller values of one of these criteria will indicate a better model

188

(Burnham & Anderson, 2002).

- Standard error of regression is an estimate of σ, standard error of the error term.
- Total sum of squares, model sum of squared, and residual sum of squares tell us how much of the initial variation in the sample were explained by the regression.
- F-statistic tries to test the hypothesis that all coefficients (except the intercept) are equal to zero. This statistic has $F(p-1, n-p)$ distribution under the null hypothesis and normality assumption, and its p-value indicates probability that the hypothesis is indeed true. Note that when errors are not normal this statistic becomes invalid, and other tests such as for example Wald test or LR test should be used.

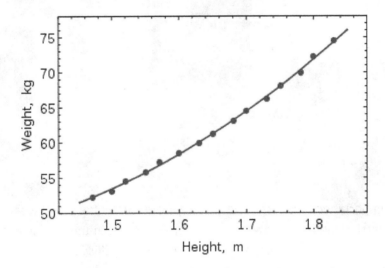

Fitted Regression

Ordinary least squares analysis often includes the use of diagnostic plots designed to detect departures of the data from the assumed form of the model. These are some of the common diagnostic plots:

- Residuals against the explanatory variables in the model. A non-linear relation between these variables suggests that the linearity of the conditional mean function may not hold. Different levels of

189

variability in the residuals for different levels of the explanatory variables suggests possible heteroscedasticity.

- Residuals against explanatory variables not in the model. Any relation of the residuals to these variables would suggest considering these variables for inclusion in the model.
- Residuals against the fitted values, $\hat{y}$.
- Residuals against the preceding residual. This plot may identify serial correlations in the residuals.

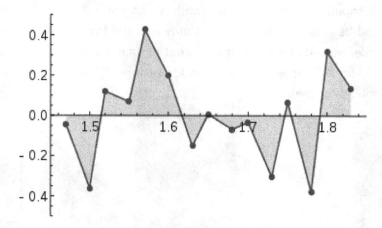

Residuals plot

An important consideration when carrying out statistical inference using regression models is how the data were sampled. In this example, the data are averages rather than measurements on individual women. The fit of the model is very good, but this does not imply that the weight of an individual woman can be predicted with high accuracy based only on her height.

Sensitivity to rounding

This example also demonstrates that coefficients determined by these calculations are sensitive to how the data is prepared. The heights were originally given rounded to the nearest inch and have been converted and rounded to the nearest centimeter. Since the conversion factor is one inch to 2.54 cm this is not an exact conversion. The original inches can be recovered by Round(x/0.0254) and then re-converted to metric without rounding. If this is done the results become:

Constant	Height	Height^2	
128.8128	-143.1620	61.96033	Converted to metric with rounding.
119.0205	-131.5076	58.50460	Converted to metric without rounding.

Using either of these equations to predict the weight of a 5' 6" (1.6764m) woman gives similar values: 62.94 kg with rounding vs. 62.98 kg without rounding. Thus a seemingly small variation in the data has a real effect on the coefficients but a small effect on the results of the equation.

While this may look innocuous in the middle of the data range it could become significant at the extremes or in the case where the fitted model is used to project outside the data range (extrapolation).

This highlights a common error: this example is an abuse of OLS which inherently requires that the errors in the dependent variable (in this case height) are zero or at least negligible. The initial rounding to nearest inch plus any actual measurement errors constitute a finite and non-negligible error. As a result the fitted parameters are not the best estimates they are presumed to be. Though not totally spurious the error in the estimation will depend upon relative size of the x and y errors.

Software

All major statistical software packages perform least squares regression analysis and inference. Simple linear regression and multiple regression using least squares can be done in some spreadsheet applications and on some calculators. While many statistical software packages can perform various types of nonparametric and robust regression, these methods are less standardized; different software packages implement different methods, and a method with a given name may be implemented differently in different packages. Specialized regression

191

software has been developed for use in fields such as survey analysis and neuroimaging.

Open Source software that perform OLS include DAP, Octave, R, and Weke. Commercial software that perform OLS include Analytica, SPSS Modeler, MATLAB, SAS Enterprise and STATISTICA.

Example Using R

Now let's look at an example concerning the number of species of tortoise on the various Galapagos Islands. There are 30 cases (Islands) and 7 variables in the dataset. We start by reading the data into R and examining it. Copy the following data and save it as a text file: gala.txt (tab delimited) in a directory, like "C/mydata/".

	Species	Endemics	Area	Elevation	Nearest	Scruz	Adjacent
Baltra	58	23	25.09	346	0.6	0.6	1.84
Bartolome	31	21	1.24	109	0.6	26.3	572.33
Caldwell	3	3	0.21	114	2.8	58.7	0.78
Champion	25	9	0.10	46	1.9	47.4	0.18
Coamano	2	1	0.05	77	1.9	1.9	903.82
Daphne.Major	18	11	0.34	119	8.0	8.0	1.84
Daphne.Minor	24	0	0.08	93	6.0	12.0	0.34
Darwin	10	7	2.33	168	34.1	290.2	2.85
Eden	8	4	0.03	71	0.4	0.4	17.95
Enderby	2	2	0.18	112	2.6	50.2	0.10
Espanola	97	26	58.27	198	1.1	88.3	0.57
Fernandina	93	35	634.49	1494	4.3	95.3	4669.32
Gardner1	58	17	0.57	49	1.1	93.1	58.27
Gardner2	5	4	0.78	227	4.6	62.2	0.21
Genovesa	40	19	17.35	76	47.4	92.2	129.49
Isabela	347	89	4669.32	1707	0.7	28.1	634.49
Marchena	51	23	129.49	343	29.1	85.9	59.56
Onslow	2	2	0.01	25			

	3.3	45.9	0.10	
Pinta	104	37	59.56	777
	29.1	119.6	129.49	
Pinzon	108	33	17.95	458
	10.7	10.7	0.03	
Las.Plazas	12	9	0.23	94
	0.5	0.6	25.09	
Rabida	70	30	4.89	367
	4.4	24.4	572.33	
SanCristobal	280	65	551.62	716
	45.2	66.6	0.57	
SanSalvador	237	81	572.33	906
	0.2	19.8	4.89	
SantaCruz	444	95	903.82	864
	0.6	0.0	0.52	
SantaFe	62	28	24.08	259
	16.5	16.5	0.52	
SantaMaria	285	73	170.92	640
	2.6	49.2	0.10	
Seymour	44	16	1.84	147
	0.6	9.6	25.09	
Tortuga	16	8	1.24	186
	6.8	50.9	17.95	
Wolf	21	12	2.85	253
	34.1	254.7	2.33	

Change the working directory to "c:/mydata" (do this by choosing "File"->"Change directory", and then inputting the directory name). And now you can simply read the data into R by:

```
> gala <- read.table("gala.txt") # read the data into R
```

Now we can take a look at the data.

```
> data(gala)
> gala
          Species Endemics Area Elevation Nearest Scruz Adjacent
   Baltra 58           23 25.09       346     0.6   0.6     1.84
Bartolome 31           21 1.24        109     0.6  26.3   572.33
--- cases deleted ---
  Tortuga 16            8 1.24        186     6.8  50.9    17.95
     Wolf 21           12 2.85        253    34.1 254.7     2.33
```

The variables are

194

Species	The number of species of tortoise found on the island
Endemics	The number of endemic species
Elevation	The highest elevation of the island (m)
Nearest	The distance from the nearest island (km)
Scruz	The distance from Santa Cruz island (km)
Adjacent	The area of the adjacent island (km2)

The data were presented by Johnson and Raven (Johnson & Raven, 1973) and also appear in Weisberg (Weisberg, 2005). We have filled in some missing values for simplicity. Fitting a linear model in R is done using the lm() command. Notice the syntax for specifying the predictors in the model. This is the so-called Wilkinson-Rogers notation. In this case, since all the variables are in the gala data frame, we must use the data= argument.

First, we generate a series of plots of various species-area relations. We consider three models: Linear, Gleason, and log-Arrhenius.

1. Linear model: $S \sim \text{Normal}(\mu, \sigma^2)$ with identity link such that $\mu = \beta_0 + \beta_1 A$.
2. Gleason model: $S \sim \text{Normal}(\mu, \sigma^2)$ with identity link such that $\mu = \beta_0 + \beta_1 \log A$.
3. log-Arrhenius model: $S \sim \text{Normal}(\mu, \sigma^2)$ with identity link such that $\mu = \beta_0 A^{\beta_1}$.

Model 1 is a Linear Model. We fit a linear model on the original scale, model 1 above and obtain the log-likelihood (with logLik) and the AIC (with AIC).

```
> model1<-lm(Species~Area,data=gala)
> logLik(model1)
'log Lik.' -177.0993 (df=3)
> AIC(model1)
[1] 360.1985
```

We superimpose the fitted model on a scatter plot of the data.

```
> plot(gala$Area,gala$Species, xlab='Area', ylab='Species')
```

```
> abline(model1,col=2, lty=2)
> mtext('Model 1: linear model', side=3, line=.5)
```

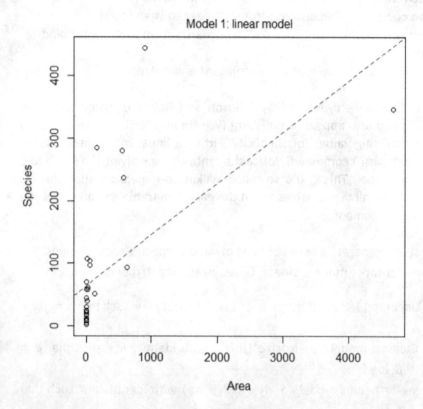

Model 1: linear model

Model 2 is a Gleason Model. The Gleason model requires a log-transformed predictor, but an untransformed response.

```
> model2<-lm(Species~log(Area),data=gala)
> logLik(model2)
'log Lik.' -169.9574 (df=3)
> AIC(model2)
[1] 345.9147

> plot(log(gala$Area), gala$Species, xlab='log(Area)',
+           ylab='Species')
> abline(model2,col=2,lty=2)
> mtext( 'Model 2: Gleason model', side=3, line=.5)
```

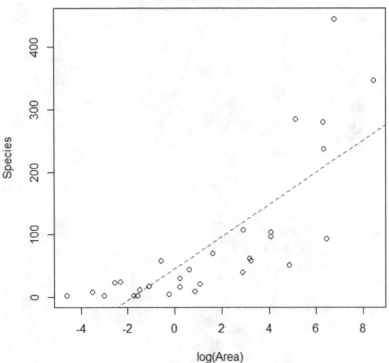

Model 2: Gleason model

Model 3 is a log-Arrhenius. The log-Arrhenius model is just an ordinary regression model in which both the response and predictor are log-transformed.

```
> model3<-lm(log(Species)~log(Area), data=gala)
> logLik(model3)
'log Lik.' -34.23973 (df=3)
> AIC(model3)
[1] 74.47946

> plot(log(gala$Area), log(gala$Species), xlab='log(Area)',
+             ylab='log(Species)')
> abline(model3,col=2,lty=2)
> mtext('Model 3: log-Arrhenius model', side=3, line=.5)
```

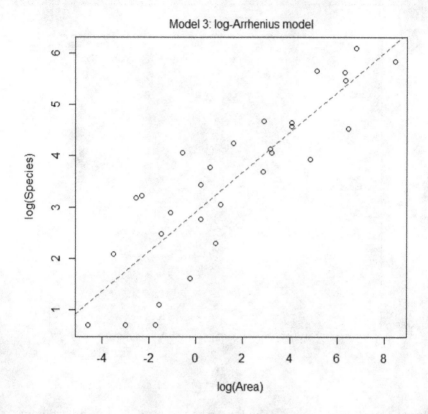

Model 3: log-Arrhenius model

Now we want to compare the models. We begin by collecting the names of our models.

```
> model.names<-c('Linear', 'Gleason', 'Log-Arrhenius')
```

Next we concatenate all the calculated log-likelihoods together.

```
> loglike <-c(logLik(model1),logLik(model2),logLik(model3))
```

Next we concatenate a list of the number of parameters estimated for each model. Each model has three parameters—β_0, β_1, and σ^2.

```
> numparms<-c(3,3,3)
```

Finally, we create our function to carry out the calculations.

```
# LL is loglikelihood,
# K is number of estimated parameters
```

```
# n is the sample size
> AIC.func<-function(LL,K,n,modelnames)
+ {
+ AIC<- -2*LL + 2*K
+   AICc<-AIC + 2*K*(K+1)/(n-K-1)
+   output<-cbind(LL,K,AIC,AICc)
+   colnames(output)<-c('LogL','K','AIC','AICc')
+   minAICc<-min(output[,"AICc"])
+   deltai<-output[,"AICc"]-minAICc
+   rel.like<-exp(-deltai/2)
+   wi<-round(rel.like/sum(rel.like),3)
+   out<-data.frame(modelnames,output,deltai,wi)
+   out
+ }
> AIC.func(loglike,numparms,dim(gala)[1],model.names)
```

	modelnames	LogL	K	AIC	AICc	deltai	wi
1	Linear	-177.09927	3	360.19853	361.12161	285.7191	0
2	Gleason	-169.95737	3	345.91473	346.83781	271.4353	0
3	Log-Arrhenius	-34.23973	3	74.47946	75.40253	0.0000	1

Based on the output we see there is only one model that has any empirical support, the log-Arrhenius model. For reasons we will not explain here, although the log-Arrhenius model fits well, it is not guaranteed to be optimal. For the Galapagos data, a model that allows there to be heteroscedasticity on the scale of the original response is to be preferred.

The previous models only examine the Species-Area relationship. We now consider additional variables: Endemics, Elevation, Nearest, Scruz, and Adjacent. We will call our model gfit.

```
> gfit <- lm(Species~Area + Elevation + Nearest + Scruz +
+             Adjacent, data=gala)
> summary(gfit)
Call:
> lm(formula = Species~Area + Elevation + Nearest + Scruz +
+             Adjacent, data=gala)
> summary(gfit)
```

```
Call:
lm(formula = Species ~ Area + Elevation + Nearest + Scruz +
Adjacent,
    data = gala)

Residuals:
    Min      1Q    Median      3Q      Max
-111.679  -34.898   -7.862   33.460  182.584

Coefficients:
             Estimate  Std. Error  t value  Pr(>|t|)
(Intercept)   7.068221  19.154198    0.369  0.715351
Area         -0.023938   0.022422   -1.068  0.296318
Elevation     0.319465   0.053663    5.953  3.82e-06 ***
Nearest       0.009144   1.054136    0.009  0.993151
Scruz        -0.240524   0.215402   -1.117  0.275208
Adjacent     -0.074805   0.017700   -4.226  0.000297 ***
---
Signif. codes: 0 '***' 0.001 '**' 0.01 '*' 0.05 '.' 0.1 ' '
1

Residual standard error: 60.98 on 24 degrees of freedom
Multiple R-squared:  0.7658,    Adjusted R-squared:  0.7171
F-statistic:   15.7 on 5 and 24 DF,  p-value: 6.838e-07
```

We can identify several useful quantities in this output. Other statistical packages tend to produce output quite similar to this. One useful feature of R is that it is possible to directly calculate quantities of interest. Of course, it is not necessary here because the lm() function does the job but it is very useful when the statistic you want is not part of the pre-packaged functions.

First we make the X-matrix

```
> x <- cbind(1,gala[,-c(1,2)])
```

and here's the response y:

```
> y <- gala$Species
```

Now let's construct $X'X$: t() does transpose and %*% does matrix multiplication:

```
> t(x) %*% x
Error: %*% requires numeric matrix/vector arguments
```

Gives a somewhat cryptic error. The problem is that matrix arithmetic can only be done with numeric values but x here derives from the data frame type. Data frames are allowed to contain character variables, which would disallow matrix arithmetic. We need to force x into the matrix form:

```
> x <- as.matrix(x)
> t(x) %*% x
                 1        Area  Elevation    Nearest
1            30.00     7851.26    11041.0     301.80
Area       7851.26 23708665.46 10852798.5   39240.84
Elevation 11041.00 10852798.53  9218227.0  109139.20
Nearest     301.80    39240.84   109139.2    8945.30
Scruz      1709.30   275516.84   616237.8   34527.34
Adjacent   7832.95  5950313.65  8553187.9   37196.67
              Scruz    Adjacent
1           1709.30     7832.95
Area      275516.84  5950313.65
Elevation 616237.80  8553187.95
Nearest    34527.34    37196.67
Scruz     231613.77   534409.98
Adjacent  534409.98 23719568.46
```

Inverses can be taken using the solve() command:

```
> xtxi <- solve(t(x) %*% x)
> xtxi
                     1          Area     Elevation
1          9.867829e-02  3.778242e-05 -1.561976e-04
Area       3.778242e-05  1.352247e-07 -2.593617e-07
Elevation -1.561976e-04 -2.593617e-07  7.745339e-07
Nearest   -2.339027e-04  1.294003e-06 -3.549366e-06
Scruz     -3.760293e-04 -4.913149e-08  3.080831e-07
```

201

```
Adjacent     2.309832e-05   4.620303e-08 -1.640241e-07
                  Nearest          Scruz        Adjacent
1             -2.339027e-04 -3.760293e-04  2.309832e-05
Area           1.294003e-06 -4.913149e-08  4.620303e-08
Elevation     -3.549366e-06  3.080831e-07 -1.640241e-07
Nearest        2.988732e-04 -3.821077e-05  1.424729e-06
Scruz         -3.821077e-05  1.247941e-05 -1.958356e-07
Adjacent       1.424729e-06 -1.958356e-07  8.426543e-08
```

A somewhat more direct way to get $(X'X)^{-1}$ is as follows:

```
> gfit <- lm(Species~Area+Elevation+Nearest+Scruz+Adjacent,
+            data=gala)
> gs <- summary(gfit)
> gs$cov.unscaled
                 (Intercept)          Area      Elevation
(Intercept)  9.867829e-02  3.778242e-05 -1.561976e-04
Area         3.778242e-05  1.352247e-07 -2.593617e-07
Elevation   -1.561976e-04 -2.593617e-07  7.745339e-07
Nearest     -2.339027e-04  1.294003e-06 -3.549366e-06
Scruz       -3.760293e-04 -4.913149e-08  3.080831e-07
Adjacent     2.309832e-05  4.620303e-08 -1.640241e-07
                   Nearest          Scruz        Adjacent
(Intercept) -2.339027e-04 -3.760293e-04  2.309832e-05
Area         1.294003e-06 -4.913149e-08  4.620303e-08
Elevation   -3.549366e-06  3.080831e-07 -1.640241e-07
Nearest      2.988732e-04 -3.821077e-05  1.424729e-06
Scruz       -3.821077e-05  1.247941e-05 -1.958356e-07
Adjacent     1.424729e-06 -1.958356e-07  8.426543e-08
```

The names() command is the way to see the components of an Splus object - you can see that there are other useful quantities that are directly available:

```
> names(gs)
> names(gfit)
```

In particular, the fitted (or predicted) values and residuals are

```
> gfit$fit
```

Baltra	Bartolome	Caldwell	Champion
116.7259460	-7.2731544	29.3306594	10.3642660
Coamano	Daphne.Major	Daphne.Minor	Darwin
-36.3839155	43.0877052	33.9196678	-9.0189919
Eden	Enderby	Espanola	Fernandina
28.3142017	30.7859425	47.6564865	96.9895982
Gardner1	Gardner2	Genovesa	Isabela
-4.0332759	64.6337956	-0.4971756	386.4035578
Marchena	Onslow	Pinta	Pinzon
88.6945404	4.0372328	215.6794862	150.4753750
Las.Plazas	Rabida	SanCristobal	SanSalvador
35.0758066	75.5531221	206.9518779	277.6763183
SantaCruz	SantaFe	SantaMaria	Seymour
261.4164131	85.3764857	195.6166286	49.8050946
Tortuga	Wolf		
52.9357316	26.7005735		

```
> gfit$res
```

Baltra	Bartolome	Caldwell	Champion
-58.725946	38.273154	-26.330659	14.635734
Coamano	Daphne.Major	Daphne.Minor	Darwin
38.383916	-25.087705	-9.919668	19.018992
Eden	Enderby	Espanola	Fernandina
-20.314202	-28.785943	49.343513	-3.989598
Gardner1	Gardner2	Genovesa	Isabela
62.033276	-59.633796	40.497176	-39.403558
Marchena	Onslow	Pinta	Pinzon
-37.694540	-2.037233	-111.679486	-42.475375
Las.Plazas	Rabida	SanCristobal	SanSalvador
-23.075807	-5.553122	73.048122	-40.676318
SantaCruz	SantaFe	SantaMaria	Seymour
182.583587	-23.376486	89.383371	-5.805095
Tortuga	Wolf		
-36.935732	-5.700573		

We can get $\hat{\beta}$ directly:

```
> xtxi %*% t(x) %*% y
                 [,1]
1        7.068220709
```

```
Area         -0.023938338
Elevation     0.319464761
Nearest       0.009143961
Scruz        -0.240524230
Adjacent     -0.074804832
```

or in a computationally efficient and stable manner:

```
> solve(t(x) %*% x, t(x) %*% y)
             [,1]
[1,]   7.068220709
[2,]  -0.023938338
[3,]   0.319464761
[4,]   0.009143961
[5,]  -0.240524230
[6,]  -0.074804832
```

We can estimate σ using the estimator in the text:

```
> root1<-sum((gfit$res)^2)
> sqrt(root1/(30-6))
[1] 60.97519
```

Compare this to the results above (Residual standard error).

We may also obtain the standard errors for the coefficients. Also diag() returns the diagonal of a matrix):

```
> sqrt(diag(xtxi))*60.97519
            1         Area    Elevation      Nearest
 19.15419834   0.02242235   0.05366281   1.05413598
       Scruz     Adjacent
  0.21540225   0.01770019
```

Finally we may compute R^2:
```
> 1-sum((gfit$res)^2)/sum((y-mean(y))^2)
[1] 0.7658469
```

11. Generalized linear model

In statistics, the generalized linear model (GLM)—not to be confused with general linear model or generalized least squares—is a flexible generalization of ordinary linear regression that allows for response variables that have error distribution models other than a normal distribution. The GLM generalizes linear regression by allowing the linear model to be related to the response variable via a link function and by allowing the magnitude of the variance of each measurement to be a function of its predicted value.

Generalized linear models were formulated by John Nelder and Robert Wedderburn as a way of unifying various other statistical models, including linear regression, logistic regression and Poisson regression (Nelder & Wedderburn, 1972). They proposed an iteratively reweighted least squares method for maximum likelihood estimation of the model parameters. Maximum-likelihood estimation remains popular and is the default method on many statistical computing packages. Other approaches, including Bayesian approaches and least squares fits to variance stabilized responses, have been developed.

Intuition

Ordinary linear regression predicts the expected value of a given unknown quantity (the response variable, a random variable) as a linear combination of a set of observed values (predictors). This implies that a constant change in a predictor leads to a constant change in the response variable (i.e. a linear-response model). This is appropriate when the response variable has a normal distribution (intuitively, when a response variable can vary essentially indefinitely in either direction with no fixed "zero value", or more generally for any quantity that only varies by a relatively small amount, e.g. human heights).

However, these assumptions are inappropriate for many types of response variables. For example, in many cases when the response variable must be positive and can vary over a wide scale, constant input changes lead to geometrically varying rather than constantly varying output changes. As an example, a model that predicts that each decrease in 10 degrees Fahrenheit leads to 1,000 fewer people going to a given beach is unlikely to generalize well over both small beaches (e.g. those where the expected attendance was 50 at the lower temperature) and large beaches (e.g. those where the expected attendance was 10,000 at the lower temperature). An even worse problem is that, since the model also implies that a drop in 10 degrees leads 1,000 fewer people going to a given beach, a beach whose expected attendance was 50 at the higher temperature would now be predicted to have the impossible attendance value of -950. Logically, a more realistic model would instead predict a constant rate of increased beach attendance (e.g. an increase in 10 degrees leads to a doubling in beach attendance, and a drop in 10 degrees leads to a halving in attendance). Such a model is termed an exponential-response model (or log-linear model, since the logarithm of the response is predicted to vary linearly).

Similarly, a model that predicts a probability of making a yes/no choice (a Bernoulli variable) is even less suitable as a linear-response model, since probabilities are bounded on both ends (they must be between 0 and 1). Imagine, for example, a model that predicts the likelihood of a given person going to the beach as a function of temperature. A reasonable model might predict, for example, that a change in 10 degrees makes a person two times more or less likely to go to the beach. But what does "twice as likely" mean in terms of a probability? It cannot literally mean to double the probability value (e.g. 50% becomes 100%, 75% becomes 150%, etc.). Rather, it is the odds that are doubling: from 2:1 odds, to 4:1 odds, to 8:1 odds, etc. Such a model is a log-odds model.

Generalized linear models cover all these situations by allowing for response variables that have arbitrary distributions (rather than simply normal distributions), and for an arbitrary function of the response variable (the link function) to vary linearly with the predicted values (rather than assuming that the response itself must vary linearly). For example, the case above of predicted number of beach attendees would typically be modeled with a Poisson distribution and a log link, while the case of predicted probability of beach attendance would typically be modeled with a Bernoulli distribution (or binomial distribution, depending on exactly how the problem is phrased) and a log-odds (or logit) link function.

Overview

In a generalized linear model (GLM), each outcome of the dependent variables, Y, is assumed to be generated from a particular distribution in the exponential family, a large range of probability distributions that includes the normal, binomial, Poisson and gamma distributions, among others. The mean, μ, of the distribution depends on the independent variables, X, through:

$$E(Y) = \mu = g^{-1}(X\beta),$$

where $E(Y)$ is the expected value of Y; $X\beta$ is the linear predictor, a linear combination of unknown parameters, β; g is the link function.

In this framework, the variance is typically a function, V, of the mean:

$$\text{Var}(Y) = V(\mu) = V\big(g^{-1}(X\beta)\big).$$

It is convenient if V follows from the exponential family distribution, but it may simply be that the variance is a function of the predicted value.

The unknown parameters, β, are typically estimated with maximum likelihood, maximum quasi-likelihood, or Bayesian techniques.

Model components

The GLM consists of three elements:

1. A probability distribution from the exponential family.

2. A linear predictor $\eta = X\beta$.

3. A link function g such that $E(Y) = \mu = g - 1(\eta)$.

Probability distribution

The overdispersed exponential family of distributions is a generalization of the exponential family and exponential dispersion model of distributions and includes those probability distributions, parameterized by θ and   , whose density functions f (or probability mass function, for the case of a discrete distribution) can be expressed in the form

$$f_Y(y|\theta, \tau) = h(y, \tau)\exp\left(\frac{b(\theta)T(y) - A(\theta)}{d(\tau)}\right).$$

τ, called the dispersion parameter, typically is known and is usually related to the variance of the distribution. The functions $h(y, \tau)$, $b(\theta)$, $T(y)$, $A(\theta)$, and $d(\tau)$ are known. Many common distributions are in this family.

For scalar Y and θ, this reduces to

$$f_Y(y|\theta, \tau) = h(y, \tau)\exp\left(\frac{b(\theta)T(y) - A(\theta)}{d(\tau)}\right).$$

θ is related to the mean of the distribution. If $b(\theta)$ is the identity function, then the distribution is said to be in canonical form (or natural form). Note that any distribution can be converted to canonical form by rewriting θ as θ' and then applying the transformation $\theta = b(\theta')$. It is always possible to convert $A(\theta)$ in terms of the new parameterization, even if $b(\theta')$ is not a one-to-one function; see comments in the page on the exponential family. If, in addition, $T(y)$ is the identity and τ is known, then θ is called the canonical parameter (or natural parameter) and is related to the mean through

$$\mu = E(Y) = \nabla A(\theta).$$

For scalar Y and θ, this reduces to

$$\mu = E(Y) = A'(\theta).$$

Under this scenario, the variance of the distribution can be shown to be (McCullagh & Nelder, 1989)

$$\text{Var}(Y) = \nabla\nabla^T A(\theta)d(\tau).$$

For scalar Y and θ, this reduces to

$$\text{Var}(Y) = A''(\theta)d(\tau).$$

Linear predictor

The linear predictor is the quantity which incorporates the information about the independent variables into the model. The symbol η (Greek "eta") denotes a linear predictor. It is related to the expected value of the data (thus, "predictor") through the link function.

η is expressed as linear combinations (thus, "linear") of unknown parameters β. The coefficients of the linear combination are represented as the matrix of independent variables X. η can thus be expressed as

$$\eta = X\beta.$$

Link function

The link function provides the relationship between the linear predictor and the mean of the distribution function. There are many commonly used link functions, and their choice can be somewhat arbitrary. It makes sense to try to match the domain of the link function to the range of the distribution function's mean.

When using a distribution function with a canonical parameter θ, the canonical link function is the function that expresses θ in terms of μ, i.e. $\theta = b(\mu)$. For the most common distributions, the mean μ is one of the parameters in the standard form of the distribution's density function, and then $b(\mu)$ is the function as defined above that maps the density function into its canonical form. When using the canonical link function,

$b(\mu) = \theta = X\beta$, which allows $X^T Y$ $X^T Y$ to be a sufficient statistic for β.

Following is a table of several exponential-family distributions in common use and the data they are typically used for, along with the canonical link functions and their inverses (sometimes referred to as the mean function, as done here).

Common distributions with typical uses and canonical link functions

Distribution	Support of distribution	Typical uses	Link name	Link function	Mean function
Normal	real: $(-\infty, \infty)$	Linear-response data	Identity	$X\beta = \mu$	$\mu = X\beta$
Exponential Gamma	real: $(0, \infty)$	Exponential-response data, scale parameters	Inverse	$X\beta = -\mu^{-1}$	$\mu = (-X\beta)^{-1}$
Inverse Gaussian	real: $(0, \infty)$		Inverse squared	$X\beta = -\mu^{-2}$	$\mu = (-X\beta)^{-1/2}$
Poisson	integer: $(0, \infty)$	count of occurrences in fixed amount of time/space	Log	$X\beta = \ln(\mu)$	$\mu = e^{X\beta}$
Bernoulli	integer: $[0,1]$	outcome of single yes/no occurrence	Logit	$X\beta = \ln\left(\dfrac{\mu}{1-\mu}\right)$	$\mu = \dfrac{1}{1+e^{X\beta}}$
Binomial	integer: $[0, N]$	count of # of "yes" occurrences out of N yes/no occurrences			
Categorical	integer: $[0, K]$ K-vector of integer: $[0,1]$, where exactly one element in the vector has the value 1	outcome of single K-way occurrence			
Multinomial	K-vector of $[0, N]$	count of occurrences of different types (1 .. K) out of N total K-way occurrences			

In the cases of the exponential and gamma distributions, the domain of the canonical link function is not the same as the permitted range of the mean. In particular, the linear predictor may be negative, which would give an impossible negative mean. When maximizing the likelihood, precautions must be taken to avoid this. An alternative is to use a noncanonical link function.

Note also that in the case of the Bernoulli, binomial, categorical and multinomial distributions, the support of the distributions is not the same type of data as the parameter being predicted. In all of these cases, the predicted parameter is one or more probabilities, i.e. real numbers in the range $[0,1]$. The resulting model is known as logistic regression (or multinomial logistic regression in the case that K-way rather than binary values are being predicted).

For the Bernoulli and binomial distributions, the parameter is a single probability, indicating the likelihood of occurrence of a single event. The Bernoulli still satisfies the basic condition of the generalized linear model in that, even though a single outcome will always be either 0 or 1, the expected value will nonetheless be a real-valued probability, i.e. the probability of occurrence of a "yes" (or 1) outcome. Similarly, in a binomial distribution, the expected value is Np, i.e. the expected proportion of "yes" outcomes will be the probability to be predicted.

For categorical and multinomial distributions, the parameter to be predicted is a K-vector of probabilities, with the further restriction that all probabilities must add up to 1. Each probability indicates the likelihood of occurrence of one of the K possible values. For the multinomial distribution, and for the vector form of the categorical distribution, the expected values of the elements of the vector can be related to the predicted probabilities similarly to the binomial and Bernoulli distributions.

Fitting

Maximum likelihood

The maximum likelihood estimates can be found using an iteratively reweighted least squares algorithm using either a Newton–Raphson method with updates of the form:

$$\boldsymbol{\beta}^{(t+1)} = \boldsymbol{\beta}^{(t)} + \mathcal{J}^{-1}(\boldsymbol{\beta}^{(t)})u(\boldsymbol{\beta}^{(t)}),$$

where $\mathcal{J}(\boldsymbol{\beta}^{(t)})$ is the observed information matrix (the negative of the Hessian matrix) and $u(\boldsymbol{\beta}^{(t)})$ is the score function; or a Fisher's scoring method:

$$\boldsymbol{\beta}^{(t+1)} = \boldsymbol{\beta}^{(t)} + I^{-1}(\boldsymbol{\beta}^{(t)})u(\boldsymbol{\beta}^{(t)}),$$

where $I(\boldsymbol{\beta}^{(t)})$ is the Fisher information matrix. Note that if the canonical link function is used, then they are the same.

Bayesian methods

In general, the posterior distribution cannot be found in closed form and so must be approximated, usually using Laplace approximations or some type of Markov chain Monte Carlo method such as Gibbs sampling.

Examples

General linear models

A possible point of confusion has to do with the distinction between generalized linear models and the general linear model, two broad statistical models. The general linear model may be viewed as a special case of the generalized linear model with identity link and responses normally distributed. As most exact results of interest are obtained only for the general linear model, the general linear model has undergone a somewhat longer historical development. Results for the generalized linear model with non-identity link are asymptotic (tending to work well with large samples).

Linear regression

A simple, very important example of a generalized linear model (also an example of a general linear model) is linear regression. In linear regression, the use of the least-squares estimator is justified by the Gauss-Markov theorem, which does not assume that the distribution is normal.

From the perspective of generalized linear models, however, it is useful to suppose that the distribution function is the normal distribution with constant variance and the link function is the identity, which is the canonical link if the variance is known.

For the normal distribution, the generalized linear model has a closed form expression for the maximum-likelihood estimates, which is convenient. Most other GLMs lack closed form estimates.

Binomial data

When the response data, Y, are binary (taking on only values 0 and 1), the distribution function is generally chosen to be the Bernoulli distribution and the interpretation of μ_i is then the probability, p, of Y_i taking on the value one.

There are several popular link functions for binomial functions; the most typical is the canonical logit link:

$$g(p) = \ln \left(\frac{p}{1 - p} \right).$$

GLMs with this setup are logistic regression models (or logit models).

In addition, the inverse of any continuous cumulative distribution function (CDF) can be used for the link since the CDF's range is $[0,1]$, the range of the binomial mean. The normal CDF Φ is a popular choice and yields the probit model. Its link is

$$g(p) = \Phi^{-1}(p).$$

The reason for the use of the probit model is that a constant scaling of the input variable to a normal CDF (which can be absorbed through equivalent scaling of all of the parameters) yields a function that is practically identical to the logit function, but probit models are more tractable in some situations than logit models. (In a Bayesian setting in which normally distributed prior distributions are placed on the parameters, the relationship between the normal priors and the normal CDF link function means that a probit model can be computed using

Gibbs sampling, while a logit model generally cannot.)

The complementary log-log function $\log(-\log(1-p))$ may also be used. This link function is asymmetric and will often produce different results from the probit and logit link functions.

The identity link is also sometimes used for binomial data to yield the linear probability model, but a drawback of this model is that the predicted probabilities can be greater than one or less than zero. In implementation it is possible to fix the nonsensical probabilities outside of $[0,1]$, but interpreting the coefficients can be difficult. The model's primary merit is that near $p = 0.5$ it is approximately a linear transformation of the probit and logit—econometricians sometimes call this the Harvard model.

The variance function for binomial data is given by:

$$\text{Var}(Y_i) = \tau \mu_i (1 - \mu_i),$$

where the dispersion parameter τ is typically fixed at exactly one. When it is not, the resulting quasi-likelihood model often described as binomial with overdispersion or quasi-binomial.

Multinomial regression

The binomial case may be easily extended to allow for a multinomial distribution as the response (also, a Generalized Linear Model for counts, with a constrained total). There are two ways in which this is usually done:

Ordered response
If the response variable is an ordinal measurement, then one may fit a model function of the form:

$$g(\mu_m) = \eta_m = \beta_0 + X_1\beta_1 + \cdots + X_p\beta_p + \gamma_2 + \cdots + \gamma_m$$
$$= \eta_1 + \gamma_2 + \cdots + \gamma_m,$$

where $\mu_m = P(Y \leq m)$, for $m > 2$. Different links g lead to

214

proportional odds models or ordered probit models.

Unordered response

If the response variable is a nominal measurement, or the data do not satisfy the assumptions of an ordered model, one may fit a model of the following form:

$$g(\mu_m) = \eta_m = \beta_{m,0} + X_1\beta_{m,1} + \cdots + X_p\beta_{m,p},$$

where $\mu_m = P(Y = m|Y \in \{1, m\})$, for $m > 2$. Different links g lead to multinomial logit or multinomial probit models. These are more general than the ordered response models, and more parameters are estimated.

Count data

Another example of generalized linear models includes Poisson regression which models count data using the Poisson distribution. The link is typically the logarithm, the canonical link. The variance function is proportional to the mean

$$\text{var}(Y_i) = \tau\mu_i,$$

where the dispersion parameter τ is typically fixed at exactly one. When it is not, the resulting quasi-likelihood model is often described as Poisson with overdispersion or quasi-Poisson.

Extensions

Correlated or clustered data

The standard GLM assumes that the observations are uncorrelated. Extensions have been developed to allow for correlation between observations, as occurs for example in longitudinal studies and clustered designs:

• Generalized estimating equations (GEEs) allow for the correlation between observations without the use of an explicit probability model for the origin of the correlations, so there is no explicit likelihood. They are suitable when the random effects and their variances are not of inherent interest, as they allow for the correlation without explaining its origin. The focus is on estimating the average response over the population ("population-averaged" effects) rather than the regression parameters that would enable prediction of the effect of changing one or more components of X on a given individual. GEEs are usually used in conjunction with Huber-White standard errors (Zeger, Liang, & Albert, 1988) (Hardin & Hilbe, 2003).

• Generalized linear mixed models (GLMMs) are an extension to GLMs that includes random effects in the linear predictor, giving an explicit probability model that explains the origin of the correlations. The resulting "subject-specific" parameter estimates are suitable when the focus is on estimating the effect of changing one or more components of X on a given individual. GLMMs are also referred to as multilevel models and as mixed model. In general, fitting GLMMs is more computationally complex and intensive than fitting GEEs.

Generalized additive models

Generalized additive models (GAMs) are another extension to GLMs in which the linear predictor η is not restricted to be linear in the covariates X but is the sum of smoothing functions applied to the x_i's:

$$\eta = \beta_0 + f_1(x_1) + f_2(x_2) + \cdots.$$

The smoothing functions f_i are estimated from the data. In general this requires a large number of data points and is computationally intensive (Hastie & Tibshirani, 1990) (Wood, 2006).

The model relates a univariate response variable, Y, to some predictor variables, x_i. An exponential family distribution is specified for Y (for example normal, binomial or Poisson distributions) along with a link function g (for example the identity or log functions) relating the expected value of Y to the predictor variables via a structure such as

$$g\big(E(Y)\big) = \eta = \beta_0 + f_1(x_1) + f_2(x_2) + \cdots f_m(x_m).$$

The functions $f_i(x_i)$ may be functions with a specified parametric form

216

(for example a polynomial, or a coefficient depending on the levels of a factor variable) or maybe specified non-parametrically, or semi-parametrically, simply as 'smooth functions', to be estimated by non-parametric means. So a typical GAM might use a scatterplot smoothing function, such as a locally weighted mean, for $f_1(x_1)$, and then use a factor model for $f_2(x_2)$. This flexibility to allow non-parametric fits with relaxed assumptions on the actual relationship between response and predictor, provides the potential for better fits to data than purely parametric models, but arguably with some loss of interpretablity.

Generalized additive model for location, scale and shape

The generalized additive model location, scale and shape (GAMLSS) is a class of statistical model that provides extended capabilities compared to the simpler generalized linear models and generalized additive models. These simpler models allow the typical values of a quantity being modelled to be related to whatever explanatory variables are available. Here the "typical value" is more formally a location parameter, which only describes a limited aspect of the probability distribution of the dependent variable. The GAMLSS approach allows other parameters of the distribution to be related to the explanatory variables; where these other parameters might be interpreted as scale and shape parameters of the distribution, although the approach is not limited to such parameters.

In GAMLSS the exponential family distribution assumption for the response variable, (Y), (essential in GLMs and GAMs), is relaxed and replaced by a general distribution family, including highly skew and/or kurtotic continuous and discrete distributions.

The systematic part of the model is expanded to allow modeling not only of the mean (or location) but other parameters of the distribution of Y as linear and/or nonlinear, parametric and/or additive non-parametric functions of explanatory variables and/or random effects.

GAMLSS is especially suited for modeling leptokurtic or platykurtic and/or positive or negative skew response variable. For count type response variable data it deals with over-dispersion by using proper over-dispersed discrete distributions. Heterogeneity also is dealt with by modeling the scale or shape parameters using explanatory variables. There are several packages written in R related to GAMLSS models (Stasinopoulos & Rigby, 2007).

A GAMLSS model assumes independent observations y_i for $i = 1, ..., n$ with probability (density) function $f(y_i|\mu_i, \sigma_i, \nu_i, \tau_i)$ conditional on $(\mu_i, \sigma_i, \nu_i, \tau_i)$ a vector of four distribution parameters, each of which can be a function to the explanatory variables. The first two population distribution parameters μ_i and σ_i are usually characterized as location and scale parameters, while the remaining parameter(s), if any, are characterized as shape parameters, e.g. skewness and kurtosis parameters, although the model may be applied more generally to the parameters of any population distribution with up to four distribution parameters, and can be generalized to more than four distribution parameters (Stasinopoulos & Rigby, 2007).

$$g_1(\mu) = \eta_1 = X_1\beta_1 + \sum_{j=1}^{J_1} h_{j1}(x_{j1})$$

$$g_2(\mu) = \eta_2 = X_2\beta_2 + \sum_{j=1}^{J_2} h_{j2}(x_{j2})$$

$$g_3(\mu) = \eta_{23} = X_3\beta_3 + \sum_{j=1}^{J_3} h_{j3}(x_{j3})$$

$$g_4(\mu) = \eta_4 = X_4\beta_4 + \sum_{j=1}^{J_4} h_{j4}(x_{j4}).$$

Where μ, σ, ν, τ and n_k are vectors of length n, $\beta_k^T = \left(\beta_{1k}, \beta_{2k}, ..., \beta_{J'_k k}\right)$ is a parameter vector of length J'_k, X_k is a fixed known design matrix of order $n \times J'_k$ and h_{jk} is a smooth non-parametric function of explanatory variable x_{jk}, $j = 1, \ldots, j_k$ and $k = 1,2,3,4$ (Nelder & Wedderburn, 1972).

Confusion with general linear models

The term "generalized linear model", and especially its abbreviation GLM, can be confused with general linear model. John Nelder has expressed regret about this in a conversation with Stephen Senn:

> Senn: I must confess to having some confusion when I was a young statistician between general linear models and generalized linear models. Do you regret the terminology?

> Nelder: I think probably I do. I suspect we should have found some more fancy name for it that would have stuck and not been confused with the general linear model, although general and generalized are not quite the same. I can see why it might have been better to have thought of something else (Senn, 2003).

Software

All the primary software packages discussed in Chapter 2 have this functionality.

Example Using R

Setting up the Model

Use data "rats" from "survival" package in R.

Data on 150 rats contain identifying "litter", ""rx" (indicator of injection of drug after initial administration of carcinogen), time in days on study (ignored initially, and "status" which is indicator of tumor, our binary response variable.

```
> library(survival)

> fitB1 = glm(cbind(status,1-status) ~ rx, family=binomial,
+ data = rats)
```

NOTE you can use the column headers as variable names if you specify the data-frame using "data="

```
> fitB1

Call:  glm(formula = cbind(status, 1 - status) ~ rx, family
= binomial,
    data = rats)

Coefficients:
(Intercept)              rx
     -1.450           1.127

Degrees of Freedom: 149 Total (i.e. Null);  148 Residual
Null Deviance:        174
Residual Deviance: 165.3          AIC: 169.3

> summary(fitB1)$coef
             Estimate Std. Error   z value      Pr(>|z|)
(Intercept) -1.450010  0.2549063 -5.688404 1.282324e-08
rx           1.127237  0.3835089  2.939272 3.289845e-03
```

Coefficients fitted by MLE, link="logit" is default for binomial-family data: this is logistic regression.

The standard error is found as sqrt of diagonal in variance:

```
> sqrt(diag(summary(fitB1)$cov.scaled))
(Intercept)          rx
  0.2549063   0.3835089
```

"Deviance" = "Residual Deviance" = -2*logLik
```
> c(fitB1$deviance, -2*logLik(fitB1))
[1] 165.2738 165.2738
```

"Null.deviance" is -2 times the logLik for the same model with only a constant term

```
> c(fitB1$null.dev,
```

```
+  -2*logLik(update(fitB1, formula = .~ 1))
+ )
[1] 173.9746 173.9746
```

NOTE the use of the "update" function to refit a model of the same type as the one previously done: in the model formula, the left-hand side term is a "." to indicate that it is the same as before. We have changed the right-hand side from rx (which automatically included intercept along with rx predictor) to one with "1" or intercept alone.

Next use "update" to change the fitB1 model not in its model formula but in its specified link within the binomial "family".

```
> fitB2 = update(fitB1, family=binomial(link="probit"))
> rbind(logit= fitB1$coef, probit= fitB2$coef,
+ rescal.probit = fitB2$coef/0.5513)
                    (Intercept)        rx
logit             -1.4500102 1.1272368
probit            -0.8778963 0.6760028
rescal.probit  -1.5924112 1.2261977
```

Recall that we use deviance and differences between them because Wilks' Theorem says that 2 times the difference between logLik for a model with p extra parameter dimensions versus logLik for a base model is equal to approximately a chi-square (p, df) variate when the base model is the true one (see Chapter 10).

Model Quality

LET's use this idea to examine the quality of the model with predictor log(time) in the model along with rx.

NOTE that we must put the expression log(time) within I( ) to have it evaluated and constructed as a new predictor within the glm fitting function.

```
> fitB3 = update(fitB1, formula= . ~ . + I(log(time)))
```

The "data" is the same now as in fitB1, so "time" is the column in the data-frame, and a `log(time)` predictor is created under "`glm`"

It is reasonable to use "`time`" as a predictor, because the range of times is not too different for rats who generate tumors, so "`time`" is not really a response variable.

```
> summary(rats$time[rats$status==1])
   Min. 1st Qu.  Median    Mean 3rd Qu.    Max.
  34.00   66.75   80.00   77.28   92.50  104.00
> summary(rats$time[rats$status==0])
   Min. 1st Qu.  Median    Mean 3rd Qu.    Max.
  45.00   83.50  104.00   93.85  104.00  104.00
```

```
> cbind(rats[1:10,], model.matrix(fitB3)[1:10,])
   litter rx time status (Intercept) rx I(log(time))
1       1  1  101      0           1  1     4.615121
2       1  0   49      1           1  0     3.891820
3       1  0  104      0           1  0     4.644391
4       2  1  104      0           1  1     4.644391
5       2  0  102      0           1  0     4.624973
6       2  0  104      0           1  0     4.644391
7       3  1  104      0           1  1     4.644391
8       3  0  104      0           1  0     4.644391
9       3  0  104      0           1  0     4.644391
10      4  1   77      0           1  1     4.343805
```

The first 4 columns are the original "rats" data. The last 3 are the design matrix columns created by `glm`. So we can look at the new model fit for significance of coefficients:

```
> summary(fitB3)$coef
                Estimate Std. Error   z value      Pr(>|z|)
(Intercept)   17.868661  4.4924813  3.977459 6.965559e-05
rx             1.194019  0.4284626  2.786751 5.323935e-03
I(log(time)) -4.355407  1.0180848 -4.278040 1.885462e-05
```

Or alternatvely compare deviances or `logLik`'s with `fitB1`

```
> c(2*(logLik(fitB3)-logLik(fitB1)), fitB1$dev-fitB3$dev)
```

```
[1] 24.37307 24.37307
```

This is LRT stat to be compared with chisq 1 df.

```
> 1-pchisq(24.373,1)
[1] 7.937339e-07
```

This is still highly significant but somewhat different p-value from the I(log(time)) coef probably because the model is still far from the right one.

We could try to enter additional terms like log(time)^2 or rx * log(time)

```
> fitB4 = update(fitB3, .~. + I(rx*log(time)) +
+ I(log(time)^2))
> summary(fitB4)$coef
                        Estimate Std. Error    z value
(Intercept)            -9.784968  52.690740 -0.1857056
rx                    -13.501206   8.732837 -1.5460274
I(log(time))           10.179730  24.364938  0.4178024
I(rx * log(time))       3.324780   1.973389  1.6848069
I(log(time)^2)         -1.871215   2.819823 -0.6635932
                       Pr(>|z|)
(Intercept)          0.85267560
rx                   0.12209794
I(log(time))         0.67609159
I(rx * log(time))    0.09202582
I(log(time)^2)       0.50695069
```

This time, the new variables do NOT look significant which we can check also through deviances:

```
> fitB3$dev - fitB4$dev
[1] 3.901065
```

This result is to be compared with chisq 2df, so it is not at all significant.

We can also do these deviance comparisons all at once by looking at an "analysis of deviance" table

```
> anova(fitB4)
Analysis of Deviance Table
Model: binomial, link: logit

Response: cbind(status, 1 - status)
Terms added sequentially (first to last)

                  Df Deviance Resid. Df Resid. Dev
NULL                               149      173.97
rx                 1   8.7008        148      165.27
I(log(time))       1  24.3731        147      140.90
I(rx * log(time))  1   3.4784        146      137.42
I(log(time)^2)     1   0.4226        145      137.00
```

As in an ANOVA table, in which RSS replaced Deviance these "Deviance values" are the amounts by which the current model-fitting line decreases the deviance: (recall that fitB1 uses rx only, fitB3 augments by log(time), and fitB4 by log(time) plus the 2 additional rx*log(tim) and log(time)^2 terms.

```
> Devs = c(fitB1$null.dev, fitB1$dev, fitB3$dev,
+ update(fitB3, .~.+I(rx*log(time)))$dev,
+ fitB4$dev)
> Devs
[1] 173.9746 165.2738 140.9007 137.4223 136.9997

> round (-diff(Devs), 3 )### successive differences of llks
[1]   8.701 24.373  3.478  0.423      ### give Deviance col
in "anova"
```

12. Logistic regression

In statistics, logistic regression, or logit regression, is a type of probabilistic statistical classification model (Bishop, 2006). It is also used to predict a binary response from a binary predictor, used for predicting the outcome of a categorical dependent variable (i.e., a class label) based on one or more predictor variables (features). That is, it is used in estimating the parameters of a qualitative response model. The probabilities describing the possible outcomes of a single trial are modeled, as a function of the explanatory (predictor) variables, using a logistic function. Frequently (and subsequently in this article) "logistic regression" is used to refer specifically to the problem in which the dependent variable is binary—that is, the number of available categories is two—while problems with more than two categories are referred to as multinomial logistic regression or, if the multiple categories are ordered, as ordered logistic regression.

Logistic regression measures the relationship between a categorical dependent variable and one or more independent variables, which are usually (but not necessarily) continuous, by using probability scores as the predicted values of the dependent variable (Bhandari & Joensson, 2008). As such it treats the same set of problems as does probit regression using similar techniques.

Fields and examples of applications

Logistic regression was put forth in the 1940s as an alternative to Fisher's 1936 classification method, linear discriminant analysis (James, Witten, Hastie, & Tibshirani, 2013). It is used extensively in numerous disciplines, including the medical and social science fields. For example, the Trauma and Injury Severity Score (TRISS), which is widely used to predict mortality in injured patients, was originally developed by Boyd et al. using logistic regression (Boyd, Tolson, & Copes, 1987). Logistic regression might be used to predict whether a patient has a given disease (e.g. diabetes), based on observed characteristics of the patient (age, gender, body mass index, results of various blood tests, etc.). Another example, a propensity model, might be to predict whether an American voter will vote Democratic or Republican, based on age, income, gender, race, state of residence, votes in previous elections, etc. (Harrell, 2010). The technique can also be used in engineering, especially for predicting the probability of failure of a given process, system or product (Strano & Colosimo, 2006) (Palei & Das, 2009). It is also used in marketing applications such as prediction of a customer's propensity to purchase a product or cease a subscription, etc. In economics it can be used to predict the likelihood of a person's choosing to be in the labor force, and a business application would be to predict the likelihood of a homeowner defaulting on a mortgage. Conditional random fields, an extension of logistic regression to sequential data, are used in natural language processing.

Basics

Logistic regression can be binomial or multinomial. Binomial or binary logistic regression deals with situations in which the observed outcome for a dependent variable can have only two possible types (for example, "dead" vs. "alive"). Multinomial logistic regression deals with situations where the outcome can have three or more possible types (e.g., "disease A" vs. "disease B" vs. "disease C"). In binary logistic regression, the outcome is usually coded as "0"or "1", as this leads to the most straightforward interpretation (Hosmer & Lemeshow, 2000). If a particular observed outcome for the dependent variable is the noteworthy possible outcome (referred to as a "success" or a "case") it is usually coded as "1" and the contrary outcome (referred to as a "failure" or a "noncase") as "0". Logistic regression is used to predict the odds of being a case based on the values of the independent variables (predictors). The odds are defined as the probability that a particular outcome is a case divided by the probability that it is a noncase.

Like other forms of regression analysis, logistic regression makes use of one or more predictor variables that may be either continuous or categorical data. Unlike ordinary linear regression, however, logistic regression is used for predicting binary outcomes of the dependent variable (treating the dependent variable as the outcome of a Bernoulli trial) rather than continuous outcomes. Given this difference, it is necessary that logistic regression take the natural logarithm of the odds of the dependent variable being a case (referred to as the logit or log-odds) to create a continuous criterion as a transformed version of the dependent variable. Thus the logit transformation is referred to as the link function in logistic regression—although the dependent variable in logistic regression is binomial, the logit is the continuous criterion upon which linear regression is conducted (Hosmer & Lemeshow, 2000).

The logit of success is then fit to the predictors using linear regression analysis. The predicted value of the logit is converted back into predicted odds via the inverse of the natural logarithm, namely the exponential function. Therefore, although the observed dependent variable in logistic regression is a zero-or-one variable, the logistic regression estimates the odds, as a continuous variable, that the dependent variable is a success (a case). In some applications the odds are all that is needed. In others, a specific yes-or-no prediction is needed for whether the dependent variable is or is not a case; this categorical prediction can be based on the computed odds of a success, with predicted odds above some chosen cut-off value being translated into a prediction of a success.

Logistic function, odds ratio, and logit

An explanation of logistic regression begins with an explanation of the logistic function, which always takes on values between zero and one (Hosmer & Lemeshow, 2000):

$$F(t) = \frac{e^t}{e^t + 1} = \frac{1}{1 + e^{t}},$$

and viewing t as a linear function of an explanatory variable x (or of a linear combination of explanatory variables), the logistic function can be written as:

$$F(x) = \frac{1}{1 + e^{-(\beta_0 + \beta_1 x)}}.$$

This will be interpreted as the probability of the dependent variable equaling a "success" or "case" rather than a failure or non-case. We also define the inverse of the logistic function, the logit:

$$g(x) = \ln \frac{F(x)}{1 - F(x)} = \beta_0 + \beta_1 x,$$

and equivalently:

$$\frac{F(x)}{1 - F(x)} = e^{(\beta_0 + \beta_1 x)}.$$

A graph of the logistic function is shown in Figure 1. The input is the value of and the output is $F(x)$. The logistic function is useful because it can take an input with any value from negative infinity to positive infinity, whereas the output is confined to values between 0 and 1 and hence is interpretable as a probability. In the above equations, refers to the logit function of some given linear combination of the predictors, denotes the natural logarithm, is the probability that the dependent variable equals a case, is the intercept from the linear regression equation (the value of the criterion when the predictor is equal to zero), is the regression coefficient multiplied by some value of the predictor, and base e denotes the exponential function.

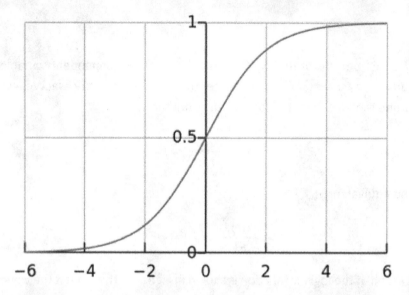

Figure 1. The logistic function, with $\beta_0 + \beta_1$ on the horizontal axis and $F(x)$ on the vertical axis

The formula for $F(x)$ illustrates that the probability of the dependent variable equaling a case is equal to the value of the logistic function of the linear regression expression. This is important in that it shows that the value of the linear regression expression can vary from negative to positive infinity and yet, after transformation, the resulting expression for the probability $F(x)$ ranges between 0 and 1. The equation for $g(x)$ illustrates that the logit (i.e., log-odds or natural logarithm of the odds) is equivalent to the linear regression expression. Likewise, the next equation illustrates that the odds of the dependent variable equaling a case is equivalent to the exponential function of the linear regression expression. This illustrates how the logit serves as a link function between the probability and the linear regression expression. Given that the logit ranges between negative infinity and positive infinity, it provides an adequate criterion upon which to conduct linear regression and the logit is easily converted back into the odds (Hosmer & Lemeshow, 2000).

Multiple explanatory variables

If there are multiple explanatory variables, then the above expression $\beta_0 + \beta_1 x$ can be revised to $\beta_0 + \beta_1 x_1 + \beta_2 x_1 + \cdots + \beta_m x_m$. Then when this is used in the equation relating the logged odds of a success to the values of the predictors, the linear regression will be a multiple regression with m explanators; the parameters β_j for all $j = 0,1,2,\ldots,m$ are all estimated.

Model fitting

Estimation

Maximum likelihood estimation
The regression coefficients are usually estimated using maximum likelihood estimation (Menard, 2002). Unlike linear regression with normally distributed residuals, it is not possible to find a closed-form expression for the coefficient values that maximizes the likelihood function, so an iterative process must be used instead, for example Newton's method. This process begins with a tentative solution, revises it slightly to see if it can be improved, and repeats this revision until improvement is minute, at which point the process is said to have converged (Menard, 2002).

In some instances the model may not reach convergence. When a model does not converge this indicates that the coefficients are not meaningful because the iterative process was unable to find appropriate solutions. A failure to converge may occur for a number of reasons: having a large proportion of predictors to cases, multicollinearity, sparseness, or complete separation.

- Having a large proportion of variables to cases results in an overly conservative Wald statistic (discussed below) and can lead to nonconvergence.
- Multicollinearity refers to unacceptably high correlations between predictors. As multicollinearity increases, coefficients remain unbiased but standard errors increase and the likelihood of model

231

convergence decreases. To detect multicollinearity amongst the predictors, one can conduct a linear regression analysis with the predictors of interest for the sole purpose of examining the tolerance statistic used to assess whether multicollinearity is unacceptably high (Menard, 2002).

- Sparseness in the data refers to having a large proportion of empty cells (cells with zero counts). Zero cell counts are particularly problematic with categorical predictors. With continuous predictors, the model can infer values for the zero cell counts, but this is not the case with categorical predictors. The reason the model will not converge with zero cell counts for categorical predictors is because the natural logarithm of zero is an undefined value, so final solutions to the model cannot be reached. To remedy this problem, researchers may collapse categories in a theoretically meaningful way or may consider adding a constant to all cells (Menard, 2002).

- Another numerical problem that may lead to a lack of convergence is complete separation, which refers to the instance in which the predictors perfectly predict the criterion – all cases are accurately classified. In such instances, one should reexamine the data, as there is likely some kind of error (Hosmer & Lemeshow, 2000).

Although not a precise number, as a general rule of thumb, logistic regression models require a minimum of 10 events per explaining variable (where event denotes the cases belonging to the less frequent category in the dependent variable) (Peduzzi, Concato, Kemper, Holford, & Feinstein, 1996).

Minimum chi-squared estimator for grouped data
While individual data will have a dependent variable with a value of zero or one for every observation, with grouped data one observation is on a group of people who all share the same characteristics (e.g., demographic characteristics); in this case the researcher observes the proportion of people in the group for whom the response variable falls into one category or the other. If this proportion is neither zero nor one for any group, the minimum chi-squared estimator involves using

232

weighted least squares to estimate a linear model in which the dependent variable is the logit of the proportion: that is, the log of the ratio of the fraction in one group to the fraction in the other group (Greene, 2011).

Evaluating goodness of fit

Goodness of fit in linear regression models is generally measured using the R^2. Since this has no direct analog in logistic regression, various methods (Greene, 2011) including the following can be used instead.

Deviance and likelihood ratio tests

In linear regression analysis, one is concerned with partitioning variance via the sum of squares calculations – variance in the criterion is essentially divided into variance accounted for by the predictors and residual variance. In logistic regression analysis, deviance is used in lieu of sum of squares calculations (Cohen, Cohen, West, & Aiken, 2002). Deviance is analogous to the sum of squares calculations in linear regression (Hosmer & Lemeshow, 2000) and is a measure of the lack of fit to the data in a logistic regression model (Cohen, Cohen, West, & Aiken, 2002). Deviance is calculated by comparing a given model with the saturated model—a model with a theoretically perfect fit. This computation is called the likelihood-ratio test (Hosmer & Lemeshow, 2000):

$$D = -2\ln\lambda(y_i) = -2\ln\frac{\text{likelihood of the fitted model}}{\text{likelihood of the saturated model}}$$

In the above equation D represents the deviance and ln represents the natural logarithm, and $\Lambda = \lambda(y_i)$. The log of the likelihood ratio (the ratio of the fitted model to the saturated model) will produce a negative value, so the product is multiplied by negative two times its natural logarithm to produce a value with an approximate χ^2-squared distribution (Hosmer & Lemeshow, 2000). Smaller values indicate better fit as the fitted model deviates less from the saturated model. When assessed upon a chi-square distribution, nonsignificant chi-square values indicate very little unexplained variance and thus, good model fit.

Conversely, a significant chi-square value indicates that a significant amount of the variance is unexplained.

Two measures of deviance are particularly important in logistic regression: null deviance and model deviance. The null deviance represents the difference between a model with only the intercept (which means "no predictors") and the saturated model (Cohen, Cohen, West, & Aiken, 2002). And, the model deviance represents the difference between a model with at least one predictor and the saturated model. In this respect, the null model provides a baseline upon which to compare predictor models. Given that deviance is a measure of the difference between a given model and the saturated model, smaller values indicate better fit. Therefore, to assess the contribution of a predictor or set of predictors, one can subtract the model deviance from the null deviance and assess the difference on a χ^2_{s-p} chi-square distribution with degree of freedom (Hosmer & Lemeshow, 2000) equal to the difference in the number of parameters estimated.

Let

$$D_{null} = -2\ln\frac{\text{likelihood of the null model}}{\text{likelihood of the saturated model}}$$

$$D_{fitted} = -2\ln\frac{\text{likelihood of the fitted model}}{\text{likelihood of the saturated model}}$$

Then

$$D_{fitted} - D_{null}$$

$$= \left(-2\ln\frac{\text{likelihood of the fitted model}}{\text{likelihood of the saturated model}}\right)$$

$$- \left(2\ln\frac{\text{likelihood of the null model}}{\text{likelihood of the saturated model}}\right)$$

$$= -2\left(\ln\frac{\text{likelihood of the fitted model}}{\text{likelihood of the saturated model}}\right.$$

$$\left. - \ln\frac{\text{likelihood of the null model}}{\text{likelihood of the saturated model}}\right)$$

$$= -2\ln\frac{\dfrac{\text{likelihood of the fitted model}}{\text{likelihood of the saturated model}}}{\dfrac{\text{likelihood of the null model}}{\text{likelihood of the saturated model}}}$$

$$= -2\ln\frac{\text{likelihood of the fitted model}}{\text{likelihood of the null model}}.$$

If the model deviance is significantly smaller than the null deviance then one can conclude that the predictor or set of predictors significantly improved model fit. This is analogous to the F-test used in linear regression analysis to assess the significance of prediction (Cohen, Cohen, West, & Aiken, 2002). A convenient result, attributed to Samuel S. Wilks, says that as the sample size n approaches∞, the test statistic $-2\ln(\Lambda)$ for a nested model will be asymptotically χ^2-distributed with degrees of freedom equal to the difference in dimensionality of the saturated model and null model (Wilks, 1938). This means that for a great variety of hypotheses, a practitioner can compute the likelihood ratio Λ for the data and compare $-2\ln(\Lambda)$ to the χ^2 value corresponding to a desired statistical significance as an approximate statistical test. This is often referred to a Wilks' Theorem.

Pseudo-R^2s

In linear regression the squared multiple correlation, R^2 is used to assess goodness-of-fit as it represents the proportion of variance in the criterion that is explained by the predictors (Cohen, Cohen, West, & Aiken, 2002). In logistic regression analysis, there is no agreed upon analogous measure, but there are several competing measures each with limitations. Three of the most commonly used indices are examined on this section beginning with the likelihood ratio R^2, R_L^2 (Cohen, Cohen, West, & Aiken, 2002):

$$R_L^2 \frac{D_{null} - D_{model}}{D_{null}}.$$

This is the most analogous index to the squared multiple correlation in linear regression (Menard, 2002). It represents the proportional reduction in the deviance, wherein the deviance is treated as a measure of variation analogous but not identical to the variance in linear regression analysis (Menard, 2002). One limitation of the likelihood ratio R^2 is that it is not monotonically related to the odds ratio (Cohen, Cohen, West, & Aiken, 2002), meaning that it does not necessarily increase as the odds ratio increases, and does not necessarily decrease as the odds ratio decreases.

The Cox and Snell R^2 is an alternative index of goodness-of-fit related to the R^2 value from linear regression. The Cox and Snell index is problematic as its maximum value is 0.75, when the variance is at its maximum (0.25). The Nagelkerke R^2 provides a correction to the Cox and Snell R^2 so that the maximum value is equal to one. Nevertheless, the Cox and Snell and likelihood ratio R^2s show greater agreement with each other than either does with the Nagelkerke R^2 (Cohen, Cohen, West, & Aiken, 2002). Of course, this might not be the case for values exceeding 0.75 as the Cox and Snell index is capped at this value. The likelihood ratio R^2 is often preferred to the alternatives as it is most analogous to R^2 in linear regression, is independent of the base rate (both Cox and Snell and Nagelkerke R^2s increase as the proportion of cases increase from 0 to 0.5) and varies between 0 and 1.

A word of caution is in order when interpreting pseudo-R^2 statistics. The reason these indices of fit are referred to as pseudo R^2 is because they do not represent the proportionate reduction in error as the R^2 in linear regression does (Cohen, Cohen, West, & Aiken, 2002). Linear regression assumes homoscedasticity, that the error variance is the same for all values of the criterion. Logistic regression will always be heteroscedastic – the error variances differ for each value of the predicted score. For each value of the predicted score there would be a different value of the proportionate reduction in error. Therefore, it is inappropriate to think of R^2 as a proportionate reduction in error in a universal sense in logistic regression (Cohen, Cohen, West, & Aiken, 2002).

Hosmer–Lemeshow test
The Hosmer–Lemeshow test uses a test statistic that asymptotically

follows a χ^2 distribution to assess whether or not the observed event rates match expected event rates in subgroups of the model population (Hosmer & Lemeshow, 2000).

Evaluating binary classification performance
If the estimated probabilities are to be used to classify each observation of independent variable values as predicting the category that the dependent variable is found in, the various methods below for judging the model's suitability in out-of-sample forecasting can also be used on the data that were used for estimation—accuracy, precision (also called positive predictive value), recall (also called sensitivity), specificity and negative predictive value. In each of these evaluative methods, an aspect of the model's effectiveness in assigning instances to the correct categories is measured.

Coefficients

After fitting the model, it is likely that researchers will want to examine the contribution of individual predictors. To do so, they will want to examine the regression coefficients. In linear regression, the regression coefficients represent the change in the criterion for each unit change in the predictor (Cohen, Cohen, West, & Aiken, 2002). In logistic regression, however, the regression coefficients represent the change in the logit for each unit change in the predictor. Given that the logit is not intuitive, researchers are likely to focus on a predictor's effect on the exponential function of the regression coefficient – the odds ratio (see definition). In linear regression, the significance of a regression coefficient is assessed by computing a t-test. In logistic regression, there are several different tests designed to assess the significance of an individual predictor, most notably the likelihood ratio test and the Wald statistic.

Likelihood ratio test

The likelihood-ratio test discussed above to assess model fit is also the recommended procedure to assess the contribution of individual "predictors" to a given model (Cohen, Cohen, West, & Aiken, 2002) (Hosmer & Lemeshow, 2000) (Menard, 2002). In the case of a single predictor model, one simply compares the deviance of the predictor model with that of the null model on a chi-square distribution with a single degree of freedom. If the predictor model has a significantly smaller deviance (c.f chi-square using the difference in degrees of freedom of the two models), then one can conclude that there is a significant association between the "predictor" and the outcome. Although some common statistical packages (e.g. SPSS) do provide likelihood ratio test statistics, without this computationally intensive test it would be more difficult to assess the contribution of individual predictors in the multiple logistic regression case. To assess the contribution of individual predictors one can enter the predictors hierarchically, comparing each new model with the previous to determine the contribution of each predictor (Cohen, Cohen, West, & Aiken, 2002). (There is considerable debate among statisticians regarding the appropriateness of so-called "stepwise" procedures. They do not preserve the nominal statistical properties and can be very misleading (Harrell, 2010).

Wald statistic

Alternatively, when assessing the contribution of individual predictors in a given model, one may examine the significance of the Wald statistic. The Wald statistic, analogous to the t-test in linear regression, is used to assess the significance of coefficients. The Wald statistic is the ratio of the square of the regression coefficient to the square of the standard error of the coefficient and is asymptotically distributed as a chi-square distribution (Menard, 2002).

$$W_j = \frac{B_j^2}{SE_{B_j}^2}.$$

Although several statistical packages (e.g., SPSS, SAS) report the Wald statistic to assess the contribution of individual predictors, the Wald statistic has limitations. When the regression coefficient is large, the standard error of the regression coefficient also tends to be large increasing the probability of Type-II error. The Wald statistic also tends to be biased when data are sparse (Cohen, Cohen, West, & Aiken, 2002).

Case-control sampling

Suppose cases are rare. Then we might wish to sample them more frequently than their prevalence in the population. For example, suppose there is a disease that affects 1 person in 10,000 and to collect our data we need to do a complete physical. It may be too expensive to do thousands of physicals of healthy people in order to get data on only a few diseased individuals. Thus, we may evaluate more diseased individuals. This is also called unbalanced data. As a rule of thumb, sampling controls at a rate of five times the number of cases is sufficient to get enough control data (Prentice & Pyke, 1979).

If we form a logistic model from such data, if the model is correct, the β_j parameters are all correct except for β_0. We can correct β_0 if we know the true prevalence as follows (Prentice & Pyke, 1979):

$$\hat{\beta}_0^* = \hat{\beta}_0 + \log \frac{\pi}{1 - \pi} \log \frac{\hat{\pi}}{1 - \hat{\pi}},$$

where π is the true prevalence and $\hat{\pi}$ is the prevalence in the sample.

Formal mathematical specification

There are various equivalent specifications of logistic regression, which fit into different types of more general models. These different specifications allow for different sorts of useful generalizations.

Setup

The basic setup of logistic regression is the same as for standard linear regression.

It is assumed that we have a series of N observed data points. Each data point i consists of a set of m explanatory variables $x_{1,i}, \ldots, x_{m,i}$ (also called independent variables, predictor variables, input variables, features, or attributes), and an associated binary-valued outcome variable Y_i (also known as a dependent variable, response variable, output variable, outcome variable or class variable), i.e. it can assume only the two possible values 0 (often meaning "no" or "failure") or 1 (often meaning "yes" or "success"). The goal of logistic regression is to explain the relationship between the explanatory variables and the outcome, so that an outcome can be predicted for a new set of explanatory variables.

Some examples:

- The observed outcomes are the presence or absence of a given disease (e.g. diabetes) in a set of patients, and the explanatory variables might be characteristics of the patients thought to be pertinent (sex, race, age, blood pressure, body-mass index, etc.).
- The observed outcomes are the votes (e.g. Democratic or Republican) of a set of people in an election, and the explanatory variables are the demographic characteristics of each person (e.g. sex, race, age, income, etc.). In such a case, one of the two outcomes is arbitrarily coded as 1, and the other as 0.

As in linear regression, the outcome variables Y are assumed to depend on the explanatory variables $x_{1,i}, \dots, x_{m,i}$.

Explanatory variables
As shown above in the above examples, the explanatory variables may be of any type: real-valued, binary, categorical, etc. The main distinction is between continuous variables (such as income, age and blood pressure) and discrete variables (such as sex or race). Discrete variables referring to more than two possible choices are typically coded using dummy variables (or indicator variables), that is, separate explanatory variables taking the value 0 or 1 are created for each possible value of the discrete variable, with a 1 meaning "variable does have the given value" and a 0 meaning "variable does not have that value". For example, a four-way discrete variable of blood type with the possible values "A, B, AB, O" can be converted to four separate two-way dummy variables, "is-A, is-B, is-AB, is-O", where only one of them has the value 1 and all the rest have the value 0. This allows for separate regression

coefficients to be matched for each possible value of the discrete variable. (In a case like this, only three of the four dummy variables are independent of each other, in the sense that once the values of three of the variables are known, the fourth is automatically determined. Thus, it is only necessary to encode three of the four possibilities as dummy variables. This also means that when all four possibilities are encoded, the overall model is not identifiable in the absence of additional constraints such as a regularization constraint. Theoretically, this could cause problems, but in reality almost all logistic regression models are fit with regularization constraints.)

Outcome variables

Formally, the outcomes Y_i are described as being Bernoulli-distributed data, where each outcome is determined by an unobserved probability p_i that is specific to the outcome at hand, but related to the explanatory variables. This can be expressed in any of the following equivalent forms:

$$Y_i | x_{1,i}, \dots, x_{m,i} \sim \text{Bernoulli}(p_i)$$
$$E[Y_i | x_{1,i}, \dots, x_{m,i}] = p_i$$
$$\Pr(Y_i = y_i | x_{1,i}, \dots, x_{m,i}) = \begin{cases} p_i & \text{if } y_i = 1 \\ 1 - p_i & \text{if } y_i = 0 \end{cases}$$
$$\Pr(Y_i = y_i | x_{1,i}, \dots, x_{m,i}) = p_i^{y_i}(1 - p_i)^{(1-y_i)}$$

The meanings of these four lines are:

1. The first line expresses the probability distribution of each Y_i: Conditioned on the explanatory variables, it follows a Bernoulli distribution with parameters p_i, the probability of the outcome of 1 for trial i. As noted above, each separate trial has its own probability of success, just as each trial has its own explanatory variables. The probability of success p_i is not observed, only the outcome of an individual Bernoulli trial using that probability.

2. The second line expresses the fact that the expected value of each Y_i is equal to the probability of success p_i, which is a general property of the Bernoulli distribution. In other words, if we run a large number of

Bernoulli trials using the same probability of success p_i, then take the average of all the 1 and 0 outcomes, then the result would be close to p_i. This is because doing an average this way simply computes the proportion of successes seen, which we expect to converge to the underlying probability of success.

3. The third line writes out the probability mass function of the Bernoulli distribution, specifying the probability of seeing each of the two possible outcomes.

4. The fourth line is another way of writing the probability mass function, which avoids having to write separate cases and is more convenient for certain types of calculations. This relies on the fact that Y_i can take only the value 0 or 1. In each case, one of the exponents will be 1, "choosing" the value under it, while the other is 0, "canceling out" the value under it. Hence, the outcome is either p_i or $1 - p_i$, as in the previous line.

Linear predictor function

The basic idea of logistic regression is to use the mechanism already developed for linear regression by modeling the probability p_i using a linear predictor function, i.e. a linear combination of the explanatory variables and a set of regression coefficients that are specific to the model at hand but the same for all trials. The linear predictor function $f(i)$ for a particular data point i is written as:

$$f(i) = \beta_0 + \beta_1 x_{1,i} + \beta_2 x_{1,i} + \cdots + \beta_m x_{m,i},$$

where $\beta_0, \dots, \beta_m$ are regression coefficients indicating the relative effect of a particular explanatory variable on the outcome.

The model is usually put into a more compact form as follows:

- The regression coefficients $\beta_0, \beta_1, \dots, \beta_m$ β , β , ..., β are grouped into a single vector $\boldsymbol{\beta}$ of size $m + 1$.
- For each data point i, an additional explanatory pseudo-variable $x_{0,i}$ is added, with a fixed value of 1, corresponding to the intercept coefficient β_0 .

- The resulting explanatory variables $x_{0,i}, x_{1,i}, \ldots, x_{m,i}$ are then grouped into a single vector $\boldsymbol{X}_i$ of size $m + 1$.

This makes it possible to write the linear predictor function as follows:

$$f(i) = \boldsymbol{\beta} \cdot \boldsymbol{X}_i,$$

using the notation for a dot product between two vectors.

As a generalized linear model

The particular model used by logistic regression, which distinguishes it from standard linear regression and from other types of regression analysis used for binary-valued outcomes, is the way the probability of a particular outcome is linked to the linear predictor function:

$$\text{logit}\big(E[Y_i|x_{1,i}, \ldots, x_{m,i}]\big) = \text{logit}(p_i)$$
$$= \ln\left(\frac{p_i}{1 - p_i}\right) = \beta_1 x_{1,i} + \beta_2 x_{1,i} + \cdots + \beta_m x_{m,i}$$

Written using the more compact notation described above, this is:

$$\text{logit}(E[Y_i|\boldsymbol{X}_i]) = \text{logit}(p_i) = \ln\left(\frac{p_i}{1 - p_i}\right) = \boldsymbol{\beta} \cdot \boldsymbol{X}_i.$$

This formulation expresses logistic regression as a type of generalized linear model, which predicts variables with various types of probability distributions by fitting a linear predictor function of the above form to some sort of arbitrary transformation of the expected value of the variable.

The intuition for transforming using the logit function (the natural log of the odds) was explained above. It also has the practical effect of converting the probability (which is bounded to be between 0 and 1) to a variable that ranges over $(-\infty, +\infty)$ — thereby matching the potential range of the linear prediction function on the right side of the equation.

Note that both the probabilities p_i and the regression coefficients are unobserved, and the means of determining them is not part of the model

243

itself. They are typically determined by some sort of optimization procedure, e.g. maximum likelihood estimation, which finds values that best fit the observed data (i.e. that give the most accurate predictions for the data already observed), usually subject to regularization conditions that seek to exclude unlikely values, e.g. extremely large values for any of the regression coefficients. The use of a regularization condition is equivalent to doing maximum a posteriori (MAP) estimation, an extension of maximum likelihood. (Regularization is most commonly done using a squared regularizing function, which is equivalent to placing a zero-mean Gaussian prior distribution on the coefficients, but other regularizers are also possible.) Whether or not regularization is used, it is usually not possible to find a closed-form solution; instead, an iterative numerical method must be used, such as iteratively reweighted least squares (IRLS) or, more commonly these days, a quasi-Newton method such as the L-BFGS method.

The interpretation of the β_j parameter estimates is as the additive effect on the log of the odds for a unit change in the jth explanatory variable. In the case of a dichotomous explanatory variable, for instance gender, e^β is the estimate of the odds of having the outcome for, say, males compared with females.

An equivalent formula uses the inverse of the logit function, which is the logistic function, i.e.:

$$E[Y_i|X_i] = p_i = (\boldsymbol{\beta} \cdot \boldsymbol{X}_i) = \frac{1}{1 + e^{-\beta \cdot X_i}}.$$

The formula can also be written (somewhat awkwardly) as a probability distribution (specifically, using a probability mass function):

$$\Pr(Y_i = y_i|X_i) = p_i^{y_i}(1 - p_i)^{(1-y_i)}$$
$$= \left(\frac{1}{1 + e^{-\beta \cdot X_i}}\right)^{y_i} \left(1 - \frac{1}{1 + e^{-\beta \cdot X_i}}\right)^{1-y_i}.$$

As a latent-variable model

The above model has an equivalent formulation as a latent-variable model. This formulation is common in the theory of discrete choice models, and makes it easier to extend to certain more complicated models with multiple, correlated choices, as well as to compare logistic regression to the closely related probit model.

Imagine that, for each trial i, there is a continuous latent variable Y_i^* (i.e. an unobserved random variable) that is distributed as follows:

$$Y_i^* = \boldsymbol{\beta} \cdot \boldsymbol{X}_i + \varepsilon,$$

Where

$$\varepsilon \sim \text{Logistic}(0,1),$$

i.e., the latent variable can be written directly in terms of the linear predictor function and an additive random error variable that is distributed according to a standard logistic distribution.

Then Y_i can be viewed as an indicator for whether this latent variable is positive:

$$Y_i = \begin{cases} 1 & \text{if } Y_i^* > 0, i.e. -\varepsilon < \boldsymbol{\beta} \cdot \boldsymbol{X}_i \\ 0 & \text{otherwise} \end{cases}.$$

The choice of modeling the error variable specifically with a standard logistic distribution, rather than a general logistic distribution with the location and scale set to arbitrary values, seems restrictive, but in fact it is not. It must be kept in mind that we can choose the regression coefficients ourselves, and very often can use them to offset changes in the parameters of the error variable's distribution. For example, a logistic error-variable distribution with a non-zero location parameter μ (which sets the mean) is equivalent to a distribution with a zero location parameter, where μ has been added to the intercept coefficient. Both situations produce the same value for Y_i^* regardless of settings of explanatory variables. Similarly, an arbitrary scale parameter s is equivalent to setting the scale parameter to 1 and then dividing all regression coefficients by s. In the latter case, the resulting value of Y_i^* will be smaller by a factor of s than in the former case, for all sets of explanatory variables — but critically, it will always remain on the same side of 0, and hence lead to the same Y_i choice.

(Note that this predicts that the irrelevancy of the scale parameter may not carry over into more complex models where more than two choices are available.)

It turns out that this formulation is exactly equivalent to the preceding one, phrased in terms of the generalized linear model and without any latent variables. This can be shown as follows, using the fact that the cumulative distribution function (CDF) of the standard logistic distribution is the logistic function, which is the inverse of the logit function, i.e.

$$Pr(\varepsilon < x) = (x).$$

Then:

$$
\begin{aligned}
Pr(Y_i = 1 | X_i) &= Pr\big((Y_i^* > 0)\big| X_i\big) \\
&= Pr(\boldsymbol{\beta} \cdot X_i + \varepsilon > 0) \\
&= Pr(\varepsilon > -\boldsymbol{\beta} \cdot X_i) \\
&= Pr(\varepsilon < \boldsymbol{\beta} \cdot X_i) \\
&= (\boldsymbol{\beta} \cdot X_i) \\
&= p_i.
\end{aligned}
$$

This formulation — which is standard in discrete choice models — makes clear the relationship between logistic regression (the "logit model") and the probit model, which uses an error variable distributed according to a standard normal distribution instead of a standard logistic distribution. Both the logistic and normal distributions are symmetric with a basic unimodal, "bell curve" shape. The only difference is that the logistic distribution has somewhat heavier tails, which means that it is less sensitive to outlying data (and hence somewhat more robust to model misspecifications or erroneous data).

As a two-way latent-variable model

Yet another formulation uses two separate latent variables:

$$Y_i^{0*} = \boldsymbol{\beta_0} \cdot \boldsymbol{X_i} + \varepsilon_0,$$

$$Y_i^{1*} = \boldsymbol{\beta_{01}} \cdot \boldsymbol{X_i} + \varepsilon_1,$$

where

$$\varepsilon_0 \sim EV_1(0,1),$$

$$\varepsilon_1 \sim EV_1(0,1),$$

where $EV_1(0,1)$ is a standard type-1 extreme value distribution: i.e.

$$Pr(\varepsilon_0 = x) = Pr(\varepsilon_1 = x) = e^{-x}e^{-e^{-x}},$$

Then

$$Y_i = \begin{cases} 1 & \text{if } Y_i^{1*} > Y_i^{0*} \\ 0 & \text{otherwise} \end{cases}.$$

This model has a separate latent variable and a separate set of regression coefficients for each possible outcome of the dependent variable. The reason for this separation is that it makes it easy to extend logistic regression to multi-outcome categorical variables, as in the multinomial logit model. In such a model, it is natural to model each possible outcome using a different set of regression coefficients. It is also possible to motivate each of the separate latent variables as the theoretical utility associated with making the associated choice, and thus motivate logistic regression in terms of utility theory. (In terms of utility theory, a rational actor always chooses the choice with the greatest associated utility.) This is the approach taken by economists when formulating discrete choice models, because it both provides a theoretically strong foundation and facilitates intuitions about the model, which in turn makes it easy to consider various sorts of extensions. (See the example below.)

The choice of the type-1 extreme value distribution seems fairly arbitrary, but it makes the mathematics work out, and it may be possible to justify its use through rational choice theory.

It turns out that this model is equivalent to the previous model, although this seems non-obvious, since there are now two sets of regression coefficients and error variables, and the error variables have a different distribution. In fact, this model reduces directly to the previous one with the following substitutions:

$$\beta = \beta_1 - \beta_0,$$

$$\varepsilon = \varepsilon_1 - \varepsilon_0.$$

An intuition for this comes from the fact that, since we choose based on the maximum of two values, only their difference matters, not the exact values — and this effectively removes one degree of freedom. Another critical fact is that the difference of two type-1 extreme-value-distributed variables is a logistic distribution, i.e. if

$$\varepsilon = \varepsilon_1 - \varepsilon_0 \sim \text{Logistic}(0,1).$$

We can demonstrate the equivalent as follows:

$$
\begin{aligned}
\Pr(Y_i = 1 | X_i) &= \Pr\left(Y_i^{1*} > Y_i^{0*} | X_i\right) \\
&= \Pr\left(Y_i^{1*} - Y_i^{0*} > 0 | X_i\right) \\
&= \Pr(\beta_1 \cdot X_i + \varepsilon_1 - (\beta_0 \cdot X_i + \varepsilon_0) > 0) \\
&= \Pr((\beta_1 \cdot X_i - \beta_0 \cdot X_i) + (\varepsilon_1 - \varepsilon_0) > 0) \\
&= \Pr((\beta_1 - \beta_0) \cdot X_i + (\varepsilon_1 - \varepsilon_0) > 0) \\
&= \Pr((\beta_1 - \beta_0) \cdot X_i + \varepsilon > 0) \\
&= \Pr(\beta \cdot X_i + \varepsilon > 0) \\
&= \Pr(\varepsilon > -\beta \cdot X_i) \\
&= \Pr(\varepsilon < \beta \cdot X_i) \\
&= (\beta \cdot X_i) \\
&= p_i.
\end{aligned}
$$

Example

As an example, consider a province-level election where the choice is between a right-of-center party, a left-of-center party, and a secessionist party (e.g. the Parti Québécois, which wants Quebec to secede from Canada (Hale & Hale, 2006)). We would then use three latent variables, one for each choice. Then, in accordance with utility theory, we can then interpret the latent variables as expressing the utility that results from making each of the choices. We can also interpret the regression coefficients as indicating the strength that the associated factor (i.e. explanatory variable) has in contributing to the utility — or more correctly, the amount by which a unit change in an explanatory variable changes the utility of a given choice. A voter might expect that the right-of-center party would lower taxes, especially on rich people. This would give low-income people no benefit, i.e. no change in utility (since they usually don't pay taxes); would cause moderate benefit (i.e. somewhat more money, or moderate utility increase) for middle-incoming people; and would cause significant benefits for high-income people. On the other hand, the left-of-center party might be expected to raise taxes and offset it with increased welfare and other assistance for the lower and middle classes. This would cause significant positive benefit to low-income people, perhaps weak benefit to middle-income people, and significant negative benefit to high-income people. Finally, the secessionist party would take no direct actions on the economy, but simply secede. A low-income or middle-income voter might expect basically no clear utility gain or loss from this, but a high-income voter might expect negative utility, since he/she is likely to own companies, which will have a harder time doing business in such an environment and probably lose money.

These intuitions can be expressed as follows:

Estimated strength of regression coefficient for different outcomes (party choices) and different values of explanatory variables

	Center-right	Center-left	Secessionist
High-income	strong +	strong −	strong −
Middle-income	moderate +	weak +	none
Low-income	none	strong +	none

This clearly shows that

1. Separate sets of regression coefficients need to exist for each choice. When phrased in terms of utility, this can be seen very easily. Different choices have different effects on net utility; furthermore, the effects vary in complex ways that depend on the characteristics of each individual, so there need to be separate sets of coefficients for each characteristic, not simply a single extra per-choice characteristic.

2. Even though income is a continuous variable, its effect on utility is too complex for it to be treated as a single variable. Either it needs to be directly split up into ranges, or higher powers of income need to be added so that polynomial regression on income is effectively done.

As a "log-linear" model

Yet another formulation combines the two-way latent variable formulation above with the original formulation higher up without latent variables, and in the process provides a link to one of the standard formulations of the multinomial logit (Greene, 2011).

Here, instead of writing the logit of the probabilities p_i as a linear predictor, we separate the linear predictor into two, one for each of the two outcomes:

$$\ln \Pr(Y_i = 0) = \boldsymbol{\beta_0} \cdot \boldsymbol{X}_i - \ln Z$$

$$\ln \Pr(Y_i = 0) = \boldsymbol{\beta_1} \cdot \boldsymbol{X}_i - \ln Z.$$

Note that two separate sets of regression coefficients have been introduced, just as in the two-way latent variable model, and the two equations appear a form that writes the logarithm of the associated probability as a linear predictor, with an extra term $- \ln Z$ at the end. This term, as it turns out, serves as the normalizing factor ensuring that the result is a distribution. This can be seen by exponentiating both sides:

$$\Pr(Y_i = 0) = \frac{1}{Z} e^{\beta_0 \cdot X_i}$$

$$\Pr(Y_i = 1) = \frac{1}{Z} e^{\beta_1 \cdot X_i}.$$

In this form it is clear that the purpose of Z is to ensure that the resulting distribution over Y_i is in fact a probability distribution, i.e. it sums to 1. This means that Z is simply the sum of all un-normalized probabilities, and by dividing each probability by Z, the probabilities become "normalized". That is:

$$Z = e^{\beta_0 \cdot X_i} + e^{\beta_1 \cdot X_i},$$

and the resulting equations are

$$\Pr(Y_i = 0) = \frac{e^{\beta_0 \cdot X_i}}{e^{\beta_0 \cdot X_i} + e^{\beta_1 \cdot X_i}}$$

$$\Pr(Y_i = 1) = \frac{e^{\beta_1 \cdot X_i}}{e^{\beta_0 \cdot X_i} + e^{\beta_1 \cdot X_i}}.$$

Or generally:

$$\Pr(Y_i = c) = \frac{e^{\beta_c \cdot X_i}}{\sum_h e^{\beta_h \cdot X_i}}.$$

This shows clearly how to generalize this formulation to more than two outcomes, as in multinomial logit (Greene, 2011).

In order to prove that this is equivalent to the previous model, note that the above model is over specified, in that $\Pr(Y_i = 0)$ and $\Pr(Y_i = 1)$

cannot be independently specified: $\Pr(Y_i = 0) + \Pr(Y_i = 1) = 1$ rather so knowing one automatically determines the other. As a result, the model is nonidentifiable, in that multiple combinations of β_0 and β_1 will produce the same probabilities for all possible explanatory variables. In fact, it can be seen that adding any constant vector to both of them will produce the same probabilities:

$$\Pr(Y_i = 1) = \frac{e^{(\beta_1 + C) \cdot X_i}}{e^{(\beta_0 + C) \cdot X_i} + e^{(\beta_1 + C) \cdot X_i}}$$

$$= \frac{e^{\beta_1 \cdot X_i} e^{C \cdot X_i}}{e^{\beta_0 \cdot X_i} e^{C \cdot X_i} + e^{\beta_1 \cdot X_i} e^{C \cdot X_i}}$$

$$= \frac{e^{\beta_1 \cdot X_i} e^{C \cdot X_i}}{e^{C \cdot X_i}(e^{\beta_0 \cdot X_i} + e^{\beta_1 \cdot X_i})}$$

$$= \frac{e^{\beta_1 \cdot X_i}}{(e^{\beta_0 \cdot X_i} + e^{\beta_1 \cdot X_i})}.$$

As a result, we can simplify matters, and restore identifiability, by picking an arbitrary value for one of the two vectors. We choose to set $\beta_0 = 0$. Then,

$$e^{\beta_0 \cdot X_i} = e^{0 \cdot X_i} = 1,$$

and so

$$\Pr(Y_i = 1) = \frac{e^{\beta_1 \cdot X_i}}{1 + e^{\beta_1 \cdot X_i}} = \frac{1}{1 + e^{-\beta_1 \cdot X_i}} = p_i,$$

which shows that this formulation is indeed equivalent to the previous formulation. (As in the two-way latent variable formulation, any settings where $\beta = \beta_1 - \beta_0$ will produce equivalent results.)

Note that most treatments of the multinomial logit model start out either by extending the "log-linear" formulation presented here or the two-way latent variable formulation presented above, since both clearly show the way that the model could be extended to multi-way outcomes (Greene, 2011). In general, the presentation with latent variables is more common in econometrics and political science, where discrete choice models and utility theory reign, while the "log-linear" formulation here is more common in computer science, e.g. machine learning and natural language processing.

As a single-layer perceptron

The model has an equivalent formulation

$$p_i = \frac{1}{1 + e^{-(\beta_{10} + \beta_1 \cdot X_{1,i} + \cdots + k \cdot X_{k,i})}}.$$

This functional form is commonly called a single-layer perceptron or single-layer artificial neural network (Da & Xiurun, 2005). A single-layer neural network computes a continuous output instead of a step function. The derivative of p_i with respect to $X = (x_1, \ldots, x_k)$ is computed from the general form:

$$y = \frac{1}{1 + e^{-f(x)}},$$

where $f(X)$ is an analytic function in X. With this choice, the single-layer neural network is identical to the logistic regression model. This function has a continuous derivative, which allows it to be used in backpropagation. This function is also preferred because its derivative is easily calculated:

$$\frac{dy}{dX} = y(1 - 4)\frac{df}{dX}.$$

In terms of binomial data

A closely related model assumes that each i is associated not with a single Bernoulli trial but with n_i independent identically distributed trials, where the observation Y_i is the number of successes observed (the sum of the individual Bernoulli-distributed random variables), and hence follows a binomial distribution:

$$Y_i \sim Bin(n_i, p_p), \text{ for } i = 1, \ldots, n.$$

An example of this distribution is the fraction of seeds (p_i) that germinate after n_i are planted. In terms of expected values, this model is expressed as follows:

$$p_i = E\left[\frac{Y_i}{n_i}\middle| X_i\right],$$

so that

$$\text{logit}\left(E\left[\frac{Y_i}{n_i}\middle| X_i\right]\right) = \text{logit}(p_i) = \ln\left(\frac{p_i}{1 - p_i}\right) = \boldsymbol{\beta} \cdot \boldsymbol{X_i},$$

Or equivalently:

$$\Pr(Y_i = y_i | \boldsymbol{X_i}) = \binom{n_i}{k_i} p_i^{y_i}(1 - p_i)^{n_i - y_i}$$

$$= \binom{n_i}{k_i}\left(\frac{1}{1 + e^{-\boldsymbol{\beta} \cdot \boldsymbol{X_i}}}\right)^{y_i}\left(1 - \frac{1}{1 + e^{-\boldsymbol{\beta} \cdot \boldsymbol{X_i}}}\right)^{1 - y_i}.$$

This model can be fit using the same sorts of methods as the above more basic model.

Bayesian logistic regression

In a Bayesian statistics context, prior distributions are normally placed on the regression coefficients, usually in the form of Gaussian distributions. Unfortunately, the Gaussian distribution is not the conjugate prior of the likelihood function in logistic regression; in fact, the likelihood function is not an exponential family and thus does not have a conjugate prior at all. As a result, the posterior distribution is difficult to calculate, even using standard simulation algorithms (e.g. Gibbs sampling).

There are various possibilities:

- Don't do a proper Bayesian analysis, but simply compute a maximum a posteriori point estimate of the parameters. This is common, for example, in "maximum entropy" classifiers in machine learning.
- Use a more general approximation method such as the Metropolis–

Hastings algorithm.

- Draw a Markov chain Monte Carlo sample from the exact posterior by using the Independent Metropolis–Hastings algorithm with heavy-tailed multivariate candidate distribution found by matching the mode and curvature at the mode of the normal approximation to the posterior and then using the Student's t shape with low degrees of freedom. This is shown to have excellent convergence properties.

- Use a latent variable model and approximate the logistic distribution using a more tractable distribution, e.g. a Student's t-distribution or a mixture of normal distributions.

- Do probit regression instead of logistic regression. This is actually a special case of the previous situation, using a normal distribution in place of a Student's t, mixture of normals, etc. This will be less accurate but has the advantage that probit regression is extremely common, and a ready-made Bayesian implementation may already be available.

- Use the Laplace approximation of the posterior distribution. This approximates the posterior with a Gaussian distribution. This is not a terribly good approximation, but it suffices if all that is desired is an estimate of the posterior mean and variance. In such a case, an approximation scheme such as variational Bayes can be used (Bishop, 2006).

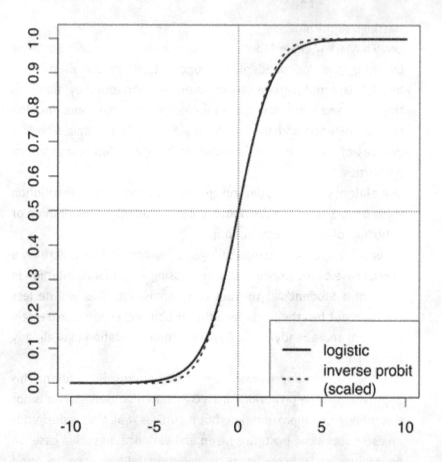

Comparison of logistic function with a scaled inverse probit function (i.e. the CDF of the normal distribution), comparing $\sigma(x)$ vs. $\Phi = \left(\sqrt{\frac{\pi}{8}}x\right)$, which makes the slopes the same at the origin. This shows the heavier tails of the logistic distribution.

Gibbs sampling with an approximating distribution

As shown above, logistic regression is equivalent to a latent variable model with an error variable distributed according to a standard logistic distribution. The overall distribution of the latent variable Y_i^* is also a logistic distribution, with the mean equal to $\beta \cdot X_i$ (i.e. the fixed quantity added to the error variable). This model considerably simplifies the application of techniques such as Gibbs sampling (George & McCullochb,

1993). However, sampling the regression coefficients is still difficult, because of the lack of conjugacy between the normal and logistic distributions. Changing the prior distribution over the regression coefficients is of no help, because the logistic distribution is not in the exponential family and thus has no conjugate prior.

One possibility is to use a more general Markov chain Monte Carlo technique (Walsh, 2004), such as the Metropolis–Hastings algorithm (Chib & Greenberg, 1995), which can sample arbitrary distributions. Another possibility, however, is to replace the logistic distribution with a similar-shaped distribution that is easier to work with using Gibbs sampling. In fact, the logistic and normal distributions have a similar shape, and thus one possibility is simply to have normally distributed errors. Because the normal distribution is conjugate to itself, sampling the regression coefficients becomes easy. In fact, this model is exactly the model used in probit regression.

However, the normal and logistic distributions differ in that the logistic has heavier tails. As a result, it is more robust to inaccuracies in the underlying model (which are inevitable, in that the model is essentially always an approximation) or to errors in the data. Probit regression loses some of this robustness.

Another alternative is to use errors distributed as a Student's t-distribution. The Student's t-distribution has heavy tails, and is easy to sample from because it is the compound distribution of a normal distribution with variance distributed as an inverse gamma distribution. In other words, if a normal distribution is used for the error variable, and another latent variable, following an inverse gamma distribution, is added corresponding to the variance of this error variable, the marginal distribution of the error variable will follow a Student's t-distribution. Because of the various conjugacy relationships, all variables in this model are easy to sample from.

The Student's t-distribution that best approximates a standard logistic distribution can be determined by matching the moments of the two

257

distributions. The Student's t-distribution has three parameters, and since the skewness of both distributions is always 0, the first four moments can all be matched, using the following equations:

$$\mu = 0$$

$$\frac{\nu}{\nu - 2} s^2 = \frac{\pi^2}{3}$$

$$\frac{6}{\nu - 4} = \frac{6}{5}.$$

This yields the following values:

$$\mu = 0$$

$$s = \sqrt{\frac{7}{9} \frac{\pi^2}{3}}$$

$$\nu = 9.$$

The following graphs compare the standard logistic distribution with the Student's t-distribution that matches the first four moments using the above-determined values, as well as the normal distribution that matches the first two moments. Note how much closer the Student's t-distribution agrees, especially in the tails. Beyond about two standard deviations from the mean, the logistic and normal distributions diverge rapidly, but the logistic and Student's t-distributions don't start diverging significantly until more than 5 standard deviations away.

(Another possibility, also amenable to Gibbs sampling, is to approximate the logistic distribution using a mixture density of normal distributions (Chen, Zhu, Wang, Zheng, & Zhang, 2013).)

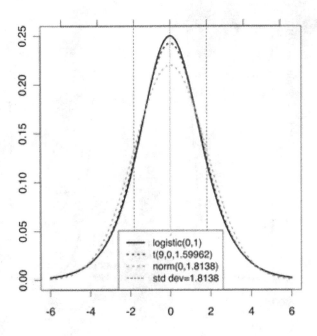

Comparison of logistic and approximating distributions (*t*, normal).

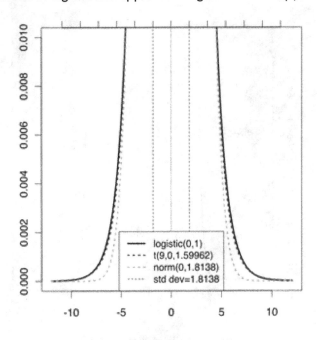

Tails of distributions.

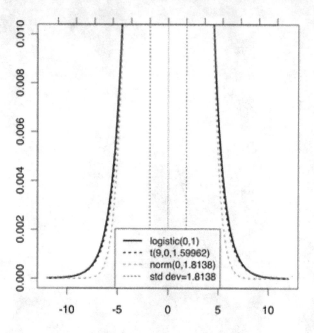

Further tails of distributions.

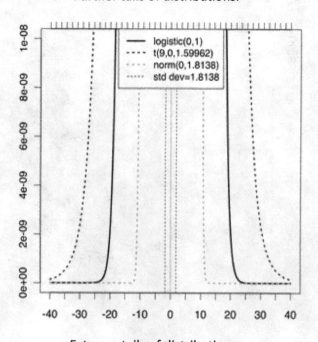

Extreme tails of distributions.

Extensions

There are large numbers of extensions:

- Multinomial logistic regression (or multinomial logit) handles the case of a multi-way categorical dependent variable (with unordered values, also called "classification"). Note that the general case of having dependent variables with more than two values is termed polytomous regression.
- Ordered logistic regression (or ordered logit) handles ordinal dependent variables (ordered values).
- Mixed logit is an extension of multinomial logit that allows for correlations among the choices of the dependent variable.
- An extension of the logistic model to sets of interdependent variables is the conditional random field.

Model suitability

A way to measure a model's suitability is to assess the model against a set of data that was not used to create the model (Mark & Goldberg, 2001). The class of techniques is called cross-validation. This holdout model assessment method is particularly valuable when data are collected in different settings (e.g., at different times or places) or when models are assumed to be generalizable.

To measure the suitability of a binary regression model, one can classify both the actual value and the predicted value of each observation as either 0 or 1 (Myers & Forgy, 1963). The predicted value of an observation can be set equal to 1 if the estimated probability that the observation equals 1 is above $1/2$, and set equal to 0 if the estimated probability is below $1/2$. Here logistic regression is being used as a binary classification model. There are four possible combined classifications:

1. prediction of 0 when the holdout sample has a 0 (True Negatives, the number of which is TN)

2. prediction of 0 when the holdout sample has a 1 (False Negatives, the number of which is FN)

3. prediction of 1 when the holdout sample has a 0 (False Positives, the number of which is FP)

4. prediction of 1 when the holdout sample has a 1 (True Positives, the number of which is TP)

These classifications are used to calculate accuracy, precision (also called positive predictive value), recall (also called sensitivity), specificity and negative predictive value:

$$\text{Accuracy} = \frac{TP + TN}{TP + FP + FN + TN}$$
$$= \text{fraction of observations with correct predicted classification}$$

$$Precision = PositivePredictiveValue = \frac{TP}{TP + FP}$$
$$= \text{Fraction of predicted positives that are correct}$$

$$NegativePredictiveVlaue = \frac{TN}{TN + FN}$$
$$= \text{fraction of predicted negatives that are correct}$$

$$Recall = Sensitivity = \frac{TP}{TP + FN}$$
$$= \text{fraction of observations that are actually 1 with}$$
a correct predicted classification

$$Specificity = \frac{TN}{TN + FP}$$
$$= \text{fraction of observations that are actually 0 with a correct predicted}$$

Software

All the primary software packages discussed in Chapter 2 have this functionality.

Examples Using R

Logistic Regression: Multiple Numerical Predictors

Inattentional Blindness (IB) refers to situations in which a person fails to see an obvious stimulus right in front of his eyes. It is hypothesized that IB could be predicted from performance on the Stroop Color Word test. This test produces three scores: "W" (word alone, i.e., a score derived from reading a list of color words such as red, green, black), "C" (color alone, in which a score is derived from naming the color in which a series of Xs are printed), and "CW" (the Stroop task, in which a score is derived from the subject's attempt to name the color in which a color word is printed when the word and the color do not agree). The data are in the following table, in which the response, "seen", is coded as 0=no and 1=yes...

	seen	W	C	CW
1	0	126	86	64
2	0	118	76	54
3	0	61	66	44
4	0	69	48	32
5	0	57	59	42
6	0	78	64	53
7	0	114	61	41
8	0	81	85	47
9	0	73	57	33
10	0	93	50	45
11	0	116	92	49
12	0	156	70	45
13	0	90	66	48
14	0	120	73	49
15	0	99	68	44
16	0	113	110	47
17	0	103	78	52
18	0	123	61	28
19	0	86	65	42
20	0	99	77	51
21	0	102	77	54
22	0	120	74	53

```
23    0 128 100 56
24    0 100  89 56
25    0  95  61 37
26    0  80  55 36
27    0  98  92 51
28    0 111  90 52
29    0 101  85 45
30    0 102  78 51
31    1 100  66 48
32    1 112  78 55
33    1  82  84 37
34    1  72  63 46
35    1  72  65 47
36    1  89  71 49
37    1 108  46 29
38    1  88  70 49
39    1 116  83 67
40    1 100  69 39
41    1  99  70 43
42    1  93  63 36
43    1 100  93 62
44    1 110  76 56
45    1 100  83 36
46    1 106  71 49
47    1 115 112 66
48    1 120  87 54
49    1  97  82 41
```

To get them into R, try this first...

```
> file = "http://ww2.coastal.edu/kingw/statistics/R-
+ tutorials/text/gorilla.csv"
> read.csv(file) -> gorilla
> str(gorilla)
'data.frame':    49 obs. of  4 variables:
 $ seen: int  0 0 0 0 0 0 0 0 0 0 ...
 $ W   : int  126 118 61 69 57 78 114 81 73 93 ...
 $ C   : int  86 76 66 48 59 64 61 85 57 50 ...
 $ CW  : int  64 54 44 32 42 53 41 47 33 45 ...
```

If that doesn't work (and it should), try copying and pasting this script into R at the command prompt...

```
### Begin copying here.
gorilla = data.frame(rep(c(0,1),c(30,19)),

c(126,118,61,69,57,78,114,81,73,93,116,156,90,120,99,113,10
3,123,

86,99,102,120,128,100,95,80,98,111,101,102,100,112,82,72,72
,

89,108,88,116,100,99,93,100,110,100,106,115,120,97),

c(86,76,66,48,59,64,61,85,57,50,92,70,66,73,68,110,78,61,65
,

77,77,74,100,89,61,55,92,90,85,78,66,78,84,63,65,71,46,70,
                83,69,70,63,93,76,83,71,112,87,82),

c(64,54,44,32,42,53,41,47,33,45,49,45,48,49,44,47,52,28,42,
51,54,

53,56,56,37,36,51,52,45,51,48,55,37,46,47,49,29,49,67,39,43
,36,
                62,56,36,49,66,54,41))
colnames(gorilla) = c("seen","W","C","CW")
str(gorilla)
### End copying here.
```

And if that does not work, well, you know what you have to do! We might begin like this...

```
> cor(gorilla)              ### a correlation matrix
            seen          W          C          CW
seen   1.00000000 -0.03922667 0.05437115 0.06300865
W     -0.03922667  1.00000000 0.43044418 0.35943580
C      0.05437115  0.43044418 1.00000000 0.64463361
CW     0.06300865  0.35943580 0.64463361 1.00000000
```

...or like this...

```
> with(gorilla, tapply(W, seen, mean))
        0           1
100.40000  98.89474
> with(gorilla, tapply(C, seen, mean))
        0           1
73.76667 75.36842
> with(gorilla, tapply(CW, seen, mean))
        0           1
46.70000 47.84211
```

The Stroop scale scores are moderately positively correlated with each other, but none of them appears to be related to the "seen" response variable, at least not to any impressive extent. There doesn't appear to be much here to look at. Let's have a go at it anyway.

Since the response is a binomial variable, a logistic regression can be done as follows...

```
> glm.out = glm(seen ~ W * C * CW, family=binomial(logit),
+ data=gorilla)
> summary(glm.out)

Call:
glm(formula = seen ~ W * C * CW, family = binomial(logit),
data = gorilla)

Deviance Residuals:
    Min       1Q   Median       3Q      Max
-1.8073  -0.9897  -0.5740   1.2368   1.7362

Coefficients:
              Estimate Std. Error z value Pr(>|z|)
(Intercept) -1.323e+02  8.037e+01  -1.646   0.0998 .
W            1.316e+00  7.514e-01   1.751   0.0799 .
C            2.129e+00  1.215e+00   1.753   0.0797 .
CW           2.206e+00  1.659e+00   1.329   0.1837
W:C         -2.128e-02  1.140e-02  -1.866   0.0621 .
W:CW        -2.201e-02  1.530e-02  -1.439   0.1502
```

```
C:CW          -3.582e-02  2.413e-02  -1.485   0.1376
W:C:CW         3.579e-04  2.225e-04   1.608   0.1078
---
```

Signif.codes:0 '***' 0.001 '**' 0.01 '*' 0.05 '.' 0.1 ' ' 1

(Dispersion parameter for binomial family taken to be 1)

```
    Null deviance: 65.438  on 48  degrees of freedom
Residual deviance: 57.281  on 41  degrees of freedom
AIC: 73.281
```

Number of Fisher Scoring iterations: 5

> anova(glm.out, test="Chisq")
Analysis of Deviance Table

Model: binomial, link: logit

Response: seen

Terms added sequentially (first to last)

	Df	Deviance	Resid. Df	Resid. Dev	Pr(>Chi)
NULL			48	65.438	
W	1	0.0755	47	65.362	0.78351
C	1	0.3099	46	65.052	0.57775
CW	1	0.1061	45	64.946	0.74467
W:C	1	2.3632	44	62.583	0.12423
W:CW	1	0.5681	43	62.015	0.45103
C:CW	1	1.4290	42	60.586	0.23193
W:C:CW	1	3.3053	41	57.281	0.06906 .

```
---
```
Signif.codes:0 '***' 0.001 '**' 0.01 '*' 0.05 '.' 0.1 ' ' 1

Two different extractor functions have been used to see the results of our analysis. What do they mean?

The first gives us what amount to regression coefficients with standard errors and a z-test, as we saw in the single variable example above. None of the coefficients are significantly different from zero (but a few are close). The deviance was reduced by 8.157 points on 7 degrees of freedom, for a p-value of...

```
> 1 - pchisq(8.157, df=7)
[1] 0.3189537
```

Overall, the model appears to have performed poorly, showing no significant reduction in deviance (no significant difference from the null model).

The second print out shows the same overall reduction in deviance, from 65.438 to 57.281 on 7 degrees of freedom. In this print out, however, the reduction in deviance is shown for each term, added sequentially first to last. Of note is the three-way interaction term, which produced a nearly significant reduction in deviance of 3.305 on 1 degree of freedom $(p = 0.069)$.

In the event you are encouraged by any of this, the following graph might be revealing...

```
> plot(glm.out$fitted)
> abline(v=30.5,col="red")
> abline(h=.3,col="green")
> abline(h=.5,col="green")
> text(15,.9,"seen = 0")
> text(40,.9,"seen = 1")
```

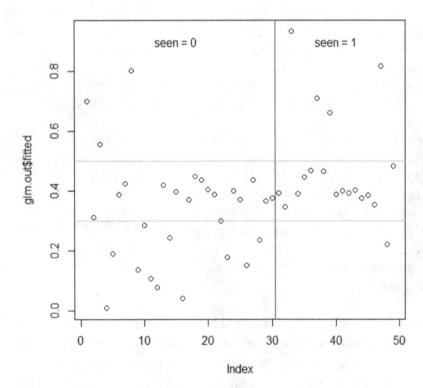

We leave it up to you to interpret this.

Logistic Regression: Categorical Predictors

Categorical data are commonly encountered in three forms: a frequency table or cross-tabulation, a flat table, or a case-by-case data frame. Let's begin with the last of these. Copy and paste the following lines ALL AT ONCE into R. That is, highlight these lines with your mouse, hit Ctrl-C on your keyboard, click at a command prompt in R, and hit Ctrl-V on your keyboard, and hit Enter if necessary, i.e., if R hasn't returned to a command prompt. On the Mac, use Command-C and Command-V. This will execute these lines as a script and create a data frame called "ucb" in your workspace. WARNING: Your workspace will also be cleared, so save anything you don't want to lose first.

```
# Begin copying here.
rm(list=ls())
```

```
gender = rep(c("female","male"),c(1835,2691))
admitted                                                    =
rep(c("yes","no","yes","no"),c(557,1278,1198,1493))
dept                                                        =
rep(c("A","B","C","D","E","F","A","B","C","D","E","F"),
        c(89,17,202,131,94,24,19,8,391,244,299,317))
dept2                                                       =
rep(c("A","B","C","D","E","F","A","B","C","D","E","F"),

c(512,353,120,138,53,22,313,207,205,279,138,351))
department = c(dept,dept2)
ucb = data.frame(gender,admitted,department)
rm(gender,admitted,dept,dept2,department)
ls()
# End copying here.
[1] "ucb"
```

Data sets that are purely categorical are not economically represented
in case-by-case data frames, and so the built-in data sets that are purely
categorical come in the form of tables (contingency tables or
crosstabulations). We have just taken the data from one of these (the
"UCBAdmissions" built-in data set) and turned it into a case-by-case
data frame. It's the classic University of California, Berkeley, admissions
data from 1973 describing admissions into six different graduate
programs broken down by gender. Let's examine the "UCBAdmissions"
data set.

```
> ftable(UCBAdmissions, col.vars="Admit")
                Admit Admitted Rejected
Gender Dept
Male    A                512      313
        B                353      207
        C                120      205
        D                138      279
        E                 53      138
        F                 22      351
Female  A                 89       19
        B                 17        8
        C                202      391
```

D	131	244
E	94	299
F	24	317

The data are from 1973 and show admissions by gender to the top six grad programs at the University of California, Berkeley. Looked at as a two-way table, there appears to be a bias against admitting women...

```
> dimnames(UCBAdmissions)
$Admit
[1] "Admitted" "Rejected"

$Gender
[1] "Male"    "Female"

$Dept
[1] "A" "B" "C" "D" "E" "F"

> margin.table(UCBAdmissions, c(2,1))
        Admit
Gender   Admitted Rejected
  Male       1198     1493
  Female      557     1278
```

However, there are also relationships between "Gender" and "Dept" as well as between "Dept" and "Admit", which means the above relationship may be confounded by "Dept" (or "Dept" might be a lurking variable, in the language of traditional regression analysis). Perhaps a logistic regression with the binomial variable "Admit" as the response can tease these variables apart.

If there is a way to conveniently get that flat table into a data frame (without splitting an infinitive), I do not know it. So I had to do this...

```
> ucb.df =
+ data.frame(gender=rep(c("Male","Female"),c(6,6)),
+ dept=rep(LETTERS[1:6],2),
+ yes=c(512,353,120,138,53,22,89,17,202,131,94,24),
+ no=c(313,207,205,279,138,351,19,8,391,244,299,317))
```

271

```
> ucb.df
   gender dept yes  no
1    Male    A 512 313
2    Male    B 353 207
3    Male    C 120 205
4    Male    D 138 279
5    Male    E  53 138
6    Male    F  22 351
7  Female    A  89  19
8  Female    B  17   8
9  Female    C 202 391
10 Female    D 131 244
11 Female    E  94 299
12 Female    F  24 317
```

Once again, we do not have a binary coded response variable, so the last two columns of this data frame will have to be bound into the columns of a table to serve as the response in the model formula...

```
> mod.form = "cbind(yes,no) ~ gender * dept"
> glm.out = glm(mod.form, family=binomial(logit),
+ data=ucb.df)
```

We used a trick here of storing the model formula in a data object, and then entering the name of this object into the glm( ) function. That way, if we made a mistake in the model formula (or want to run an alternative model), we have only to edit the "mod.form" object to do it.

Let's see what we have found...

```
> options(show.signif.stars=F)   # turn off significance
                                 # stars (optional)
> anova(glm.out, test="Chisq")
Analysis of Deviance Table

Model: binomial, link: logit

Response: cbind(yes, no)

Terms added sequentially (first to last)
```

	Df	Deviance	Resid. Df	Resid. Dev	Pr(>Chi)
NULL			11	877.06	
gender	1	93.45	10	783.61	< 2.2e-16
dept	5	763.40	5	20.20	< 2.2e-16
gender:dept	5	20.20	0	0.00	0.001144

This is a saturated model, meaning we have used up all our degrees of freedom, and there is no residual deviance left over at the end. Saturated models always fit the data perfectly. In this case, it appears the saturated model is required to explain the data adequately. If we leave off the interaction term, for example, we will be left with a residual deviance of 20.2 on 5 degrees of freedom, and the model will be rejected ($p = 0.001144$). It appears all three terms are making a significant contribution to the model.

How they are contributing appears if we use the other extractor...

```
> summary(glm.out)
```

```
Call:
glm(formula = mod.form, family = binomial(logit), data =
ucb.df)
```

```
Deviance Residuals:
 [1] 0 0 0 0 0 0 0 0 0 0 0 0
```

Coefficients:

	Estimate	Std. Error	z value	Pr(>|z|)
(Intercept)	1.5442	0.2527	6.110	9.94e-10
genderMale	-1.0521	0.2627	-4.005	6.21e-05
deptB	-0.7904	0.4977	-1.588	0.11224
deptC	-2.2046	0.2672	-8.252	< 2e-16
deptD	-2.1662	0.2750	-7.878	3.32e-15
deptE	-2.7013	0.2790	-9.682	< 2e-16
deptF	-4.1250	0.3297	-12.512	< 2e-16
genderMale:deptB	0.8321	0.5104	1.630	0.10306
genderMale:deptC	1.1770	0.2996	3.929	8.53e-05

```
genderMale:deptD   0.9701    0.3026   3.206   0.00135
genderMale:deptE   1.2523    0.3303   3.791   0.00015
genderMale:deptF   0.8632    0.4027   2.144   0.03206
```

(Dispersion parameter for binomial family taken to be 1)

```
    Null deviance:   8.7706e+02  on 11  degrees of freedom
Residual deviance:  -1.6676e-13  on  0  degrees of freedom
AIC: 92.94
```

Number of Fisher Scoring iterations: 3

These are the regression coefficients for each predictor in the model, with the base level of each factor being suppressed. Remember, we are predicting log odd"...

```
> exp(-1.0521)         # antilog of the genderMale coefficient
[1] 0.3492037
> 1/exp(-1.0521)
[1] 2.863658
```

This shows that men were actually at a significant *disadvantage* when department and the interaction are controlled. The odds of a male being admitted were only 0.35 times the odds of a female being admitted. The reciprocal of this turns it on its head. All else being equal, the odds of female being admitted were 2.86 times the odds of a male being admitted.

Each coefficient compares the corresponding predictor to the base level. So...

```
> exp(-2.2046)
[1] 0.1102946
```

...the odds of being admitted to department C were only about 1/9th the odds of being admitted to department A, all else being equal. If you want to compare, for example, department C to department D, do this...

```
> exp(-2.2046) / exp(-2.1662)        # C:A / D:A leaves C:D
```

[1] 0.9623279

All else equal, the odds of being admitted to department C were 0.96 times the odds of being admitted to department D. (To be honest, I am not sure I am comfortable with the interaction in this model. You might want to examine the interaction, and if you think it doesn't merit inclusion, run the model again without it. Statistics are nice, but in the end it's what makes sense that should rule the day.)

13. Robust regression

In robust statistics, robust regression is a form of regression analysis designed to circumvent some limitations of traditional parametric and non-parametric methods. Regression analysis seeks to find the relationship between one or more independent variables and a dependent variable. Certain widely used methods of regression, such as ordinary least squares, have favorable properties if their underlying assumptions are true, but can give misleading results if those assumptions are not true; thus ordinary least squares is said to be not robust to violations of its assumptions. Robust regression methods are designed to be not overly affected by violations of assumptions by the underlying data-generating process (Andersen, 2008).

In particular, least squares estimates for regression models are highly sensitive to (not robust against) outliers. While there is no precise definition of an outlier, outliers are observations which do not follow the pattern of the other observations. This is not normally a problem if the outlier is simply an extreme observation drawn from the tail of a normal distribution, but if the outlier results from non-normal measurement error or some other violation of standard ordinary least squares assumptions, then it compromises the validity of the regression results if a non-robust regression technique is used.

Applications

Heteroscedastic errors

One instance in which robust estimation should be considered is when there is a strong suspicion of heteroscedasticity. In the homoscedastic model, it is assumed that the variance of the error term is constant for all values of x. Heteroscedasticity allows the variance to be dependent on x, which is more accurate for many real scenarios. For example, the variance of expenditure is often larger for individuals with higher income than for individuals with lower incomes. Software packages usually default to a homoscedastic model, even though such a model may be less accurate than a heteroscedastic model. One simple approach (Tofallis, 2008) is to apply least squares to percentage errors as this reduces the influence of the larger values of the dependent variable compared to ordinary least squares.

Presence of outliers

Another common situation in which robust estimation is used occurs when the data contain outliers. In the presence of outliers that do not come from the same data-generating process as the rest of the data, least squares estimation is inefficient and can be biased. Because the least squares predictions are dragged towards the outliers, and because the variance of the estimates is artificially inflated, the result is that outliers can be masked. (In many situations, including some areas of geostatistics and medical statistics, it is precisely the outliers that are of interest.)

Although it is sometimes claimed that least squares (or classical statistical methods in general) are robust, they are only robust in the sense that the type I error rate does not increase under violations of the model. In fact, the type I error rate tends to be lower than the nominal level when outliers are present, and there is often a dramatic increase in the type II error rate. The reduction of the type I error rate has been labelled as the conservatism of classical methods. Other labels might include inefficiency or inadmissibility.

History and unpopularity of robust regression

Despite their superior performance over least squares estimation in many situations, robust methods for regression are still not widely used. Several reasons may help explain their unpopularity (Hampel, Ronchetti, Rousseeuw, & Stahel, 2005). One possible reason is that there are several competing methods and the field got off to many false starts. Also, computation of robust estimates is much more computationally intensive than least squares estimation; in recent years however, this objection has become less relevant as computing power has increased greatly. Another reason may be that some popular statistical software packages failed to implement the methods (Stromberg, 2004). The belief of many statisticians that classical methods are robust may be another reason.

Although uptake of robust methods has been slow, modern mainstream statistics text books often include discussion of these methods (for example, the books by Seber and Lee (Seber, Lee, & J., 2003), and by Faraway (Faraway, 2004); for a good general description of how the various robust regression methods developed from one another see Andersen's book (Andersen, 2008)). Also, modern statistical software packages such as R, Stata and S-PLUS include considerable functionality for robust estimation (see, for example, the books by Venables and Ripley (Venables & Ripley, 2002), and by Maronna et al. (Maronna, Martin, & Yohai, 2006)).

Methods for robust regression

Least squares alternatives

The simplest methods of estimating parameters in a regression model that are less sensitive to outliers than the least squares estimates, is to use least absolute deviations. Even then, gross outliers can still have a considerable impact on the model, motivating research into even more robust approaches.

In 1973, Huber introduced M-estimation for regression. The M in M-estimation stands for "maximum likelihood type". The method is robust to outliers in the response variable, but turned out not to be resistant to outliers in the explanatory variables (leverage points). In fact, when there are outliers in the explanatory variables, the method has no advantage over least squares.

In the 1980s, several alternatives to M-estimation were proposed as attempts to overcome the lack of resistance. See the book by Rousseeuw and Leroy for a very practical review. Least trimmed squares (LTS) is a viable alternative and is currently (2007) the preferred choice of

Rousseeuw and Leroy (Rousseeuw & Leroy, 2003). The Theil–Sen estimator has a lower breakdown point than LTS but is statistically efficient and popular. Another proposed solution was S-estimation. This method finds a line (plane or hyperplane) that minimizes a robust estimate of the scale (from which the method gets the S in its name) of the residuals. This method is highly resistant to leverage points, and is robust to outliers in the response. However, this method was also found to be inefficient.

MM-estimation attempts to retain the robustness and resistance of S-estimation, whilst gaining the efficiency of M-estimation. The method proceeds by finding a highly robust and resistant S-estimate that minimizes an M-estimate of the scale of the residuals (the first M in the method's name). The estimated scale is then held constant whilst a close-by M-estimate of the parameters is located (the second M).

Parametric alternatives

Another approach to robust estimation of regression models is to replace the normal distribution with a heavy-tailed distribution. A t-distribution with between 4 and 6 degrees of freedom has been reported to be a good choice in various practical situations. Bayesian robust regression, being fully parametric, relies heavily on such distributions.

Under the assumption of t-distributed residuals, the distribution is a location-scale family. That is, $x \leftarrow (x - \mu)/\sigma$. The degrees of freedom of the t-distribution is sometimes called the kurtosis parameter. Lange, Little and Taylor (1989) discuss this model in some depth from a non-Bayesian point of view. A Bayesian account appears in Gelman et al. (Gelman, 2005).

An alternative parametric approach is to assume that the residuals follow a mixture of normal distributions; in particular, a contaminated normal distribution in which the majority of observations are from a specified normal distribution, but a small proportion are from a normal distribution with much higher variance. That is, residuals have probability $1 - \varepsilon$ of coming from a normal distribution with variance σ^2, where ε is small, and probability ε of coming from a normal distribution with variance $c\sigma^2$ for some $c > 1$

$$e_i \sim (1 - \varepsilon)N(0, \sigma^2) + \varepsilon N(0, c\sigma^2).$$

Typically, $\varepsilon < 0.1$. This is sometimes called the ε-contamination model.

Parametric approaches have the advantage that likelihood theory provides an 'off the shelf' approach to inference (although for mixture models such as the ε-contamination model, the usual regularity conditions might not apply), and it is possible to build simulation models from the fit. However, such parametric models still assume that the underlying model is literally true. As such, they do not account for skewed residual distributions or finite observation precisions.

Unit weights

Another robust method is the use of unit weights (Wainer & Thissen, 1976), a method that can be applied when there are multiple predictors of a single outcome. Ernest Burgess (Burgess, 1928) used unit weights to predict success on parole. He scored 21 positive factors as present (e.g., "no prior arrest" = 1) or absent ("prior arrest" = 0), then summed to yield a predictor score, which was shown to be a useful predictor of parole success. Samuel S. Wilks (Wilks, 1938) showed that nearly all sets of regression weights sum to composites that are very highly correlated with one another, including unit weights, a result referred to as Wilk's theorem (Ree, Carretta, & Earles, 1998). Robyn Dawes (Dawes, 1979) examined decision making in applied settings, showing that simple models with unit weights often outperformed human experts. Bobko, Roth, and Buster (Bobko, Roth, & Buster, 2007) reviewed the literature on unit weights, and they concluded that decades of empirical studies show that unit weights perform similar to ordinary regression weights on cross validation.

Example: BUPA liver data

The BUPA liver data have been studied by various authors, including Breiman (Breiman L. , Statistical Modeling: the Two Cultures, 2001). The data can be found via the classic data sets page and there is some discussion in the article on the Box-Cox transformation. A plot of the logs of ALT versus the logs of γGT appears below. The two regression lines are those estimated by ordinary least squares (OLS) and by robust MM-estimation. The analysis was performed in R using software made available by Venables and Ripley (Venables & Ripley, 2002).

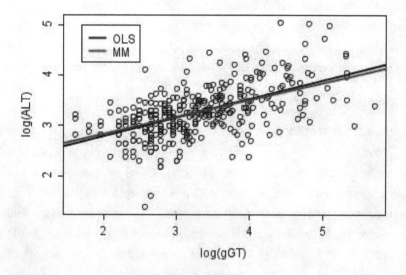

The two regression lines appear to be very similar (and this is not unusual in a data set of this size). However, the advantage of the robust approach comes to light when the estimates of residual scale are considered. For ordinary least squares, the estimate of scale is 0.420, compared to 0.373 for the robust method. Thus, the relative efficiency of ordinary least squares to MM-estimation in this example is 1.266. This inefficiency leads to loss of power in hypothesis tests, and to unnecessarily wide confidence intervals on estimated parameters.

Outlier detection

Another consequence of the inefficiency of the ordinary least squares fit is that several outliers are masked. Because the estimate of residual scale is inflated, the scaled residuals are pushed closer to zero than when a more appropriate estimate of scale is used. The plots of the scaled residuals from the two models appear below. The variable on the x-axis is just the observation number as it appeared in the data set. Rousseeuw and Leroy (Rousseeuw & Leroy, 2003) contains many such plots.

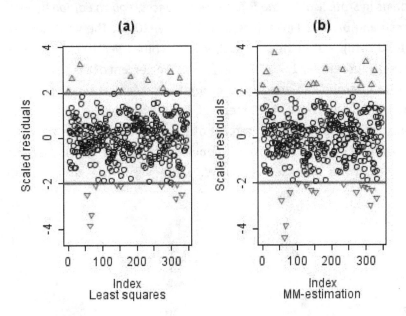

The horizontal reference lines are at 2 and -2 so that any observed scaled residual beyond these boundaries can be considered to be an outlier. Clearly, the least squares method leads to many interesting observations being masked.

While in one or two dimensions outlier detection using classical methods can be performed manually, with large data sets and in high dimensions the problem of masking can make identification of many outliers impossible. Robust methods automatically detect these observations, offering a serious advantage over classical methods when outliers are present.

Software

The best packages for this functionality include R, MATLAB, and SAS.

Example Using R

For our data analysis in R below, we will use the crime dataset that appears in *Statistical Methods for Social Sciences, Fourth Edition* by Alan Agresti and Barbara Finlay (Argresti & Finlay, 2008). The variables are state id (sid), state name (state), violent crimes per 100,000 people (crime), murders per 1,000,000 (murder), the percent of the population living in metropolitan areas (pctmetro), the percent of the population that is white (pctwhite), percent of population with a high school education or above (pcths), percent of population living under poverty line (poverty), and percent of population that are single parents (single). It has 51 observations. We are going to use poverty and single to predict crime.

```
> library(foreign)
> cdata <-
+ read.dta("http://www.ats.ucla.edu/stat/data/crime.dta")
> summary(cdata)
      sid              state              crime
 Min.   : 1.0    Length:51         Min.   :   82.0
 1st Qu.:13.5    Class :character  1st Qu.:  326.5
 Median :26.0    Mode  :character  Median :  515.0
 Mean   :26.0                      Mean   :  612.8
 3rd Qu.:38.5                      3rd Qu.:  773.0
 Max.   :51.0                      Max.   : 2922.0
     murder            pctmetro          pctwhite
 Min.   : 1.600   Min.   : 24.00   Min.   :31.80
 1st Qu.: 3.900   1st Qu.: 49.55   1st Qu.:79.35
 Median : 6.800   Median : 69.80   Median :87.60
 Mean   : 8.727   Mean   : 67.39   Mean   :84.12
 3rd Qu.:10.350   3rd Qu.: 83.95   3rd Qu.:92.60
 Max.   :78.500   Max.   :100.00   Max.   :98.50
     pcths            poverty           single
 Min.   :64.30    Min.   : 8.00    Min.   : 8.40
 1st Qu.:73.50    1st Qu.:10.70    1st Qu.:10.05
```

```
Median :76.70    Median :13.10    Median :10.90
Mean   :76.22    Mean   :14.26    Mean   :11.33
3rd Qu.:80.10    3rd Qu.:17.40    3rd Qu.:12.05
Max.   :86.60    Max.   :26.40    Max.   :22.10
```

In most cases, we begin by running an OLS regression and doing some diagnostics. We will begin by running an OLS regression and looking at diagnostic plots examining residuals, fitted values, Cook's distance, and leverage.

```
> summary(ols <- lm(crime ~ poverty + single, data =
+           cdata))

Call:
lm(formula = crime ~ poverty + single, data = cdata)

Residuals:
    Min      1Q  Median      3Q     Max
-811.14 -114.27  -22.44  121.86  689.82

Coefficients:
             Estimate Std. Error t value Pr(>|t|)
(Intercept) -1368.189    187.205  -7.308 2.48e-09
poverty         6.787      8.989   0.755    0.454
single        166.373     19.423   8.566 3.12e-11

Residual standard error: 243.6 on 48 degrees of freedom
Multiple R-squared: 0.7072,    Adjusted R-squared: 0.695
F-statistic: 57.96 on 2 and 48 DF,   p-value: 1.578e-13

> opar <- par(mfrow = c(2, 2), oma = c(0, 0, 1.1, 0))
> plot(ols, las = 1)
```

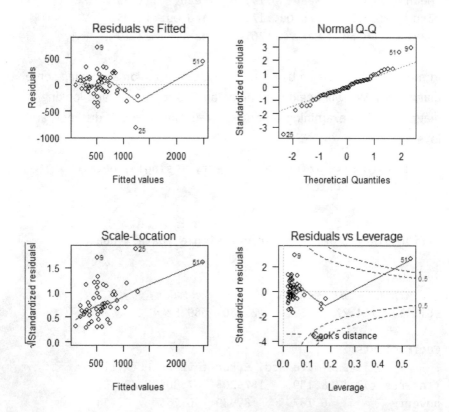

lm(crime ~ poverty + single)

From these plots, we can identify observations 9, 25, and 51as possibly problematic to our model. We can look at these observations to see which states they represent.

```
> cdata[c(9, 25, 51), 1:2]
   sid state
9    9    fl
25  25    ms
51  51    dc
```

DC, Florida and Mississippi have either high leverage or large residuals. We can display the observations that have relatively large values of Cook's D. A conventional cut-off point is $\frac{4}{n}$, where **n** is the number of observations in the data set. We will use this criterion to select the values to display.

```
> library(MASS)
> d1 <- cooks.distance(ols)
> r <- stdres(ols)
> a <- cbind(cdata, d1, r)
> a[d1 > 4/51, ]
    sid state crime murder pctmetro pctwhite pcths poverty
1    1    ak   761    9.0     41.8     75.2  86.6     9.1
9    9    fl  1206    8.9     93.0     83.5  74.4    17.8
25  25    ms   434   13.5     30.7     63.3  64.3    24.7
51  51    dc  2922   78.5    100.0     31.8  73.1    26.4
    single          d1           r
1     14.3 0.1254750 -1.397418
9     10.6 0.1425891  2.902663
25    14.7 0.6138721 -3.562990
51    22.1 2.6362519  2.616447
```

We probably should drop DC to begin with since it is not even a state. We include it in the analysis just to show that it has large Cook's D and demonstrate how it will be handled by rlm. Now we will look at the residuals. We will generate a new variable called absr1, which is the absolute value of the residuals (because the sign of the residual doesn't matter). We then print the ten observations with the highest absolute residual values.

```
> rabs <- abs(r)
> a <- cbind(cdata, d1, r, rabs)
> asorted <- a[order(-rabs), ]
> asorted[1:10, ]
    sid state crime murder pctmetro pctwhite pcths poverty
25  25    ms   434   13.5     30.7     63.3  64.3    24.7
9    9    fl  1206    8.9     93.0     83.5  74.4    17.8
51  51    dc  2922   78.5    100.0     31.8  73.1    26.4
46  46    vt   114    3.6     27.0     98.4  80.8    10.0
26  26    mt   178    3.0     24.0     92.6  81.0    14.9
21  21    me   126    1.6     35.7     98.5  78.8    10.7
1    1    ak   761    9.0     41.8     75.2  86.6     9.1
31  31    nj   627    5.3    100.0     80.8  76.7    10.9
```

```
14   14    il   960    11.4       84.0      81.0  76.2      13.6
20   20    md   998    12.7       92.8      68.9  78.4       9.7
     single        d1       r      rabs
25    14.7 0.61387212 -3.562990 3.562990
9     10.6 0.14258909  2.902663 2.902663
51    22.1 2.63625193  2.616447 2.616447
46    11.0 0.04271548 -1.742409 1.742409
26    10.8 0.01675501 -1.460885 1.460885
21    10.6 0.02233128 -1.426741 1.426741
1     14.3 0.12547500 -1.397418 1.397418
31     9.6 0.02229184  1.354149 1.354149
14    11.5 0.01265689  1.338192 1.338192
20    12.0 0.03569623  1.287087 1.287087
```

Now let's run our first robust regression. Robust regression is done by iterated re-weighted least squares (IRLS). The command for running robust regression is rlm in the MASS package. There are several weighting functions that can be used for IRLS. We are going to first use the Huber weights in this example. We will then look at the final weights created by the IRLS process. This can be very useful.

```
> summary(rr.huber <- rlm(crime ~ poverty + single, data =
+            cdata))

Call: rlm(formula = crime ~ poverty + single, data = cdata)
Residuals:
    Min      1Q  Median      3Q     Max
-846.09 -125.80  -16.49  119.15  679.94

Coefficients:
              Value      Std. Error t value
(Intercept) -1423.0373   167.5899    -8.4912
poverty         8.8677     8.0467     1.1020
single        168.9858    17.3878     9.7186

Residual standard error: 181.8 on 48 degrees of freedom

> hweights <- data.frame(state = cdata$state, resid =
+            rr.huber$resid, weight = rr.huber$w)
```

```
> hweights2 <- hweights[order(rr.huber$w), ]
> hweights2[1:15, ]
    state      resid     weight
25     ms -846.08536 0.2889618
9      fl  679.94327 0.3595480
46     vt -410.48310 0.5955740
51     dc  376.34468 0.6494131
26     mt -356.13760 0.6864625
21     me -337.09622 0.7252263
31     nj  331.11603 0.7383578
14     il  319.10036 0.7661169
1      ak -313.15532 0.7807432
20     md  307.19142 0.7958154
19     ma  291.20817 0.8395172
18     la -266.95752 0.9159411
2      al  105.40319 1.0000000
3      ar   30.53589 1.0000000
4      az  -43.25299 1.0000000
```

We can see that roughly, as the absolute residual goes down, the weight goes up. In other words, cases with a large residuals tend to be down-weighted. This output shows us that the observation for Mississippi will be down-weighted the most. Florida will also be substantially down-weighted. All observations not shown above have a weight of 1. In OLS regression, all cases have a weight of 1. Hence, the more cases in the robust regression that have a weight close to one, the closer the results of the OLS and robust regressions.

Next, let's run the same model, but using the bisquare weighting function. Again, we can look at the weights.

```
> rr.bisquare <- rlm(crime ~ poverty + single, data =
+               cdata, psi = psi.bisquare)
> summary(rr.bisquare)

Call: rlm(formula = crime ~ poverty + single, data = cdata,
psi = psi.bisquare)
Residuals:
    Min      1Q  Median      3Q      Max
```

-905.59 -140.97   -14.98   114.65   668.38

Coefficients:
	Value	Std. Error	t value
(Intercept)	-1535.3338	164.5062	-9.3330
poverty	11.6903	7.8987	1.4800
single	175.9303	17.0678	10.3077

Residual standard error: 202.3 on 48 degrees of freedom

```
> biweights <- data.frame(state = cdata$state, resid =
+             rr.bisquare$resid, weight = rr.bisquare$w)
> biweights2 <- biweights[order(rr.bisquare$w), ]
> biweights2[1:15, ]
   state     resid        weight
25    ms -905.5931 0.007652565
9     fl  668.3844 0.252870542
46    vt -402.8031 0.671495418
26    mt -360.8997 0.731136908
31    nj  345.9780 0.751347695
18    la -332.6527 0.768938330
21    me -328.6143 0.774103322
1     ak -325.8519 0.777662383
14    il  313.1466 0.793658594
20    md  308.7737 0.799065530
19    ma  297.6068 0.812596833
51    dc  260.6489 0.854441716
50    wy -234.1952 0.881660897
5     ca  201.4407 0.911713981
10    ga -186.5799 0.924033113
```

We can see that the weight given to Mississippi is dramatically lower using the bisquare weighting function than the Huber weighting function and the parameter estimates from these two different weighting methods differ. When comparing the results of a regular OLS regression and a robust regression, if the results are very different, you will most likely want to use the results from the robust regression. Large differences suggest that the model parameters are being highly influenced by outliers. Different functions have advantages and drawbacks. Huber weights can have difficulties with severe outliers, and bisquare weights can have difficulties converging or may yield multiple solutions.

As you can see, the results from the two analyses are fairly different, especially with respect to the coefficients of `single` and the constant (`intercept`). While normally we are not interested in the constant, if you had centered one or both of the predictor variables, the constant would be useful. On the other hand, you will notice that `poverty` is not statistically significant in either analysis, whereas `single` is significant in both analyses.

14. k-nearest neighbor algorithm

In pattern recognition, the k-Nearest Neighbors algorithm (or k-NN for short) is a non-parametric method used for classification and regression (Altman N. , 1992). In both cases, the input consists of the k closest training examples in the feature space. The output depends on whether k-NN is used for classification or regression:

- In k-NN classification, the output is a class membership. An object is classified by a majority vote of its neighbors, with the object being assigned to the class most common among its k nearest neighbors (k is a positive integer, typically small). If $k = 1$, then the object is simply assigned to the class of that single nearest neighbor.
- In k-NN regression, the output is the property value for the object. This value is the average of the values of its k nearest neighbors.

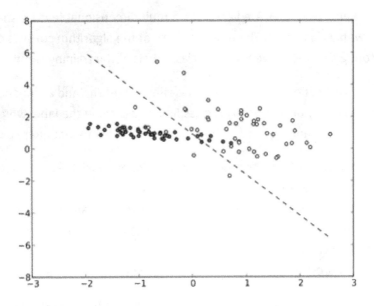

k-NN is a type of instance-based learning, or lazy learning, where the function is only approximated locally and all computation is deferred until classification. The k-NN algorithm is among the simplest of all machine learning algorithms.

Both for classification and regression, it can be useful to weight the contributions of the neighbors, so that the nearer neighbors contribute more to the average than the more distant ones. For example, a common weighting scheme consists in giving each neighbor a weight of $1/d$, where d is the distance to the neighbor.

The neighbors are taken from a set of objects for which the class (for k-NN classification) or the object property value (for k-NN regression) is known. This can be thought of as the training set for the algorithm, though no explicit training step is required.

A shortcoming of the k-NN algorithm is that it is sensitive to the local structure of the data.

Algorithm

The training examples are vectors in a multidimensional feature space, each with a class label. The training phase of the algorithm consists only of storing the feature vectors and class labels of the training samples.

In the classification phase, k is a user-defined constant, and an unlabeled vector (a query or test point) is classified by assigning the label which is most frequent among the k training samples nearest to that query point.

A commonly used distance metric for continuous variables is Euclidean distance. For discrete variables, such as for text classification, another metric can be used, such as the overlap metric (or Hamming distance). Often, the classification accuracy of k-NN can be improved significantly if the distance metric is learned with specialized algorithms such as Large Margin Nearest Neighbor or Neighborhood components analysis.

A drawback of the basic "majority voting" classification occurs when the class distribution is skewed. That is, examples of a more frequent class tend to dominate the prediction of the new example, because they tend to be common among the k nearest neighbors due to their large number

(Coomans & Massart, 1982). One way to overcome this problem is to weight the classification, taking into account the distance from the test point to each of its k nearest neighbors. The class (or value, in regression problems) of each of the k nearest points is multiplied by a weight proportional to the inverse of the distance from that point to the test point. Another way to overcome skew is by abstraction in data representation. For example in a self-organizing map (SOM), each node is a representative (a center) of a cluster of similar points, regardless of their density in the original training data. k-NN can then be applied to the SOM.

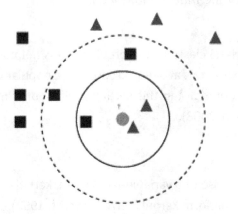

Example of k-NN classification.

The test sample (green circle) should be classified either to the first class of blue squares or to the second class of red triangles. If k = 3 (solid line circle) it is assigned to the second class because there are 2 triangles and only 1 square inside the inner circle. If k = 5 (dashed line circle) it is assigned to the first class (3 squares vs. 2 triangles inside the outer circle).

Parameter selection

The best choice of k depends upon the data; generally, larger values of k reduce the effect of noise on the classification (Everitt, Landau, Leese, & Stahl), but make boundaries between classes less distinct. A good k can be selected by various heuristic techniques (see hyperparameter optimization). The special case where the class is predicted to be the class of the closest training sample (i.e. when $k = 1$) is called the nearest neighbor algorithm.

The accuracy of the k-NN algorithm can be severely degraded by the presence of noisy or irrelevant features, or if the feature scales are not consistent with their importance. Much research effort has been put into selecting or scaling features to improve classification. A particularly popular approach is the use of evolutionary algorithms to optimize feature scaling (Nigsch, et al., 2006). Another popular approach is to scale features by the mutual information of the training data with the training classes.

In binary (two class) classification problems, it is helpful to choose k to be an odd number as this avoids tied votes. One popular way of choosing the empirically optimal k in this setting is via bootstrap method (Hall, Park, & Samworth, 2008).

Properties

k-NN is a special case of a variable-bandwidth, kernel density "balloon" estimator with a uniform kernel (Terrell & Scott, 1992).

The naive version of the algorithm is easy to implement by computing the distances from the test example to all stored examples, but it is computationally intensive for large training sets. Using an appropriate nearest neighbor search algorithm makes k-NN computationally tractable even for large data sets. Many nearest neighbor search algorithms have been proposed over the years; these generally seek to reduce the number of distance evaluations actually performed.

k-NN has some strong consistency results. As the amount of data approaches infinity, the algorithm is guaranteed to yield an error rate no worse than twice the Bayes error rate (the minimum achievable error rate given the distribution of the data) (Cover & Hart, 1967). k-NN is guaranteed to approach the Bayes error rate for some value of k (where k increases as a function of the number of data points). Various improvements to k-NN are possible by using proximity graphs (Toussaint, 2005).

Feature extraction

When the input data to an algorithm is too large to be processed and it is suspected to be notoriously redundant (e.g. the same measurement in both feet and meters) then the input data will be transformed into a reduced representation set of features (also named features vector). Transforming the input data into the set of features is called Feature extraction. If the features extracted are carefully chosen it is expected that the features set will extract the relevant information from the input data in order to perform the desired task using this reduced representation instead of the full size input. Feature extraction is performed on raw data prior to applying k-NN algorithm on the transformed data in feature space.

An example of a typical Computer vision computation pipeline for face recognition using k-NN including feature extraction and dimension reduction pre-processing steps (usually implemented with OpenCV):

1. Haar face detection

2. Mean-shift tracking analysis

3. PCA or Fisher LDA projection into feature space, followed by k-NN classification

Dimension reduction

For high-dimensional data (e.g., with number of dimensions more than 10) dimension reduction is usually performed prior to applying the k-NN algorithm in order to avoid the effects of the curse of dimensionality (Beyer, 1999).

The curse of dimensionality in the k-NN context basically means that Euclidean distance is unhelpful in high dimensions because all vectors are almost equidistant to the search query vector (imagine multiple points lying more or less on a circle of with the query point at the center; the distance from the query to all data points in the search space is almost the same).

Feature extraction and dimension reduction can be combined in one step using principal component analysis (PCA), linear discriminant analysis (LDA), or canonical correlation analysis (CCA) techniques as a pre-processing step, followed by clustering by k-NN on feature vectors in reduced-dimension space. In machine learning this process is also called low-dimensional embedding (Shaw & Jebara, 2009).

For very-high-dimensional datasets (e.g. when performing a similarity search on live video streams, DNA data or high-dimensional time series) running a fast approximate k-NN search using locality sensitive hashing, "random projections" (Bingham & M., 2001), "sketches" (Shasha, 2004) or other high-dimensional similarity search techniques from VLDB toolbox might be the only feasible option.

Decision boundary

Nearest neighbor rules in effect implicitly compute the decision boundary. It is also possible to compute the decision boundary explicitly, and to do so efficiently, so that the computational complexity is a function of the boundary complexity (Bremne, et al., 2005).

Data reduction

Data reduction is one of the most important problems for work with huge data sets. Usually, only some of the data points are needed for accurate classification. Those data are called the prototypes and can be found as follows:

1. Select the class-outliers, that is, training data that are classified incorrectly by k-NN (for a given k)

2. Separate the rest of the data into two sets: (i) the prototypes that are used for the classification decisions and (ii) the absorbed points that can

be correctly classified by k-NN using prototypes. The absorbed points can then be removed from the training set.

Selection of class-outliers

A training example surrounded by examples of other classes is called a class outlier. Causes of class outliers include:

- random error
- insufficient training examples of this class (an isolated example appears instead of a cluster)
- missing important features (the classes are separated in other dimensions which we do not know)
- too many training examples of other classes (unbalanced classes) that create a "hostile" background for the given small class

Class outliers with k-NN produce noise. They can be detected and separated for future analysis. Given two natural numbers, $k > r > 0$, a training example is called a (k, r)NN class-outlier if its k nearest neighbors include more than r examples of other classes.

CNN for data reduction

Condensed nearest neighbor (CNN, the Hart algorithm) is an algorithm designed to reduce the data set for k-NN classification (Hart, 1968). It selects the set of prototypes U from the training data, such that 1NN with U can classify the examples almost as accurately as 1NN does with the whole data set.

Given a training set X, CNN works iteratively:

1. Scan all elements of X, looking for an element x whose nearest prototype from U has a different label than x.

2. Remove x from X and add it to U

3. Repeat the scan until no more prototypes are added to U.

Use U instead of X for classification. The examples that are not prototypes are called "absorbed" points.

It is efficient to scan the training examples in order of decreasing border ratio (Mirkes, 2011).

The border ratio of a training example x is defined as

$$a(x) = \|x' - y\|/\|x - y\|$$

where $\|x - y\|$ is the distance to the closest example y having a different color than x, and $\|x' - y\|$ is the distance from y to its closest example x' with the same label as x.

The border ratio is in the interval [0,1] because $\|x' - y\|$ never exceeds $\|x - y\|$. This ordering gives preference to the borders of the classes for inclusion in the set of prototypes U. A point of a different label than x is called external to x. The calculation of the border ratio is illustrated by the figure on the right. The data points are labeled by colors: the initial point is x and its label is red. External points are blue and green. The closest to x external point is y. The closest to y red point is x'. The border ratio $a(x) = \|x' - y\|/\|x - y\|$ is the attribute of the initial point x.

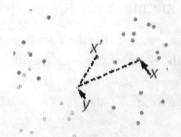

Calculation of the border ratio.

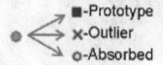

■-Prototype
x-Outlier
o-Absorbed

Three types of points: prototypes, class-outliers, and absorbed points.

Below is an illustration of CNN in a series of figures. There are three classes (red, green and blue). Figure 1: initially there are 60 points in each class. Figure 2 shows the 1NN classification map: each pixel is classified by 1NN using all the data. Figure 3 shows the 5NN classification map. White areas correspond to the unclassified regions, where 5NN voting is tied (for example, if there are two green, two red and one blue points among 5 nearest neighbors). Figure 4 shows the reduced data set. The crosses are the class-outliers selected by the (3,2)NN rule (all the three nearest neighbors of these instances belong to other classes); the squares are the prototypes, and the empty circles are the absorbed points. The left bottom corner shows the numbers of the class-outliers, prototypes and absorbed points for all three classes. The number of prototypes varies from 15% to 20% for different classes in this example. Figure 5 shows that the 1NN classification map with the prototypes is very similar to that with the initial data set. The figures were produced using the Mirkes applet (Mirkes, 2011).

CNN model reduction for k-NN classifiers

Figure 1. The data Set

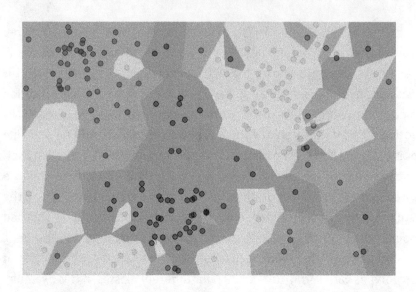

Figure 2. The 1NN classification map.

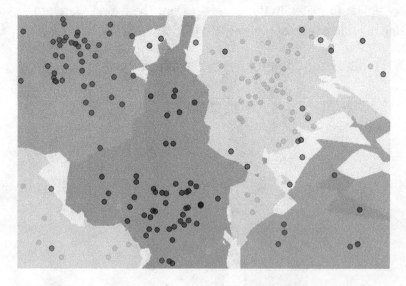

Figure 3. The 5NN classification map.

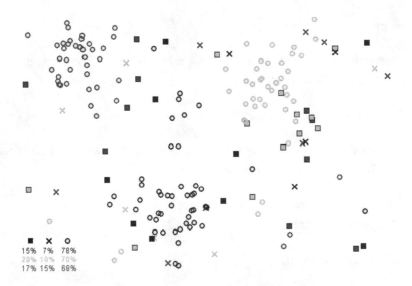

Figure 4. The CNN reduced dataset.

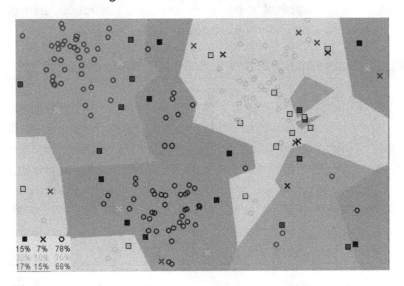

Figure 5. The 1NN classification map based on the CNN extracted prototypes.

k-NN regression

In k-NN regression, the k-NN algorithm is used for estimating continuous variables. One such algorithm uses a weighted average of the k nearest neighbors, weighted by the inverse of their distance. This algorithm works as follows:

1. Compute the Euclidean or Mahalanobis distance from the query example to the labeled examples.

2. Order the labeled examples by increasing distance.

3. Find a heuristically optimal number k of nearest neighbors, based on RMSE. This is done using cross validation.

4. Calculate an inverse distance weighted average with the k-nearest multivariate neighbors.

Validation of results

A confusion matrix or "matching matrix" is often used as a tool to validate the accuracy of k-NN classification. More robust statistical methods such as likelihood-ratio test can also be applied.

Algorithms for hyperparameter optimization

Grid search

The *de facto* standard way of performing hyperparameter optimization is **grid search**, which is simply an exhaustive searching through a manually specified subset of the hyperparameter space of a learning algorithm. A grid search algorithm must be guided by some performance metric, typically measured by cross-validation on the training set (Hsu, Chang, & Lin, 2010) or evaluation on a held-out validation set.

Since the parameter space of a machine learner may include real-valued or unbounded value spaces for certain parameters, manually set bounds and discretization may be necessary before applying grid search.

For example, a typical soft-margin SVM classifier equipped with an RBF kernel has at least two hyperparameters that need to be tuned for good performance on unseen data: a regularization constant C and a kernel hyperparameter γ. Both parameters are continuous, so to perform grid search, one selects a finite set of "reasonable" values for each, say

$$C \in \{10,100,1000\}$$

$$\gamma \in \{0.1,0.2,0.5,1.0\}$$

Grid search then trains an SVM with each pair (C,γ) in the Cartesian product of these two sets and evaluates their performance on a held-out validation set (or by internal cross-validation on the training set, in which case multiple SVMs are trained per pair). Finally, the grid search algorithm outputs the settings that achieved the highest score in the validation procedure.

Grid search suffers from the curse of dimensionality, but is often embarrassingly parallel because typically the hyperparameter settings it evaluates are independent of each other (Bergstra & Bengio, 2012).

Alternatives

Since grid searching is an exhaustive and therefore potentially expensive method, several alternatives have been proposed. In particular, a randomized search that simply samples parameter settings a fixed number of times has been found to be more effective in high-dimensional spaces than exhaustive search (Bergstra & Bengio, 2012).

For specific learning algorithms, specialized model selection algorithms can be used. E.g., Chapelle *et al.* present a gradient descent algorithm for minimizing the estimated generalization error of a support vector machine (Chapelle, Vapnik, Bousquet, & Mukherjee, 2002).

Software

To perform the k-NN method, it is best to use R, k-NN Forest, or SPSS Modeler.

Example Using R

In this example, we will show how to use R's knn() function which implements the k-Nearest Neighbors (kNN) algorithm in a simple scenario which you can extend to cover your more complex and practical scenarios. The function knn() is part of the `class` package.

To simplify the demonstration of *kNN* and make it easy to follow, we will have only two classes used in object classification, which we label *A* and *B*.

Objects in classes *A* and *B* have two numeric attributes/properties that we map to *X* and *Y* Cartesian coordinates so that we can plot class instances (cases) as points on a 2-D chart. In other words, our cases are represented as points with *X* and *Y* coordinates ($p(X, Y)$).

Our simple classes *A* and *B* will have 3 object instances (cases) each.

Class *A* will include points with coordinates (0,0), (1,1), and (2,2). Class *B* will include points with coordinates (6,6), (5.5, 7), and (6.5, 5).

In R, we can write down the above arrangement as follows:

Class *A* training object instances (cases)

```
> A1=c(0,0)
> A2=c(1,1)
> A3=c(2,2)
```

Class *B* training objects instances (cases)

```
> B1=c(6,6)
> B2=c(5.5,7)
> B3=c(6.5,5)
```

Here is how the classification training objects for class *A* and class *B* are arranged on the chart.

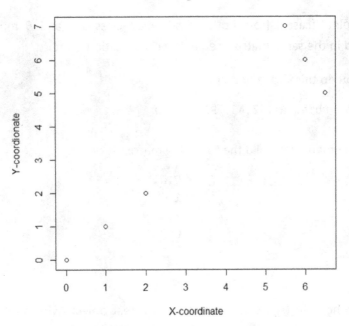

Figure 6. Classification Training Data Set, using plot(train ,main = "The knn Algorithm Demo", xlab = "X-coordinate", ylab = "Y-coordinate")

The knn() function is housed in the class package (it is also in the FNN package) and is invoked as follows:

```
knn(train, test, cl, k),
```

where

- **train** is a matrix or a data frame of training (classification) cases
- **test** is a matrix or a data frame of test case(s) (one or more rows)
- **cl** is a vector of classification labels (with the number of elements matching the number of classes in the training data set)
- **k** is an integer value of closest cases (the k in the k-Nearest Neighbor Algorithm); normally, it is a small odd integer number

For full description of the knn() function, read its help page that you can see by typing ?knn in the R console.

The points (cases) from both classification classes A and B must be packed in the same matrix used in the classification exercise.

In R you do this with a one-liner:

```
> train=rbind(A1,A2,A3, B1,B2,B3)
```

This command will build the following matrix:

A1:	0.0	0
A2:	1.0	1
A3:	2.0	2
B1:	6.0	6
B2:	5.5	7
B3: 6.5 5		

Now, when we try out classification of a test object (with properties expressed as X and Y coordinates), the *kNN* algorithm will use the **Euclidean distance metric** calculated for every row (case) in the training matrix to find the closest one for $k = 1$ and the majority of closest ones for $k > 1$ (where k should be an odd number).

We also need to construct the c1 parameter (the vector of classification labels). We can do this with this command:

```
> cl=factor(c(rep("A",3),rep("B",3)))
```

This command uses the factor() function to create a vector of factors (discrete, enumerated values) that are used as class literals. In our setup, we have two factors (a.k.a. levels): A and B.

The rep() function replicates the first parameter (a printable symbol) the number of times passed on to it as the second parameter.

The resulting factor vector has the following content: A A A B B B (3 A's followed by 3 B's to match the layout of our train cases – we have 3 cases of A followed by 3 cases of B).

To run the knn() function, we need to supply the test case(s). In our runs, we will start with a single test object that we create as follows:

```
> test=c(4,4)
```

which corresponds to a point sitting approximately in the middle of the distance between A and B.

At this point, we have everything in place to run knn(). Let's do it for $k = 1$ (classification by its proximity to a single neighbor).

For more informative reports of test object classification results, we are going to use the summary() function that can polymorphically act on its input parameter depending on its type. In our case, the input parameter to the summary() function is the output of the knn() function.

This is how the nested call looks like:

```
> summary(knn(train, test, cl, k = 1))
```

Here is the complete code listing that you can copy and paste into the R console.

```
# Class A cases
A1=c(0,0)
A2=c(1,1)
A3=c(2,2)

# Class B cases
B1=c(6,6)
B2=c(5.5,7)
B3=c(6.5,5)

# Build the classification matrix
train=rbind(A1,A2,A3, B1,B2,B3)

# Class labels vector (attached to each class instance)
cl=factor(c(rep("A",3),rep("B",3)))
```

```
# The object to be classified
test=c(4, 4)

# Load the class package that holds the knn() function
library(class)

# call knn() and get its summary
summary(knn(train, test, cl, k = 1))

# End of listing
```

After pasting the above code in the R console, press **ENTER** to submit it to the R interpreter for execution.

You should see the following output in your console:

```
A                                                    B
0 1
```

This result indicates that the test case has been classified as belonging to class B.

Type in the following command in console:

```
> test=c(3.5, 3.5)
```

Visually, this test case point looks to be closer to the cluster of the A class cases (points). Let's verify our assumption.

Repeat the same knn `summary` command as we did a moment ago:

```
> summary(knn(train, test, cl, k = 1))
```

The result comes back as we expected:

```
A                                                    B
1 0
```

The point has been classified as belonging to class A.

Let's increase the number of closest neighbors that are involved in voting during the classification step.

Type in the following command:

```
> summary(knn(train, test, cl, k = 3))
```

Now, the positions of class B points make them closer as a whole (according to the Euclidean distance metric) to the test point, so the (3.5, 3.5) case is classified as belonging to class B this time.

A   B
0 1

If you wish, you can further experiment with the k number (this is one of the exercises data scientists perform trying out better fitting classification models).

Now, let's build a matrix of test cases containing four points:

(4,4) - should be classified as B
(3,3) - should be classified as A
(5,6) - should be classified as B
(7,7) - should be classified as B

As a result, we should be expecting our test batch to have 3 cases (points) classified as belonging to the B class and one A case.

Type in the following code:

```
> test = matrix (c(4,4,3,3,5,6,7,7), ncol=2, byrow=TRUE)
```

This command will help us map our points into a two-column matrix containing the X and Y coordinates of our test points.

Now run again the previous knn summary command:

```
> summary(knn(train, test, cl, k = 3))
```

R should print the following summary of its classification job:

A   B
1 3

Which supports our assumptions.

15. Analysis of variance

Analysis of variance (ANOVA) is a collection of statistical models used to analyze the differences between group means and their associated procedures (such as "variation" among and between groups), developed by R.A. Fisher. In the ANOVA setting, the observed variance in a particular variable is partitioned into components attributable to different sources of variation. In its simplest form, ANOVA provides a statistical test of whether or not the means of several groups are equal, and therefore generalizes the t-test to more than two groups. As doing multiple two-sample t-tests would result in an increased chance of committing a statistical type I error, ANOVAs are useful in comparing (testing) three or more means (groups or variables) for statistical significance.

Motivating example

The analysis of variance can be used as an exploratory tool to explain observations. A dog show provides an example. A dog show is not a random sampling of the breed: it is typically limited to dogs that are male, adult, pure-bred and exemplary. A histogram of dog weights from a show might plausibly be rather complex, like the yellow-orange distribution shown in the illustrations. Suppose we wanted to predict the weight of a dog based on a certain set of characteristics of each dog. Before we could do that, we would need to explain the distribution of weights by dividing the dog population into groups based on those characteristics. A successful grouping will split dogs such that a) each group has a low variance of dog weights (meaning the group is relatively homogeneous) and b) the mean of each group is distinct (if two groups have the same mean, then it isn't reasonable to conclude that the groups are, in fact, separate in any meaningful way).

In the illustrations below, each group is identified as X_1, X_2, etc. In the first illustration, we divide the dogs according to the product (interaction) of two binary groupings: young vs old, and short-haired vs long-haired (thus, group 1 is young, short-haired dogs, group 2 is young, long-haired dogs, etc.). Since the distributions of dog weight within each of the groups (shown in blue) has a large variance, and since the means are very close across groups, grouping dogs by these characteristics does not produce an effective way to explain the variation in dog weights: knowing which group a dog is in does not allow us to make any reasonable statements as to what that dog's weight is likely to be. Thus, this grouping fails to fit the distribution we are trying to explain (yellow-orange).

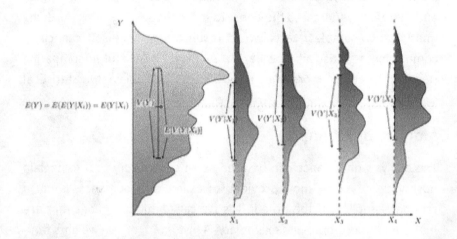

No fit.

An attempt to explain the weight distribution by grouping dogs as (pet vs working breed) and (less athletic vs more athletic) would probably be somewhat more successful (fair fit). The heaviest show dogs are likely to be big strong working breeds, while breeds kept as pets tend to be smaller and thus lighter. As shown by the second illustration, the distributions have variances that are considerably smaller than in the first case, and the means are more reasonably distinguishable.

314

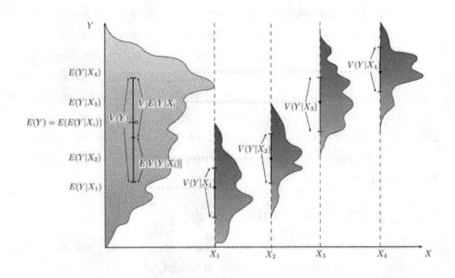

Fair fit

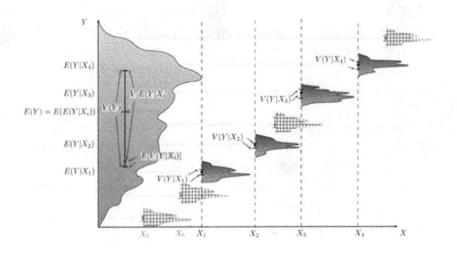

Very good fit

However, the significant overlap of distributions, for example, means that we cannot reliably say that X_1 and X_2 are truly distinct (i.e., it is perhaps reasonably likely that splitting dogs according to the flip of a coin—by pure chance—might produce distributions that look similar).

An attempt to explain weight by breed is likely to produce a very good fit. All Chihuahuas are light and all St. Bernards are heavy. The difference in weights between Setters and Pointers does not justify separate breeds. The analysis of variance provides the formal tools to justify these intuitive judgments. A common use of the method is the analysis of experimental data or the development of models. The method has some advantages over correlation: not all of the data must be numeric and one result of the method is a judgment in the confidence in an explanatory relationship.

Background and terminology

ANOVA is a particular form of statistical hypothesis testing heavily used in the analysis of experimental data. A statistical hypothesis test is a method of making decisions using data. A test result (calculated from the null hypothesis and the sample) is called statistically significant if it is deemed unlikely to have occurred by chance, assuming the truth of the null hypothesis. A statistically significant result, when a probability (p-value) is less than a threshold (significance level), justifies the rejection of the null hypothesis, but only if the a priori probability of the null hypothesis is not high.

In the typical application of ANOVA, the null hypothesis is that all groups are simply random samples of the same population. For example, when studying the effect of different treatments on similar samples of patients, the null hypothesis would be that all treatments have the same effect (perhaps none). Rejecting the null hypothesis would imply that different treatments result in altered effects.

By construction, hypothesis testing limits the rate of Type I errors (false positives leading to false scientific claims) to a significance level. Experimenters also wish to limit Type-II errors (false negatives resulting in missed scientific discoveries). The Type II error rate is a function of several things including sample size (positively correlated with experiment cost), significance level (when the standard of proof is high, the chances of overlooking a discovery are also high) and effect size (when the effect is obvious to the casual observer, Type II error rates are low).

The terminology of ANOVA is largely from the statistical design of experiments. The experimenter adjusts factors and measures responses in an attempt to determine an effect. Factors are assigned to experimental units by a combination of randomization and blocking to ensure the validity of the results. Blinding keeps the weighing impartial. Responses show a variability that is partially the result of the effect and is partially random error.

ANOVA is the synthesis of several ideas and it is used for multiple purposes. As a consequence, it is difficult to define concisely or precisely.

Classical ANOVA for balanced data does three things at once:

1. As exploratory data analysis, an ANOVA is an organization of an additive data decomposition, and its sums of squares indicate the variance of each component of the decomposition (or, equivalently, each set of terms of a linear model).

2. Comparisons of mean squares, along with F-tests ... allow testing of a nested sequence of models.

3. Closely related to the ANOVA is a linear model fit with coefficient estimates and standard errors (Gelman, 2005).

In short, ANOVA is a statistical tool used in several ways to develop and confirm an explanation for the observed data.

Additionally:

1. It is computationally elegant and relatively robust against violations of its assumptions.

2. ANOVA provides industrial strength (multiple sample comparison) statistical analysis.

3. It has been adapted to the analysis of a variety of experimental designs.

As a result: ANOVA "has long enjoyed the status of being the most used (some would say abused) statistical technique in psychological research." (Howell, 2002) ANOVA "is probably the most useful technique in the field of statistical inference." (Montgomery, 2001)

ANOVA is difficult to teach, particularly for complex experiments, with split-plot designs being notorious (Gelman, 2005). In some cases the proper application of the method is best determined by problem pattern recognition followed by the consultation of a classic authoritative test (Gelman, 2005).

Design-of-experiments terms

(Condensed from the NIST Engineering Statistics handbook: Section 5.7. A Glossary of DOE Terminology.) (NIST, 2012)

Balanced design
An experimental design where all cells (i.e. treatment combinations) have the same number of observations.

Blocking
A schedule for conducting treatment combinations in an experimental study such that any effects on the experimental results due to a known change in raw materials, operators, machines, etc., become concentrated in the levels of the blocking variable. The reason for blocking is to isolate a systematic effect and prevent it from obscuring the main effects. Blocking is achieved by restricting randomization.

Design
A set of experimental runs which allows the fit of a particular model and the estimate of effects.

DOE
Design of experiments. An approach to problem solving involving collection of data that will support valid, defensible, and supportable

conclusions (NIST, 2012).

Effect
How changing the settings of a factor changes the response. The effect of a single factor is also called a main effect.

Error
Unexplained variation in a collection of observations. DOE's typically require understanding of both random error and lack of fit error.

Experimental unit
The entity to which a specific treatment combination is applied.

Factors
Process inputs an investigator manipulates to cause a change in the output.

Lack-of-fit error
Error that occurs when the analysis omits one or more important terms or factors from the process model. Including replication in a DOE allows separation of experimental error into its components: lack of fit and random (pure) error.

Model
Mathematical relationship which relates changes in a given response to changes in one or more factors.

Random error
Error that occurs due to natural variation in the process. Random error is typically assumed to be normally distributed with zero mean and a constant variance. Random error is also called experimental error.

Randomization
A schedule for allocating treatment material and for conducting treatment combinations in a DOE such that the conditions in one run neither depend on the conditions of the previous run nor predict the conditions in the subsequent runs.

Replication
Performing the same treatment combination more than once. Including replication allows an estimate of the random error independent of any lack of fit error.

Responses
The output(s) of a process. Sometimes called dependent variable(s).

Treatment
A treatment is a specific combination of factor levels whose effect is to be compared with other treatments.

Classes of models

There are three classes of models used in the analysis of variance, and these are outlined here.

Fixed-effects models

The fixed-effects model of analysis of variance applies to situations in which the experimenter applies one or more treatments to the subjects of the experiment to see if the response variable values change. This allows the experimenter to estimate the ranges of response variable values that the treatment would generate in the population as a whole.

Random-effects models

Random effects models are used when the treatments are not fixed. This occurs when the various factor levels are sampled from a larger population. Because the levels themselves are random variables, some assumptions and the method of contrasting the treatments (a multi-variable generalization of simple differences) differ from the fixed-effects model (Montgomery, 2001).

Mixed-effects models

A mixed-effects model contains experimental factors of both fixed and random-effects types, with appropriately different interpretations and analysis for the two types.

Example: Teaching experiments could be performed by a university department to find a good introductory textbook, with each text considered a treatment. The fixed-effects model would compare a list of candidate texts. The random-effects model would determine whether important differences exist among a list of randomly selected texts. The mixed-effects model would compare the (fixed) incumbent texts to randomly selected alternatives.

Defining fixed and random effects has proven elusive, with competing definitions arguably leading toward a linguistic quagmire (Gelman, 2005).

Assumptions of ANOVA

The analysis of variance has been studied from several approaches, the most common of which uses a linear model that relates the response to the treatments and blocks. Note that the model is linear in parameters but may be nonlinear across factor levels. Interpretation is easy when data is balanced across factors but much deeper understanding is needed for unbalanced data.

Textbook analysis using a normal distribution

The analysis of variance can be presented in terms of a linear model, which makes the following assumptions about the probability distribution of the responses (Snedecor & Cochran, 1989) (Cochran & Cox, 1992):

- Independence of observations – this is an assumption of the model that simplifies the statistical analysis.
- Normality – the distributions of the residuals are normal.
- Equality (or "homogeneity") of variances, called homoscedasticity — the variance of data in groups should be the same.

The separate assumptions of the textbook model imply that the errors are independently, identically, and normally distributed for fixed effects models, that is, that the errors (ε's) are independent and $\varepsilon \sim N(0, \sigma^2)$.

Randomization-based analysis

In a randomized controlled experiment, the treatments are randomly assigned to experimental units, following the experimental protocol. This randomization is objective and declared before the experiment is carried out. The objective random-assignment is used to test the significance of the null hypothesis, following the ideas of C. S. Peirce (Peirce, 1992) and Ronald A. Fisher (Fisher & Prance, 1974). This design-based analysis was discussed and developed by Francis J. Anscombe at Rothamsted Experimental Station and by Oscar Kempthorne (Hinkelmann & Kempthorne, 2008) at Iowa State University (Anscombe, 1948). Kempthorne and his students make an assumption of unit treatment additivity, which is discussed in the books of Kempthorne and David R. Cox (Cox, 1992).

Unit-treatment additivity

In its simplest form, the assumption of unit-treatment additivity[states that the observed response $y_{i,j}$ from experimental unit i when receiving treatment j can be written as the sum of the unit's response y_i and the treatment-effect t_j, that is (Kempthorne, 1979) (Cox, 1992) (Hinkelmann & Kempthorne, 2008)

$$y_{i,j} = y_i + t_j.$$

The assumption of unit-treatment additivity implies that, for every treatment j, the jth treatment have exactly the same effect t_j on every experiment unit.

The assumption of unit treatment additivity usually cannot be directly falsified, according to Cox and Kempthorne (Cox, 1992) (Kempthorne, 1979). However, many consequences of treatment-unit additivity can be falsified. For a randomized experiment, the assumption of unit-treatment additivity implies that the variance is constant for all treatments. Therefore, by contraposition, a necessary condition for unit-treatment additivity is that the variance is constant.

The use of unit treatment additivity and randomization is similar to the

322

design-based inference that is standard in finite-population survey sampling.

Derived linear model

Kempthorne uses the randomization-distribution and the assumption of unit-treatment additivity to produce a derived linear model, very similar to the textbook model discussed previously (Hinkelmann & Kempthorne, 2008).] The test statistics of this derived linear model are closely approximated by the test statistics of an appropriate normal linear model, according to approximation theorems and simulation studies (Hinkelmann & Kempthorne, 2008). However, there are differences. For example, the randomization-based analysis results in a small but (strictly) negative correlation between the observations (Bailey, 2008) (Hinkelmann & Kempthorne, 2008). In the randomization-based analysis, there is no assumption of a normal distribution and certainly no assumption of independence. On the contrary, the observations are dependent.

The randomization-based analysis has the disadvantage that its exposition involves tedious algebra and extensive time. Since the randomization-based analysis is complicated and is closely approximated by the approach using a normal linear model, most teachers emphasize the normal linear model approach. Few statisticians object to model-based analysis of balanced randomized experiments.

Statistical models for observational data

However, when applied to data from non-randomized experiments or observational studies, model-based analysis lacks the warrant of randomization (Kempthorne, 1979). For observational data, the derivation of confidence intervals must use subjective models, as emphasized by Ronald A. Fisher and his followers. In practice, the estimates of treatment-effects from observational studies generally are often inconsistent. In practice, "statistical models" and observational data are useful for suggesting hypotheses that should be treated very cautiously by the public (Freedman, 2005).

323

Summary of assumptions

The normal-model based ANOVA analysis assumes the independence, normality and homogeneity of the variances of the residuals. The randomization-based analysis assumes only the homogeneity of the variances of the residuals (as a consequence of unit-treatment additivity) and uses the randomization procedure of the experiment. Both these analyses require homoscedasticity, as an assumption for the normal-model analysis and as a consequence of randomization and additivity for the randomization-based analysis.

However, studies of processes that change variances rather than means (called dispersion effects) have been successfully conducted using ANOVA (Montgomery, 2001). There are no necessary assumptions for ANOVA in its full generality, but the F-test used for ANOVA hypothesis testing has assumptions and practical limitations which are of continuing interest.

Problems which do not satisfy the assumptions of ANOVA can often be transformed to satisfy the assumptions. The property of unit-treatment additivity is not invariant under a "change of scale", so statisticians often use transformations to achieve unit-treatment additivity. If the response variable is expected to follow a parametric family of probability distributions, then the statistician may specify (in the protocol for the experiment or observational study) that the responses be transformed to stabilize the variance (Hinkelmann & Kempthorne, 2008). Also, a statistician may specify that logarithmic transforms be applied to the responses, which are believed to follow a multiplicative model (Cox, 1992) (Bailey, 2008). According to Cauchy's functional equation theorem, the logarithm is the only continuous transformation that transforms real multiplication to addition.

Characteristics of ANOVA

ANOVA is used in the analysis of comparative experiments, those in which only the difference in outcomes is of interest. The statistical significance of the experiment is determined by a ratio of two variances.

This ratio is independent of several possible alterations to the experimental observations: Adding a constant to all observations does not alter significance. Multiplying all observations by a constant does not alter significance. So ANOVA statistical significance results are independent of constant bias and scaling errors as well as the units used in expressing observations. In the era of mechanical calculation it was common to subtract a constant from all observations (when equivalent to dropping leading digits) to simplify data entry (Montgomery, 2001) (Cochran & Cox, 1992). This is an example of data coding.

Logic of ANOVA

The calculations of ANOVA can be characterized as computing a number of means and variances, dividing two variances and comparing the ratio to a handbook value to determine statistical significance. Calculating a treatment effect is then trivial, "the effect of any treatment is estimated by taking the difference between the mean of the observations which receive the treatment and the general mean." (Cochran & Cox, 1992)

Partitioning of the sum of squares

ANOVA uses traditional standardized terminology. The definitional equation of sample variance is $s^2 = \frac{1}{n-q}\sum(y_i - \bar{y})^2$, where the divisor is called the degrees of freedom (DF), the summation is called the sum of squares (SS), the result is called the mean square (MS) and the squared terms are deviations from the sample mean. ANOVA estimates 3 sample variances: a total variance based on all the observation deviations from the grand mean, an error variance based on all the observation deviations from their appropriate treatment means and a treatment variance. The treatment variance is based on the deviations of treatment means from the grand mean, the result being multiplied by the number of observations in each treatment to account for the difference between the variance of observations and the variance of means.

The fundamental technique is a partitioning of the total sum of squares

SS into components related to the effects used in the model. For example, the model for a simplified ANOVA with one type of treatment at different levels:

$$SS_{\text{Total}} = SS_{\text{Error}} + SS_{\text{Treatments}}.$$

The number of degrees of freedom DF can be partitioned in a similar way: one of these components (that for error) specifies a chi-squared distribution which describes the associated sum of squares, while the same is true for "treatments" if there is no treatment effect:

$$DF_{\text{Total}} = DF_{\text{Error}} + DF_{\text{Treatments}}.$$

The F-test

The F-test is used for comparing the factors of the total deviation. For example, in one-way, or single-factor ANOVA, statistical significance is tested for by comparing the F test statistic

$$F =$$

variance between treatments/variance within treatments

$$F = \frac{MS_{\text{Treatments}}}{MS_{\text{Error}}} = \frac{SS_{\text{Treatments}}/(I-1)}{SS_{\text{Error}}/(n_T - I)}$$

where MS is mean square, I = number of treatments and n_T = total number of cases to the F-distribution with $I - 1$, $n_T - I$ degrees of freedom. Using the F-distribution is a natural candidate because the test statistic is the ratio of two scaled sums of squares each of which follows a scaled chi-squared distribution.

The expected value of F is $1 + n\sigma^2_{\text{Treatment}}/\sigma^2_{\text{Error}}$ (where n is the treatment sample size) which is 1 for no treatment effect. As values of F increase above 1, the evidence is increasingly inconsistent with the null hypothesis. Two apparent experimental methods of increasing F are increasing the sample size and reducing the error variance by tight experimental controls.

There are two methods of concluding the ANOVA hypothesis test, both of which produce the same result:

- The textbook method is to compare the observed value of F with the critical value of F determined from tables. The critical value of F is a function of the degrees of freedom of the numerator and the denominator and the significance level (α). If $F \geq F_{\text{Critical}}$, the null hypothesis is rejected.
- The computer method calculates the probability (p-value) of a value of F greater than or equal to the observed value. The null hypothesis is rejected if this probability is less than or equal to the significance level (α).

The ANOVA F-test is known to be nearly optimal in the sense of minimizing false negative errors for a fixed rate of false positive errors (i.e. maximizing power for a fixed significance level). For example, to test the hypothesis that various medical treatments have exactly the same effect, the F-test's p-values closely approximate the permutation test's p-values: The approximation is particularly close when the design is balanced (Hinkelmann & Kempthorne, 2008). Such permutation tests characterize tests with maximum power against all alternative hypotheses, as observed by Rosenbaum (Rosenbaum, 2002). The ANOVA F–test (of the null-hypothesis that all treatments have exactly the same effect) is recommended as a practical test, because of its robustness against many alternative distributions (Moore & McCabe, 2003).

Extended logic

ANOVA consists of separable parts; partitioning sources of variance and hypothesis testing can be used individually. ANOVA is used to support other statistical tools. Regression is first used to fit more complex models to data, then ANOVA is used to compare models with the objective of selecting simple(r) models that adequately describe the data. "Such models could be fit without any reference to ANOVA, but ANOVA tools could then be used to make some sense of the fitted models, and to test hypotheses about batches of coefficients." (Gelman, 2005) "[W]e think of the analysis of variance as a way of understanding and structuring multilevel models—not as an alternative to regression but as a tool for summarizing complex high-dimensional inferences ..." (Gelman, 2005)

ANOVA for a single factor

The simplest experiment suitable for ANOVA analysis is the completely randomized experiment with a single factor. More complex experiments with a single factor involve constraints on randomization and include completely randomized blocks and Latin squares (and variants: Graeco-Latin squares, etc.). The more complex experiments share many of the complexities of multiple factors. A relatively complete discussion of the analysis (models, data summaries, ANOVA table) of the completely randomized experiment is available.

ANOVA for multiple factors

ANOVA generalizes to the study of the effects of multiple factors. When the experiment includes observations at all combinations of levels of each factor, it is termed factorial. Factorial experiments are more efficient than a series of single factor experiments and the efficiency grows as the number of factors increases (Montgomery, 2001). Consequently, factorial designs are heavily used.

The use of ANOVA to study the effects of multiple factors has a complication. In a 3-way ANOVA with factors x, y and z, the ANOVA model includes terms for the main effects (x, y, z) and terms for interactions (xy, xz, yz, xyz). All terms require hypothesis tests. The proliferation of interaction terms increases the risk that some hypothesis test will produce a false positive by chance. Fortunately, experience says that high order interactions are rare (Belle, 2008). The ability to detect interactions is a major advantage of multiple factor ANOVA. Testing one factor at a time hides interactions, but produces apparently inconsistent experimental results (Montgomery, 2001).

Caution is advised when encountering interactions; Test interaction terms first and expand the analysis beyond ANOVA if interactions are found. Texts vary in their recommendations regarding the continuation of the ANOVA procedure after encountering an interaction. Interactions complicate the interpretation of experimental data. Neither the calculations of significance nor the estimated treatment effects can be taken at face value. "A significant interaction will often mask the significance of main effects." (Montgomery, 2001) Graphical methods are recommended to enhance understanding. Regression is often useful. A lengthy discussion of interactions is available in Cox (1958) (Cox, 1992). Some interactions can be removed (by transformations) while others cannot.

A variety of techniques are used with multiple factor ANOVA to reduce expense. One technique used in factorial designs is to minimize replication (possibly no replication with support of analytical trickery) and to combine groups when effects are found to be statistically (or practically) insignificant. An experiment with many insignificant factors may collapse into one with a few factors supported by many replications (Montgomery, 2001).

Worked numeric examples

Several fully worked numerical examples are available in Neter, J., et al, *Applied Linear Statistical Models*. A simple case uses one-way (a single factor) analysis. A more complex case uses two-way (two-factor) analysis.

Associated analysis

Some analysis is required in support of the design of the experiment while other analysis is performed after changes in the factors are formally found to produce statistically significant changes in the responses. Because experimentation is iterative, the results of one experiment alter plans for following experiments.

Preparatory analysis

The number of experimental units

In the design of an experiment, the number of experimental units is planned to satisfy the goals of the experiment. Experimentation is often sequential.

Early experiments are often designed to provide mean-unbiased estimates of treatment effects and of experimental error. Later experiments are often designed to test a hypothesis that a treatment effect has an important magnitude; in this case, the number of experimental units is chosen so that the experiment is within budget and has adequate power, among other goals.

Reporting sample size analysis is generally required in psychology. "Provide information on sample size and the process that led to sample size decisions." (Wilkinson, 1999) The analysis, which is written in the experimental protocol before the experiment is conducted, is examined in grant applications and administrative review boards.

Besides the power analysis, there are less formal methods for selecting the number of experimental units. These include graphical methods based on limiting the probability of false negative errors, graphical methods based on an expected variation increase (above the residuals) and methods based on achieving a desired confident interval (Montgomery, 2001).

Power analysis

Power analysis is often applied in the context of ANOVA in order to assess the probability of successfully rejecting the null hypothesis if we assume a certain ANOVA design, effect size in the population, sample size and significance level. Power analysis can assist in study design by determining what sample size would be required in order to have a reasonable chance of rejecting the null hypothesis when the alternative hypothesis is true (Moore & McCabe, 2003) (Howell, 2002).

Effect size

Several standardized measures of effect have been proposed for ANOVA to summarize the strength of the association between a predictor(s) and the dependent variable (e.g., η^2, ω^2, or f^2) or the overall standardized difference (Ψ) of the complete model. Standardized effect-size estimates facilitate comparison of findings across studies and disciplines. However, while standardized effect sizes are commonly used in much of the professional literature, a non-standardized measure of effect size that has immediately "meaningful" units may be preferable for reporting purposes (Wilkinson, 1999).

Followup analysis

It is always appropriate to carefully consider outliers. They have a disproportionate impact on statistical conclusions and are often the result of errors.

Model confirmation

It is prudent to verify that the assumptions of ANOVA have been met. Residuals are examined or analyzed to confirm homoscedasticity and gross normality (Montgomery, 2001). Residuals should have the appearance of (zero mean normal distribution) noise when plotted as a function of anything including time and modeled data values. Trends hint at interactions among factors or among observations. One rule of thumb: "If the largest standard deviation is less than twice the smallest standard deviation, we can use methods based on the assumption of equal standard deviations and our results will still be approximately correct." (Moore & McCabe, 2003)

Follow-up tests

A statistically significant effect in ANOVA is often followed up with one or more different follow-up tests. This can be done in order to assess which groups are different from which other groups or to test various other focused hypotheses. Follow-up tests are often distinguished in terms of whether they are planned (*a priori*) or *post hoc*. Planned tests are determined before looking at the data and post hoc tests are performed after looking at the data.

Often one of the "treatments" is none, so the treatment group can act as a control. Dunnett's test (a modification of the t-test) tests whether each of the other treatment groups has the same mean as the control (Montgomery, 2001).

Post hoc tests such as Tukey's range test most commonly compare every group mean with every other group mean and typically incorporate some method of controlling for Type I errors. Comparisons, which are most commonly planned, can be either simple or compound. Simple comparisons compare one group mean with one other group mean. Compound comparisons typically compare two sets of group means where one set has two or more groups (e.g., compare average group means of group A, B and C with group D). Comparisons can also look at tests of trend, such as linear and quadratic relationships, when the independent variable involves ordered levels.

Following ANOVA with pair-wise multiple-comparison tests has been criticized on several grounds (Hinkelmann & Kempthorne, 2008) (Wilkinson, 1999). There are many such tests (10 in one table) and recommendations regarding their use are vague or conflicting (Howell, 2002) (Montgomery, 2001).

Study designs and ANOVAs

There are several types of ANOVA. Many statisticians base ANOVA on the design of the experiment (Cochran & Cox, 1992), especially on the protocol that specifies the random assignment of treatments to subjects; the protocol's description of the assignment mechanism should include a specification of the structure of the treatments and of any blocking. It is also common to apply ANOVA to observational data using an appropriate statistical model.

Some popular designs use the following types of ANOVA:

• One-way ANOVA is used to test for differences among two or more independent groups (means), e.g., different levels of urea application in a crop. Typically, however, the one-way ANOVA is used to test for differences among at least three groups, since the two-group case can be covered by a t-test. When there are only two means to compare, the t-test and the ANOVA F-test are equivalent; the relation between ANOVA and t is given by $F = t^2$.

- Factorial ANOVA is used when the experimenter wants to study the interaction effects among the treatments.
- Repeated measures ANOVA is used when the same subjects are used for each treatment (e.g., in a longitudinal study).
- Multivariate analysis of variance (MANOVA) is used when there is more than one response variable.

ANOVA cautions

Balanced experiments (those with an equal sample size for each treatment) are relatively easy to interpret; unbalanced experiments offer more complexity. For single factor (one way) ANOVA, the adjustment for unbalanced data is easy, but the unbalanced analysis lacks both robustness and power (Montgomery, 2001). For more complex designs the lack of balance leads to further complications. "The orthogonality property of main effects and interactions present in balanced data does not carry over to the unbalanced case. This means that the usual analysis of variance techniques do not apply. Consequently, the analysis of unbalanced factorials is much more difficult than that for balanced designs." (Montgomery, 2001) In the general case, "The analysis of variance can also be applied to unbalanced data, but then the sums of squares, mean squares, and F-ratios will depend on the order in which the sources of variation are considered." (Gelman, 2005) The simplest techniques for handling unbalanced data restore balance by either throwing out data or by synthesizing missing data. More complex techniques use regression.

ANOVA is (in part) a significance test. The American Psychological Association holds the view that simply reporting significance is insufficient and that reporting confidence bounds is preferred

(Wilkinson, 1999).

While ANOVA is conservative (in maintaining a significance level) against multiple comparisons in one dimension, it is not conservative against comparisons in multiple dimensions (Wilkinson, 1999).

Generalizations

ANOVA is considered to be a special case of linear regression (Gelman, 2005) which in turn is a special case of the general linear model (Howell, 2002). All consider the observations to be the sum of a model (fit) and a residual (error) to be minimized. The Kruskal–Wallis test and the Friedman test are nonparametric tests, which do not rely on an assumption of normality (Montgomery, 2001).

History

While the analysis of variance reached fruition in the 20th century, antecedents extend centuries into the past according to Stigler (Stigler, 1986). These include hypothesis testing, the partitioning of sums of squares, experimental techniques and the additive model. Laplace was performing hypothesis testing in the 1770s. The development of least-squares methods by Laplace and Gauss circa 1800 provided an improved method of combining observations (over the existing practices of astronomy and geodesy). It also initiated much study of the contributions to sums of squares. Laplace soon knew how to estimate a variance from a residual (rather than a total) sum of squares. By 1827 Laplace was using least squares methods to address ANOVA problems regarding measurements of atmospheric tides. Before 1800 astronomers had isolated observational errors resulting from reaction times (the "personal equation") and had developed methods of reducing the errors. The experimental methods used in the study of the personal equation were later accepted by the emerging field of psychology which developed strong (full factorial) experimental methods to which randomization and blinding were soon added. An eloquent non-mathematical explanation of the additive effects model was available in

1885 (Stigler, 1986).

Sir Ronald Fisher introduced the term "variance" and proposed a formal analysis of variance in a 1918 article *The Correlation Between Relatives on the Supposition of Mendelian Inheritance* (Fisher R. A., 1918). His first application of the analysis of variance was published in 1921 (Fisher R. A., Probable Error" of a Coefficient of Correlation Deduced from a Small Sample, 1921). Analysis of variance became widely known after being included in Fisher's 1925 book, *Statistical Methods for Research Workers* (Edwards, 1925).

Randomization models were developed by several researchers. The first was published in Polish by Neyman in 1923 (Scheffé, 1959).

One of the attributes of ANOVA which ensured its early popularity was computational elegance. The structure of the additive model allows solution for the additive coefficients by simple algebra rather than by matrix calculations. In the era of mechanical calculators this simplicity was critical. The determination of statistical significance also required access to tables of the F function which were supplied by early statistics texts.

Software

All the primary software packages discussed in Chapter 2 have this functionality.

Example Using R

This example requires the R `stats` package. There are three groups with seven observations per group. We denote group i values by y_i:

```
> y1 = c(18.2, 20.1, 17.6, 16.8, 18.8, 19.7, 19.1)
> y2 = c(17.4, 18.7, 19.1, 16.4, 15.9, 18.4, 17.7)
> y3 = c(15.2, 18.8, 17.7, 16.5, 15.9, 17.1, 16.7)
> local({pkg <- select.list(sort(.packages(all.available =
+ TRUE)), graphics=TRUE)
+ if(nchar(pkg)) library(pkg, character.only=TRUE)})
```

Now we combine them into one long vector, with a second vector, group, identifying group membership:

```
> y = c(y1, y2, y3)
> n = rep(7, 3)
> n
[1] 7 7 7
> group = rep(1:3, n)
> group
 [1] 1 1 1 1 1 1 1 2 2 2 2 2 2 2 3 3 3 3 3 3 3
```

Here are summaries by group and for the combined data. First we show stem-leaf diagrams.

```
> tmp = tapply(y, group, stem)

  The decimal point is at the |

  16 | 8
  17 | 6
  18 | 28
  19 | 17
  20 | 1


  The decimal point is at the |

  15 | 9
  16 | 4
  17 | 47
  18 | 47
  19 | 1


  The decimal point is at the |

  15 | 29
  16 | 57
  17 | 17
```

```
18 | 8
```

```
> stem(y)
```

```
  The decimal point is at the |

  15 | 299
  16 | 4578
  17 | 14677
  18 | 24788
  19 | 117
  20 | 1
```

Now we show summary statistics by group and overall. We locally define a temporary function, tmpfn, to make this easier.

```
> tmpfn = function(x) c(sum = sum(x), mean = mean(x),
+              var = var(x),n = length(x))
> tapply(y, group, tmpfn)
$`1`
         sum        mean         var           n
  130.300000   18.614286    1.358095    7.000000

$`2`
         sum        mean         var           n
  123.600000   17.657143    1.409524    7.000000

$`3`
         sum        mean         var           n
  117.900000   16.842857    1.392857    7.000000

> tmpfn(y)
         sum        mean         var           n
  371.800000   17.704762    1.798476   21.000000
```

While we could show you how to use R to mimic the computation of SS by hand, it is more natural to go directly to the ANOVA table.

```
> data = data.frame(y = y, group = factor(group))
> fit = lm(y ~ group, data)
```

337

```
> anova(fit)
Analysis of Variance Table

Response: y
          Df Sum Sq Mean Sq F value  Pr(>F)
group      2 11.007  5.5033  3.9683 0.03735 *
Residuals 18 24.963  1.3868
---
Signif. codes:  0 '***' 0.001 '**' 0.01 '*' 0.05 '.' 0.1 '
' 1
```

The anova(fit) object can be used for other computations on the handout and in class. For instance, the tabled F values can be found by the following. First we extract the treatment and error degrees of freedom. Then we use qt to get the tabled F values.

```
> df = anova(fit)[, "Df"]
> names(df) = c("trt", "err")
> df
trt err
  2  18
> alpha = c(0.05, 0.01)
> qf(alpha, df["trt"], df["err"], lower.tail = FALSE)
[1] 3.554557 6.012905
```

A confidence interval on the pooled variance can be computed as well using the anova(fit) object. First we get the residual sum of squares, SSTrt, then we divide by the appropriate chi-square tabled values.

```
> anova(fit)["Residuals", "Sum Sq"]
[1] 24.96286
> anova(fit)["Residuals", "Sum Sq"]/qchisq(c(0.025, 0.975),
18)
[1] 3.0328790 0.7918086
anova(fit)["Residuals", "Sum Sq"]/qchisq(c(0.025, 0.975),
18,lower.tail = FALSE)
[1] 0.7918086 3.0328790
```

16. Support vector machines

In machine learning, support vector machines (SVMs, also support vector networks (Cortes & Vapnik, 1995)) are supervised learning models with associated learning algorithms that analyze data and recognize patterns, used for classification and regression analysis. Given a set of training examples, each marked as belonging to one of two categories, an SVM training algorithm builds a model that assigns new examples into one category or the other, making it a non-probabilistic binary linear classifier. An SVM model is a representation of the examples as points in space, mapped so that the examples of the separate categories are divided by a clear gap that is as wide as possible. New examples are then mapped into that same space and predicted to belong to a category based on which side of the gap they fall on.

In addition to performing linear classification, SVMs can efficiently perform a non-linear classification using what is called the kernel trick, implicitly mapping their inputs into high-dimensional feature spaces.

Definition

More formally, a support vector machine constructs a hyperplane or set of hyperplanes in a high- or infinite-dimensional space, which can be used for classification, regression, or other tasks. Intuitively, a good separation is achieved by the hyperplane that has the largest distance to the nearest training data point of any class (so-called functional margin), since in general the larger the margin the lower the generalization error of the classifier.

Whereas the original problem may be stated in a finite dimensional space, it often happens that the sets to discriminate are not linearly separable in that space. For this reason, it was proposed that the original finite-dimensional space be mapped into a much higher-dimensional space, presumably making the separation easier in that space. To keep the computational load reasonable, the mappings used by SVM schemes are designed to ensure that dot products may be computed easily in terms of the variables in the original space, by defining them in terms of a kernel function $K(x, y)$ selected to suit the problem (Press, Teukolsky, Vetterling, & Flannery, 2007). The hyperplanes in the higher-dimensional space are defined as the set of points whose dot product with a vector in that space is constant. The vectors defining the hyperplanes can be chosen to be linear combinations with parameters α_i of images of feature vectors that occur in the data base. With this choice of a hyperplane, the points in the feature space that are mapped into the hyperplane are defined by the relation: $\sum_i \alpha_i K(x_i, x) =$ constant. Note that if $K(x, y)$ becomes small as grows further away from, each term in the sum measures the degree of closeness of the test point to the corresponding data base point x_i. In this way, the sum of kernels above can be used to measure the relative nearness of each test point to the data points originating in one or the other of the sets to be discriminated. Note the fact that the set of points mapped into any hyperplane can be quite convoluted as a result, allowing much more complex discrimination between sets which are not convex at all in the original space.

History

The original SVM algorithm was invented by Vladimir N. Vapnik and the current standard incarnation (soft margin) was proposed by Corinna Cortes and Vapnik in 1993 and published in 1995 (Cortes & Vapnik, 1995).

Motivation

Classifying data is a common task in machine learning. Suppose some given data points each belong to one of two classes, and the goal is to decide which class a new data point will be in. In the case of support vector machines, a data point is viewed as a p-dimensional vector (a list of p numbers), and we want to know whether we can separate such points with a $(p-1)$-dimensional hyperplane. This is called a linear classifier. There are many hyperplanes that might classify the data. One reasonable choice as the best hyperplane is the one that represents the largest separation, or margin, between the two classes. So we choose the hyperplane so that the distance from it to the nearest data point on each side is maximized. If such a hyperplane exists, it is known as the maximum-margin hyperplane and the linear classifier it defines is known as a maximum margin classifier; or equivalently, the perceptron of optimal stability.

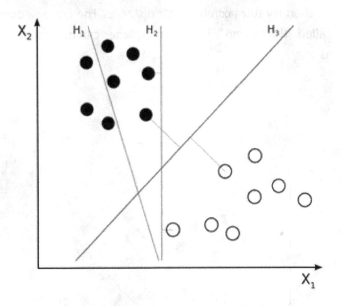

H_1 does not separate the classes. H_2 does, but small margin. H_3 separates them with the maximum margin.

Linear SVM

Given some training data $\mathcal{D}$ a set of n points of the form only with a

$$\mathcal{D} = \{(x_i, y_i) | x_i \in \mathbb{R}^p, y_i \in \{-1,1\}\}_{i=1}^n$$

where the y_i is either 1 or −1, indicating the class to which the point x_i belongs. Each x_i is a p-dimensional real vector. We want to find the maximum-margin hyperplane that divides the points having $y_i = 1$ from those having $y_i = -1$. Any hyperplane can be written as the set of points x satisfying

$$w \cdot x - b = 0,$$

341

where · denotes the dot product and w the (not necessarily normalized) normal vector to the hyperplane. The parameter $\frac{b}{\|w\|}$ determines the offset of the from the origin along the normal vector w.

If the training data are linearly separable, we can select two hyperplanes in a way that they separate the data and there are no points between them, and then try to maximize their distance. The region bounded by them is called "the margin". These hyperplanes can be described by the equations

$$w \cdot x - b = 1,$$

and

$$w \cdot x - b = -1,$$

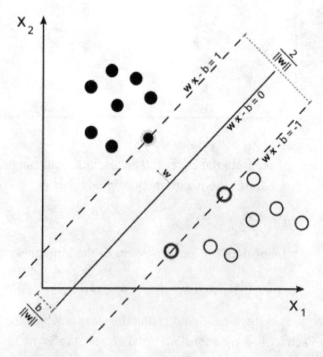

Maximum-margin hyperplane and margins for an SVM trained with samples from two classes. Samples on the margin are called the support vectors.

By using geometry, we find the distance between these two hyperplanes is $\frac{2}{\|w\|}$, so we want to minimize $\|w\|$. As we also have to prevent data points from falling into the margin, we add the following constraint: for each i either

$$w \cdot x - b \geq 1, \text{ for } x_i \text{ of the first class,}$$

or

This can be rewritten as:

$$w \cdot x - b \leq 1, \text{ for } x_i \text{ of the second class.}$$

This can be written as:

$$y_i(w \cdot x_i - b) \geq 1, \text{ for all } 1 \leq i \leq n. \tag{1}$$

We can put this together to get the optimization problem:

Minimize (in w, b)

$$\|w\|$$

subject to (for any $i = 1, \dots, n$)

$$y_i(w \cdot x_i - b) \geq 1.$$

Primal form

The optimization problem presented in the preceding section is difficult to solve because it depends on $\|w\|$, the norm of w, which involves a square root. Fortunately it is possible to alter the equation by substituting $\|w\|$ with $\frac{1}{2}\|w\|^2$ (the factor of 1/2 being used for mathematical convenience) without changing the solution (the minimum of the original and the modified equation have the same w and b). This is a quadratic programming optimization problem. More clearly:

$$\arg\min_{(w,b)} \frac{1}{2} \|w\|^2,$$

subject to (for any $i = 1, \ldots, n$)

$$y_i(w \cdot x_i - b) \geq 1.$$

By introducing Lagrange multipliers α, the previous constrained problem can be expressed as

$$\arg\min_{w,b} \max_{\alpha \geq 0} \left\{ \frac{1}{2} \|w\|^2 - \sum_{i=1}^{n} \alpha_i [y_i(w \cdot x_i - b) - 1] \right\},$$

that is, we look for a saddle point. In doing so all the points which can be separated as $y_i(w \cdot x_i - b) > 1$ do not matter since we must set the corresponding α_i to zero.

This problem can now be solved by standard quadratic programming techniques and programs. The "stationary" Karush–Kuhn–Tucker condition implies that the solution can be expressed as a linear combination of the training vectors

$$w = \sum_{i=1}^{n} \alpha_i y_i x_i.$$

Only a few α_i will be greater than zero. The corresponding x_i are exactly the support vectors, which lie on the margin and satisfy $y_i(w \cdot x_i - b) = 1$. From this one can derive that the support vectors also satisfy

$$w \cdot x_i - b = 1/y_i = y_i \iff b = w \cdot x_i - y_i,$$

which allows one to define the offset b. In practice, it is more robust to average over all support vectors:

$$b = \frac{1}{N_{SV}} \sum_{i=1}^{N_{SV}} (w \cdot x_i - y_i).$$

344

Dual form

Writing the classification rule in its unconstrained dual form reveals that the maximum-margin hyperplane and therefore the classification task is only a function of the support vectors, the subset of the training data that lie on the margin.

Using the fact that $\|w\|^2 = w \cdot w$ and substituting $w = \sum_{i=1}^{n} \alpha_i y_i x_i$, one can show that the dual of the SVM reduces to the following optimization problem: Maximize (in α_i)

$$\tilde{L}(\alpha) = \sum_{i=1}^{n} \alpha_i - \frac{1}{2} \sum_{i,j} \alpha_i \alpha_j y_i y_j x_i^T x_j = \sum_{i=1}^{n} \alpha_i - \frac{1}{2} \sum_{i,j} \alpha_i \alpha_j y_i y_j k(x_i x_j),$$

subject to (for any $i = 1, \dots, n$)

$$\alpha_i \geq 0,$$

and to the constraint from the minimization in b

$$\sum_{i=1}^{n} \alpha_i y_i = 0.$$

Here the kernel is defined by $k(x_i, x_j) = x_i \cdot x_j$. W can be computed thanks to the α terms:

$$w = \sum_{i} \alpha_i y_i x_i.$$

Biased and unbiased hyperplanes

For simplicity reasons, sometimes it is required that the hyperplane pass through the origin of the coordinate system. Such hyperplanes are called unbiased, whereas general hyperplanes not necessarily passing through the origin are called biased. An unbiased hyperplane can be enforced by setting $b = 0$ in the primal optimization problem. The corresponding dual is identical to the dual given above without the equality constraint

$$\sum_{i=1}^{n} \alpha_i y_i = 0.$$

Soft margin

In 1995, Corinna Cortes and Vladimir N. Vapnik suggested a modified maximum margin idea that allows for mislabeled examples (Cortes & Vapnik, 1995). If there exists no hyperplane that can split the "yes" and "no" examples, the Soft Margin method will choose a hyperplane that splits the examples as cleanly as possible, while still maximizing the distance to the nearest cleanly split examples. The method introduces non-negative slack variables, ξ_i, which measure the degree of misclassification of the data x_i

$$y_i(\boldsymbol{w} \cdot \boldsymbol{x}_i - b) \geq 1 - \xi_i, 1 \leq i \leq n. \tag{2}$$

The objective function is then increased by a function which penalizes non-zero ξ_i, and the optimization becomes a trade-off between a large margin and a small error penalty. If the penalty function is linear, the optimization problem becomes:

$$\arg \min_{w,\xi,b} \left\{ \frac{1}{2} \|\boldsymbol{w}\|^2 + C \sum_{i=1}^{n} \xi_i \right\},$$

subject to (for any $i = 1, \dots, n$)

$$y_i(\boldsymbol{w} \cdot \boldsymbol{x}_i - b) \geq 1 - \xi_i, \qquad \xi_i \geq 0.$$

This constraint along with the objective of minimizing $\|\boldsymbol{w}\|$ can be solved using Lagrange multipliers as done above. One has then to solve the following problem:

$$\arg \min_{w,\xi,b} \max_{\alpha,\beta} \left\{ \frac{1}{2} \|\boldsymbol{w}\|^2 + C \sum_{i=1}^{n} \xi_i \right.$$

$$\left. - \sum_{i=1}^{n} \alpha_i [y_i(\boldsymbol{w} \cdot \boldsymbol{x}_i - b) - 1 + \xi_i] - \sum_{i=1}^{n} \beta_i \xi_i \right\},$$

with $\alpha_i, \beta_i \geq 0.$.

Dual form

Maximize (in α_i)

$$\tilde{L}(\alpha) = \sum_{i=1}^{n} \alpha_i - \frac{1}{2} \sum_{i,j} \alpha_i \alpha_j y_i y_j k(x_i x_j),$$

subject to (for any $i = 1, \dots, n$)

$$0 \leq \alpha_i \leq C,$$

and

$$\sum_{i=1}^{n} \alpha_i y_i = 0.$$

The key advantage of a linear penalty function is that the slack variables vanish from the dual problem, with the constant C appearing only as an additional constraint on the Lagrange multipliers. For the above formulation and its huge impact in practice, Cortes and Vapnik received the 2008 ACM Paris Kanellakis Award. Nonlinear penalty functions have been used, particularly to reduce the effect of outliers on the classifier, but unless care is taken the problem becomes non-convex, and thus it is considerably more difficult to find a global solution.

Nonlinear classification

The original optimal hyperplane algorithm proposed by Vapnik in 1963 was a linear classifier. However, in 1992, Bernhard E. Boser, Isabelle M. Guyon and Vladimir N. Vapnik suggested a way to create nonlinear classifiers by applying the kernel trick (originally proposed by Aizerman et al. (Aizerman, Braverman, & Rozonoer, 1964)) to maximum-margin hyperplanes (Boser, Guyon, & Vapnik, 1992). The resulting algorithm is formally similar, except that every dot product is replaced by a nonlinear kernel function. This allows the algorithm to fit the maximum-margin hyperplane in a transformed feature space. The transformation may be nonlinear and the transformed space high dimensional; thus though the classifier is a hyperplane in the high-dimensional feature space, it may be nonlinear in the original input space.

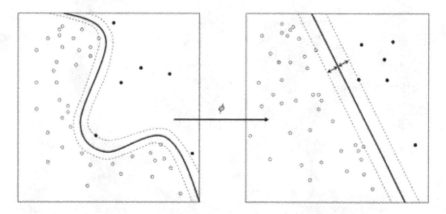

Figure 1. Kernel machine

If the kernel used is a Gaussian radial basis function, the corresponding feature space is a Hilbert space of infinite dimensions. Maximum margin classifiers are well regularized, so the infinite dimensions do not spoil the results. Some common kernels include:

- Polynomial (homogeneous): $k(x_i, x_j) = (x_i \cdot x_j)^d$
- Polynomial (inhomogeneous): $k(x_i, x_j) = (x_i \cdot x_j + 1)^d$
- Gaussian radial basis function: $k(x_i, x_j) = \exp\left(-\gamma \|x_i - x_j\|^2\right)$, for $\gamma > 0$. Sometimes parametrized using $\gamma = 1/2\sigma^2$
- Hyperbolic tangent:, $k(x_i, x_j) = \tanh(\kappa x_i \cdot x_j + c)$ for some (not every) $\kappa > 0$ and $c > 0$.

The kernel is related to the transform $\varphi(x_i)$ by the equation $k(x_i, x_j) = \varphi(x_i) \cdot \varphi(x_j)$. The value w is also in the transformed space, with $w = \sum_i \alpha_i y_i \varphi(x_i)$. Dot products with w for classification can again be computed by the kernel trick, i.e. $w \cdot \varphi(x_i) = \sum_i \alpha_i y_i k(x_i, x)$. However, there does not in general exist a value w′ such that $w \cdot$

$$\varphi(x_i) = k(w', w) \,.$$

Properties

SVMs belong to a family of generalized linear classifiers and can be interpreted as an extension of the perceptron. They can also be considered a special case of Tikhonov regularization. A special property is that they simultaneously minimize the empirical classification error and maximize the geometric margin; hence they are also known as maximum margin classifiers.

A comparison of the SVM to other classifiers has been made by Meyer, Leisch and Hornik (Meyer, Leisch, & Hornik, 2003).

Parameter selection

The effectiveness of SVM depends on the selection of kernel, the kernel's parameters, and soft margin parameter C. A common choice is a Gaussian kernel, which has a single parameter γ. The best combination of C and γ is often selected by a grid search with exponentially growing sequences of C and γ, for example, $C \in \{2^{-5}, 2^{-3}, \dots, 2^{13}, 2^{15}\}$; $\gamma \in \{2^{-15}, 2^{-13}, \dots, 2^1, 2^3\}$. Typically, each combination of parameter choices is checked using cross validation, and the parameters with best cross-validation accuracy are picked. The final model, which is used for testing and for classifying new data, is then trained on the whole training set using the selected parameters (Hsu, Chang, & Lin, 2010).

Issues

Potential drawbacks of the SVM are the following three aspects:

- Uncalibrated class membership probabilities
- The SVM is only directly applicable for two-class tasks. Therefore, algorithms that reduce the multi-class task to several binary problems have to be applied; see the multi-class SVM section.
- Parameters of a solved model are difficult to interpret.

Extensions

Multiclass SVM

Multiclass SVM aims to assign labels to instances by using support vector machines, where the labels are drawn from a finite set of several elements.

The dominant approach for doing so is to reduce the single multiclass problem into multiple binary classification problems (Duan & Keerthi, 2005). Common methods for such reduction include (Hsu, Chang, & Lin, 2010):

- Building binary classifiers which distinguish between (i) one of the labels and the rest (one-versus-all) or (ii) between every pair of classes (one-versus-one). Classification of new instances for the one-versus-all case is done by a winner-takes-all strategy, in which the classifier with the highest output function assigns the class (it is important that the output functions be calibrated to produce comparable scores). For the one-versus-one approach, classification is done by a max-wins voting strategy, in which every classifier assigns the instance to one of the two classes, then the vote for the assigned class is increased by one vote, and finally the class with the most votes determines the instance classification.
- Directed acyclic graph SVM (DAGSVM) (Platt, Cristianini, & Shawe-Taylor, 2000).
- Error-correcting output codes (Dietterich & Bakiri, 1995).

Crammer and Singer proposed a multiclass SVM method which casts the multiclass classification problem into a single optimization problem, rather than decomposing it into multiple binary classification problems (Crammer & Singer, 2001). See also Lee, Lin and Wahba (Lee, Lin, & Wahba, 2001).

Transductive support vector machines

Transductive support vector machines extend SVMs in that they could also treat partially labeled data in semi-supervised learning by following the principles of transduction (Joachims, 1999). Here, in addition to the training set $\mathcal{D}$, the learner is also given a set

$$\mathcal{D}^* = \{x_i^* | x_i^* \in \mathbb{R}^p\}_{i=1}^k$$

of test examples to be classified. Formally, a transductive support vector machine is defined by the following primal optimization problem:[2]

Minimize (in w, b, y^*)

$$\frac{1}{2}\|w\|^2$$

subject to (for any $i = 1, \dots, n$ and any $j = 1, \dots, k$)

$$y_i(w \cdot x_i - b) \geq 1,$$

$$y_j^*(w \cdot x_j^* - b) \geq 1,$$

and

$$y_j^* \in \{-1,1\}.$$

Transductive support vector machines were introduced by Vladimir N. Vapnik in 1998.

Structured SVM

SVMs have been generalized to structured SVMs, where the label space is structured and of possibly infinite size.

Regression

A version of SVM for regression was proposed in 1996 by Vladimir N. Vapnik, Harris Drucker, Christopher J. C. Burges, Linda Kaufman and Alexander J. Smola (Drucker, Burges, Kaufman, Smola, & Vapnik, 1996). This method is called support vector regression (SVR). The model produced by support vector classification (as described above) depends only on a subset of the training data, because the cost function for building the model does not care about training points that lie beyond the margin. Analogously, the model produced by SVR depends only on a subset of the training data, because the cost function for building the model ignores any training data close to the model prediction (within a threshold). Another SVM version known as least squares support vector machine (LS-SVM) has been proposed by Suykens and Vandewalle (Suykens & Vandewalle, 1999).

Interpreting SVM models

The SVM algorithm has been widely applied in the biological and other sciences. Permutation tests based on SVM weights have been suggested as a mechanism for interpretation of SVM models (Cuingnet, et al., 2011). Support vector machine weights have also been used to interpret SVM models in the past. Posthoc interpretation of support vector machine models in order to identify features used by the model to make predictions is a relatively new area of research with special significance in the biological sciences.

Implementation

The parameters of the maximum-margin hyperplane are derived by solving the optimization. There exist several specialized algorithms for quickly solving the QP problem that arises from SVMs, mostly relying on heuristics for breaking the problem down into smaller, more-manageable chunks. A common method is Platt's sequential minimal optimization (SMO) algorithm, which breaks the problem down into 2-dimensional sub-problems that may be solved analytically, eliminating the need for a numerical optimization algorithm (Platt J. , 1999).

Another approach is to use an interior point method that uses Newton-like iterations to find a solution of the Karush–Kuhn–Tucker conditions of the primal and dual problems (Ferris & Munson, 2002). Instead of solving a sequence of broken down problems, this approach directly solves the problem as a whole. To avoid solving a linear system involving the large kernel matrix, a low rank approximation to the matrix is often used in the kernel trick.

The special case of linear support vector machines can be solved more efficiently by the same kind of algorithms used to optimize its close cousin, logistic regression; this class of algorithms includes sub-gradient descent (e.g., PEGASOS (Shalev-Shwartz, Singer, & Srebro, 2007)) and coordinate descent (e.g., LIBLINEAR (Fan, Chang, Hsieh, Wang, & C.J., 2008)). The general kernel SVMs can also be solved more efficiently using sub-gradient descent (e.g. P-packSVM (Zhu, Chen, Wang, Zhu, & Chen, 2009)), especially when parallelization is allowed.

Kernel SVMs are available in many machine learning toolkits, including LIBSVM, MATLAB, SVMlight, scikit-learn, Shogun, Weka, Shark [8], JKernelMachines [9] and others.

Applications

SVMs can be used to solve various real world problems:

- SVMs are helpful in text and hypertext categorization as their application can significantly reduce the need for labeled training instances in both the standard inductive and transductive settings.
- Classification of images can also be performed using SVMs. Experimental results show that SVMs achieve significantly higher search accuracy than traditional query refinement schemes after just three to four rounds of relevance feedback.
- SVMs are also useful in medical science to classify proteins with up to 90% of the compounds classified correctly.
- Hand-written characters can be recognized using SVM

Software

Software for SVM modeling include Gini-SVM in Octave, kernlab in R, SVMlight, SPSS Modeler, and MATLAB.

Example Using R

Ksvm in `kernlab`

Package **kernlab** (Karatzoglou, Smola, Hornik, & Zeileis, 2004) aims to provide the R user with basic kernel functionality (e.g., like computing a kernel matrix using a particular kernel), along with some utility functions commonly used in kernel-based methods like a quadratic programming solver, and modern kernel-based algorithms based on the functionality that the package provides. It also takes advantage of the inherent modularity of kernel-based methods, aiming to allow the user to switch between kernels on an existing algorithm and even create and use own kernel functions for the various kernel methods provided in the package.

kernlab uses R's new object model described in "Programming with Data" (Chambers, 1998) which is known as the S4 class system and is implemented in package methods. In contrast to the older S3 model for objects in R, classes, slots, and methods relationships must be declared explicitly when using the S4 system. The number and types of slots in an instance of a class have to be established at the time the class is defined. The objects from the class are validated against this definition and have to comply with it at any time. S4 also requires formal declarations of methods, unlike the informal system of using function names to identify a certain method in S3. Package **kernlab** is available from CRAN (http://CRAN.R-project. org/) under the GPL license.

The `ksvm()` function, **kernlab**'s implementation of SVMs, provides a standard formula interface along with a matrix interface. `ksvm()` is mostly programmed in R but uses, through the `.call` interface, the optimizers found in `bsvm` and `libsvm` (Chang & Lin, 2011) which provide a very efficient C++ version of the Sequential Minimization Optimization (SMO). The SMO algorithm solves the SVM quadratic problem (QP) without using any numerical QP optimization steps. Instead, it chooses to solve the smallest possible optimization problem involving two elements of α_1 because the must obey one linear equality constraint. At every step, SMO chooses two α_1 to jointly optimize and finds the optimal values for these α_1 analytically, thus avoiding numerical QP optimization, and updates the SVM to reflect the new optimal values.

The SVM implementations available in ksvm() include the C-SVM classification algorithm along with the v-SVM classification. Also included is a bound constraint version of C classification (C-BSVM) which solves a slightly different QP problem ((Mangasarian & Musicant, 1999), including the offset β in the objective function) using a modified version of the TRON (Lin & More, 1999) optimization software. For regression, ksvm() includes the E-SVM regression algorithm along with the v-SVM regression formulation. In addition, a bound constraint version (E-BSVM) is provided, and novelty detection (one-class classification) is supported.

For classification problems which include more than two classes (multi-class case) two options are available: a one-against-one (pairwise) classification method or the native multi-class formulation of the SVM (spocsvc). The optimization problem of the native multi-class SVM implementation is solved by a decomposition method proposed in Hsu and Lin (Hsu & Lin, 2002) where optimal working sets are found (that is, sets of α_1 values which have a high probability of being non-zero). The QP sub-problems are then solved by a modified version of the TRON optimization software.

The ksvm() implementation can also compute class-probability output by using Platt's probability methods along with the multi-class extension of the method in Wu et al. (Wu, Lin, & Weng, 2003). The prediction method can also return the raw decision values of the support vector model:

```
> library("kernlab")
> data("iris")
> irismodel <- ksvm(Species ~ ., data = iris,
+ type = "C-bsvc", kernel = "rbfdot",
+ kpar = list(sigma = 0.1), C = 10,
+ prob.model = TRUE)
> irismodel
```

Support Vector Machine object of class "ksvm"

SV type: C-bsvc (classification)
 parameter : cost C = 10

Gaussian Radial Basis kernel function.
 Hyperparameter : sigma = 0.1

Number of Support Vectors : 32

Objective Function Value : -5.8442 -3.0652 -136.9786
Training error : 0.02
Probability model included.

```
> predict(irismodel, iris[c(3, 10, 56, 68, 107, 120), -5]
+              , type = "probabilities")
         setosa   versicolor   virginica
[1,] 0.985040508 0.007941886 0.007017606
[2,] 0.981634222 0.010962854 0.007402924
[3,] 0.004004929 0.970726183 0.025268888
[4,] 0.007777874 0.990465191 0.001756935
[5,] 0.012370962 0.103044282 0.884584756
[6,] 0.010869688 0.205778364 0.783351948

> predict(irismodel, iris[c(3, 10, 56, 68, 107, 120), -5]
+              , type = "decision")
          [,1]        [,2]        [,3]
[1,] -1.460398 -1.1910251 -3.8868836
[2,] -1.357355 -1.1749491 -4.2107843
[3,]  1.647272  0.7655001 -1.3205306
[4,]  1.412721  0.4736201 -2.7521640
[5,]  1.844763  1.0000000  1.0000019
[6,]  1.848985  1.0069010  0.6742889
```

ksvm allows for the use of any valid user defined kernel function by just defining a function which takes two vector arguments and returns its Hilbert Space dot product in scalar form.

```
> k <- function(x, y) { (sum(x * y) + 1) * exp(0.001
+            * sum((x - y)^2))}
```

```
> class(k) <- "kernel"
> data("promotergene")
> gene <- ksvm(Class ~ ., data = promotergene,
+ kernel = k, C = 10, cross = 5)
> gene
Support Vector Machine object of class "ksvm"

SV type: C-svc  (classification)
 parameter : cost C = 10

Number of Support Vectors : 44

Objective Function Value : -23.3052
Training error : 0.084906
Cross validation error : 0.151082
```

The implementation also includes the following computationally efficiently implemented kernels: Gaussian RBF, polynomial, linear, sigmoid, Laplace, Bessel RBF, spline, and ANOVA RBF.

N -fold cross-validation of an SVM model is also supported by ksvm, and the training error is reported by default.

The problem of model selection is partially addressed by an empirical observation for the popular Gaussian RBF kernel (Caputo, Sim, Furesjo, & Smola), where the optimal values of the width hyper-parameter σ are shown to lie in between the 0.1 and 0.9 quantile of the $\|x - x'\|^2$ statistics. The sigest() function uses a sample of the training set to estimate the quantiles and returns a vector containing the values of the quantiles. Pretty much any value within this interval leads to good performance.

The object returned by the ksvm() function is an S4 object of class ksvm with slots containing the coefficients of the model (support vectors), the parameters used (C , v, etc.), test and cross-validation error, the kernel function, information on the problem type, the data scaling parameters, etc. There are accessor functions for the information contained in the slots of the ksvm object.

The decision values of binary classification problems can also be visualized via a contour plot with the plot() method for the ksvm objects. This function is mainly for simple problems. An example is shown in Figure 2.

```
> x <- rbind(matrix(rnorm(120), , 2), matrix(rnorm(120,
+ mean = 3), , 2))
> y <- matrix(c(rep(1, 60), rep(-1, 60)))
> svp <- ksvm(x, y, type = "C-svc", kernel = "rbfdot",
+ kpar = list(sigma = 2))
> plot(svp)
```

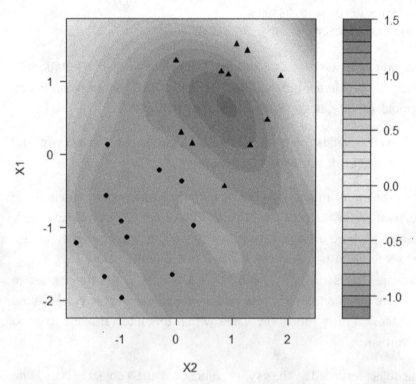

Figure 2: A contour plot of the fitted decision values for a simple binary classification problem.

svm in e1071

Package **e1071** provides an interface to **libsvm** (Chang and Lin 2001, current version: 2.8 (Chang & Lin, 2011)), complemented by visualization and tuning functions. libsvm is a fast and easy-to-use implementation of the most popular SVM formulations (C and v classification, E and v regression, and novelty detection). It includes the most common kernels (linear, polynomial, RBF, and sigmoid), only extensible by changing the C++ source code of libsvm. Multi-class classification is provided using the one-against-one voting scheme. Other features include the computation of decision and probability values for predictions (for both classification and regression), shrinking heuristics during the fitting process, class weighting in the classification mode, handling of sparse data, and the computation of the training error using cross-validation. libsvm is distributed under a very permissive, BSD-like license.

The R implementation is based on the S3 class mechanisms. It basically provides a training function with standard and formula interfaces, and a predict() method. In addition, a plot() method visualizing data, support vectors, and decision boundaries if provided. Hyper- parameter tuning is done using the tune() framework in e1071 performing a grid search over specified parameter ranges.

The sample session starts with a C classification task on the iris data, using the radial basis function kernel with fixed hyperparameters C and γ:

```
> library("e1071")
> model <- svm(Species ~ ., data = iris_train,
+          method = "C-classification", kernel = "radial",
+          cost = 10, gamma = 0.1)
> summary(model)

Call:

svm(formula = Species ~ ., data = iris_train, method =
+            "C-classification", kernel = "radial", cost
= 10, +      gamma = 0.1)

Parameters:
SVM-Type:    C-classification
```

359

```
SVM-Kernel:              radial cost: 10 gamma:
              0.1

Number  of  Support  Vectors:          27 ( 12 12 3 )

Number  of  Classes:      3

Levels:
setosa  versicolor  virginica
```

We can visualize a 2-dimensional projection of the data with highlighting classes and support vectors (see Figure 3.)

```
> plot(model,  iris_train,  Petal.Width  ~  Petal.Length
+    ,  slice  = list(Sepal.Width  = 3, Sepal.Length  = 4))
```

Predictions from the model, as well as decision values from the binary classifiers, are obtained using the predict() method:

```
> (pred  <-  predict(model,  head(iris),  decision.values  =
TRUE))

[1]  setosa  setosa  setosa  setosa  setosa  setosa
Levels:  setosa  versicolor  virginica

> attr(pred,  "decision.values")
```

	setosa/versicolor versicolor/virginica		setosa/virginica
1	1.401032	1.185293	4.242854
2	1.27702	1.149088	4.240565
3	1.466205	1.191251	3.904643
4	1.376632	1.149488	3.799572
5	1.437044	1.191163	3.953461
6	1.168084	1.091338	3.86014

```
Levels: setosa versicolor virginica
```

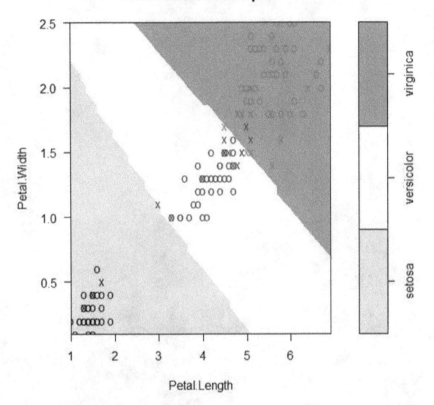

Figure 3: SVM plot visualizing the iris data. Support vectors are shown as '*X*', true classes are highlighted through symbol color, predicted class regions are visualized using colored background.

Probability values can be obtained in a similar way.

361

17. Gradient boosting

Gradient boosting is a machine learning technique for regression problems, which produces a prediction model in the form of an ensemble of weak prediction models, typically decision trees. It builds the model in a stage-wise fashion like other boosting methods do, and it generalizes them by allowing optimization of an arbitrary differentiable loss function. The gradient boosting method can also be used for classification problems by reducing them to regression with a suitable loss function.

The method was invented by Jerome H. Friedman in 1999 and was published in a series of two papers, the first of which (Friedman, Greedy Function Approximation: A Gradient Boosting Machine, 1995) introduced the method, and the second one (Friedman, Stochastic Gradient Boosting, 1999) described an important tweak to the algorithm, which improves its accuracy and performance.

Algorithm

In many supervised learning problems one has an output variable y and a vector of input variables x connected together via a joint probability distribution $P(x, y)$. Using a training set of known values of x and corresponding values of y, the goal is to find an approximation $\hat{F}(x)$ to a function $F^*(x)$ that minimizes the expected value of some specified loss function $L(y, F(x))$:

$$F^* = \arg\min_F \mathbb{E}_{x,y}\left[L\big(y, F(x)\big)\right]$$

Gradient boosting method assumes a real-valued y and seeks an approximation $\hat{F}(x)$ in the form of a weighted sum of functions $h_i(x)$ from some class $\mathcal{H}$, called base (or weak) learners:

$$F(x) = \sum_{i=1}^{M} \gamma_i h_i(x) + \text{constant}.$$

In accordance with the empirical risk minimization principle, the method tries to find an approximation $\hat{F}(x)$ that minimizes the average value of the loss function on the training set. It does so by starting with a model, consisting of a constant function $F_0(x)$, and incrementally expanding it in a greedy fashion:

$$F_0(x) = \arg\min_{\gamma} \sum_{i=1}^{n} L(y_i, \gamma),$$

$$F_m(x) = F_{m-1}(x) + \arg\min_{f \in \mathcal{H}} \sum_{i=1}^{n} L\big(y_i, F_{m-1}(x_i) + f(x_i)\big),$$

where f is restricted to be a function from the class $\mathcal{H}$ of base learner functions.

However, the problem of choosing at each step the best f for an arbitrary loss function L is a hard optimization problem in general, and so we will "cheat" by solving a much easier problem instead.

The idea is to apply a steepest descent step to this minimization problem. If we only cared about predictions at the points of the training set, and f were unrestricted, we'd update the model per the following equation, where we view $L(y, f)$ not as a functional of f, but as a function of a vector of values $f(x_1), \dots, f(x_n)$:

$$F_m(x) = F_{m-1}(x) - \gamma_m \sum_{i=1}^{n} \nabla_f L\big(y_i, F_{m-1}(x_i)\big),$$

$$\gamma_m = \arg\min_{\gamma} \sum_{i=1}^{n} L\left(y_i, F_{m-1}(x_i) - \gamma \frac{\partial L\big(y_i, F_{m-1}(x_i)\big)}{\partial f(x_i)}\right).$$

But as f must come from a restricted class of functions (that's what allows us to generalize), we will just choose the one that most closely approximates the gradient of L. Having chosen f, the multiplier γ is then selected using line search just as shown in the second equation above.

In pseudocode, the generic gradient boosting method is (Friedman, Greedy Function Approximation: A Gradient Boosting Machine, 1995) (Hastie, Tibshirani, & Friedman, 2009):

Input: training set $\{(x_i, y_i)\}_{i=1}^{n}$, a differentiable loss function $L(y, F(x))$ number of iterations M.

Algorithm:

1. Initialize model with a constant value:

$$F_0(x) = \arg\min_{\gamma} \sum_{i=1}^{n} L(y_i, \gamma),$$

2. For $m = 1$ to M:

    a. Compute so-called pseudo-residuals:

$$r_{im} = -\left[\frac{\partial L(y_i, F(x_i))}{\partial F(x_i)}\right]_{F(x)=F_{m-1}(x)} \quad , for\ i = 1, \dots n.$$

    b. Fit a base learner $h_m(x)$ to pseudo-residuals, i.e. train it using the training set $\{(x_i, r_{im})\}_{i=1}^{n}$.

    c. Compute multiplier γ_m by solving the following one-dimensional optimization problem:

$$\gamma_m = \arg\min_{\gamma} \sum_{i=1}^{n} L(y_i, F_{m-1}(x_i) + \gamma h_m(x_i)).$$

    d. Update the model:

$$F_m(x) = F_{m-1}(x) + \gamma_m h_m(x).$$

3. Output $F_m(x)$.

Gradient tree boosting

Gradient boosting is typically used with decision trees (especially CART trees) of a fixed size as base learners. For this special case Friedman proposes a modification to gradient boosting method which improves the quality of fit of each base learner.

Generic gradient boosting at the m-th step would fit a decision tree $h_m(x)$ to pseudo-residuals. Let J be the number of its leaves. The tree partitions the input space into J disjoint regions $R_{1m}, \ldots, R_{Jm}$ and predicts a constant value in each region. Using the indicator notation, the output of $h_m(x)$ for input x can be written as the sum:

$$h_m(x) = \sum_{j=1}^{J} b_{jm} I(x \in R_{jm}),$$

Where b_{jm} is the value predicted in the region R_{jm}.

Then the coefficients b_{jm} are multiplied by some value γ_m, chosen using line search so as to minimize the loss function, and the model is updated as follows:

$$F_m(x) = F_{m-1}(x) + \gamma_m h_m(x),$$

$$\gamma_m = \arg \min_{\gamma} \sum_{i=1}^{n} L\big(y_i, F_{m-1}(x_i) + \gamma h_m(x_i)\big).$$

Friedman proposes to modify this algorithm so that it chooses a separate optimal value γ_{jm} for each of the tree's regions, instead of a single γ_m for the whole tree. He calls the modified algorithm "TreeBoost". The coefficients from the tree-fitting procedure can be then simply discarded and the model update rule becomes:

$$F_m(x) = F_{m-1}(x) + \sum_{j=1}^{J} \gamma_{jm} I(x \in R_{jm}),$$

$$\gamma_{jm} = \arg\min_{\gamma} \sum_{x_i \in R_{jm}}^{n} L\big(y_i, F_{m-1}(x_i) + \gamma h_m(x_i)\big).$$

Size of trees

J, the number of terminal nodes in trees, is the method's parameter which can be adjusted for a data set at hand. It controls the maximum allowed level of interaction between variables in the model. With $J = 2$ (decision stumps), no interaction between variables is allowed. With $J = 3$ the model may include effects of the interaction between up to two variables, and so on.

Hastie et al. (Hastie, Tibshirani, & Friedman, 2009) comment that typically $4 \leq J \leq 8$ work well for boosting and results are fairly insensitive to the choice of J in this range, $J = 2$ is insufficient for many applications, and $J > 10$ is unlikely to be required.

Regularization

Fitting the training set too closely can lead to degradation of the model's generalization ability. Several so-called regularization techniques reduce this overfitting effect by constraining the fitting procedure.

One natural regularization parameter is the number of gradient boosting iterations M (i.e. the number of trees in the model when the base learner is a decision tree). Increasing M reduces the error on training set, but setting it too high may lead to overfitting. An optimal value of M is often selected by monitoring prediction error on a separate validation data set. Besides controlling M, several other regularization techniques are used.

Shrinkage

An important part of gradient boosting method is regularization by shrinkage which consists in modifying the update rule as follows:

$$F_m(x) = F_{m-1}(x) + v \cdot \gamma_m h_m(x), \qquad 0 < v \leq 1,$$

where parameter v is called the "learning rate".

Empirically it has been found that using small learning rates (such as $v <$ 0.1) yields dramatic improvements in model's generalization ability over gradient boosting without shrinking ($v = 1$) (Hastie, Tibshirani, & Friedman, 2009). However, it comes at the price of increasing computational time both during training and querying: lower learning rate requires more iterations.

Stochastic gradient boosting

Soon after the introduction of gradient boosting Friedman proposed a minor modification to the algorithm, motivated by Breiman's bagging method (Friedman, Stochastic Gradient Boosting, 1999). Specifically, he proposed that at each iteration of the algorithm, a base learner should be fit on a subsample of the training set drawn at random without replacement. Friedman observed a substantial improvement in gradient boosting's accuracy with this modification.

Subsample size is some constant fraction f of the size of the training set. When $f = 1$, the algorithm is deterministic and identical to the one described above. Smaller values of f introduce randomness into the algorithm and help prevent overfitting, acting as a kind of regularization. The algorithm also becomes faster, because regression trees have to be fit to smaller datasets at each iteration. Friedman (Friedman, Stochastic Gradient Boosting, 1999) obtained that $0.5 \leq f \leq 0.8$ leads to good results for small and moderate sized training sets. Therefore, f is typically set to 0.5, meaning that one half of the training set is used to build each base learner.

Also, like in bagging, subsampling allows one to define an out-of-bag estimate of the prediction performance improvement by evaluating predictions on those observations which were not used in the building of the next base learner. Out-of-bag estimates help avoid the need for an independent validation dataset, but often underestimate actual performance improvement and the optimal number of iterations (Ridgeway, 2007).

Number of observations in leaves

Gradient tree boosting implementations often also use regularization by limiting the minimum number of observations in trees' terminal nodes (this parameter is called `n.minobsinnode` in the R `gbm` package). It is used in the tree building process by ignoring any splits that lead to nodes containing fewer than this number of training set instances.

Imposing this limit helps to reduce variance in predictions at leaves.

Usage

Recently, gradient boosting has gained some popularity in the field of learning to rank. The commercial web search engines Yahoo (Ridgeway, 2007) and Yandex (Cossock & Zhang, 2008) use variants of gradient boosting in their machine-learned ranking engines.

Names

The method goes by a wide variety of names. The title of the original publication refers to it as a "Gradient Boosting Machine" (GBM). That same publication and a later one by J. Friedman also use the names "Gradient Boost", "Stochastic Gradient Boosting" (emphasizing the random subsampling technique), "Gradient Tree Boosting" and "TreeBoost" (for specialization of the method to the case of decision trees as base learners.)

A popular open-source implementation for R calls it "Generalized Boosting Model". Sometimes the method is referred to as "functional gradient boosting", "Gradient Boosted Models" and its tree version is also called "Gradient Boosted Decision Trees" (GBDT) or "Gradient Boosted Regression Trees" (GBRT). Commercial implementations from Salford Systems use the names "Multiple Additive Regression Trees" (MART) and TreeNet, both trademarked.

Software

Software packages for gradient boosting include Mboost in R, sklearn.ensemble in scikit-learn, MATLAB, SPSS Modeler, and STATISTICA.

Example Using R

The aim of this example is to compute accurate predictions for the body fat of women based on available anthropometric measurements. Observations of 71 German women are available with the data set bodyfat (Nieto-Garcia, Bush, & Keyl, 1990) included in R's mboost-package. We first load the package and the data set.

```
> library("mboost") ## load package
> data("bodyfat", package = "TH.data") ## load data
```

The response variable is the body fat measured by DXA (DEXfat), which can be seen as the gold standard to measure body fat. However, DXA measurements are too expensive and complicated for a broad use. Anthropometric measurements as waist or hip circumferences are in comparison very easy to measure in a standard screening. A prediction formula only based on these measures could therefore be a valuable alternative with high clinical relevance for daily usage. The available variables and anthropometric measurements in the data set are presented in Table 1.

Table 1: Available variables in the bodyfat data, for details see (Nieto-Garcia, Bush, & Keyl, 1990).

Name	Description
DEXfat	body fat measured by DXA (response variable)
age	age of the women in years
waistcirc	waist circumference
hipcirc	hip circumference
elbowbreadth	breadth of the elbow
kneebreadth	breadth of the knee
anthro3a	sum of logarithm of three anthropometric measurements
anthro3b	sum of logarithm of three anthropometric measurements
anthro3c	sum of logarithm of three anthropometric measurements
anthro4	sum of logarithm of four anthropometric measurements

In the original publication, the presented prediction formula was based on a linear model with backward-elimination for variable selection. The resulting final model utilized hip circumference (hipcirc), knee breadth (kneebreadth) and a compound covariate (anthro3a), which is defined as the sum of the logarithmic measurements of chin skinfold, triceps skinfold and subscapular skinfold:

```
> ## Reproduce formula of Garcia et al., 2005
> lm1 <- lm(DEXfat ~ hipcirc + kneebreadth + anthro3a, data
+           = bodyfat)
> coef(lm1)
(Intercept)     hipcirc kneebreadth     anthro3a
-75.2347840   0.5115264   1.9019904   8.9096375
```

A very similar model can be easily fitted by boosting, applying glmboost() with default settings:

```
> ## Estimate same model by glmboost
> glm1 <- glmboost(DEXfat ~ hipcirc + kneebreadth +
+           anthro3a, data = bodyfat)
> coef(glm1, off2int=TRUE) ## off2int adds the offset to the
intercept
(Intercept)     hipcirc kneebreadth     anthro3a
-75.2073365   0.5114861   1.9005386   8.9071301
```

Note that in this case we used the default settings in control and the default family Gaussian() leading to boosting with the L_2 loss.

We now want to consider all available variables as potential predictors. One way is to simply specify "." on the right side of the formula:

```
> glm2 <- glmboost(DEXfat ~ ., data = bodyfat)
```

As an alternative one can explicitly provide the whole formula by using the paste() function. Therefore, one could essentially call:

```
> preds <- names(bodyfat[, names(bodyfat) != "DEXfat"])
##names of predictors
> fm <- as.formula(paste("DEXfat ~", paste(preds, collapse
+                        = "+")))
## build formula
```

```
> fm
+                   DEXfat ~ age+waistcirc + hipcirc + elbowbreadth
+
+                   kneebreadth + anthro3a + anthro3b + anthro3c +
+                   anthro4
```

and provide fm to the `formula` argument in `glmboost()`. Note that a solution using the `paste()` function is somewhat unavoidable when we intend to combine different base-learners for plenty of predictors in `gamboost()`. Note that at this iteration (`mstop` is still 100 as it is the default value) `anthro4a` is not included in the resulting model as the corresponding base-learner was never selected in the update step. The function `coef()` by default only displays the selected variables but can be forced to show all effects by specifying `which` = "":

```
> coef(glm2,    ## usually the argument 'which' is used to
                ## specify single base-
+ which = "") ## learners via partial matching; with which
                ## = "" we select all.
(Intercept) age  waistcirc hipcirc elbowbreadth kneebreadth
-98.816608 0.0136   0.1897   0.3516      -0.384      1.7366
anthro3a anthro3b anthro3c anthro4
3.326860   3.6565   0.5954        0
attr(,"offset")
[1] 30.78282
```

A plot of the coefficient paths, similar to the ones commonly known from the LARS algorithm (Efron et al. 2004), can be easily produced by using `plot()` on the `glmboost` object (see Figure 1):

```
> plot(glm2, off2int = TRUE) ## default plot, offset added
>                            ## to intercept
> ## now change ylim to the range of the coefficients
> ## without intercept (zoom-in)
> plot(glm2, ylim = range(coef(glm2, which = preds)))
```

glmboost.formula(formula = DEXfat ~ ., data = bodyfat)

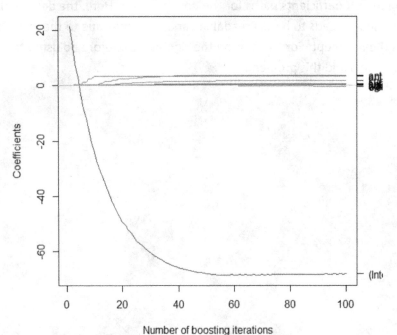

Number of boosting iterations

glmboost.formula(formula = DEXfat ~ ., data = bodyfat)

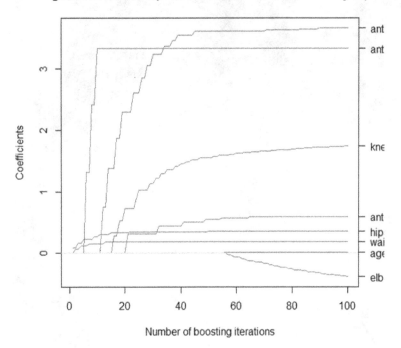

Number of boosting iterations

Figure 1: Coefficients paths for the body fat data: Here, the default plot on the left leads to hardly readable variable names due to the inclusion of the intercept. For the plot on the right we therefore adjusted the y-scale to avoid this problem.

18. Artificial neural network

In computer science and related fields, artificial neural networks (ANNs) are computational models inspired by an animal's central nervous systems (in particular the brain) which is capable of machine learning as well as pattern recognition. Artificial neural networks are generally presented as systems of interconnected "neurons" which can compute values from inputs.

For example, a neural network for handwriting recognition is defined by a set of input neurons which may be activated by the pixels of an input image. After being weighted and transformed by a function (determined by the network's designer), the activations of these neurons are then passed on to other neurons. This process is repeated until finally, an output neuron is activated. This determines which character was read.

Like other machine learning methods - systems that learn from data - neural networks have been used to solve a wide variety of tasks that are hard to solve using ordinary rule-based programming, including computer vision and speech recognition.

Background

An artificial neural network is an interconnected group of nodes, akin to the vast network of neurons in a brain. Here, each circular node represents an artificial neuron and an arrow represents a connection from the output of one neuron to the input of another.

Examinations of the human's central nervous system inspired the concept of neural networks. In an Artificial Neural Network, simple artificial nodes, known as "neurons", "neurodes", "processing elements" or "units", are connected together to form a network which mimics a biological neural network.

There is no single formal definition of what an artificial neural network is. However, a class of statistical models may commonly be called "Neural" if they possess the following characteristics:

1. consist of sets of adaptive weights, i.e. numerical parameters that are tuned by a learning algorithm, and

2. are capable of approximating non-linear functions of their inputs.

The adaptive weights are conceptually connection strengths between neurons, which are activated during training and prediction.

Neural networks are similar to biological neural networks in performing functions collectively and in parallel by the units, rather than there being a clear delineation of subtasks to which various units are assigned. The term "neural network" usually refers to models employed in statistics, cognitive psychology and artificial intelligence. Neural network models which emulate the central nervous system are part of theoretical neuroscience and computational neuroscience.

In modern software implementations of artificial neural networks, the approach inspired by biology has been largely abandoned for a more practical approach based on statistics and signal processing. In some of these systems, neural networks or parts of neural networks (like artificial neurons) form components in larger systems that combine both adaptive and non-adaptive elements. While the more general approach of such systems is more suitable for real-world problem solving, it has little to do with the traditional artificial intelligence connectionist models. What they do have in common, however, is the principle of non-linear, distributed, parallel and local processing and adaptation. Historically, the use of neural networks models marked a paradigm shift in the late eighties from high-level (symbolic) artificial intelligence, characterized by expert systems with knowledge embodied in if-then rules, to low-level (sub-symbolic) machine learning, characterized by knowledge embodied in the parameters of a dynamical system.

History

Warren McCulloch and Walter Pitts (McCulloch & Pitts, 1943) created a computational model for neural networks based on mathematics and algorithms. They called this model threshold logic. The model paved the way for neural network research to split into two distinct approaches. One approach focused on biological processes in the brain and the other focused on the application of neural networks to artificial intelligence.

In the late 1940s psychologist Donald Hebb (Hebb, 1949) created a hypothesis of learning based on the mechanism of neural plasticity that is now known as Hebbian learning. Hebbian learning is considered to be a 'typical' unsupervised learning rule and its later variants were early models for long term potentiation. These ideas started being applied to computational models in 1948 with Turing's B-type machines.

Farley and Wesley A. Clark first used computational machines, then called calculators, to simulate a Hebbian network at MIT (Farley & Clark, 1954). Other neural network computational machines were created by Rochester, Holland, Habit, and Duda (Rochester, Holland, Habit, & Duda, 1956).

Frank Rosenblatt created the perceptron, an algorithm for pattern recognition based on a two-layer learning computer network using simple addition and subtraction (Rosenblatt, 1958). With mathematical notation, Rosenblatt also described circuitry not in the basic perceptron, such as the exclusive-or circuit, a circuit whose mathematical computation could not be processed until after the backpropagation algorithm was created by Paul Werbos (Werbos, 1975).

Neural network research stagnated after the publication of machine learning research by Marvin Minsky and Seymour Papert (Minsky & Papert, 1969). They discovered two key issues with the computational machines that processed neural networks. The first issue was that single-layer neural networks were incapable of processing the exclusive-or circuit. The second significant issue was that computers were not sophisticated enough to effectively handle the long run time required by large neural networks. Neural network research slowed until computers achieved greater processing power. Also key later advances was the backpropagation algorithm which effectively solved the exclusive-or problem (Werbos, 1975).

377

The parallel distributed processing of the mid-1980s became popular under the name connectionism. The text by David E. Rumelhart and James McClelland (Rumelhart & McClelland, 1986) provided a full exposition on the use of connectionism in computers to simulate neural processes.

Neural networks, as used in artificial intelligence, have traditionally been viewed as simplified models of neural processing in the brain, even though the relation between this model and brain biological architecture is debated, as it is not clear to what degree artificial neural networks mirror brain function (Russell, 1996).

In the 1990s, neural networks were overtaken in popularity in machine learning by support vector machines and other, much simpler methods such as linear classifiers. Renewed interest in neural nets was sparked in the 2000s by the advent of deep learning.

Recent improvements

Computational devices have been created in CMOS, for both biophysical simulation and neuromorphic computing. More recent efforts show promise for creating nanodevices (Yang, et al., 2008) for very large scale principal components analyses and convolution. If successful, these efforts could usher in a new era of neural computing (Strukov, Snider, Stewart, & Williams, 2008) that is a step beyond digital computing, because it depends on learning rather than programming and because it is fundamentally analog rather than digital even though the first instantiations may in fact be with CMOS digital devices.

Variants of the back-propagation algorithm as well as unsupervised methods by Geoff Hinton and colleagues at the University of Toronto (Hinton, Osindero, & Teh, 2006) can be used to train deep, highly nonlinear neural architectures similar to the 1980 Neocognitron by Kunihiko Fukushima (Fukushima, 1980), and the "standard architecture of vision" (Riesenhuber & Poggio, 1999), inspired by the simple and complex cells identified by David H. Hubel and Torsten Wiesel in the primary visual cortex. Deep learning feedforward networks, such as convolutional neural networks, alternate convolutional layers and max-pooling layers, topped by several pure classification layers.

Successes in pattern recognition contests since 2009

Between 2009 and 2012, the recurrent neural networks and deep feedforward neural networks developed in the research group of Jürgen Schmidhuber at the Swiss AI Lab IDSIA have won eight international competitions in pattern recognition and machine learning (Schmidhuber, 2012). For example, multi-dimensional long short term memory (LSTM) (Graves & Schmidhuber, 2009) won three competitions in connected handwriting recognition at the 2009 International Conference on Document Analysis and Recognition (ICDAR), without any prior knowledge about the three different languages to be learned.

Fast GPU-based implementations of this approach by Dan Ciresan and colleagues at IDSIA have won several pattern recognition contests, including the IJCNN 2011 Traffic Sign Recognition Competition (Ciresan, Meier, & Schmidhuber, 2012), the ISBI 2012 Segmentation of Neuronal Structures in Electron Microscopy Stacks challenge (Ciresan, Giusti, Gambardella, & Schmidhuber, 2012), and others. Their neural networks also were the first artificial pattern recognizers to achieve human-competitive or even superhuman performance (Ciresan, Giusti, Gambardella, & Schmidhuber, 2012) on important benchmarks such as traffic sign recognition (IJCNN 2012), or the MNIST handwritten digits problem of Yann LeCun at NYU. Deep, highly nonlinear neural architectures similar to the 1980 neocognitron by Kunihiko Fukushima (Fukushima, 1980) and the "standard architecture of vision (Riesenhuber & Poggio, 1999)" can also be pre-trained by unsupervised methods (Hinton, Osindero, & Teh, 2006) of Geoff Hinton's lab at University of Toronto. A team from this lab won a 2012 contest sponsored by Merck to design software to help find molecules that might lead to new drugs (Markoff, 2012).

Models

Neural network models in artificial intelligence are usually referred to as

379

artificial neural networks (ANNs); these are essentially simple mathematical models defining a function $f: x \rightarrow y$ or a distribution over x or both x and y, but sometimes models are also intimately associated with a particular learning algorithm or learning rule. A common use of the phrase ANN model really means the definition of a class of such functions (where members of the class are obtained by varying parameters, connection weights, or specifics of the architecture such as the number of neurons or their connectivity).

Network function

The word network in the term 'artificial neural network' refers to the inter–connections between the neurons in the different layers of each system. An example system has three layers. The first layer has input neurons which send data via synapses to the second layer of neurons, and then via more synapses to the third layer of output neurons. More complex systems will have more layers of neurons with some having increased layers of input neurons and output neurons. The synapses store parameters called "weights" that manipulate the data in the calculations.

An ANN is typically defined by three types of parameters:

1. The interconnection pattern between the different layers of neurons

2. The learning process for updating the weights of the interconnections

3. The activation function that converts a neuron's weighted input to its output activation

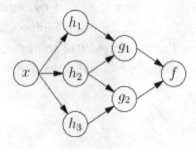

ANN dependency graph

Mathematically, a neuron's network function $f(x)$ is defined as a composition of other functions $g_i(x)$, which can further be defined as a composition of other functions. This can be conveniently represented as a network structure, with arrows depicting the dependencies between variables. A widely used type of composition is the *nonlinear weighted sum*, where $f(x) = \kappa(\sum_i w_i g_i(x))$, where κ (commonly referred to as the activation function) is some predefined function, such as the hyperbolic tangent. It will be convenient for the following to refer to a collection of functions g_i as simply a vector $g = (g_1, g_2, \ldots, g_n)$.

This figure depicts such a decomposition of f, with dependencies between variables indicated by arrows. These can be interpreted in two ways.

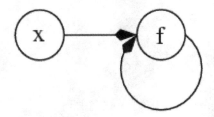

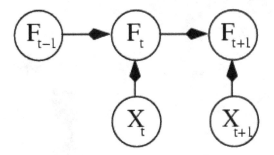

Two separate depictions of the recurrent ANN dependency graph

The first view is the functional view: the input x is transformed into a 3-

381

dimensional vector h, which is then transformed into a 2-dimensional vector g, which is finally transformed into f. This view is most commonly encountered in the context of optimization.

The second view is the probabilistic view: the random variable $F = f(G)$ depends upon the random variable $G = g(H)$, which depends upon $H = h(x)$, which depends upon the random variable x. This view is most commonly encountered in the context of graphical models.

The two views are largely equivalent. In either case, for this particular network architecture, the components of individual layers are independent of each other (e.g., the components of g are independent of each other given their input h). This naturally enables a degree of parallelism in the implementation.

Networks such as the previous one are commonly called feedforward, because their graph is a directed acyclic graph. Networks with cycles are commonly called recurrent. Such networks are commonly depicted in the manner shown at the top of the figure, where f is shown as being dependent upon itself. However, an implied temporal dependence is not shown.

Learning

What has attracted the most interest in neural networks is the possibility of learning. Given a specific task to solve, and a class of functions F, learning means using a set of observations to find $f^* \in F$ which solves the task in some optimal sense.

This entails defining a cost function $C: F \to \mathbb{R}$ such that, for the optimal solution f^*, $C(f^*) \leq C(f) \, \forall f \in F$— i.e., no solution has a cost less than the cost of the optimal solution.

The cost function C is an important concept in learning, as it is a measure of how far away a particular solution is from an optimal solution to the problem to be solved. Learning algorithms search through the solution space to find a function that has the smallest possible cost.

For applications where the solution is dependent on some data, the cost must necessarily be a function of the observations, otherwise we would not be modeling anything related to the data. It is frequently defined as a statistic to which only approximations can be made. As a simple example, consider the problem of finding the model f, which minimizes $C = E[(f(x) - y)^2]$, for data pairs (x, y) drawn from some distribution $\mathcal{D}$. In practical situations we would only have N samples from $\mathcal{D}$ and thus, for the above example, we would only minimize $\hat{C} =$

$\frac{1}{N}\sum_{i=1}^{N}(f(x_i) - y_i)^2$. Thus, the cost is minimized over a sample of the data rather than the entire data set.

When $N \to \infty$ some form of online machine learning must be used, where the cost is partially minimized as each new example is seen. While online machine learning is often used when $\mathcal{D}$ is fixed, it is most useful in the case where the distribution changes slowly over time. In neural network methods, some form of online machine learning is frequently used for finite datasets.

Choosing a cost function

While it is possible to define some arbitrary ad hoc cost function, frequently a particular cost will be used, either because it has desirable properties (such as convexity) or because it arises naturally from a particular formulation of the problem (e.g., in a probabilistic formulation the posterior probability of the model can be used as an inverse cost). Ultimately, the cost function will depend on the desired task. An overview of the three main categories of learning tasks is provided below:

Learning paradigms

There are three major learning paradigms, each corresponding to a particular abstract learning task. These are supervised learning, unsupervised learning and reinforcement learning.

Supervised learning

In supervised learning, we are given a set of example pairs $(x, y), x \in X, y \in Y$ and the aim is to find a function $f: X \to Y$ in the allowed class of functions that matches the examples. In other words, we wish to infer the mapping implied by the data; the cost function is related to the mismatch between our mapping and the data and it implicitly contains prior knowledge about the problem domain.

A commonly used cost is the mean-square error, which tries to minimize the average squared error between the network's output, $f(x)$, and the target value y over all the example pairs. When one tries to minimize this cost using gradient descent for the class of neural networks called multilayer perceptrons, one obtains the common and well-known backpropagation algorithm for training neural networks.

Tasks that fall within the paradigm of supervised learning are pattern recognition (also known as classification) and regression (also known as function approximation). The supervised learning paradigm is also applicable to sequential data (e.g., for speech and gesture recognition). This can be thought of as learning with a "teacher," in the form of a function that provides continuous feedback on the quality of solutions obtained thus far.

Unsupervised learning

In unsupervised learning, some data x is given and the cost function to be minimized, that can be any function of the data x and the network's output, f.

The cost function is dependent on the task (what we are trying to model) and our a *priori* assumptions (the implicit properties of our model, its parameters and the observed variables).

As a trivial example, consider the model $f(x) = a$ where a is a constant and the cost $C = E[(f(x) - y)^2]$. Minimizing this cost will give us a value of a that is equal to the mean of the data. The cost function can be much more complicated. Its form depends on the application: for example, in compression it could be related to the mutual information between x and $f(x)$, whereas in statistical modeling, it could be related to the posterior probability of the model given the data. (Note that in both of those examples those quantities would be maximized rather than minimized).

Tasks that fall within the paradigm of unsupervised learning are in general estimation problems; the applications include clustering, the estimation of statistical distributions, compression and filtering.

Reinforcement learning

In reinforcement learning, data x are usually not given, but generated by an agent's interactions with the environment. At each point in time t, the agent performs an action y_t and the environment generates an observation x_t and an instantaneous cost c_t, according to some (usually unknown) dynamics. The aim is to discover a *policy* for selecting actions that minimizes some measure of a long-term cost; i.e., the expected cumulative cost. The environment's dynamics and the long-term cost for each policy are usually unknown, but can be estimated.

More formally the environment is modelled as a Markov decision process (MDP) with states $s_1, \dots, s_n \in S$ and actions $a_1, \dots, a_m \in A$ with the following probability distributions: the instantaneous cost distribution $P(c_t|s_t)$, the observation distribution $P(x_t|s_t)$ and the transition $P(s_{t+1}|s_t, a_t)$, while a policy is defined as conditional distribution over actions given the observations. Taken together, the two then define a Markov chain (MC). The aim is to discover the policy that minimizes the cost; i.e., the MC for which the cost is minimal.

ANNs are frequently used in reinforcement learning as part of the overall algorithm (Hoskins & Himmelblau, 1992). Dynamic programming has been coupled with ANNs (Neuro dynamic programming) by Bertsekas and Tsitsiklis and applied to multi-dimensional nonlinear problems (Bertsekas, 1996) such as those involved in vehicle routing (Secomandi, 2000), natural resources management (de Rigo, Rizzoli, Soncini-Sessa, Weber, & Zenesi, 2001) (Damas, et al., 2000) or medicine (Deng & Ferris, 2008) because of the ability of ANNs to mitigate losses of accuracy even when reducing the discretization grid density for numerically approximating the solution of the original control problems.

Tasks that fall within the paradigm of reinforcement learning are control problems, games and other sequential decision making tasks.

Learning algorithms

Training a neural network model essentially means selecting one model from the set of allowed models (or, in a Bayesian framework, determining a distribution over the set of allowed models) that minimizes the cost criterion. There are numerous algorithms available for training neural network models; most of them can be viewed as a straightforward application of optimization theory and statistical estimation.

Most of the algorithms used in training artificial neural networks employ some form of gradient descent. This is done by simply taking the derivative of the cost function with respect to the network parameters and then changing those parameters in a gradient-related direction.

Evolutionary methods (de Rigo, Castelletti, Rizzoli, Soncini-Sessa, & Weber, 2005), gene expression programming (Ferreira, 2006), simulated annealing (Da & Xiurun, 2005), expectation-maximization, non-parametric methods and particle swarm optimization (Wu & Chen, 2009) are some commonly used methods for training neural networks.

Employing artificial neural networks

Perhaps the greatest advantage of ANNs is their ability to be used as an arbitrary function approximation mechanism that 'learns' from observed data. However, using them is not so straightforward, and a relatively good understanding of the underlying theory is essential.

- Choice of model: This will depend on the data representation and the application. Overly complex models tend to lead to problems with learning.
- Learning algorithm: There are numerous trade-offs between learning algorithms. Almost any algorithm will work well with the correct hyperparameters for training on a particular fixed data set. However, selecting and tuning an algorithm for training on unseen data requires a significant amount of experimentation.
- Robustness: If the model, cost function and learning algorithm are selected appropriately the resulting ANN can be extremely robust.

With the correct implementation, ANNs can be used naturally in online

387

learning and large data set applications. Their simple implementation and the existence of mostly local dependencies exhibited in the structure allows for fast, parallel implementations in hardware.

Applications

The utility of artificial neural network models lies in the fact that they can be used to infer a function from observations. This is particularly useful in applications where the complexity of the data or task makes the design of such a function by hand impractical.

Real-life applications

The tasks artificial neural networks are applied to tend to fall within the following broad categories:

- Function approximation, or regression analysis, including time series prediction, fitness approximation and modeling.
- Classification, including pattern and sequence recognition, novelty detection and sequential decision making.
- Data processing, including filtering, clustering, blind source separation and compression.
- Robotics, including directing manipulators, prosthesis.
- Control, including Computer numerical control.

Application areas include the system identification and control (vehicle control, process control, natural resources management), quantum chemistry (Balabin & Lomakina, 2009), game-playing and decision making (backgammon, chess, poker), pattern recognition (radar systems, face identification, object recognition and more), sequence recognition (gesture, speech, handwritten text recognition), medical diagnosis, financial applications (e.g. automated trading systems), data mining (or knowledge discovery in databases, "KDD"), visualization and e-mail spam filtering.

Artificial neural networks have also been used to diagnose several cancers. An ANN based hybrid lung cancer detection system named

388

HLND improves the accuracy of diagnosis and the speed of lung cancer radiology (Ganesan, 2010). These networks have also been used to diagnose prostate cancer. The diagnoses can be used to make specific models taken from a large group of patients compared to information of one given patient. The models do not depend on assumptions about correlations of different variables. Colorectal cancer has also been predicted using the neural networks. Neural networks could predict the outcome for a patient with colorectal cancer with more accuracy than the current clinical methods. After training, the networks could predict multiple patient outcomes from unrelated institutions (Bottaci, 1997).

Neural networks and neuroscience

Theoretical and computational neuroscience is the field concerned with the theoretical analysis and the computational modeling of biological neural systems. Since neural systems are intimately related to cognitive processes and behavior, the field is closely related to cognitive and behavioral modeling.

The aim of the field is to create models of biological neural systems in order to understand how biological systems work. To gain this understanding, neuroscientists strive to make a link between observed biological processes (data), biologically plausible mechanisms for neural processing and learning (biological neural network models) and theory (statistical learning theory and information theory).

Types of models

Many models are used in the field, defined at different levels of abstraction and modeling different aspects of neural systems. They range from models of the short-term behavior of individual neurons, models of how the dynamics of neural circuitry arise from interactions between individual neurons and finally to models of how behavior can arise from abstract neural modules that represent complete subsystems. These include models of the long-term, and short-term plasticity, of neural systems and their relations to learning and memory from the individual neuron to the system level.

Types of artificial neural networks

Artificial neural network types vary from those with only one or two layers of single direction logic, to complicated multi–input many directional feedback loops and layers. On the whole, these systems use algorithms in their programming to determine control and organization of their functions. Most systems use "weights" to change the parameters of the throughput and the varying connections to the neurons. Artificial neural networks can be autonomous and learn by input from outside "teachers" or even self-teaching from written-in rules.

Theoretical properties

Computational power

The multi-layer perceptron (MLP) is a universal function approximator, as proven by the Cybenko theorem. However, the proof is not constructive regarding the number of neurons required or the settings of the weights. Work by Hava Siegelmann and Eduardo D. Sontag has provided a proof that a specific recurrent architecture with rational valued weights (as opposed to full precision real number-valued weights) has the full power of a Universal Turing Machine (Siegelmann & Sontag, 1991) using a finite number of neurons and standard linear connections. They have further shown that the use of irrational values for weights results in a machine with super-Turing power.

Capacity

Artificial neural network models have a property called 'capacity', which roughly corresponds to their ability to model any given function. It is related to the amount of information that can be stored in the network and to the notion of complexity.

Convergence

Nothing can be said in general about convergence since it depends on a number of factors. Firstly, there may exist many local minima. This depends on the cost function and the model. Secondly, the optimization method used might not be guaranteed to converge when far away from a local minimum. Thirdly, for a very large amount of data or parameters, some methods become impractical. In general, it has been found that theoretical guarantees regarding convergence are an unreliable guide to practical application.

Generalization and statistics

In applications where the goal is to create a system that generalizes well in unseen examples, the problem of over-training has emerged. This arises in convoluted or over-specified systems when the capacity of the network significantly exceeds the needed free parameters. There are two schools of thought for avoiding this problem: The first is to use cross-validation and similar techniques to check for the presence of overtraining and optimally select hyperparameters such as to minimize the generalization error. The second is to use some form of regularization. This is a concept that emerges naturally in a probabilistic (Bayesian) framework, where the regularization can be performed by selecting a larger prior probability over simpler models; but also in statistical learning theory, where the goal is to minimize over two quantities: the 'empirical risk' and the 'structural risk', which roughly corresponds to the error over the training set and the predicted error in unseen data due to overfitting.

Supervised neural networks that use an MSE cost function can use formal statistical methods to determine the confidence of the trained model. The MSE on a validation set can be used as an estimate for variance. This value can then be used to calculate the confidence interval of the output of the network, assuming a normal distribution. A confidence analysis made this way is statistically valid as long as the output probability distribution stays the same and the network is not modified.

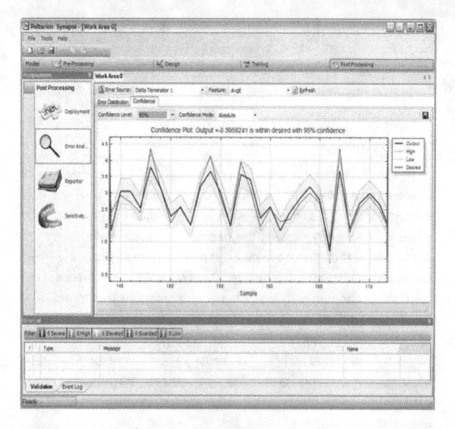

Confidence analysis of a neural network

By assigning a softmax activation function, a generalization of the logistic function, on the output layer of the neural network (or a softmax component in a component-based neural network) for categorical target variables, the outputs can be interpreted as posterior probabilities. This is very useful in classification as it gives a certainty measure on classifications. The softmax activation function is:

$$y_i = \frac{e^{x_i}}{\sum_{i=1}^{c} e^{x_j}}.$$

Dynamic properties

Various techniques originally developed for studying disordered magnetic systems (i.e., the spin glass) have been successfully applied to simple neural network architectures, such as the Hopfield network.

Influential work by E. Gardner and B. Derrida has revealed many interesting properties about perceptrons with real-valued synaptic weights, while later work by W. Krauth and M. Mezard has extended these principles to binary-valued synapses.

Criticism

A common criticism of neural networks, particularly in robotics, is that they require a large diversity of training for real-world operation. This is not surprising, since any learning machine needs sufficient representative examples in order to capture the underlying structure that allows it to generalize to new cases. Dean Pomerleau, in his research presented in the paper "Knowledge-based Training of Artificial Neural Networks for Autonomous Robot Driving," uses a neural network to train a robotic vehicle to drive on multiple types of roads (single lane, multi-lane, dirt, etc.). A large amount of his research is devoted to (1) extrapolating multiple training scenarios from a single training experience, and (2) preserving past training diversity so that the system does not become overtrained (if, for example, it is presented with a series of right turns – it should not learn to always turn right). These issues are common in neural networks that must decide from amongst a wide variety of responses, but can be dealt with in several ways, for example by randomly shuffling the training examples, by using a numerical optimization algorithm that does not take too large steps when changing the network connections following an example, or by grouping examples in so-called mini-batches.

A. K. Dewdney, a former Scientific American columnist, wrote in 1997, "Although neural nets do solve a few toy problems, their powers of computation are so limited that I am surprised anyone takes them seriously as a general problem-solving tool." (Dewdney, p. 82)

Arguments for Dewdney's position are that to implement large and effective software neural networks, much processing and storage resources need to be committed. While the brain has hardware tailored to the task of processing signals through a graph of neurons, simulating even a most simplified form on Von Neumann technology may compel a neural network designer to fill many millions of database rows for its connections – which can consume vast amounts of computer memory and hard disk space. Furthermore, the designer of neural network systems will often need to simulate the transmission of signals through many of these connections and their associated neurons – which must often be matched with incredible amounts of CPU processing power and time. While neural networks often yield effective programs, they too often do so at the cost of efficiency (they tend to consume considerable amounts of time and money).

Arguments against Dewdney's position are that neural nets have been successfully used to solve many complex and diverse tasks, ranging from autonomously flying aircraft (NASA, 2003) to detecting credit card fraud.

Technology writer Roger Bridgman commented on Dewdney's statements about neural nets:

Neural networks, for instance, are in the dock not only because they have been hyped to high heaven, (what hasn't?) but also because you could create a successful net without understanding how it worked: the bunch of numbers that captures its behavior would in all probability be "an opaque, unreadable table...valueless as a scientific resource".

In spite of his emphatic declaration that science is not technology, Dewdney seems here to pillory neural nets as bad science when most of those devising them are just trying to be good engineers. An unreadable table that a useful machine could read would still be well worth having (Bridgman).

In response to this kind of criticism, one should note that although it is true that analyzing what has been learned by an artificial neural network is difficult, it is much easier to do so than to analyze what has been learned by a biological neural network. Furthermore, researchers involved in exploring learning algorithms for neural networks are gradually uncovering generic principles which allow a learning machine to be successful. For example, Bengio and LeCun (2007) wrote an article regarding local vs non-local learning, as well as shallow vs deep architecture. Some other criticisms came from believers of hybrid models (combining neural networks and symbolic approaches). They advocate the intermix of these two approaches and believe that hybrid models can better capture the mechanisms of the human mind (Sun and Bookman, 1990).

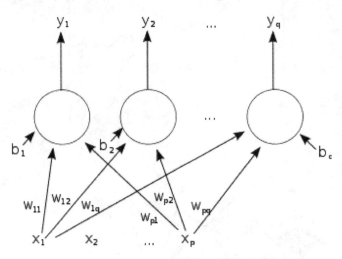

A single-layer feedforward artificial neural network. Arrows originating from x_2 are omitted for clarity. There are p inputs to this network and q outputs. In this system, the value of the qth output, y_q would be calculated as $y_q = \Sigma(x_i * w_{iq})$

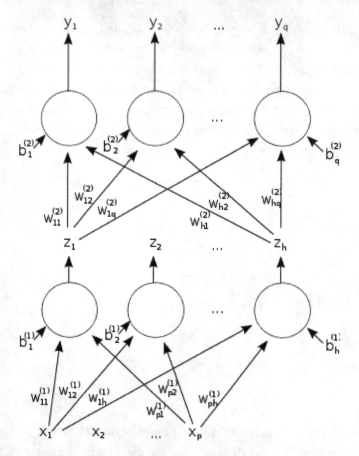

A two-layer feedforward artificial neural network.

Neural network software

Simulators

Neural network simulators are software applications that are used to simulate the behavior of artificial or biological neural networks. They focus on one or a limited number of specific types of neural networks. They are typically stand-alone and not intended to produce general neural networks that can be integrated in other software. Simulators usually have some form of built-in visualization to monitor the training process. Some simulators also visualize the physical structure of the neural network.

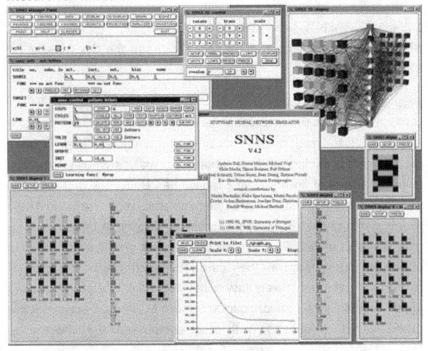

SNNS research neural network simulator

Historically, the most common type of neural network software was intended for researching neural network structures and algorithms. The primary purpose of this type of software is, through simulation, to gain a better understanding of the behavior and properties of neural networks. Today in the study of artificial neural networks, simulators have largely been replaced by more general component based development environments as research platforms.

Commonly used artificial neural network simulators include the Stuttgart Neural Network Simulator (SNNS), Emergent, JavaNNS, Neural Lab and NetMaker

In the study of biological neural networks however, simulation software is still the only available approach. In such simulators the physical biological and chemical properties of neural tissue, as well as the electromagnetic impulses between the neurons are studied.

Commonly used biological network simulators include Neuron, GENESIS, NEST and Brian. Other simulators are XNBC and the NN Toolbox for MATLAB.

Data analysis simulators
Unlike the research simulators, the data analysis simulators are intended for practical applications of artificial neural networks. Their primary focus is on data mining and forecasting. Data analysis simulators usually have some form of preprocessing capabilities. Unlike the more general development environments data analysis simulators use a relatively simple static neural network that can be configured. A majority of the data analysis simulators on the market use back propagating networks or self-organizing maps as their core. The advantage of this type of software is that it is relatively easy to use. Some data analysis simulators are dedicated neural network packages, such as Neural Designer. Some others work in conjunction with other computational environments, such as NeuralTools for Microsoft Excel.

Simulators for teaching neural network theory
When the Parallel Distributed Processing volumes[1] [2][3] were released in 1986-87, they provided some relatively simple software. The original PDP software did not require any programming skills, which led to its adoption by a wide variety of researchers in diverse fields. The original PDP software was developed into a more powerful package called PDP++, which in turn has become an even more powerful platform called Emergent. With each development, the software has become more powerful, but also more daunting for use by beginners.

In 1997, the tLearn software was released to accompany a book.[4] This was a return to the idea of providing a small, user-friendly, simulator that was designed with the novice in mind. tLearn allowed basic feed forward networks, along with simple recurrent networks, both of which can be trained by the simple back propagation algorithm. tLearn has not been updated since 1999.

In 2011, the Basic Prop simulator was released. Basic Prop is a self-contained application, distributed as a platform neutral JAR file, that provides much of the same simple functionality as tLearn.

Development Environments

Development environments for neural networks differ from the software described above primarily on two accounts – they can be used to develop custom types of neural networks and they support deployment of the neural network outside the environment. In some cases they have advanced preprocessing, analysis and visualization capabilities.

Component based

A more modern type of development environments that are currently favored in both industrial and scientific use are based on a component based paradigm. The neural network is constructed by connecting adaptive filter components in a pipe filter flow. This allows for greater flexibility as custom networks can be built as well as custom components used by the network. In many cases this allows a combination of adaptive and non-adaptive components to work together. The data flow is controlled by a control system which is exchangeable as well as the adaptation algorithms. The other important feature is deployment capabilities. With the advent of component-based frameworks such as .NET and Java, component based development environments are capable of deploying the developed neural network to these frameworks as inheritable components. In addition some software can also deploy these components to several platforms, such as embedded systems.

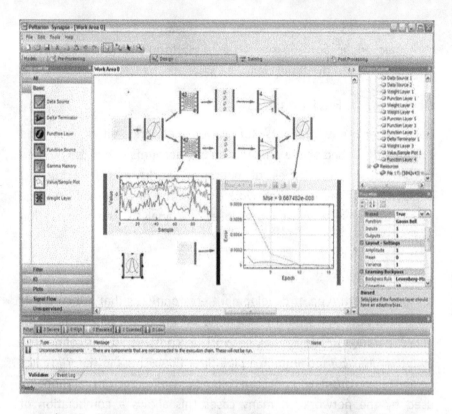

Peltarion Synapse component based development environment.

Component based development environments include: Peltarion Synapse, NeuroDimension NeuroSolutions, Scientific Software Neuro Laboratory, and the LIONsolver integrated software. Free open source component based environments include Encog and Neuroph.

Criticism
A disadvantage of component-based development environments is that they are more complex than simulators. They require more learning to fully operate and are more complicated to develop.

Custom neural networks

The majority implementations of neural networks available are however custom implementations in various programming languages and on various platforms. Basic types of neural networks are simple to implement directly. There are also many programming libraries that contain neural network functionality and that can be used in custom implementations.

Standards

In order for neural network models to be shared by different applications, a common language is necessary. Recently, the Predictive Model Markup Language (PMML) has been proposed to address this need.

PMML is an XML-based language which provides a way for applications to define and share neural network models (and other data mining models) between PMML compliant applications.

PMML provides applications a vendor-independent method of defining models so that proprietary issues and incompatibilities are no longer a barrier to the exchange of models between applications. It allows users to develop models within one vendor's application, and use other vendors' applications to visualize, analyze, evaluate or otherwise use the models. Previously, this was very difficult, but with PMML, the exchange of models between compliant applications is now straightforward.

PMML Consumers and Producers

A range of products are being offered to produce and consume PMML. This ever growing list includes the following neural network products:

- R: produces PMML for neural nets and other machine learning models via the package `pmml`.
- SAS Enterprise Miner: produces PMML for several mining models, including neural networks, linear and logistic regression, decision trees, and other data mining models.
- SPSS: produces PMML for neural networks as well as many other mining models.
- STATISTICA: produces PMML for neural networks, data mining models and traditional statistical models.

Example Using R

In this example a neural network (or Multilayer perceptron depending on naming convention) will be build that is able to take a number and calculate the square root (or as close to as possible). The R library 'neuralnet' will be used to train and build the neural network.

The example will produce the neural network shown in the image below. It is going to take a single input (the number that you want square rooting) and produce a single output (the square root of the input). The middle of the image contains 10 hidden neurons which will be trained.

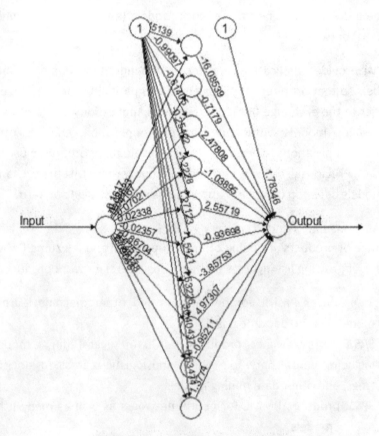

Error: 0.001006 Steps: 5096

The output of the script will look like:

Input Expected Output Neural Net Output

```
     Input        Expected Output      Neural Net Output
       1                1                 0.9623402772
       4                2                 2.0083461217
       9                3                 2.9958221776
      16                4                 4.0009548085
      25                5                 5.0028838579
      36                6                 5.9975810435
      49                7                 6.9968278722
      64                8                 8.0070028670
      81                9                 9.0019220736
     100               10                 9.9222007864
```

As you can see the neural network does a reasonable job at finding the square root, the largest error in in finding the square root of 1 which is out by ~4%

Onto the code:

```
install.packages('neuralnet')
library("neuralnet")

#Going to create a neural network to perform sqare
#rooting
#Type ?neuralnet for more information on the
#neuralnet library

#Generate 50 random numbers uniformly distributed
#between 0 and 100
#And store them as a dataframe

> traininginput <-  as.data.frame(runif(50, min=0,
+             max=100))
> trainingoutput <- sqrt(traininginput)

#Column bind the data into one variable
> trainingdata <- cbind(traininginput,trainingoutput)
> colnames(trainingdata) <- c("Input","Output")

#Train the neural network
#Going to have 10 hidden layers
#Threshold is a numeric value specifying the threshold for
```

the partial
#derivatives of the error function as stopping criteria.
>   net.sqrt   <-   neuralnet(Output~Input,trainingdata,
hidden=10, threshold=0.01)
> print(net.sqrt)

Call: neuralnet(formula = Output ~ Input, data =
trainingdata, hidden = 10,   threshold = 0.01)

1 repetition was calculated.

          Error Reached Threshold Steps
1 0.0003125347103   0.009401234527 7413

#Plot the neural network
> plot(net.sqrt)

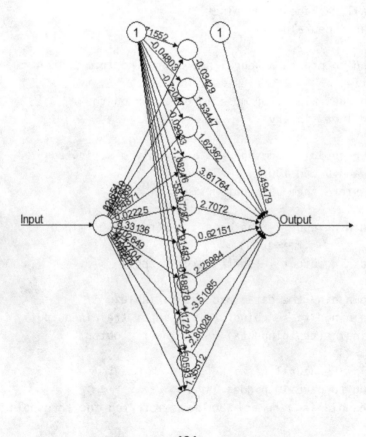

```
#Test the neural network on some training data
> testdata <- as.data.frame((1:10)^2)
#Generate some squared numbers through the neural #network

#Lets see what properties net.sqrt has
> ls(net.results)
 [1] "act.fct"        "call"            "covariate"
 [4] "data"           "err.fct" "generalized.weights"
 [7] "linear.output" "model.list"       "net.result"
[10] "response"      "result.matrix"  "startweights"
[13] "weights"

#Lets see the results
> print(net.results$net.result)
[[1]]
            [,1]
1   5.0490045485
2   7.4625475299
3   5.4268560491
4   9.3944183247
5   7.3261826045
6   9.7116754748
7   7.7005230133
8   6.1877876553
9   9.0208308800
10  5.7323789090
11  8.8662469974
12  9.6321471501
13  5.5556127899
14  8.8963448461
15  6.5228214924
16  4.6004103084
17  5.1903750160
18  7.4088926123
19  4.6820958475
20  8.7562521802
21  8.9002614981
22  9.9683150949
23  0.8709360456
```

```
24 5.7191690479
25 9.5527300575
26 4.2271915852
27 9.3130169284
28 6.6324229956
29 6.4189621322
30 9.0096296704
31 5.7399327728
32 3.5851960402
33 8.0773241098
34 9.3700866302
35 2.7618057270
36 8.8809443763
37 7.2225438175
38 3.5564655707
39 8.2756946858
40 4.2854133636
41 8.8574145651
42 5.8292858082
43 6.3127094368
44 2.6722212606
45 7.0154300338
46 8.3787559152
47 9.5958246251
48 4.8688678386
49 6.5017337465
50 8.3502796644


#Lets display a better version of the results
> cleanoutput <- cbind(testdata,sqrt(testdata),
+            as.data.frame(net.results$net.result))
> colnames(cleanoutput) <- c("Input","Expected
+            Output","Neural Net Output")
> print(cleanoutput)
Input  Expected Output Neural Net Output
1      1               1    5.0490045485
2      4               2    7.4625475299
3      9               3    5.4268560491
4      16              4    9.3944183247
5      25              5    7.3261826045
```

6	36	6	9.7116754748
7	49	7	7.7005230133
8	64	8	6.1877876553
9	81	9	9.0208308800
10	100	10	5.7323789090
11	1	1	8.8662469974
12	4	2	9.6321471501
13	9	3	5.5556127899
14	16	4	8.8963448461
15	25	5	6.5228214924
16	36	6	4.6004103084
17	49	7	5.1903750160
18	64	8	7.4088926123
19	81	9	4.6820958475
20	100	10	8.7562521802
21	1	1	8.9002614981
22	4	2	9.9683150949
23	9	3	0.8709360456
24	16	4	5.7191690479
25	25	5	9.5527300575
26	36	6	4.2271915852
27	49	7	9.3130169284
28	64	8	6.6324229956
29	81	9	6.4189621322
30	100	10	9.0096296704
31	1	1	5.7399327728
32	4	2	3.5851960402
33	9	3	8.0773241098
34	16	4	9.3700866302
35	25	5	2.7618057270
36	36	6	8.8809443763
37	49	7	7.2225438175
38	64	8	3.5564655707
39	81	9	8.2756946858
40	100	10	4.2854133636
41	1	1	8.8574145651
42	4	2	5.8292858082
43	9	3	6.3127094368
44	16	4	2.6722212606
45	25	5	7.0154300338

46	36	6	8.3787559152
47	49	7	9.5958246251
48	64	8	4.8688678386
49	81	9	6.5017337465
50	100	10	8.3502796644

19. Uplift modeling

Uplift modeling, also known as incremental modeling, true lift modeling, or net-lift modeling is a predictive modeling technique that directly models the incremental impact of a treatment (such as a direct marketing action) on an individual's behavior.

Uplift modeling has applications in customer relationship management for up-sell, cross-sell and retention modeling. It has also been applied to personalized medicine. Unlike the related Differential Prediction concept in psychology, Uplift modeling assumes an active agent.

Introduction

Uplift modeling uses a randomized scientific control to not only measure the effectiveness of a marketing action but also to build a predictive model that predicts the incremental response to the marketing action. It is a data mining technique that has been applied predominantly in the financial services, telecommunications and retail direct marketing industries to up-sell, cross-sell, churn and retention activities.

Measuring uplift

The uplift of a marketing campaign is usually defined as the difference in response rate between a treated group and a randomized control group. This allows a marketing team to isolate the effect of a marketing action and measure the effectiveness or otherwise of that individual marketing action. Honest marketing teams will only take credit for the incremental effect of their campaign.

The uplift problem statement

The uplift problem can be stated as follow, given the following:

- cases $P = \{1, .., n\}$,
- treatments $J = \{1, ..., U\}$,
- expected return $R(i, t)$ for each case i and treatment t,

- non-negative integers $n_1, \dots, n_U$ such that

$$n_1 + \cdots + n_U = n$$

find a treatment assignment

$$f : P \to J$$

So that the total return

$$\sum_{i=1}^{n} R_{if(i)}$$

is maximized, subject to the constraints that the number of cases assigned to treatment j is not to exceed $n_j, (j = 1, .., U)$.

Example: Marketing action case

- P: a group of customers,
- two treatments:

1. treatment 1: exercise some marketing action; R_{i1} is the expected return if treatment 1 is given to customer i,
2. treatment 2: exercise no the marketing action; let R_{i2} be the expected return if treatment 2 is given to customer i.

Solution to the maximization problem:

$$\sum_{i=1}^{n} R_{if(i)} = \left(\sum_{i \in (f=1)} R_{i1} \right) + \left(\sum_{i \in (f=2)} R_{i2} \right)$$

$$= \left(\sum_{i \in (f=1)} R_{i1} \right) + \left(\sum_{i=1}^{n} R_{i2} - \sum_{i \in (f=1)} R_{i2} \right)$$

$$= \left(\sum_{i \in (f=1)} R_{i1} - R_{i2} \right) + \left(\sum_{i=1}^{n} R_{i2} \right)$$

The second sum does not involve f, so maximizing total return is

410

equivalent to maximizing the first term

$$\sum_{i \in (f=1)} (R_{i1} - R_{i2})$$

As for to the solution to the problem when we consider only the reponses to treatment 1, to attain the maximum return:

- assign treatment 1 to the customers with the n_1 largest values of $R_{i1} - R_{i2}$
- assign treatment 2 to the remaining customers

The difference $R_{i1} - R_{i2}$ is called net lift, uplift, incremental response, differential response, etc.

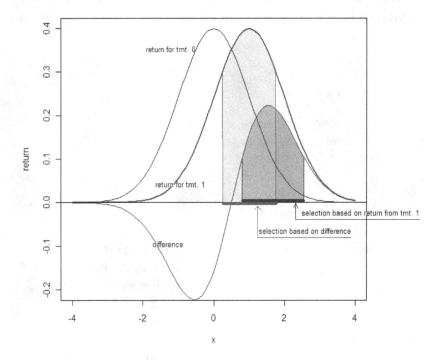

If we consider only the response to treatment 1, and base targeting on a model built out of responses to previous marketing actions, we are not proceeding as if to maximize $\sum_{i=1}^{n} R_{if(i)}$. Such maximization would not yield the maximum return. We need to consider the return from cases subjected to **no** marketing action.

Now, consider a model with a binary response, e.g., Yes = 1, No = 0. Then the netlift is:

$$Prob(1) = \frac{\exp(score_1)}{1 + \exp(score_1)};$$

$$Prob(0) = \frac{\exp(score_0)}{1 + \exp(score_0)};$$

$$netlift = Prob(1) - Prob(0),$$

where $Prob(1)$ is the probability of a response equal to 1, $Prob(0)$ is the probability of a response = 0, $score_1$ is the model scores for responses equal to 1, and $score_0$ is the model scores for responses equal to 0.

The incremental response lift, with all initial vales set to 0, can be obtained using the following pseudo code:

```
prob1 = exp(score_1)/(1+exp(score_1));
prob0 = exp(score_0)/(1+exp(score_0));
netlift = prob1 - prob0;

if  treatment flag = 1 then
mail total = mail total +  1;
if  response = 1 then mail response = mail response +  1;
expected netlift mailed = expected netlift mailed + netlift;
expected anyway mailed = expected anyway mailed + prob(0);
expected mail response = expected mail response + prob(1);
end;
else do;
nomail totoal = nomail total + 1;
if response = 1 then nomail response = nomail response + 1;
end;
```

The associated probabilities and netlift pseudo code is:

412

```
if last pentile;
empirical prob mail = mail response/mail total;
empirical prob nomail = nomail response/nomail total;
empirical netlift = empirical prob mail - empirical prob
nomail;
percent gain = 100* empirical netlift/ empirical prob nomail;
empirical expected buyanyway mailed = mail total* empirical
prob nomail;
empirical expected netlift = mailresp - empirical expected
buyanyway mailed;
```

The table below shows the details of a campaign showing the number of responses and calculated response rate for a hypothetical marketing campaign. This campaign would be defined as having a response rate uplift of 5%. It has created 50,000 incremental responses (100,000 - 50,000).

Group	Number of Customers	Responses	Response Rate
Treated	1,000,000	100,000	10%
Control	1,000,000	50,000	5%

Traditional response modeling

Traditional response modeling typically takes a group of treated customers and attempts to build a predictive model that separates the likely responders from the non-responders through the use of one of a number of predictive modeling techniques. Typically this would use decision trees or regression analysis.

This model would only use the treated customers to build the model.

In contrast uplift modeling uses both the treated and control customers to build a predictive model that focuses on the incremental response. To understand this type of model it is proposed that there is a fundamental segmentation that separates customers into the following groups (Lo, 2002):

413

- The Persuadables : customers who only respond to the marketing action because they were targeted
- The Sure Things : customers who would have responded whether they were targeted or not
- The Lost Causes : customers who will not respond irrespective of whether or not they are targeted
- The Do Not Disturbs or Sleeping Dogs : customers who are less likely to respond because they were targeted

The only segment that provides true incremental responses is the Persuadables.

Uplift modeling provides a scoring technique that can separate customers into the groups described above. Traditional response modeling often targets the Sure Things being unable to distinguish them from the Persuadables.

Example: Simulation-Educators.com

Majority of direct marketing campaigns are based on purchase propensity models, selecting customer email, paper mail or other marketing contact lists based on customers' probability to make a purchase. Simulation-Educators.com offers training courses in modeling and simulation topics. The following is an example of a of standard purchase propensity model output for a mailing campaign for such courses.

Scoring Rank	Response Rate	Lift
1	28.1%	3.41
2	17.3%	2.10
3	9.6%	1.17
4	8.4%	1.02
5	4.8%	0.58
6	3.9%	0.47
7	3.3%	0.40
8	3.4%	0.41
9	3.5%	0.42

Scoring Rank	Response Rate	Lift
10	0.1%	0.01
Total	8.2%	

Table 1. Example of standard purchase propensity model output used to generate direct campaign mailing list at Simulation-Educators.com

This purchase propensity model had a 'nice' lift (rank's response rate over total response rate) for the top 4 ranks on the validation data set. Consequently, we would contact customers included in top 4 ranks. After the catalog campaign had been completed, we conducted post analysis of mailing list performance vs. control group. The control group consisted of customers who were not contacted, grouped by the same purchase probability scoring ranks.

	Mailing Group	Control Group	
Scoring Rank	Response Rate	Response Rate	Incremental Response Rate
1	26.99%	27.90%	-0.91%
2	20.34%	20.90%	-0.56%
3	10.70%	10.04%	0.66%
4	8.90%	7.52%	1.38%
Total	16.70%	16.55%	0.15%

Table 2. Campaign Post analysis

As shown the table 2, the top four customer ranks selected by propensity model perform well for both mailing group and control group. However, even though mailing/test group response rate was at decent level – 16.7%, our incremental response rate (mailing group net of control group) for combined top 4 ranks was only 0.15%. With such low incremental response rate, our undertaking would be likely generating a negative ROI.

What was the reason that our campaign shown such poor incremental results? The purchase propensity model did its job well and we did send an offer to people who were likely to make a purchase. Apparently, modeling based on expected purchase propensity is not always the right solution for a successful direct marking campaign. Since there was no increase in response rate over control group, we could have been contacting customers who would have bought our product without promotional direct mail. Customers in top ranks of purchase propensity model may not need a nudge or they are buying in response to a contact via other channels. If that is the case, the customers in the lower purchase propensity ranks would be more 'responsive' to a marketing contact.

We should be predicting incremental impact – additional purchases generated by a campaign, not purchases that would be made without the contact. Our marketing mailing can be substantially more cost efficient if we don't mail customers who are going to buy anyway.

Since customers very rarely use promo codes from catalogs or click on web display ads, it is difficult to identify undecided, swing customer based on the promotion codes or web display click-throughs.

Net lift models predict which customer segments are likely to make a purchase ONLY if prompted by a marketing undertaking.

Purchasers from mailing group include customers that needed a nudge, however, all purchasers in the holdout/control group did not need our catalog to make their purchasing decision. All purchasers in the control group can be classified as 'need no contact'. Since we need a model that would separate 'need contact' purchasers from 'no contact' purchasers, the net lift models look at differences in purchasers in mailing (contact) group versus purchasers from control group.

In order to classify our customers into these groups we need mailing group and control group purchases results from similar prior campaigns. If there are no comparable historic undertakings, we have to create a small scale trial before the main rollout.

Uplift modeling approach—probability decomposition models

Segments used in probability decomposition models:

	Contacted Group	Control Group
Purchasers prompted by contact	A	D
Purchasers not needing contact	B	E
Non Purchasers	C	F

Figure 2. Segments in probability decomposition models

Standard purchase propensity models are only capable of predicting all purchasers (combined segments A and B). The probability decomposition model predicts purchasers segments that need to be contacted (segment A) by leveraging two logistic regression models, as shown in the formula below (Zhong, 2009).

P(A I AUBUC) =	P(AUB I AUBUC) x	(2 - 1/P(AUB I AUBUE))
Probability of purchase prompted by contact	Probability of purchase out of contact group	Probability of purchaser being in contact group out of all purchasers

Summary of probability decomposition modeling process:

1. Build stepwise logistic regression purchase propensity model (M1) and record model score for every customer in a modeled population.
2. Use past campaign results or small scale trial campaign results to create a dataset with two equal size sections of purchasers from contact group and control group. Build a stepwise regression logistic model predicting which purchasers are from the contact group. The main task of this model will be to penalize the score of model built in the step 1 when purchaser is not likely to need contact.
3. Calculate net purchasers score based on probability decomposition formula

Results of the probability decomposition modeling process

Scoring Rank	Contact Group Response %	Control Group Response %	Incremental Response Rate
1	18.8%	12.9%	5.9%
2	7.8%	5.4%	2.4%
3	6.9%	4.5%	2.5%
4	4.3%	3.6%	0.7%
5	3.9%	3.5%	0.4%
6	4.1%	4.1%	0.0%
7	3.7%	4.0%	-0.2%
8	4.7%	4.1%	0.6%
9	5.0%	6.7%	-1.7%
10	11.0%	15.7%	-4.7%

Table 3. Post analysis of campaign leveraging probability decomposition model for Simulation-Educators.com

Scoring Ranks 1 thru 6 show positive incremental response rates. The scoring ranks are ordered based on the incremental response rates.

Return on investment

Because uplift modeling focuses on incremental responses only, it provides very strong return on investment cases when applied to traditional demand generation and retention activities. For example, by only targeting the persuadable customers in an outbound marketing campaign, the contact costs and hence the return per unit spend can be dramatically improved (Radcliffe & Surry, 2011).

Removal of negative effects

One of the most effective uses of uplift modeling is in the removal of negative effects from retention campaigns. Both in the telecommunications and financial services industries often retention campaigns can trigger customers to cancel a contract or policy. Uplift modeling allows these customers, the Do Not Disturbs, to be removed from the campaign.

Application to A/B and Multivariate Testing

It is rarely the case that there is a single treatment and control group. Often the "treatment" can be a variety of simple variations of a message or a multi-stage contact strategy that is classed as a single treatment. In the case of A/B or multivariate testing, uplift modeling can help in understanding whether the variations in tests provide any significant uplift compared to other targeting criteria such as behavioral or demographic indicators.

Methods for modeling

Example of Logistic Regression

We now use a special case of binary response variable to describe our proposed methodology. If Y_i is a binary response variable representing whether customer i responds to a campaign, we consider the following set of independent variables: X_i, T_i, and $X_i * T_i$ where $T_i = 1$ if i is in the treatment group and $T_i = 0$ if i is in the control group. We may model the response rate using a linear logistic regression

$$P_i \, E(Y_i|X_i) = \frac{\exp(\alpha + \beta'X_i + \gamma T_i + \delta'X_iT_i)}{1 + \exp(\alpha + \beta'X_i + \gamma T_i + \delta'X_iT_i)},$$

where $\alpha, \beta, \gamma, \delta$ are parameters to be estimated.

In the logistic equation, α denotes the intercept, β is a vector of parameters measuring the main effects of the independent variables, γ denotes the main treatment effect, and δ measures additional effects of the independent variables due to treatment. In reality, some variable reduction procedure will usually be applied to narrow down the list of X_i, T_i, and $X_i * T_i$ first before estimating the parameters in the equation.

Then

$P_i|\text{treatment} - P_i|\text{control}$

$$= \frac{\exp(\alpha + \gamma + \beta'X_i + \delta'X_i)}{1 + \exp(\alpha + \gamma + \beta'X_i + \delta'X_i)} - \frac{\exp(\alpha + \beta'X_i)}{1 + \exp(\alpha + \beta'X_i)}.$$

419

That is, the parameter estimates obtained in first equation can be used in this equation to predict the treatment and control difference in response rate for each i in a new data set. Then the data set can be sorted by the predicted difference between treatment and control. Those with high positive predicted differences will be selected for next campaign targeting.

The procedure then is to build a logistic regression model for the treatment sample and a separate one for the control sample. Then the uplift model subtracts probabilities predicted by both.

Example of Decision Tree

Rzepakowski and Jaroszewicz (Rzepakowski & Jaroszewicz, 2010) propose an approach that employs decision trees with:

- Spliting criteria based on Information Theory
- Pruning strategy designed for uplift modeling
- Multiclass problems and multiway splits possible
- If the control group is empty, the criterion should reduce to one of classical splitting criteria used for decision tree learning

The approach uses splitting criteria based on three distribution divergences. A distribution divergence is a measure of how much two probability distributions differ. The Kullback-Leibler divergence is a well-known and widely used information theoretic measure. It can be used to measure the difference between treatment and control groups:

$$KL\big(P_T(Class):P_C(Class)\big) = KL\big(P_T(Y)|P_C(Y)\big)$$
$$= \sum_{y\in Y} P_T(y)\log\frac{P_T(y)}{P_C(y)}.$$

The squared Euclidean distance is less frequently applied to compare distributions, but has been used in literature, and applied for example to Schema Matching:

$$Euclid\big(P_T(Y)\big|P_C(Y)\big) = \sum_{y \in \text{Dom}\,(Class)} \big(P_T{}^T(y) - P_C(y)\big)^2.$$

The third, Chi-squared divergence has been used, e.g., to measure interestingness of rules:

$$\chi^2\big(P_T(Y)\big|P_C(Y)\big) = \sum_{y \in \text{Dom}\,(Class)} \frac{\big(P^T(y) - P_C(y)\big)^2}{P_C(y)}.$$

Rzepakowski and Jaroszewicz (Rzepakowski & Jaroszewicz, 2010) argue that the squared Euclidean distance has some important advantages that make it an attractive alternative to the Kullback-Leibler and chi-squared measures.

KL-divergence is conditional on a split Ω. The KL becomes

$$KL(P_T(Y)\big|P_C(Y)\big|\Omega) = \sum_{\omega \in \Omega} \frac{M(\Omega)}{M} KL\big(P_T(Y|\omega)\big|P_C(Y|\omega)\big),$$

where $M = M_T + M_C$ (the sum of the training cases in the treatment and control groups) and $M(\Omega) = M_T(\Omega) + M_C(\Omega)$ (the sum of the number of training cases in which the outcome of the uplift Ω is ω in treatment and control groups) (Rzepakowski & Jaroszewicz, 2010).

We then define KL_{gain} as the increase in the KL divergence from a split Ω relative to the KL-divergence in the parent node

$$KL_{gain}(\Omega) = KL(P_T(Y)\big|P_C(Y)\big|\Omega) - KL\big(P_T(Y)\big|P_C(Y)\big).$$

The final split criterion is (Rzepakowski & Jaroszewicz, 2010)

$$KL_{ratio}(\Omega) = \frac{KL_{gain}(\Omega)}{KL_{norm}(\Omega)},$$

where $KL_{norm}(\Omega)$ is a normalization factor that punishes:

- splits with different treatment/control proportions on each branch

- splits with unbalanced number of cases on each branch

Decision tree pruning is a step which has decisive influence on the generalization performance of the model. There are several pruning methods, based on statistical tests, minimum description length principle, etc.

The authors devised the maximum class probability difference which can be viewed as a generalization of classification accuracy to the uplift case. The idea is to look at the differences between treatment and control probabilities in the root of the subtree and in its leaves, and prune if, overall, the differences in leaves are not greater than the difference in the root. In each node, they only look at the class for which the difference was largest on the training set, and in addition, remember the sign of that difference such that only differences that have the same sign in the training and validation sets contribute to the increase in our analog of accuracy. This procedure is consistent with the goal of maximizing the difference between treatment and control probabilities (Rzepakowski & Jaroszewicz, 2010). They define

$$Diff\,(Class, node) = P_T(Class|node) - P_C(Class|node)$$

Maximum class probability difference (MD) is

$$MD(node) = max_{Class}\,|\text{Diff}\,(Class|node)|,$$

and the sign of this difference

$$sign(node) = sgn\big(\text{Diff}\,(Class^*, node)\big).$$

These are employed on separate validation sets using a bottom up procedure. The subtree kept if

- On validation set: MD of the subtree is greater than if it was replaced with a leaf
- And the sign of MD is the same in training and validation sets

In their experimental evaluation, Rzepakowski and Jaroszewicz

(Rzepakowski & Jaroszewicz, 2010) produce the following uplift curves using for the splice dataset (The SPLICE dataset: Classification, 2010).

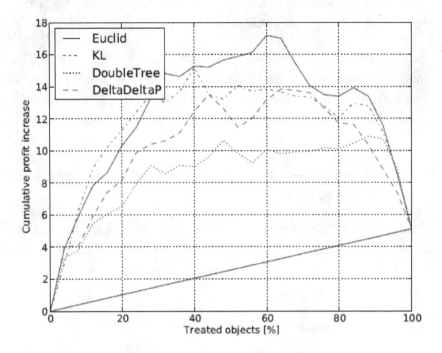

Note: The R package entropy provides the functionality for performing Kullback-Leibler (KL.plugin) and chi-squared (chi2.plugin) measures. Given two samples from splice, we have:

```
> data1<-mydata[sample(1:nrow(mydata),100,replace=FALSE),]
> data2<-mydata[sample(1:nrow(mydata),100,replace=FALSE),]
> colnames(data1)[colnames(data1)=="RESP"] <- "RESP1"
> colnames(data2)[colnames(data2)=="RESP"] <- "RESP2"
> RESP1 = c(0.21, 0.24, 0.55)
> RESP2 = c(0.26, 0.25, 0.49)

> KL.plugin(RESP1, RESP2)
[1] 0.008884248 # the KL-distance

> chi2.plugin(RESP1,RESP2)
[1] 0.01736232  # the Chi2-distance
```

History of uplift modeling

The first appearance of true response modeling appears to be in the work of Radcliffe and Surry (Radcliffe & Surry, 1999).

Victor Lo also published on this topic in The True Lift Model (Lo, 2002), and more recently Radcliffe (Radcliffe, Using Control Groups to Target on Predicted Lift: Building and Assessing Uplift Models, 2007). Radcliffe also provides a very useful frequently asked questions (FAQ) section on his web site, Scientific Marketer (Uplift Modelling FAQ, 2007).

Similar approaches have been explored in personalized medicine (Cai, Tian, Wong, & Wei, 2009).

Uplift modeling is a special case of the older psychology concept of Differential Prediction. In contrast to differential prediction, uplift modeling assumes an active agent, and uses the uplift measure as an optimization metric.

Implementations

- uplift package for R
- JMP by SAS
- Portrait Uplift by Pitney Bowes
- Uplift node for KNIME by Dymatrix

Example Using R

upliftRF

This example shows the function modelProfile ('uplift' package in R), which can be used to profile a fitted uplift model—we use upliftRF for this example. Given a vector of scores (uplift predictions), it computes basic summary statistics for each predictor by score quantile.

```
> library(uplift)
> ### Simulate data
> set.seed(12345)
> dd <- sim_pte(n = 1000, p = 5, rho = 0, sigma = sqrt(2),
```

```
+ beta.den = 4)
> dd$treat <- ifelse(dd$treat == 1, 1, 0) # required coding
                                          # for upliftRF
```

upliftRF is the model used for predictions from a Fitted Uplift
Random Forest Model (CRAN-project, 2012):

```
> ### Fit upliftRF model
> fit1 <- upliftRF(y ~ X1 + X2 + X3 + X4 + X5 + trt(treat),
+ data = dd,
+ mtry = 3,
+ ntree = 50,
+ split_method = "KL",
+ minsplit = 100,
+ verbose = TRUE)
```

where

data	A data frame containing the variables in the model. It should include a variable reflecting the binary treatment assignment of each observation (coded as 0/1).
x, formula	a data frame of predictors or a formula describing the model to be fitted. A special term of the form trt() must be used in the model equation to identify the binary treatment variable. For example, if the treatment is represented by a variable named treat, then the right hand side of the formula must include the term +trt(treat).
y	a binary response (numeric) vector.
ct	a binary (numeric) vector representing the treatment assignment (coded as 0/1).
mtry	the number of variables to be tested in each node; the default is floor(sqrt(ncol(x))).
ntree	the number of trees to generate in the forest; default is ntree = 100.
split_method	the split criteria used at each node of each tree; Possible values are: "ED" (Euclidean distance), "Chisq" (Chi-squared divergence), "KL" (Kullback-Leibler divergence), "Int" (Interaction method).
interaction.depth	The maximum depth of variable interactions. 1 implies an additive model, 2 implies a model with up to 2-way interactions, etc. The default is to grow trees to maximal

	depth, constrained on the arguments specified in `minsplit` and `minbucket`.
bag.fraction	the fraction of the training set observations randomly selected for the purpose of fitting each tree in the forest.
minsplit	the minimum number of observations that must exist in a node in order for a split to be attempted.
minbucket_ct0	the minimum number of control observations in any terminal <leaf> node.
minbucket_ct1	the minimum number of treatment observations in any terminal <leaf> node.
keep.inbag	if set to TRUE, an `nrow(x)` by `ntree` matrix is returned, whose entries are the "in-bag" samples in each tree.
verbose	print status messages?

Output

```
uplift: status messages enabled; set "verbose" to false to
disable
upliftRF: starting. Sat Jul 12 16:11:35 2014
10 out of 50 trees so far...
20 out of 50 trees so far...
30 out of 50 trees so far...
40 out of 50 trees so far...
```

predict

`predict` is a generic function for predictions from the results of various model fitting functions. In this instance we use `fit1` derived from fitting the data with the `upliftRF` model.

```
> ### Fitted values on train data
> pred <- predict(fit1, dd)
> ### Compute uplift predictions
> uplift_pred <- pred[, 1] - pred[, 2]
> ### Put together data, predictions and add some dummy
> ### factors for illustration only
> dd2 <- data.frame(dd, uplift_pred, F1 = gl(2, 50, labels
+ = c("A", "B")),
+ F2 = gl(4, 25, labels = c("a", "b", "c", "d")))
```

modelProfile

This function can be used to profile a fitted uplift model. Given a vector of scores (uplift predictions), it computes basic summary statistics for each predictor by score quantile (CRAN-project, 2012).

```
> ### Profile data based on fitted model
> modelProfile(uplift_pred ~ X1 + X2 + X3 + F1 + F2,
+ data = dd2,
+ groups = 10,
+ group_label = "D",
+ digits_numeric = 2,
+ digits_factor = 4,
+ exclude_na = FALSE,
+ LaTex = FALSE)
```

where,

uplift_pred ~ X1 + X2 + X3 + F1 + F2	a formula expression of the form score ~ predictors, where the LHS of the model formula should include the predictions from a fitted model.
data	a data.frame in which to interpret the variables named in the formula.
groups	number of groups of equal observations in which to partition the data set to show results. The default value is 10 (deciles). Other possible values are 5 and 20.
group_label	possible values are "I" or "D", for group number labels which are increasing or decreasing with the model score, respectively.
digits_numeric	number of digits to show for numeric predictors.
digits_factor	number of digits to show for factor predictors.
exclude_na	should the results exclude observations with missing values in any of the variables named in the formula?
LaTex	should the function output LaTex code?

Output

	Group				
	1	2	3	4	5
n	102	98	100	100	100

427

```
uplift_pred  Avg.     0.329    0.229    0.154    0.070   0.011
x1           Avg.     0.853    0.642    0.327    0.296   0.137
x2           Avg.    -0.637   -0.483   -0.139   -0.133  -0.155
x3           Avg.     0.834    0.523    0.320    0.114  -0.103
F1 A         Pctn.   43.140   48.980   52.000   54.000  50.000
   B         Pctn.   56.860   51.020   48.000   46.000  50.000
F2 a         Pctn.   24.510   24.490   21.000   26.000  26.000
   b         Pctn.   18.630   24.490   31.000   28.000  24.000
   c         Pctn.   27.450   25.510   27.000   22.000  25.000
   d         Pctn.   29.410   25.510   21.000   24.000  25.000

     6          7          8          9         10       All
    100        100        100        100        100      1000
  -0.054     -0.117     -0.194     -0.273     -0.387    -0.023
   0.001     -0.266     -0.593     -0.676     -0.779    -0.005
   0.287      0.067      0.056      0.346      0.957     0.016
  -0.038     -0.339     -0.325     -0.499     -0.748    -0.026
  48.00      51.000     52.000     51.000     50.000    50.000
  52.00      49.000     48.000     49.000     50.000    50.000
  24.00      34.000     21.000     20.000     29.000    25.000
  24.00      17.000     31.000     31.000     21.000    25.000
  27.00      22.000     20.000     29.000     25.000    25.000
  25.00      27.000     28.000     20.000     25.000    25.000
```

The netlift for this model appears on the line labeled "uplift_pred", with the first four entries represent quantiles and the last entry represent the overall model netlift of 1.1%

varImportance

This function extracts variable importance from upliftRF or ccif fitted objects (CRAN-project, 2012).

```
> varImportance(fit1, plotit = TRUE, normalize = TRUE)
```

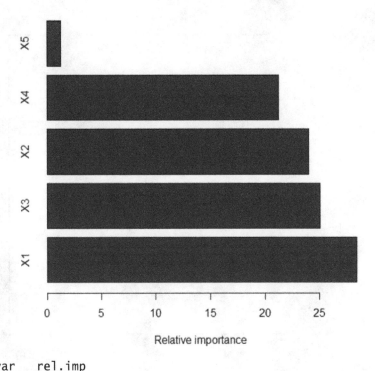

```
   var    rel.imp
1  x1  28.436811
2  x3  25.067272
3  x2  24.001705
4  x4  21.240306
5  x5   1.253906
```

Performance

This function provides a method for assessing performance for uplift models (CRAN-project, 2012).

```
> dd_new <- sim_pte(n = 1000, p = 20, rho = 0, sigma =
+ sqrt(2), beta.den = 4)
> dd_new$treat <- ifelse(dd_new$treat == 1, 1, 0)
>
> pred <- predict(fit1, dd_new)
> perf <- performance(pred[, 1], pred[, 2], dd_new$y,
+ dd_new$treat, direction = 1)
> plot(perf[, 8] ~ perf[, 1], type ="l", xlab = "Decile",
+ ylab = "uplift")
```

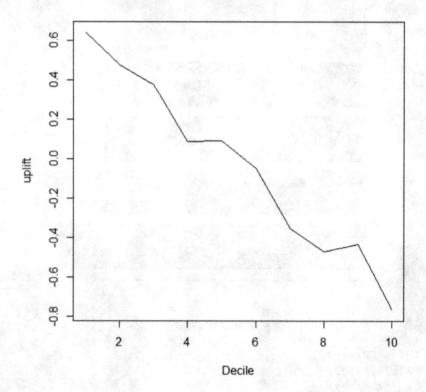

20. Time Series

A time series is a sequence of data points, measured typically at successive points in time spaced at uniform time intervals. Examples of time series are the daily closing value of the Dow Jones Industrial Average and the annual flow volume of the Nile River at Aswan. Time series are very frequently plotted via line charts. Time series are used in statistics, signal processing, pattern recognition, econometrics, mathematical finance, weather forecasting, earthquake prediction, electroencephalography, control engineering, astronomy, and communications engineering.

Time series analysis comprises methods for analyzing time series data in order to extract meaningful statistics and other characteristics of the data. Time series forecasting is the use of a model to predict future values based on previously observed values. While regression analysis is often employed in such a way as to test theories that the current values of one or more independent time series affect the current value of another time series, this type of analysis of time series is not called "time series analysis", which focuses on comparing values of a single time series or multiple dependent time series at different points in time (Imdadullah, 2014).

Time series data have a natural temporal ordering. This makes time series analysis distinct from other common data analysis problems, in which there is no natural ordering of the observations (e.g. explaining people's wages by reference to their respective education levels, where the individuals' data could be entered in any order). Time series analysis is also distinct from spatial data analysis where the observations typically relate to geographical locations (e.g. accounting for house prices by the location as well as the intrinsic characteristics of the houses). A stochastic model for a time series will generally reflect the fact that observations close together in time will be more closely related than observations further apart. In addition, time series models will often make use of the natural one-way ordering of time so that values for a given period will be expressed as deriving in some way from past values, rather than from future values (see time reversibility.)

Time series analysis can be applied to real-valued, continuous data, discrete numeric data, or discrete symbolic data (i.e. sequences of characters, such as letters and words in the English language) (Lin, Keogh, Lonardi, & Chiu, 2003).

Methods for time series analyses

Methods for time series analyses may be divided into two classes: frequency-domain methods and time-domain methods. The former include spectral analysis and recently wavelet analysis; the latter include auto-correlation and cross-correlation analysis. In time domain correlation analyses can be made in a filter-like manner using scaled correlation, thereby mitigating the need to operate in frequency domain.

Additionally, time series analysis techniques may be divided into parametric and non-parametric methods. The parametric approaches assume that the underlying stationary stochastic process has a certain structure which can be described using a small number of parameters (for example, using an autoregressive or moving average model). In these approaches, the task is to estimate the parameters of the model that describes the stochastic process. By contrast, non-parametric approaches explicitly estimate the covariance or the spectrum of the process without assuming that the process has any particular structure.

Methods of time series analysis may also be divided into linear and non-linear, and univariate and multivariate.

Analysis

There are several types of motivation and data analysis available for time series which are appropriate for different purposes.

Motivation

In the context of statistics, econometrics, quantitative finance, seismology, meteorology, and geophysics the primary goal of time series analysis is forecasting. In the context of signal processing, control engineering and communication engineering it is used for signal detection and estimation, while in the context of data mining, pattern recognition and machine learning time series analysis can be used for clustering, classification, query by content, anomaly detection as well as forecasting.

Exploratory analysis

The clearest way to examine a regular time series manually is with a line chart such as the one shown for tuberculosis in the United States, made with a spreadsheet program. The number of cases was standardized to a rate per 100,000 and the percent change per year in this rate was calculated. The nearly steadily dropping line shows that the TB incidence was decreasing in most years, but the percent change in this rate varied by as much as +/- 10%, with 'surges' in 1975 and around the early 1990s. The use of both vertical axes allows the comparison of two time series in one graphic. Other techniques include:

- Autocorrelation analysis to examine serial dependence
- Spectral analysis to examine cyclic behavior which need not be related to seasonality. For example, sun spot activity varies over 11 year cycles (Bloomfield, 1976). Other common examples include celestial phenomena, weather patterns, neural activity, commodity prices, and economic activity.
- Separation into components representing trend, seasonality, slow and fast variation, and cyclical irregularity: see trend estimation and decomposition of time series

Prediction and forecasting

- Fully formed statistical models for stochastic simulation purposes,

433

so as to generate alternative versions of the time series, representing what might happen over non-specific time-periods in the future

- Simple or fully formed statistical models to describe the likely outcome of the time series in the immediate future, given knowledge of the most recent outcomes (forecasting).
- Forecasting on time series is usually done using automated statistical software packages and programming languages, such as R, S, SAS, SPSS, Minitab, Pandas (Python) and many others.

Classification

- Assigning time series pattern to a specific category, for example identify a word based on series of hand movements in sign language.

Regression analysis (method of prediction)

- Estimating future value of a signal based on its previous behavior, e.g. predict the price of AAPL stock based on its previous price movements for that hour, day or month, or predict position of Apollo 11 spacecraft at a certain future moment based on its current trajectory (i.e. time series of its previous locations) (Lawson & Hanson, 1995).
- Regression analysis is usually based on statistical interpretation of time series properties in time domain, pioneered by statisticians George Box and Gwilym Jenkins in the 50s: see Box–Jenkins in Chapter 1.

Signal estimation

- This approach is based on harmonic analysis and filtering of signals in the frequency domain using the Fourier transform, and spectral density estimation, the development of which was significantly accelerated during World War II by mathematician Norbert Wiener (Wiener, 1942), electrical engineers Rudolf E. Kálmán (Kálmán, 1960), Dennis Gabor (Allibone, 1980) and others for filtering signals from noise and predicting signal values at a certain point in time.

434

Segmentation

- Splitting a time-series into a sequence of segments. It is often the case that a time-series can be represented as a sequence of individual segments, each with its own characteristic properties. For example, the audio signal from a conference call can be partitioned into pieces corresponding to the times during which each person was speaking. In time-series segmentation, the goal is to identify the segment boundary points in the time-series, and to characterize the dynamical properties associated with each segment. One can approach this problem using change-point detection, or by modeling the time-series as a more sophisticated system, such as a Markov jump linear system.

Models

Models for time series data can have many forms and represent different stochastic processes. When modeling variations in the level of a process, three broad classes of practical importance are the autoregressive (AR) models, the integrated (I) models, and the moving average (MA) models. These three classes depend linearly on previous data points (Gershenfeld, 1999). Combinations of these ideas produce autoregressive moving average (ARMA) and autoregressive integrated moving average (ARIMA) models. The autoregressive fractionally integrated moving average (ARFIMA) model generalizes the former three. Extensions of these classes to deal with vector-valued data are available under the heading of multivariate time-series models and sometimes the preceding acronyms are extended by including an initial "V" for "vector", as in VAR for vector autoregression. An additional set of extensions of these models is available for use where the observed time-series is driven by some "forcing" time-series (which may not have a causal effect on the observed series): the distinction from the multivariate case is that the forcing series may be deterministic or under the experimenter's control. For these models, the acronyms are extended with a final "X" for "exogenous".

Non-linear dependence of the level of a series on previous data points is of interest, partly because of the possibility of producing a chaotic time series. However, more importantly, empirical investigations can indicate the advantage of using predictions derived from non-linear models, over those from linear models, as for example in nonlinear autoregressive exogenous models.

Among other types of non-linear time series models, there are models to represent the changes of variance over time (heteroskedasticity). These models represent autoregressive conditional heteroskedasticity (ARCH) and the collection comprises a wide variety of representation (GARCH, TARCH, EGARCH, FIGARCH, CGARCH, etc.). Here changes in variability are related to, or predicted by, recent past values of the observed series. This is in contrast to other possible representations of locally varying variability, where the variability might be modelled as being driven by a separate time-varying process, as in a doubly stochastic model.

In recent work on model-free analyses, wavelet transform based methods (for example locally stationary wavelets and wavelet decomposed neural networks) have gained favor. Multiscale (often referred to as multiresolution) techniques decompose a given time series, attempting to illustrate time dependence at multiple scales. See also Markov switching multifractal (MSMF) techniques for modeling volatility evolution.

A Hidden Markov model (HMM) is a statistical Markov model in which the system being modeled is assumed to be a Markov process with unobserved (hidden) states. An HMM can be considered as the simplest dynamic Bayesian network. HMM models are widely used in speech recognition, for translating a time series of spoken words into text.

Notation

A number of different notations are in use for time-series analysis. A common notation specifying a time series X that is indexed by the natural numbers is written

$$X = \{X_1, X_2, \dots\}.$$

Another common notation is

$$Y = \{Y_1 : t \in T\},$$

where T is the index set.

Conditions

There are two sets of conditions under which much of the theory is built:

- Stationary process
- Ergodic process

However, ideas of stationarity must be expanded to consider two important ideas: strict stationarity and second-order stationarity. Both models and applications can be developed under each of these conditions, although the models in the latter case might be considered as only partly specified.

In addition, time-series analysis can be applied where the series are seasonally stationary or non-stationary. Situations where the amplitudes of frequency components change with time can be dealt with in time-frequency analysis which makes use of a time–frequency representation of a time-series or signal (Boashash, 2003).

Autoregressive model

An autoregressive (AR) model is a representation of a type of random process; as such, it describes certain time-varying processes in nature, economics, etc. The autoregressive model specifies that the output variable depends linearly on its own previous values. It is a special case of the more general ARMA model of time series.

Definition

The notation AR(p) indicates an autoregressive model of order p. The AR(p) model is defined as

$$X_t = c \sum_{i=1}^{p} \varphi_i X_{t-1} + \varepsilon_t,$$

where $\varphi_1, \ldots, \varphi_p$ are the parameters of the model, c is a constant, and ε_t is white noise. This can be equivalently written using the backshift operator B as

$$X_t = c \sum_{i=1}^{p} \varphi_i B^i X_t + \varepsilon_t,$$

so that, moving the summation term to the left side and using polynomial notation, we have

$$\phi(B)X_t = c + \varepsilon_t.$$

An autoregressive model can thus be viewed as the output of an all-pole infinite impulse response filter whose input is white noise.

Some constraints are necessary on the values of the parameters of this model in order that the model remains wide-sense stationary. For example, processes in the AR(1) model with $|\varphi_1| \geq 1$ are not stationary. More generally, for an AR(p) model to be wide-sense stationary, the roots of the polynomial $z^p - \sum_{i=1}^{p} \varphi_i z^{p-1}$ must lie within the unit circle, i.e., each root z_i must satisfy $|z_i| < 1$.

Characteristic polynomial

The autocorrelation function of an AR(p) process can be expressed as

$$\rho(\tau) = \sum_{k=1}^{p} a_k y_k^{-|\tau|},$$

Where y_k are the roots of the polynomial

$$\phi(B) = 1 - \sum_{k=1}^{p} \varphi_k B^k,$$

438

where B is the backshift operator, where $\varphi(.)$ is the function defining the autoregression, and where φ_k are the coefficients in the autoregression.

Graphs of AR(p) processes

The simplest AR process is AR(0), which has no dependence between the terms. Only the error/innovation/noise term contributes to the output of the process, so in the figure, AR(0) corresponds to white noise.

For an AR(1) process with a positive φ, only the previous term in the process and the noise term contribute to the output. If φ is close to 0, then the process still looks like white noise, but as φ approaches 1, the output gets a larger contribution from the previous term relative to the noise. This results in a "smoothing" or integration of the output, similar to a low pass filter.

For an AR(2) process, the previous two terms and the noise term contribute to the output. If both φ_1 and φ_2 are positive, the output will resemble a low pass filter, with the high frequency part of the noise decreased. If φ_1 is positive while φ_2 is negative, then the process favors changes in sign between terms of the process. The output oscillates. This can be likened to edge detection or detection of change in direction.

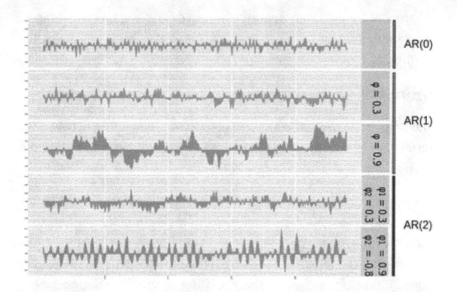

AR(0)

$\phi = 0.3$ AR(1)

$\phi = 0.9$

$\phi_1 = 0.3$ $\phi_2 = 0.3$ AR(2)

$\phi_1 = 0.9$ $\phi_2 = -0.8$

AR(0); AR(1) with AR parameter 0.3; AR(1) with AR parameter 0.9; AR(2) with AR parameters 0.3 and 0.3; and AR(2) with AR parameters 0.9 and −0.8.

Partial autocorrelation function

The partial autocorrelation function (PACF) plays an important role in data analyses aimed at identifying the extent of the lag in an autoregressive model. The use of this function was introduced as part of the Box–Jenkins approach to time series modelling, where by plotting the partial autocorrelative functions one could determine the appropriate lags p in an AR (p) model or in an extended ARIMA (p, d, q) model.

Description

Given a time series z_t, the partial autocorrelation of lag k, denoted $\alpha(k)$, is the autocorrelation between z_t and $z_{\{t+k\}}$ with the linear dependence of $z_{\{t+1\}}$ through to $z_{\{t+k-1\}}$ removed; equivalently, it is the autocorrelation between z_t and $z_{\{t+k\}}$ that is not accounted for by lags 1 to $k - 1$, inclusive.

440

$$\alpha(1) = \text{Cor}(z_t, z_{t+1})$$

$$\alpha(k) = \text{Cor}\left(z_{t+k} - P_{t,k}(z_{t+k}), z_t - P_{t,k}(z_t)\right), \text{ for } k \geq 2.$$

where $P_{t,k}(x)$ denotes the projection of x onto the space spanned by $z_{\{t+1\}}, \dots, z_{\{t+k-1\}}$.

There are algorithms, not discussed here, for estimating the partial autocorrelation based on the sample autocorrelations. See (Box, Jenkins, & Reinsel, 2008) for the mathematical details. These algorithms derive from the exact theoretical relation between the partial autocorrelation function and the autocorrelation function.

Partial autocorrelation plots (Box & Jenkins, 1976) are a commonly used tool for identifying the order of an autoregressive model. The partial autocorrelation of an AR(p) process is zero at lag $p + 1$ and greater. If the sample autocorrelation plot indicates that an AR model may be appropriate, then the sample partial autocorrelation plot is examined to help identify the order. One looks for the point on the plot where the partial autocorrelations for all higher lags are essentially zero. Placing on the plot an indication of the sampling uncertainty of the sample PACF is helpful for this purpose: this is usually constructed on the basis that the true value of the PACF, at any given positive lag, is zero. This can be formalized as described below.

An approximate test that a given partial correlation is zero (at a 5% significance level) is given by comparing the sample partial autocorrelations against the critical region with upper and lower limits given by $\pm\sqrt{1.96}$, where n is the record length (number of points) of the time-series being analyzed. This approximation relies on the assumption that the record length is moderately large (say $n > 30$) and that the underlying process has finite second moment.

Example Using R

The data sets used in this example are available in astsa, the R package. We're going to get astsa by loading the package:

441

```
> install.packages("astsa")  # install it ... you'll be
                             # asked to choose the closest
                             # CRAN mirror
> require(astsa)             # then load it (has to be done at
                             # the start of each session)
```

We will examine the Johnson & Johnson data set. It is included in `astsa` as `jj`. First, look at it.

```
> data(jj)   # load the data - you don't have to do this
             # anymore with astsa, but you do in general
> jj         # print it to the screen
           Qtr1        Qtr2        Qtr3        Qtr4
1960   0.710000    0.630000    0.850000    0.440000
1961   0.610000    0.690000    0.920000    0.550000
1962   0.720000    0.770000    0.920000    0.600000
1963   0.830000    0.800000    1.000000    0.770000
1964   0.920000    1.000000    1.240000    1.000000
1965   1.160000    1.300000    1.450000    1.250000
1966   1.260000    1.380000    1.860000    1.560000
1967   1.530000    1.590000    1.830000    1.860000
1968   1.530000    2.070000    2.340000    2.250000
1969   2.160000    2.430000    2.700000    2.250000
1970   2.790000    3.420000    3.690000    3.600000
1971   3.600000    4.320000    4.320000    4.050000
1972   4.860000    5.040000    5.040000    4.410000
1973   5.580000    5.850000    6.570000    5.310000
1974   6.030000    6.390000    6.930000    5.850000
1975   6.930000    7.740000    7.830000    6.120000
1976   7.740000    8.910000    8.280000    6.840000
1977   9.540000   10.260000    9.540000    8.729999
1978  11.880000   12.060000   12.150000    8.910000
1979  14.040000   12.960000   14.850000    9.990000
1980  16.200000   14.670000   16.020000   11.610000
```

and you see that `jj` is a collection of 84 numbers called a *time series object*.

If you're a Matlab (or similar) user, you may think `jj` is an 84 × 1 vector, but it's not. It has order and length, but no dimensions (no rows, no columns). R calls these kinds of objects "vectors" so you have to be careful. In R, "matrices" have dimensions but "vectors" do not.

```
> jj[1]         # the first element
 [1] 0.71
> jj[84]        # the last element
 [1] 11.61
> jj[1:4]       # the first 4 elements
 [1] 0.71 0.63 0.85 0.44
> jj[-(1:80)] # everything EXCEPT the first 80 elements
 [1] 16.20 14.67 16.02 11.61
> length(jj)  # the number of elements
 [1] 84
> dim(jj)       # but no dimensions ...
 NULL
> nrow(jj)      # ... no rows
 NULL
> ncol(jj)      # ... and no columns
 NULL
#-- if you want it to be a column vector (in R, a matrix),
# an easy way to go is:
> jjm = as.matrix(jj)
> dim(jjm)
 [1] 84  1
```

Now, we will make a monthly time series object that starts in June of the year 2293.

```
> options(digits=2) # the default is 7, but it's
                     # more than I want now
> ?options           # to see your options (it's the
                     # help file)
> ?rnorm             # we're using it on the next line

> (zardoz = ts(rnorm(48), start=c(2293,6), frequency=12))
         Jan     Feb     Mar     Apr     May     Jun
2293                                             0.7068
2294 -0.7945 -0.3213 -0.6600 -1.7642 -0.1160  1.0249
```

```
2295   0.9165  -0.6305   0.1905  -0.6670   1.6646   1.3500
2296   0.1763  -1.1184   0.2646   0.4811   0.4172  -0.5041
2297  -0.5879  -0.5253   0.3565   0.1063   1.6780
          Jul      Aug      Sep      Oct      Nov      Dec
2293   0.5821   1.0142  -0.4541   2.0240   2.1897   0.0094
2294   0.1773  -0.1605  -0.3028   1.1558   0.6289  -0.4785
2295   0.8064   0.5731  -0.9938  -0.4923   1.5854  -0.1910
2296  -0.2051  -0.3705  -0.4146   0.7438  -1.3559   0.7894
2297
```

```
# use window() if you want a part of a ts object
(oz = window(zardoz, start=2293, end=c(2295,12)))
          Jan      Feb      Mar      Apr      May      Jun
2293                                                0.7068
2294  -0.7945  -0.3213  -0.6600  -1.7642  -0.1160   1.0249
2295   0.9165  -0.6305   0.1905  -0.6670   1.6646   1.3500
          Jul      Aug      Sep      Oct      Nov      Dec
2293   0.5821   1.0142  -0.4541   2.0240   2.1897   0.0094
2294   0.1773  -0.1605  -0.3028   1.1558   0.6289  -0.4785
2295   0.8064   0.5731  -0.9938  -0.4923   1.5854  -0.1910
```

Note that the Johnson and Johnson data are *quarterly* earnings, hence it has frequency=4. The time series zardoz is monthly data, hence it has frequency=12. You also get some nice things with the ts object, for example:

```
> time(jj)
     Qtr1 Qtr2 Qtr3 Qtr4
1960 1960 1960 1960 1961
1961 1961 1961 1962 1962
1962 1962 1962 1962 1963
1963 1963 1963 1964 1964
1964 1964 1964 1964 1965
1965 1965 1965 1966 1966
1966 1966 1966 1966 1967
1967 1967 1967 1968 1968
1968 1968 1968 1968 1969
1969 1969 1969 1970 1970
1970 1970 1970 1970 1971
```

```
1971 1971 1971 1972 1972
1972 1972 1972 1972 1973
1973 1973 1973 1974 1974
1974 1974 1974 1974 1975
1975 1975 1975 1976 1976
1976 1976 1976 1976 1977
1977 1977 1977 1978 1978
1978 1978 1978 1978 1979
1979 1979 1979 1980 1980
1980 1980 1980 1980 1981
```

```
> cycle(jj)
     Qtr1 Qtr2 Qtr3 Qtr4
1960    1    2    3    4
1961    1    2    3    4
1962    1    2    3    4
1963    1    2    3    4
1964    1    2    3    4
1965    1    2    3    4
1966    1    2    3    4
1967    1    2    3    4
1968    1    2    3    4
1969    1    2    3    4
1970    1    2    3    4
1971    1    2    3    4
1972    1    2    3    4
1973    1    2    3    4
1974    1    2    3    4
1975    1    2    3    4
1976    1    2    3    4
1977    1    2    3    4
1978    1    2    3    4
1979    1    2    3    4
1980    1    2    3    4
```

Now try a plot of the Johnson and Johnson data:

```
> plot(jj, ylab="Earnings per Share", main="J & J")
```

445

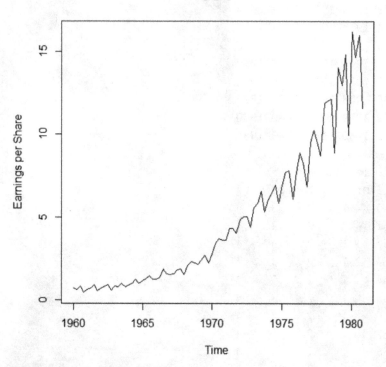

Try these and see what happens:

```
> plot(jj, ylab="Earnings per Share", main="J & J")
> plot(jj, type="o", col="blue", lty="dashed")
```

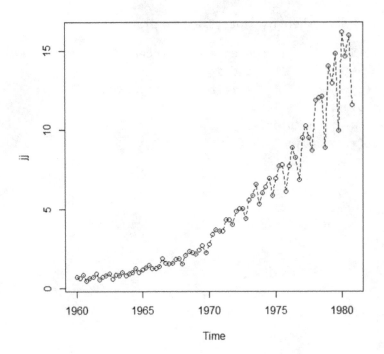

logged and diffed

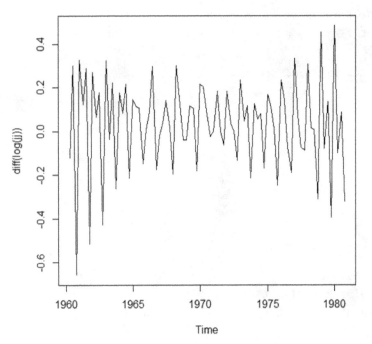

and while you're here try `plot.ts` and `ts.plot`:

```
> x = -5:5          # sequence of integers from -5 to 5
> y = 5*cos(x)      # guess
> par(mfrow=c(3,2)) # multifigure setup:3 rows,2 cols
#---  plot:
> plot(x, main="plot(x)")
> plot(x, y, main="plot(x,y)")
```

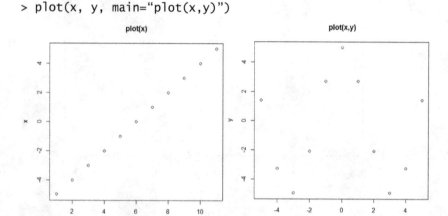

```
#---  plot.ts:
> plot.ts(x, main="plot.ts(x)")
> plot.ts(x, y, main="plot.ts(x,y)")
```

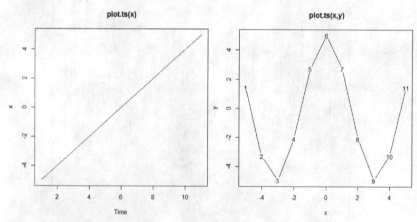

```
#---  ts.plot:
> ts.plot(x, main="ts.plot(x)")
> ts.plot(ts(x), ts(y), col=1:2, main="ts.plot(x,y)")
```

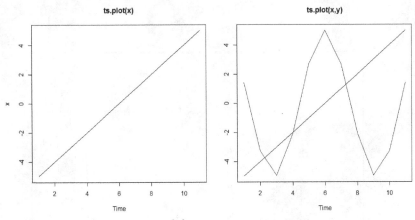

```
# note- x and y are ts objects
#---  the help files [? and help() are the same]:
> ?plot.ts
> help(ts.plot)
> ?par         # might as well skim the graphical
# parameters help file while you're here
```

Note that if your data are a time series object, plot() will do the trick (for a simple time plot, that is). Otherwise, plot.ts() will coerce the graphic into a time plot.

We now look at filtering/smoothing the Johnson & Johnson series using a two-sided moving average? Try this:

$$f_{jj}(t)= \text{⅛ } jj(t-2)+\text{¼ } jj(t-1)+\text{¼ } jj(t)+\text{¼ } jj(t+1)+\text{⅛ } jj(t+2)$$

and we'll add a lowess (?lowess) fit for fun.

```
> k = c(.5,1,1,1,.5)                 # k is the vector of
                                     # weights
> (k = k/sum(k))
[1] 0.12 0.25 0.25 0.25 0.12
> fjj = filter(jj, sides=2, k)   # ?filter for help
> plot(jj)
> lines(fjj, col="red")              # adds a line to the
                                     # existing plot
> lines(lowess(jj), col="blue", lty="dashed")
```

449

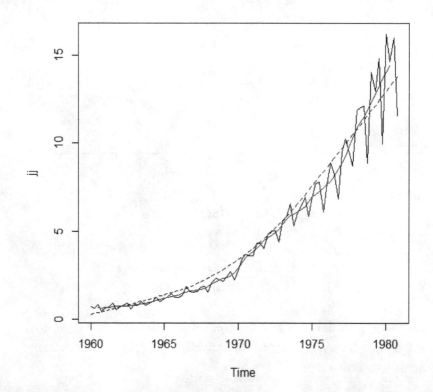

We difference the logged data and call it dljj. Then we examine dljj:

```
> dljj = diff(log(jj))    # difference the logged data
> plot(dljj)              # plot it (not shown)
> shapiro.test(dljj)      # test for normality


        Shapiro-Wilk normality test

data:  dljj
W = 0.97, p-value = 0.07211


> par(mfrow=c(2,1))           # set up the graphics
> hist(dljj, prob=TRUE, 12)   # histogram
> lines(density(dljj))        # smooth it - ?density for
                              # details
> qqnorm(dljj)                # normal Q-Q plot
```

```
qqline(dljj)                        # add a line
```

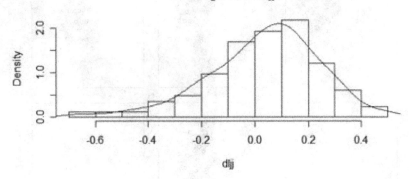

Histogram of dljj

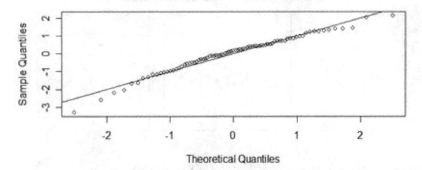

Normal Q-Q Plot

Let's check out the correlation structure of `dljj` using various techniques. First, we'll look at a grid of scatterplots of `dljj(t-lag)` vs `dljj(t)` for `lag=1,2,...,9`.

```
> lag.plot(dljj, 9, do.lines=FALSE)
> lag1.plot(dljj, 9)  # if you have astsa loaded (not
                      # shown)
# why the do.lines=FALSE? Because you get a phase
# plane if it's TRUE
```

Notice the large positive correlation at lags 4 and 8 and the negative correlations at a few other lags:

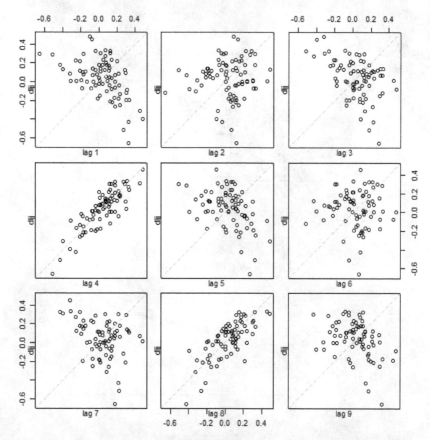

Now let's take a look at the ACF and PACF of dljj:

```
> par(mfrow=c(2,1)) # The power of accurate observation is
commonly called cynicism
                      # by those who have not got it. -
                      # George Bernard Shaw
> acf(dljj, 20)       # ACF to lag 20 - no graph shown...
                      # keep reading
> pacf(dljj, 20)      # PACF to lag 20 - no graph shown...
  # keep reading
  # !!NOTE!! acf2 on the line below is ONLY available in
  # astsa and tsa3
> acf2(dljj)          # this is what you'll see below
        ACF  PACF
[1,] -0.51 -0.51
[2,]  0.07 -0.26
```

```
 [3,]  -0.40 -0.70
 [4,]   0.73  0.27
 [5,]  -0.37  0.16
 [6,]   0.00 -0.11
 [7,]  -0.25 -0.01
 [8,]   0.56  0.11
 [9,]  -0.28  0.05
[10,]  -0.01  0.12
[11,]  -0.22 -0.03
[12,]   0.45 -0.03
[13,]  -0.21  0.04
[14,]  -0.04 -0.08
[15,]  -0.15 -0.04
[16,]   0.35 -0.04
[17,]  -0.14 -0.04
[18,]  -0.08 -0.06
[19,]  -0.09 -0.02
[20,]   0.27  0.01
```

Series: dljj

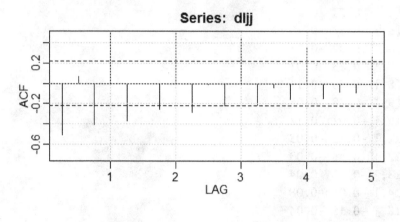

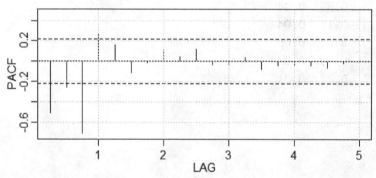

Note that the LAG axis is in terms of frequency, so 1,2,3,4,5 correspond to lags 4,8,12,16,20 because frequency=4 here. If you don't like this type of labeling, you can replace dljj in any of the above by ts(dljj, freq=1);   e.g.,   acf(ts(dljj,   freq=1),   20)

Moving on, we will try a structural decomposition of log(jj) = trend + season + error using lowess. stl decomposes a time series into seasonal, trend and irregular components using loess:

```
> plot(dog <- stl(log(jj), "per"))
```

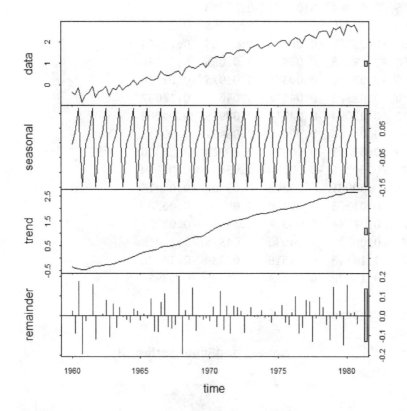

Now we inspect the residuals. The third column of the resulting series (the seasonal and trend components are in columns 1 and 2). Also, check out the ACF of the residuals, acf(dog$time.series[,3]); the residuals aren't white—not even close. You can do a little (very little) better using a local seasonal window, plot(dog <- stl(log(jj), s.win=4)), as opposed to the global one used by specifying "per". Type ?stl for details. There is also something called structTS that will fit parametric structural models.

```
> dog$time.series[,3]
          Qtr1       Qtr2      Qtr3       Qtr4
1960   0.02215  -0.08811   0.17311  -0.19320
1961  -0.02563   0.00128   0.15874  -0.11700
1962  -0.00070   0.00594   0.07749  -0.10622
1963   0.06021  -0.05831   0.03865  -0.00231
```

```
1964 -0.01744 -0.03189  0.03428  0.02085
1965 -0.02364  0.00713 -0.01013  0.08639
1966 -0.07779 -0.07984  0.06758  0.11055
1967 -0.05578 -0.06423 -0.04485  0.19954
1968 -0.19148  0.02416 -0.02055  0.14136
1969 -0.07448 -0.00568 -0.01975 -0.01118
1970 -0.02523  0.04521 -0.05630  0.12087
1971 -0.07094  0.04718 -0.08955  0.04868
1972  0.04208  0.02030 -0.08487  0.00411
1973  0.03857 -0.00395 -0.00329  0.02490
1974 -0.00825 -0.00284 -0.03440  0.01659
1975 -0.00061  0.05262 -0.03305 -0.04415
1976  0.01273  0.09466 -0.08980 -0.06100
1977  0.07734  0.06977 -0.13041 -0.00992
1978  0.09135  0.04030 -0.04335 -0.12358
1979  0.14248 -0.01616  0.02089 -0.14976
1980  0.15572  0.00999  0.01320 -0.03985
```

```
> acf(dog$time.series[,3])
```

Series dog$time.series[, 3]

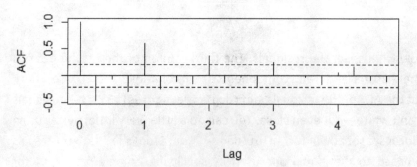

```
> (dog <- stl(log(jj), s.win=4))
 Call:
 stl(x = log(jj), s.window = 4)

Components
        seasonal    trend  remainder
1960 Q1  0.01916  -0.4519    0.09023
1960 Q2  0.01526  -0.4462   -0.03109
1960 Q3  0.26000  -0.4405    0.01801
```

1961 Q4	-0.28969	-0.4313	-0.09997
1961 Q1	0.01511	-0.4221	-0.08730
1961 Q2	0.01780	-0.4005	0.01163
1962 Q3	0.25312	-0.3789	0.04238
1962 Q4	-0.27300	-0.3492	0.02432
1962 Q1	-0.00453	-0.3194	-0.00455
1962 Q2	0.02202	-0.2988	0.01545
1962 Q3	0.21718	-0.2782	-0.02233
1963 Q4	-0.22169	-0.2524	-0.03669
1963 Q1	0.01153	-0.2266	0.02878
1963 Q2	0.00073	-0.1889	-0.03501
1964 Q3	0.16983	-0.1511	-0.01875
1964 Q4	-0.17003	-0.1023	0.01097
1964 Q1	-0.00309	-0.0535	-0.02677
1964 Q2	0.00602	0.0042	-0.01017
1964 Q3	0.14459	0.0618	0.00869
1965 Q4	-0.11427	0.1141	0.00018
1965 Q1	-0.04741	0.1664	0.02947
1965 Q2	0.00316	0.2085	0.05070
1966 Q3	0.14976	0.2507	-0.02886
1966 Q4	-0.06786	0.2918	-0.00078
1966 Q1	-0.06882	0.3329	-0.03298
1966 Q2	-0.02312	0.3742	-0.02902
1966 Q3	0.13941	0.4155	0.06564
1967 Q4	-0.01120	0.4497	0.00618
1967 Q1	-0.11103	0.4839	0.05242
1967 Q2	-0.02181	0.5131	-0.02753
1968 Q3	0.11854	0.5423	-0.05649
1968 Q4	0.02228	0.5864	0.01193
1968 Q1	-0.11897	0.6304	-0.08621
1968 Q2	0.01133	0.6855	0.03071
1968 Q3	0.08966	0.7406	0.01993
1969 Q4	-0.02660	0.7874	0.05012
1969 Q1	-0.09150	0.8343	0.02735
1969 Q2	0.04411	0.8823	-0.03847
1970 Q3	0.08638	0.9302	-0.02338
1970 Q4	-0.07156	0.9976	-0.11510
1970 Q1	-0.05319	1.0649	0.01429
1970 Q2	0.05824	1.1411	0.03030
1970 Q3	0.05955	1.2173	0.02882

1971	Q4	-0.08087	1.2810	0.08078
1971	Q1	-0.02609	1.3448	-0.03778
1971	Q2	0.06553	1.3931	0.00465
1972	Q3	0.03255	1.4414	-0.01064
1972	Q4	-0.08781	1.4816	0.00492
1972	Q1	0.01104	1.5219	0.04814
1972	Q2	0.05223	1.5619	0.00329
1972	Q3	0.04568	1.6019	-0.03018
1973	Q4	-0.12674	1.6418	-0.03116
1973	Q1	0.02589	1.6817	0.01164
1973	Q2	0.03871	1.7178	0.00992
1974	Q3	0.07733	1.7540	0.05121
1974	Q4	-0.13238	1.7827	0.01926
1974	Q1	0.00579	1.8115	-0.02051
1974	Q2	0.04614	1.8376	-0.02902
1974	Q3	0.08777	1.8638	-0.01568
1975	Q4	-0.14423	1.8943	0.01639
1975	Q1	0.00430	1.9248	0.00678
1975	Q2	0.08107	1.9535	0.01186
1976	Q3	0.06046	1.9822	0.01534
1976	Q4	-0.17937	2.0086	-0.01767
1976	Q1	0.03279	2.0350	-0.02141
1976	Q2	0.10977	2.0668	0.01060
1976	Q3	0.02502	2.0986	-0.00978
1977	Q4	-0.19056	2.1400	-0.02663
1977	Q1	0.06892	2.1814	0.00521
1977	Q2	0.10404	2.2287	-0.00448
1978	Q3	0.01320	2.2760	-0.03373
1978	Q4	-0.20842	2.3194	0.05578
1978	Q1	0.10866	2.3628	0.00340
1978	Q2	0.07325	2.3992	0.01741
1978	Q3	0.05540	2.4357	0.00627
1979	Q4	-0.24968	2.4681	-0.03123
1979	Q1	0.12905	2.5005	0.01236
1979	Q2	0.05291	2.5328	-0.02389
1980	Q3	0.08080	2.5652	0.05200
1980	Q4	-0.26610	2.5961	-0.02845
1980	Q1	0.13433	2.6271	0.02360
1980	Q2	0.04708	2.6576	-0.01892
1980	Q3	0.08768	2.6882	-0.00204

1981 Q4 -0.27051 2.7183   0.00406

Notation Used

Set Theory

Set: $\{\}$

A set: A

Element of a set: A a_i for $i = 1, \ldots, n$

Set union: $A \cup B$

Set intersection: $A \cap B$

Set complement: A^c, $\neg A$

Element of: $a \in A$

Such that: $|$

Natural numbers: $\mathbb{N}$

Integers: $\mathbb{Z}$

Real numbers: $\mathbb{R}$

Indexed set: $\{y_i, x_i\}_{i=1}^n$

Probability and statistics

Probability function: $P(A)$, $Pr(a)$, $Prob(A)$

Conditional probability: $P(A|B)$

Probability of events intersection: $P(A \cap B)$

Probability of events union: $P(A \cup B)$

probability density function (pdf): $f(x)$

Cumulative distribution function (cdf): $F(x)$

Paramete:r y

Parameter estimate: $\hat{y}$

population mean: μ

expectation value: $E(x)$

conditional expectation: $E(X|Y)$

variance: $Var(X)$

variance: σ^2

standard deviation: σ_X

covariance: $cov(X, Y)$

correlation: $corr(X, Y)$

correlation: ρ_{XY}

lower / first quartile: Q_1

median / second quartile: Q_2

upper / third quartile: Q_3

Sample mean: $\bar{x}$

Sample variance: s^2

Sample standard deviation: s

Error: ε

Regression coefficient: β_i

Regression coefficient estimate: $\hat{\beta}_i$

distribution of X: $X\sim$

Normal (Gaussian) distribution: $N(\mu, \sigma^2)$

uniform distribution: $U(a, b)$

exponential distribution: $exp(\lambda)$ or e^λ

gamma distribution: $gamma(c, \lambda)$ or $\Gamma(\lambda)$

chi-square distribution: χ^2

F distribution: $F(k_1, k_2)$

Poisson distribution: $Poisson(\lambda)$

Bernoulli distribution: $Bern(p)$

Linear Algebra

Vector x, $\vec{x}$

Matrix X

Element of a vector x_i for $i = 1, \dots, n$

Element of a matrix x_{mn} for m=number of rows, n=number of columns

Matrix size (dimension): $m \times n$

Vector cross product: $\times$

Vector dot product: $\cdot$

Norm: $\|x\|$

Rank of a matrix: $rank(A)$

Matrix transpose: A^T or A'

Matrix inverse: A^{-1}

Hermitian matrix: A^*

Matrix dimension: $dim(A)$

j-th diagonal of a matrix: $a^{(j)}$

Algebra and Calculus

generic argument: $(.)$

Very small number: ε

Mapping: $f \rightarrow g$

Maps over d: $\xrightarrow{d}$

Derivative: $\frac{dy}{dx}$

Partial derivative: $\frac{\partial f(x,y)}{\partial x}$

Integral: $\int(.)$

Double integral: $\iint(.)$

closed interval: $[a, b]$

open interval: (a, b)

maximize: $max(a, b)$

maximize subject to:
$min\ x$
$|\ condition$

minimize: $min(a, b)$

Argument of the minimum:
$$\arg\min_{a \in A}(.)\ (.)$$

Laplace transform: $\mathcal{L}$

Weierstrass elliptic function: $\wp$

Natural logarithm: $ln(.)$

Function: $f(x)$

Composite function: $f(g(x))$,
$f \circ g$

Iteration i of $F(x)$: $F_i(x)$

Combination: $\binom{n}{k}$

Factoiral: $!$

Distance between x and y:
$||x - y||$

If and only if: Iff, $\leftrightarrow$, $\Leftrightarrow$

approximately equal: $\approx$

Proportional to: $\propto$

Plur or minus: $\pm$

Such that: :

Summation: $\sum(.)$

Double summation: $\sum\sum(.)$

Sum from i=1,...,n: $\sum_{i=1}^{n}(.)$

Sum of all $i \in f(i)$: $\sum_{i \in f(i)}(.)$

Gradient: ∇

Not sign: $\neg$

Glossary

A Priori Probability: A priori probability is the probability estimate prior to receiving new information. See also Bayes Theorem and posterior probability.

Attribute: In data analysis or data mining, an attribute is a characteristic or feature that is measured for each observation (record) and can vary from one observation to another. It might be measured in continuous values (e.g. time spent on a web site), or in categorical values (e.g. red, yellow, green). The terms "attribute" and "feature" are used in the machine learning community, "variable" is used in the statistics community. They are synonyms.

Autoregression: Autoregression refers to a special branch of regression analysis aimed at analysis of time series. It rests on autoregressive models - that is, models where the dependent variable is the current value and the independent variables are N previous values of the time series. The N is called "the order of the autoregression".

Autoregression and Moving Average (ARMA) Models: The autoregression and moving average (ARMA) models are used in time series analysis to describe stationary time series. These models represent time series that are generated by passing white noise through a recursive and through a nonrecursive linear filter, consecutively. In other words, the ARMA model is a combination of an autoregressive (AR) model and a moving average (MA) model.

Autoregressive (AR) Models: The autoregressive (AR) models are used in time series analysis to describe stationary time series. These models represent time series that are generated by passing the white noise through a recursive linear filter. The output of such a filter at the moment t image is a weighted sum of m image previous values of the filter output. The integer parameter m image is called the order of the AR-model.

Average Deviation: The average deviation or the average absolute deviation is a measure of dispersion. It is the average of absolute deviations of the individual values from the median or from the mean.

Bagging: In predictive modeling, bagging is an ensemble method that uses bootstrap replicates of the original training data to fit predictive models. For each record, the predictions from all available models are then averaged for the final prediction. For a classification problem, a majority vote of the models is used. Bagging is short for "bootstrap aggregating."

Bayes´ Theorem: Bayes theorem is a formula for revising a priori probabilities after receiving new information. The revised probabilities are called posterior probabilities. For example, consider the probability that you will develop a specific cancer in the next year. An estimate of this probability based on general population data would be a prior estimate; a revised (posterior) estimate would be based on both on the population data and the results of a specific test for cancer.

Boosting: In predictive modeling, boosting is an iterative ensemble method that starts out by applying a classification algorithm and generating classifications. The classifications are then assessed, and a second round of model-fitting occurs in which the records classified incorrectly in the first round are given a higher weight in the second round. This procedure is repeated a number of times, and the final classifier results from a merger of the various iterations, with lesser weights typically accorded to the very last rounds. The idea is to concentrate the iterative learning process on the hard-to-classify cases.

Chi-Square Test: Chi-square test (or χ^2-test) is a statistical test for testing the null hypothesis that the distribution of a discrete random variable coincides with a given distribution. It is one of the most popular goodness-of-fit tests.

Classification and Regression Trees (CART): Classification and regression trees (CART) are a set of techniques for classification and prediction. The technique is aimed at producing rules that predict the value of an outcome (target) variable from known values of predictor (explanatory) variables. The predictor variables may be a mixture of categorical and continuous variables.

Classification Trees: Classification trees are one of the CART techniques. The main distinction from regression trees (another CART technique) is that the dependent variable Y image is categorical.

Coefficient of Determination: In regression analysis, the coefficient of determination is a measure of goodness-of-fit (i.e. how well or tightly the data fit the estimated model). The coefficient is defined as the ratio of two sums of squares: $R^2 = SSR / SSE$, where SSR is the sum of squares due to regression, SST is the total sum of squares. By "sum of squares" we mean the sum of squared deviations between actual values and the mean (SST), or between predicted values and the mean (SSR). The coefficient of determination takes on values between 0 and 1, with values closer to 1 implying a better fit.

Collinearity: In regression analysis, collinearity of two variables means that strong correlation exists between them, making it difficult or impossible to estimate their individual regression coefficients reliably.

Conditional Probability: When probabilities are quoted without specification of the sample space, it could result in ambiguity when the sample space is not self-evident. To avoid this, the sample space can be explicitly made known. The probability of an event A given sample space S, denoted by $P(A|S)$, is nothing but the conditional probability of A given S.

Covariance: covariance is a measure of how much two random variables change together. If the greater values of one variable mainly correspond with the greater values of the other variable, and the same holds for the smaller values, i.e., the variables tend to show similar behavior, the covariance is positive. In the opposite case, when the greater values of one variable mainly correspond to the smaller values of the other, i.e., the variables tend to show opposite behavior, the covariance is negative. The sign of the covariance therefore shows the tendency in the linear relationship between the variables.

Data Mining: Data mining is concerned with finding latent patterns in large data bases. The goal is to discover unsuspected relationships that are of practical importance, e.g., in business.

Degrees of Freedom: For a set of data points in a given situation (e.g. with mean or other parameter specified, or not), degrees of freedom is the minimal number of values which should be specified to determine all the data points.

Dependent variable: Dependent variables are also called response variables, outcome variables, target variables or output variables. The terms "dependent" and "independent" here have no direct relation to the concept of statistical dependence or independence of events.

Deviance: Deviance is a quality of fit statistic for a model that is often used for statistical hypothesis testing. It is a generalization of the idea of using the sum of squares of residuals in ordinary least squares to cases where model-fitting is achieved by maximum likelihood.

Effect: In design of experiments, the effect of a factor is an additive term of the model, reflecting the contribution of the factor to the response.

Estimator: A statistic, measure, or model, applied to a sample, intended to estimate some parameter of the population that the sample came from.

Explanatory Variable: Explanatory variable is a synonym for independent variable.

Factor: In design of experiments, factor is an independent variable manipulated by the experimenter.

Failure rate: The failure rate is defined for non-repairable populations as the (instantaneous) rate of failure for the survivors to time t during the next instant of time. The failure rate (or hazard rate) $h(t)$ and is:

$h(t) = f(t)/(1 - F(t)) = f(t)/R(t) =$ instantaneous failure rate.

Filter: A filter is an algorithm for processing a time series or random process.

General Linear Model: General (or generalized) linear models (GLM), in contrast to linear models, allow you to describe both additive and non-additive relationship between a dependent variable and N independent variables. The independent variables in GLM may be continuous as well as discrete.

Hazard function: The hazard function, conventionally denoted λ, is defined as the event rate at time t conditional on survival until time t or later (that is, $T \geq t$).

Hazard rate: see failure rate.

Heteroscedasticity: Heteroscedasticity generally means unequal variation of data, e.g. unequal variance.

Heteroscedasticity in regression: In regression analysis, heteroscedasticity means a situation in which the variance of the dependent variable varies across the data. Heteroscedasticity complicates analysis because many methods in regression analysis are based on an assumption of equal variance.

Independent Events: Two events A and B are said to be independent if $P(AB) = P(A)P(B)$. To put it differently, events A and B are independent if the occurrence or non-occurrence of A does not influence the occurrence of non-occurrence of B and vice-versa.

Independent Variables: Statistical models normally specify how one set of variables, called dependent variables, functionally depend on another set of variables, called independent variables. The term "independent" reflects only the functional relationship between variables within a model. Several models based on the same set of variables may differ by how the variables are subdivided into dependent and independent variables. Alternative names for independent variables (especially in data mining and predictive modeling) are input variables, predictors or features.

Inferential Statistics: Inferential statistics is the body of statistical techniques that deal with the question "How reliable is the conclusion or estimate that we derive from a set of data?" The two main techniques are confidence intervals and hypothesis tests.

k-Nearest Neighbors Prediction: The k-nearest neighbors (k-NN) prediction is a method to predict a value of a target variable in a given record, using as a reference point a training set of similar objects. The basic idea is to choose k objects from the training set that are closest to the given object in terms of the predictor variables, then to form the weighted average of target variable for those k objects. The weights are usually chosen inversely proportionally to the distances from the target object.

Kurtosis: Kurtosis measures the "heaviness of the tails" of a distribution (in compared to a normal distribution). Kurtosis is positive if the tails are "heavier" then for a normal distribution, and negative if the tails are "lighter" than for a normal distribution. The normal distribution has kurtosis of zero.

Latent Variable: A latent variable describes an unobservable construct and cannot be observed or measured directly.

Least Squares Method: In a narrow sense, the Least Squares Method is a technique for fitting a straight line through a set of points in such a way that the sum of the squared vertical distances from the observed points to the fitted line is minimized. In a wider sense, the Least Squares Method is a general approach to fitting a model of the data-generating mechanism to the observed data.

Likelihood Function: Likelihood function is a fundamental concept in statistical inference. It indicates how likely a particular population is to produce an observed sample.

Likelihood ratio test: a likelihood ratio test is a statistical test used to compare the fit of two models, one of which (the null model) is a special case of the other (the alternative model). The test is based on the likelihood ratio, which expresses how many times more likely the data are under one model than the other.

Linear regression: In statistics, linear regression is an approach for modeling the relationship between a scalar dependent variable y and one or more explanatory variables denoted X. The case of one explanatory variable is called simple linear regression. For more than one explanatory variable, the process is called multiple linear regression.

Linkage Function: A linkage function is an essential prerequisite for hierarchical cluster analysis. Its value is a measure of the "distance" between two groups of objects (i.e. between two clusters).

Logit: Logit is a nonlinear function of probability. If p is the probability of an event, then the corresponding logit is given by the formula: $logit(p)log(p/(1-p))$.

Logistic regression: In statistics, logistic regression, or logit regression, is a type of probabilistic statistical classification model. It is also used to predict a binary response from a binary predictor, used for predicting the outcome of a categorical dependent variable (i.e., a class label) based on one or more predictor variables (features). That is, it is used in estimating the parameters of a qualitative response model.

Machine Learning: Analytics in which computers "learn" from data to produce models or rules that apply to those data and to other similar data. Predictive modeling techniques such as neural nets, classification and regression trees (decision trees), naive Bayes, k-nearest neighbor, and support vector machines are generally included. One characteristic of these techniques is that the form of the resulting model is flexible, and adapts to the data.

Markov chain: A Markov chain, named after Andrey Markov, is a mathematical system that undergoes transitions from one state to another on a state space. It is a random process usually characterized as memoryless: the next state depends only on the current state and not on the sequence of events that preceded it. This specific kind of "memorylessness" is called the Markov property.

Mean Squared Error (MLE): The mean squared error is a measure of performance of a point estimator. It measures the average squared difference between the estimator and the parameter. For an unbiased estimator, the mean squared error is equal to the variance of the estimator.

Multicollinearity: In regression analysis, multicollinearity refers to a situation of collinearity of independent variables, often involving more than two independent variables, or more than one pair of collinear variables. Multicollinearity means redundancy in the set of variables.

Naive Bayes Classification: The Naive Bayes method is a method of classification applicable to categorical data, based on Bayes theorem. For a record to be classified, the categories of the predictor variables are noted and the record is classified according to the most frequent class among the same values of those predictor variables in the training set. A rigorous application of the Bayes theorem would require availability of all possible combinations of the values of the predictor variables. When the number of variables is large enough, this requires a training set of unrealistically large size (and, indeed, even a huge training set is unlikely to cover all possible combinations). The naive Bayes method overcomes this practical limitation of the rigorous Bayes approach to classification.

Neural Network: A neural network (NN) is a network of many simple processors ("units"), each possibly having a small amount of local memory. The units are connected by communication channels ("connections") which usually carry numeric (as opposed to symbolic) data, encoded by any of various means. The units operate only on their local data and on the inputs they receive via the connections. The restriction to local operations is often relaxed during training.

Null Hypothesis: In hypothesis testing, the null hypothesis is the one you are hoping can be disproven by the observed data. Typically, it asserts that chance variation is responsible for an effect seen in observed data (for example, a difference between treatment and placebo, an apparent correlation between one variable and another, a divergence between a sample measure and some benchmark, etc.)

Odds ratio: In statistics, the odds ratio (usually abbreviated "OR") is one of three main ways to quantify how strongly the presence or absence of property A is associated with the presence or absence of property B in a given population.

p-value: The p-value is the probability that the null model could, by random chance variation, produce a sample as extreme as the observed sample (as measured by some sample statistic of interest.)

Parameter: A Parameter is a numerical value that describes one of the characteristics of a probability distribution or population. For example, a binomial distribution is completely specified if the number of trials and probability of success are known. Here, the number of trials and the probability of success are two parameters. A normal distribution is completely specified if its mean and standard deviation are known.

Posterior Probability: Posterior probability is a revised probability that takes into account new available information. For example, let there be two urns, urn A having 5 black balls and 10 red balls and urn B having 10 black balls and 5 red balls. Now if an urn is selected at random, the probability that urn A is chosen is 0.5. This is the *a priori* probability. If we are given an additional piece of information that a ball was drawn at random from the selected urn, and that ball was black, what is the probability that the chosen urn is urn A? Posterior probability takes into account this additional information and revises the probability downward from 0.5 to 0.333 according to Bayes' theorem, because a black ball is more probable from urn B than urn A.

Probit: Probit is a nonlinear function of probability p: $probit(p) = \Theta^{-1}(p)$, where $\Theta^{-1}(.)$ is the function inverse to the cumulative distribution function $\Theta(.)$ of the standard normal distribution. In contrast to the probability p itsef (which takes on values from 0 to 1), the values of the probit of p are from minus- to plus-infinity.

R-squared: See Coefficient of determination.

Random Error: The random error is the fluctuating part of the overall error that varies from measurement to measurement. Normally, the random error is defined as the deviation of the total error from its mean value.

Random variable: a random variable is a variable whose value is subject to variations due to chance (i.e. randomness, in a mathematical sense). A random variable can take on a set of possible different values, each with an associated probability (if discrete) or a probability density function (if continuous), in contrast to other mathematical variables.

Regression Analysis: Regression analysis provides a "best-fit" mathematical equation for the relationship between the dependent variable (response) and independent variable(s) (covariates).

Regression Trees: Regression trees is one of the CART techniques. The main distinction from classification trees (another CART technique) is that the dependent variable Y image is continuous.

Regularization: Regularization refers to a wide variety of techniques used to bring structure to statistical models in the face of data size, complexity and sparseness. Advances in digital processing, storage and retrieval have led to huge and growing data sets ("Big Data"). Regularization is used to allow models to usefully model such data without overfitting. A very simple example is linear regression; other examples are smoothing techniques.

Residuals: Residuals are differences between the observed values and the values predicted by some model. Analysis of residuals allows you to estimate the adequacy of a model for particular data; it is widely used in regression analysis.

Sample: A sample is a portion of the elements of a population. A sample is chosen to make inferences about the population by examining or measuring the elements in the sample.

Sample Space: The set of all possible outcomes of a particular experiment is called the sample space for the experiment. If a coin is tossed twice, the sample space is {HH, HT, TH, TT}, where TH, for example, means getting tails on the first toss and heads on the second toss.

Seasonal Decomposition: The seasonal decomposition is a method used in time series analysis to represent a time series as a sum (or, sometimes, a product) of three components—the linear trend, the periodic (seasonal) component, and random residuals.

Serial Correlation: In analysis of time series, the Nth order serial correlation is the correlation between the current value and the Nth previous value of the same time series. For this reason serial correlation is often called "autocorrelation".

Simple Linear Regression: The simple linear regression is aimed at finding the "best-fit" values of two parameters - A and B in the following regression equation: $Y_i = A X_i + B + E_i$, $i = 1, p, \mathcal{R}, N$, where Y_i, X_i, and E_i are the values of the dependent variable, of the independent variable, and of the random error, respectively. Parameter A is called "the slope of the regression line", B - "the y-intercept of the regression line".

Singularity: In regression analysis, singularity is the extreme form of multicollinearity - when a perfect linear relationship exists between variables or, in other terms, when the correlation coefficient is equal to 1.0 or -1.0.

Standard error: The standard error measures the variability of an

473

estimator (or sample statistic) from sample to sample. By formula, $STDEER = STDEV/\sqrt{N}$.

Stationary process: a stationary process is a stochastic process whose joint probability distribution does not change when shifted in time. Consequently, parameters such as the mean and variance, if they are present, also do not change over time and do not follow any trends.

Statistical inference: statistical inference is the process of drawing conclusions from data that are subject to random variation, for example, observational errors or sampling variation.

Statistical Significance: Outcomes to an experiment or repeated events are statistically significant if they differ from what chance variation might produce.

Stochastic process: a stochastic process, or sometimes random process is a collection of random variables, representing the evolution of some system of random values over time.

t-test: A t-test is a statistical hypothesis test based on a test statistic whose sampling distribution is a t-distribution. Various t-tests, strictly speaking, are aimed at testing hypotheses about populations with normal probability distribution. However, statistical research has shown that t-tests often provide quite adequate results for non-normally distributed populations too.

Time Series: A time series is a sequence of data points, measured typically at successive points in time spaced at uniform time intervals. Examples of time series are the daily closing value of the Dow Jones Industrial Average and the annual flow volume of the Nile River at Aswan.

Training Set: A training set is a portion of a data set used to fit (train) a model for prediction or classification of values that are known in the training set, but unknown in other (future) data. The training set is used in conjunction with validation and/or test sets that are used to evaluate different models.

Type I Error: In a test of significance, Type I error is the error of rejecting the null hypothesis when it is true -- of saying an effect or event is statistically significant when it is not. The projected probability of committing type I error is called the level of significance.

Type II Error: In a test of significance, Type II error is the error of accepting the null hypothesis when it is false -- of failing to declare a real difference as statistically significant. Obviously, the bigger your samples, the more likely your test is to detect any difference that exists. The probability of detecting a real difference of specified size (i.e. of not committing a Type II error) is called the power of the test.

Validation Set: A validation set is a portion of a data set used in data mining to assess the performance of prediction or classification models that have been fit on a separate portion of the same data set (the training set). Typically both the training and validation set are randomly selected, and the validation set is used as a more objective measure of the performance of various models that have been fit to the training data (and whose performance with the training set is therefore not likely to be a good guide to their performance with data that they were not fit to).

Variance: Variance is a measure of dispersion. It is the average squared distance between the mean and each item in the population or in the sample.

References

Aharon, M., Elad, M., & Bruckstein, A. (2006). K-SVD: An Algorithm for Designing Overcomplete Dictionaries for Sparse Representation. *IEEE Transactions onSignal Processing, 54*(11), 4311-4322.

Aizerman, M., Braverman, E., & Rozonoer, L. (1964). Theoretical foundations of the potential function method in pattern recognition learning. *Automation and Remote Control, 25*, 821–837.

Akbarzadeh, V. (2013). *Line Estimation*. Retrieved from Machine Learning Made Simple: http://mlmadesimple.com/2014/05/07/line-estimation/

Allibone, T. E. (1980). Dennis Gabor. 5 June 1900-9 February 1979. *Biographical Memoirs of Fellows of the Royal Society, 26*, 106. doi:10.1098/rsbm.1980.0004

Altman, N. (1992). An introduction to kernel and nearest-neighbor nonparametric regression. *The American Statistician, 46*(3), 175–185. doi:10.1080/00031305.1992.10475879

Altman, N. S. (1992). An introduction to kernel and nearest-neighbor nonparametric regression. *The American Statistician, 46*(3), 175–185. doi:10.1080/00031305.1992.10475879

Altmann, A., Tolosi, L., Sander, O., & Lengauer, T. (2010). Permutation importance:a corrected feature importance measure. *Bioinformatics*. doi:10.1093/bioinformatics/btq134

Altschul, J. H., Sebastian, L., & Heidelberg, K. (2004). *Predictive Modeling in the Military: Similar Goals, Divergent Paths.* SRI Foundation.

Amemiya, T. (1985). *Advanced econometrics.* Boston: Harvard University Press.

Amit, Y., & Geman, D. (1997). Shape quantization and recognition with randomized trees. *Neural Computation, 9*(7), 1545–1588. doi:10.1162/neco.1997.9.7.1545

(2010). *Analysis of Alternatives (AoA) Handbook.* Air Force Materiel Command. Kirtland AFB: Office of Aerospace Studies. Retrieved 2014, from http://www.prim.osd.mil/Documents/AoA_Handbook.pdf

Andersen, R. (2008). *Modern Methods for Robust Regression.* Sage University Paper Series on Quantitative Applications in the Social Sciences.

Anscombe, F. J. (1948). The Validity of Comparative Experiments. *Journal of the Royal Statistical Society. Series A (General) , 111*(3), 181–211. doi:10.2307/2984159

Argresti, A., & Finlay, B. (2008). *Statistical Methods for the Social Sciences* (4th ed.). Pearson.

Aslam, J. A., Popa, R. A., & Rivest, R. (2007). On Estimating the Size and Confidence of a Statistical Audit. *Proceedings of the Electronic Voting Technology Workshop (EVT '07).* Boston, MA. Retrieved from http://people.csail.mit.edu/rivest/pubs/APR07.pdf

Bailey, K. (1994). Numerical Taxonomy and Cluster Analysis. In *Typologies and Taxonomies* (p. 34).

Bailey, R. A. (2008). *Design of Comparative Experiments.* Cambridge University Press.

Balabin, R., & Lomakina, E. (2009). Neural network approach to quantum-chemistry data: Accurate prediction of density functional theory energies. *J. Chem. Phys, 131*(7). doi:10.1063/1.3206326

Barkin, E. (2011). *CRM + Predictive Analytics: Why It All Adds Up.* New York: Destination CRM. Retrieved 2014, from http://www.destinationcrm.com/Articles/Editorial/Magazine-Features/CRM---Predictive-Analytics-Why-It-All-Adds-Up-74700.aspx

Barros, R. C., Cerri, R., Jaskowiak, P. A., & Carvalho, A. C. (2011). A bottom-up oblique decision tree induction algorithm. *Proceedings of the 11th International Conference on Intelligent Systems Design and Applications (ISDA 2011)* (pp. 450 - 456). IEEE. doi:10.1109/ISDA.2011.6121697

Barros, R., Basgalupp, M., Carvalho, A., & Freitas, A. (2011). A Survey of Evolutionary Algorithms for Decision-Tree Induction. *IEEE Transactions on Systems, Man and Cybernetics, Part C: Applications and Reviews, 42*(3), 291-312.

Belle, G. v. (2008). *Statistical rules of thumb* (2nd ed.). Hoboken, N.J: Wiley.

Ben-Gal I. Dana A., S. N. (2014). Efficient Construction of Decision Trees by the Dual Information Distance Method. *Quality Technology & Quantitative Management (QTQM), 11*(1), 133-147. Retrieved from http://www.eng.tau.ac.il/~bengal/DID.pdf

Bengio, Y. (2009). *Learning Deep Architectures for AI.* Now Publishers Inc.: 1-3.

Ben-Israel, A., & Greville, T. (2003). *Generalized Inverses.* New York: Springer-Verlag. Retrieved from http://books.google.com/books?id=o3-97W8vCdIC&printsec=frontcover&dq=isbn:038700293

Bergstra, J., & Bengio, Y. (2012). Random Search for Hyper-Parameter Optimization. *J. Machine Learning Research, 13*, 281–305. Retrieved from http://jmlr.org/papers/volume13/bergstra12a/bergstra12a.pdf

Bertsekas, D. T. (1996). Neuro-dynamic programming. *Athena Scientific,*

152.

Beyer, K. (1999). When is "nearest neighbor" meaningful? *Database Theory—ICDT'99*, (pp. 217-235).

Bhandari, M., & Joensson, A. (2008). *Clinical Research for Surgeons.* Thieme.

Bingham, E., & M., H. (2001). Random projection in dimensionality reduction: applications to image and text data. *of the seventh ACM SIGKDD international conference on Knowledge discovery and data mining.* ACM.

Bishop, C. (2005). *Neural networks for pattern recognition.* Oxford University Press.

Bishop, C. (2006). *Pattern Recognition and Machine Learning.* New York: Springer. Retrieved from http://www.hua.edu.vn/khoa/fita/wp-content/uploads/2013/08/Pattern-Recognition-and-Machine-Learning-Christophe-M-Bishop.pdf

Bliss, C. I. (1934). The Method of Probits. *Science, 79*(2037), 38–39. doi:10.1126/science.79.2037.38

Bloomfield, P. (1976). *Fourier analysis of time series: An introduction.* New York: Wiley.

Boashash, B. (2003). *Time-Frequency Signal Analysis and Processing: A Comprehensive Reference.* Oxford: Elsevier Science.

Bobko, P., Roth, P. L., & Buster, M. A. (2007). The usefulness of unit weights in creating composite scores: A literature review, application to content validity, and meta-analysis. *Organizational Research Methods, 10,* 689-709. doi:10.1177/1094428106294734

Boser, B., Guyon, I., & Vapnik, V. (1992). A training algorithm for optimal margin classifiers. *Proceedings of the fifth annual workshop on*

Computational learning theory - COLT '92, (p. 144). doi:10.1145/130385.130401

Bottaci, L. (1997). Artificial Neural Networks Applied to Outcome Prediction for Colorectal Cancer Patients in Separate Institutions. *The Lancet, 350.* Retrieved from http://www.lcc.uma.es/~jja/recidiva/042.pdf

Box, G. E., Jenkins, G. M., & Reinsel, G. C. (2008). *Time Series Analysis, Forecasting and Control* (4th ed.). Hoboken, NJ: Wiulley.

Box, G., & Jenkins, G. (1976). *Time Series Analysis: forecasting and control* (Revised ed.). Oakland, CA: Holden-Day.

Boyd, C. R., Tolson, M. A., & Copes, W. S. (1987). Evaluating trauma care: The TRISS method. Trauma Score and the Injury Severity Score. *The Journal of trauma, 27*(4), 370–378.

Bramer, M. (2007). *Principles of Data Mining.* London: Springer London. doi:10.1007/978-1-84628-766-4

Breiman, L. (1994). *Bagging Predictors.* Technical Report No. 421, University of California, Department of Statistics, Berkeley. Retrieved from http://statistics.berkeley.edu/sites/default/files/tech-reports/421.pdf

Breiman, L. (1996). Bagging predictors. *Machine Learning, 24*(2), 123-140. Retrieved from http://link.springer.com/article/10.1023%2FA%3A1018054314350

Breiman, L. (2001). Random Forests. *Machine Learning, 45*(1), 5-32. doi:10.1023/A:1010933404324

Breiman, L. (2001). Statistical Modeling: the Two Cultures. *Statistical Science, 16*(3), 199–231. doi:10.1214/ss/1009213725

Breiman, L., Friedman, J. H., Olshen, R. A., & Stone, C. J. (1984). *Classification and regression trees.* Monterey, CA: Wadsworth & Brooks/Cole Advanced Books & Software.

Bremne, r. D., Demaine E, Erickson, J., Iacono, J., Langerman, S., P., M., & Toussaint, G. (2005). Output-sensitive algorithms for computing nearest-neighbor decision boundaries. *Discrete and Computational Geometry, 33*(4), 593–604. doi:10.1007/s00454-004-1152-0

Bridgman, R. (n.d.). *Defence of neural networks.*

Bryll, R. (2003). Attribute bagging: improving accuracy of classifier ensembles by using random feature subsets. *Pattern Recognition, 20*(6), 1291–1302.

Buck, D. (2005). A Hands-On Introduction to SAS DATA Step Programming. *Proceedings of the Thirtieth Annual SAS® Users Group International Conference.* SAS Institute. Retrieved from http://www2.sas.com/proceedings/sugi30/134-30.pdf

Burgess, E. W. (1928). Factors determining success or failure on parole. In A. Bruce, *The Workings of the Indeterminate Sentence Law and Parole in Illinois* (pp. 205-249). Springfield, IL: Illinois State Parole Board.

Burnham, K. P., & Anderson, D. (2002). *Model Selection and Multi-Model Inference.* New York: Springer.

Cai, T., Tian, L., Wong, P. H., & Wei, L. J. (2009). Analysis of Randomized Comparative Clinical Trial Data for Personalized Treatment Selections. *Harvard University Biostatistics Working Paper Series, Paper 97.*

Caputo, B., Sim, K., Furesjo, F., & Smola, A. (n.d.). Appearance-based Object Recognition using SVMs: Which Kernel Should I Use? *Proceedings of NIPS Workshop on Statistical Methods for*

Computational Experiments in Visual Processing and Computer Vision (p. 2002). Whistler.

Carlin, B., & Louis, T. (2000). *Bayes and Empirical Bayes Methods for Data Analysis.* Chapman & Hall/CRC.

Caruana, R., & Niculescu-Mizil, A. (2006). empirical comparison of supervised learning algorithms. *Proceedings of the 23rd international conference on Machine learning.* doi:10.1.1.122.5901

Cattell, R. B. (1943). The description of personality: Basic traits resolved into clusters. *Journal of Abnormal and Social Psychology, 38,* 476–506. doi:doi:10.1037/h0054116

Chambers, J. (1998). *Programming with Data.* New York: Springer-Verlag.

Chang, C., & Lin, C. (2011). LIBSVM : a library for support vector machines. *ACM Transactions on Intelligent Systems and Technology, 2,* 27:1-27:27.

Chapelle, O., Vapnik, V., Bousquet, O., & Mukherjee, S. (2002). Choosing multiple parameters for support vector machines. *Machine Learning, 46,* 131–159.

Chen, J., Zhu, J., Wang, Z., Zheng, X., & Zhang, B. (2013). Scalable Inference for Logistic-Normal Topic Models. In *Advances in Neural Information Processing Systems* (p. 2445{2453).

Chib, S., & Greenberg, E. (1995). Understanding the metropolis-hastings algorithm. *The American Statistician, 49*(4). doi:10.1080/00031305.1995.10476177

Chipman, H., George, E., & McCulloch, R. (1998). Bayesian CART model search. *Journal of the American Statistical Association, 93*(443), 935-948.

Chong, J., Jin, Y., & Phillips, M. (2013). *The Entrepreneur's Cost of Capital: Incorporating Downside Risk in the Buildup Method.* Pasadena: MacroRisk.com. Retrieved 2014, from http://www.macrorisk.com/wp-content/uploads/2013/04/MRA-WP-2013-e.pdf

Ciresan, D. C., Meier, U. J., & Schmidhuber, J. (2012). Multi-Column Deep Neural Network for Traffic Sign Classification. *Neural Networks.*

Ciresan, D., Giusti, A., Gambardella, L., & Schmidhuber, J. (2012). Deep Neural Networks Segment Neuronal Membranes in Electron Microscopy Images. *Advances in Neural Information Processing Systems (NIPS 2012),* . Lake Tahoe.

Ciresan, D., Meier, U., & Schmidhuber, J. (2012). Multi-column Deep Neural Networks for Image Classification. *IEEE Conf. on Computer Vision and Pattern Recognition CVPR 2012.*

Cochran, W., & Cox, G. (1992). *Experimental designs* (2nd ed.). New York: Wiley.

Cohen, J., Cohen, P., West, S., & Aiken, L. (2002). *Applied Multiple Regression/Correlation Analysis for the Behavioral Sciences* (3rd ed.). Routledge.

Conz, N. (2008). *Insurers Shift to Customer-focused Predictive Analytics Technologies.* New York: Insurance & Technology. Retrieved 2014, from http://www.insurancetech.com/business-intelligence/insurers-shift-to-customer-focused-predi/210600271

Coomans, D., & Massart, D. (1982). Alternative k-nearest neighbour rules in supervised pattern recognition : Part 1. k-Nearest neighbour classification by using alternative voting rules. *Analytica Chimica Acta, 136,* 15-27.

Cortes, C., & Vapnik, V. (1995). Support-vector networks. *Machine*

Learning, 20(3), 273. doi:10.1007/BF00994018

Cossock, D., & Zhang, T. (2008). *Statistical Analysis of Bayes Optimal Subset Ranking.* Retrieved from http://www.stat.rutgers.edu/home/tzhang/papers/it08-ranking.pdf

Cover, T., & Hart, P. (1967). Nearest neighbor pattern classification. *IEEE Transactions on Information Theory, 13*(1), 21–27. doi:10.1109/TIT.1967.1053964

Cox, D. (1992). *Planning of experiments.* New York: Wiley.

Crammer, K., & Singer, Y. (2001). On the Algorithmic Implementation of Multiclass Kernel-based Vector Machines. *J. of Machine Learning Research, 2,* 265–292. Retrieved from http://jmlr.org/papers/volume2/crammer01a/crammer01a.pdf

CRAN-project. (2012). *R uplift-package help.* Retrieved from R Statistical Data Analysis: http://127.0.0.1:24928/doc/html/Search?pattern=uplift

Criminisi, A., Shotton, J., & Konukoglu, E. (2011). Forests: A Unified Framework for Classification, Regression, Density Estimation, Manifold Learning and Semi-Supervised Learning. *Foundations and Trends in Computer Vision, 7,* 81–227. doi:10.1561/0600000035

Cuingnet, R., C., R., Chupin, M., Lehéricy, S., Dormont, D., Benali, H., . . . Colliot, O. (2011). Spatial regularization of SVM for the detection of diffusion alterations associated with stroke outcome. *Medical Image Analysis, 15*(5), 729-737.

Da, Y., & Xiurun, G. (2005). An improved PSO-based ANN with simulated annealing technique. In T. e. Villmann, *New Aspects in Neurocomputing: 11th European Symposium on Artificial Neural Networks.* New York: Elsevier.

doi:10.1016/j.neucom.2004.07.002

Damas, M., Salmeron, M., Diaz, A., Ortega, J., Prieto, A., & Olivares, G. (2000). Genetic algorithms and neuro-dynamic programming: application to water supply networks. *Proceedings of 2000 Congress on Evolutionary Computation.* La Jolla, Ca: IEEE. doi:10.1109/CEC.2000.870269

Das, K., & Vidyashankar, G. (2006). *Competitive Advantage in Retail Through Analytics: Developing Insights, Creating Value.* New York: Information Management. Retrieved 2014, from http://www.information-management.com/infodirect/20060707/1057744-1.html

Davidson, R., & Mackinnon, .. G. (1993). *Estimation and inference in econometrics.* Oxford University Press.

Dawes, R. M. (1979). The robust beauty of improper linear models in decision making. *American Psychologist, 34,* 571-582. doi:10.1037/0003-066X.34.7.571

de Rigo, D., Castelletti, A., Rizzoli, A., Soncini-Sessa, R., & Weber, E. (2005). A selective improvement technique for fastening Neuro-Dynamic Programming in Water Resources Network Management. *Proceedings of the 16th IFAC World Congress – IFAC-PapersOnLine.* Prague, Czech Republic: IFAC. doi:10.3182/20050703-6-CZ-1902.02172

de Rigo, D., Rizzoli, A. E., Soncini-Sessa, R., Weber, E., & Zenesi, P. (2001). Neuro-dynamic programming for the efficient management of reservoir networks. *Proceedings of MODSIM 2001, International Congress on Modelling and Simulation.* Canberra, Australia. doi:10.5281/zenodo.7481

Defays, D. (1977). An efficient algorithm for a complete link method. *The Computer Journal (British Computer Society), 20*(4), 364–366. doi:doi:10.1093/comjnl/20.4.364

Deng, G., & Ferris, M. (2008). Neuro-dynamic programming for fractionated radiotherapy planning. *Springer Optimization and Its Applications, 12*, 47–70. doi:10.1007/978-0-387-73299-2_3

Deng, H., Runger, G., & Tuv, E. (2011). Bias of importance measures for multi-valued attributes and solutions. *Proceedings of the 21st International Conference on Artificial Neural Networks (ICANN)*, (pp. 293–300).

Devroye, L., Györfi, L., & Lugosi, G. (1996). *A Probabilistic Theory of Pattern Recognition.* New York: Springer-Verlag.

Dietterich, T. (2000). An Experimental Comparison of Three Methods for Constructing Ensembles of Decision Trees: Bagging, Boosting, and Randomization. *Machine Learning*, 139–157.

Dietterich, T., & Bakiri, G. (1995). Solving Multiclass Learning Problems via Error-Correcting Output Codes. *Journal of Artificial Intelligence Research, 2*(2), 263–286. Retrieved from http://www.jair.org/media/105/live-105-1426-jair.pdf

Draper, N., & Smith, H. (1998). *Applied Regression Analysis* (3rd ed.). New Tork: John Wiley.

Drucker, H., Burges, C. J., Kaufman, L., Smola, A., & Vapnik, V. N. (1996). Support Vector Regression Machines. *Advances in Neural Information Processing Systems 9, NIPS 1996* (pp. 155–161). MIT Press.

Duan, K., & Keerthi, S. (2005). Which Is the Best Multiclass SVM Method? An Empirical Study. *Lecture Notes in Computer Science, 3541*, 278. doi:10.1007/11494683_28

Eckerson, W. (2007). *Extending the Value of Your Data Warehousing Investment.* The Data Warehouse Institute. Retrieved 2014, from http://tdwi.org/articles/2007/05/10/predictive-analytics.aspx?sc_lang=en

Edwards, A. (1925). R. A. Fisher, Statistical Methods for Research Workers. In I. Grattan-Guinness (Ed.), *Landmark Writings in Western Mathematics: Case Studies, 1640-1940.* Amsterdam: Elsevier.

Estivill-Castro, V. (2002, June 20). Why so many clustering algorithms — A Position Paper. *ACM SIGKDD Explorations Newsletter, 4*(1), 65–75. doi:doi:10.1145/568574.568575

Everitt, B. S., Landau, S., Leese, M., & Stahl, D. (n.d.). Miscellaneous Clustering Methods. In *Cluster Analysis* (5th ed.). Chichester, UK: John Wiley & Sons, Ltd.

Fan, R., Chang, K., Hsieh, C., Wang, K., & C.J., L. (2008). LIBLINEAR: A library for large linear classification. *Journal of Machine Learning Research, 9*, 1871–1874.

Faraway, J. J. (2004). *Linear Models with R.* Chapman & Hall/CRC.

Farley, B., & Clark, W. (1954). Simulation of Self-Organizing Systems by Digital Computer. *IRE Transactions on Information Theory, 4*(4), 76–84. doi:10.1109/TIT.1954.1057468

Ferreira, C. (2006). Designing Neural Networks Using Gene Expression Programming. In A. Abraham, B. de Baets, M. Köppen, & B. Nickolay, *Applied Soft Computing Technologies: The Challenge of Complexity* (pp. 517–536). Springer-Verlag. Retrieved from http://www.gene-expression-programming.com/webpapers/Ferreira-ASCT2006.pdf

Ferris, M. C., & Munson, T. S. (2002). Interior-Point Methods for Massive Support Vector Machines. *SIAM Journal on Op, 13*(3), 783. doi:10.1137/S1052623400374379

Fisher, R. A. (1918). The Correlation Between Relatives on the Supposition of Mendelian Inheritance. *Philosophical Transactions of the Royal Society of Edinburgh, 52*, 399–433.

Fisher, R. A. (1921). Probable Error" of a Coefficient of Correlation Deduced from a Small Sample. *1*, 3-32. Retrieved from http://hdl.handle.net/2440/15169

Fisher, R., & Prance, G. (1974). *The Design of Experiments* (9th ed.). Hafner Press.

Fletcher, H. (2011). *The 7 Best Uses for Predictive Analytics in Multichannel Marketing.* Philadelphia: Target Marketing. Retrieved 2014, from http://www.targetmarketingmag.com/article/7-best-uses-predictive-analytics-modeling-multichannel-marketing/1#

Freedman, D. A. (2005). *Statistical Models: Theory and Practice.* Cambridge University Press.

Freund, Y., & Schapire, R. E. (1999). Large Margin Classification Using the Perceptron Algorithm. *Machine Learning, 37*(3), 277. doi:10.1023/A:1007662407062

Friedman, J. H. (1991). Multivariate Adaptive Regression Splines. *The Annals of Statistics, 19*(1), 1-67. doi:10.1214/aos/1176347963

Friedman, J. H. (1993). Estimating Functions of Mixed Ordinal and Categorical Variables Using Adaptive Splines. In Morgenthaler, Ronchetti, & Stahel, *New Directions in Statistical Data Analysis and Robustness.* Birkhauser.

Friedman, J. H. (1993). *Fast MARS.* Stanford University Department of Statistics.

Friedman, J. H. (1995). Greedy Function Approximation: A Gradient Boosting Machine. *IMS 1999.* Retrieved from http://statweb.stanford.edu/~jhf/ftp/trebst.pdf

Friedman, J. H. (1998). Data Mining and Statistics: What's the connection? *Computing Science and Statistics, 29*(1), 3–9.

Friedman, J. H. (1999). Stochastic Gradient Boosting. Retrieved from https://statweb.stanford.edu/~jhf/ftp/stobst.pdf

Fukushima, K. (1980). Neocognitron: A self-organizing neural network model for a mechanism of pattern recognition unaffected by shift in position. *Biological Cybernetics, 36*(4), 93–202. doi:10.1007/BF00344251

Ganesan, N. (2010). Application of Neural Networks in Diagnosing Cancer Disease Using Demographic Data. *International Journal of Computer Applications, 1*(26), 76-85. Retrieved from http://www.ijcaonline.org/journal/number26/pxc387783.pdf

Geisser, S. (1993). *Predictive Inference: An Introduction.* New York: Chapman & Hall.

Gelman, A. (2005). Analysis of variance? Why it is more important than ever. *The Annals of Statistics, 33*, 1–53. doi:10.1214/009053604000001048

George, E., & McCullochb, R. (1993). Variable Selection via Gibbs Sampling. *Journal of the American Statistical Association, 88*(423). doi:10.1080/01621459.1993.10476353

Gershenfeld, N. (1999). *The Nature of Mathematical Modeling.* New York: Cambridge University Press.

Goldberg, D. E., & Holland, J. H. (1988). Genetic algorithms and machine learning. *Machine Learning, 3*(2), 95–99.

Good, I. (1953). The population frequencies of species and the estimation of population parameters. *Biometrika, 40*(3-4), 237–264. doi:10.1093/biomet/40.3-4.237

Graves, A., & Schmidhuber, J. (2009). Handwriting Recognition with Multidimensional Recurrent Neural Networks. In Y. Bengio, D. S., J. Lafferty, C. K. Williams, & A. Culotta, *Advances in Neural Information Processing Systems 22 (NIPS'22)* (pp. 545–552).

Vancouver, BC.

Greene, W. (2011). *Econometric Analysis* (7th ed.). New York: Prentice Hall.

Hale, G., & Hale, G. (2006). *Uneasy Partnership: The Politics of Business and Government in Canada.* Toronto: University of Toronto Press.

Hall, P., Park, B., & Samworth, R. (2008). Choice of neighbor order in nearest-neighbor classification. *Annals of Statistics, 36*(5), 2135–2152. doi:10.1214/07-AOS537

Halper, F. (2011, November 1). The Top 5 Trends in Predictive Analytics. *Information Management.* Retrieved 2014, from http://www.information-management.com/issues/21_6/the-top-5-trends-in-redictive-an-alytics-10021460-1.html

Hampel, F. R., Ronchetti, E. M., Rousseeuw, P. J., & Stahel, W. A. (2005). *Robust Statistics: The Approach Based on Influence Functions.* New York: Wiley.

Hardin, J., & Hilbe, J. (2003). *Generalized Estimating Equations.* London: Chapman and Hall/CRC.

Harrell, F. (2010). *Regression Modeling Strategies: With Applications to Linear Models, Logistic Regression, and Survival Analysis.* New York: Springer-Verlag.

Hart, P. (1968). The Condensed Nearest Neighbor Rule. *IEEE Transactions on Information Theory, 18,* 515-516. doi:10.1109/TIT.1968.1054155

Hastie, T. J., & Tibshirani, R. J. (1990). *Generalized Additive Models.* London: Chapman & Hall/CRC.

Hastie, T., Tibshirani, R., & Friedman, J. H. (2001). *The elements of statistical learning : Data mining, inference, and prediction.* New

York: Springer Verlag.

Hastie, T., Tibshirani, R., & Friedman, J. H. (2009). 10. Boosting and Additive Trees. In *The Elements of Statistical Learning* (pp. 337–384). New York: Springer.

Hayashi, F. (2000). *Econometrics.* Princeton: Princeton University Press.

Hayward, R. (2004). Clinical decision support tools: Do they support clinicians? *FUTURE Practice*, 66-68.

Hebb, D. (1949). *The Organization of Behavior.* New York: Wiley.

Henschen, D. (2009, February 9). Oh My Darling! SPSS Says Goodbye Clementine, Hello 'PASW'. *Information Week*. Retrieved from http://www.informationweek.com/software/information-management/oh-my-darling!-spss-says-goodbye-clementine-hello-pasw/d/d-id/1078486?

Hinkelmann, K., & Kempthorne, O. (2008). *The Design and Analysis of Experiments* (2nd ed.). New York: Wiley.

Hinton, G. E., Osindero, S., & Teh, Y. (2006). A fast learning algorithm for deep belief nets. *Neural Computation, 18*(7), 1527–1554. doi:10.1162/neco.2006.18.7.1527

Ho, T. (1995). Random Decision Forest. *Proceedings of the 3rd International Conference on Document Analysis and Recognition*, (pp. 278–282). Montreal, QC. Retrieved from http://cm.bell-labs.com/cm/cs/who/tkh/papers/odt.pdf

Ho, T. (1998). The Random Subspace Method for Constructing Decision Forests. *IEEE Transactions on Pattern Analysis and Machine Intelligence*, 832–844. doi:10.1109/34.709601

Hofmann, M., & Klinkenberg, R. (2013). *RapidMiner: Data Mining Use Cases and Business Analytics Applications* (Vols. Chapman & Hall/CRC Data Mining and Knowledge Discovery Series, 33). CRC

Press.

Hopfield, J. (2007). Hopfield network. *Scholarpedia, 2*(5), 1977. doi:10.4249

Horváth, T., & Yamamoto, A. (2003). Inductive Logic Programming. In *Lecture Notes in Computer Science* (Vol. 2835). doi:10.1007/b13700

Hoskins, J., & Himmelblau, D. (1992). Process control via artificial neural networks and reinforcement learning. *Computers & Chemical Engineering, 16*(4), 241–251. doi:10.1016/0098-1354(92)80045-B

Hosmer, D. W., & Lemeshow, S. (2000). *Applied Logistic Regression* (2nd ed.). New York: Wiley-Interscience Publication.

Hothorn, T., Hornik, A., & Zeileis. (2006). Unbiased Recursive Partitioning: A Conditional Inference Framework. *Journal of Computational and Graphical Statistics, 15*(3), 651–674. doi:10.1198/106186006X133933

Howell, D. C. (2002). *Statistical methods for psychology.* Pacific Grove, CA: Duxbury/Thomson Learning.

Hsu, C., & Lin, C. (2002). A Simple Decomposition Method for Support Vector Machines. *Machine Learning, 46*, 291–314. Retrieved from http://www.csie.ntu.edu.tw/~cjlin/papers/decomp.ps.gz.

Hsu, C.-W., Chang, C.-C., & Lin, C.-J. (2010). *A practical guide to support vector classification.* National Taiwan University. Retrieved from http://www.csie.ntu.edu.tw/~cjlin/papers/guide/guide.pdf

Hyafil, L., & Rivest, R. (1976). Constructing Optimal Binary Decision Trees is NP-complete. *Information Processing Letters, 5*(1), 15–17. doi:10.1016/0020-0190(76)90095-8

I., B.-G., A., D., N., S., & Singer, G. (2014). Efficient Construction of

493

Decision Trees by the Dual Information Distance Method. *Quality Technology & Quantitative Management (QTQM), 11*(1), 133-147. Retrieved from http://www.eng.tau.ac.il/~bengal/DID.pdf

Imdadullah, M. (2014). Time Series Analysis. *Basic Statistics and Data Analysis.* Retrieved 2014, from http://itfeature.com/time-series-analysis-and-forecasting/time-series-analysis-forecasting

James, G., Witten, D., Hastie, T., & Tibshirani, R. (2013). *An Introduction to Statistical Learning.* New York: Springer.

Jekabsons, G. (2011). *ARESLab: Adaptive Regression Splines toolbox.* Retrieved from Open source regression software for Matlab/Octave: http://www.cs.rtu.lv/jekabsons/regression.html

Joachims, T. (1999). Transductive Inference for Text Classification using Support Vector Machines. *Proceedings of the 1999 International Conference on Machine Learning,* (pp. 200-209).

John, G. H., & Langley, P. (1995). Estimating Continuous Distributions in Bayesian Classifiers. *Proc. Eleventh Conf. on Uncertainty in Artificial Intelligence* (pp. 338–345). Morgan Kaufmann.

Johnson, M., & Raven, P. (1973). Species number and endemism: The Galapagos Archipelago revisited. *Science, 179*, 893-895.

Johnson, N. L., Kotz, S., & Kemp, A. (1992). *Discrete multivariate distributions* (2nd ed.). New York: John Wiley & Sons.

Kálmán, R. (1960). A new approach to linear filtering and prediction problems. *Journal of Basic Engineering, 82*(1), 35–45. doi:10.1115/1.3662552

Kaplan, E. L., & Meier, P. (1958). Nonparametric estimation from incomplete observations. *J. Amer. Statist. Assn., 53*(282), 457–481. Retrieved from http://www.jstor.org/stable/2281868

Karatzoglou, A., Smola, A., Hornik, K., & Zeileis, A. (2004). kernlab – An S4 Package for Kernel. *Journal of Statistical Software, 11*(9). Retrieved from http://www.jstatsoft.org/counter.php?id=105&url=v11/i09/v11i09.pdf&ct=1

Kass, G. V. (1980). An exploratory technique for investigating large quantities of categorical data. *Applied Statistics, 29*(2), 119–127. doi:10.2307/2986296

Kempthorne, O. (1979). *The Design and Analysis of Experiments* ((Corrected reprint of (1952) Wiley ed.) ed.). (R. Krieger, Ed.) New York: Wiley.

Kibriya, A., Frank, E., Pfahringer, B., & Holmes, G. (2008). *Multinomial Naive Bayes for Text Categorization Revisited.* University of \Vaikato, Department of Computer Science, Hamilton, New Zealand.

King, G. (2014, January). Restructuring the Social Sciences: Reflections from Harvard's Institute for Quantitative Social Science. *PS*, 165-172. doi:doi:10.1017/S1049096513001534

Kleinberg, E. (1996). An Overtraining-Resistant Stochastic Modeling Method for Pattern Recognition. *Annals of Statistics, 24*(6), 2319–2349. doi:10.1214/aos/1032181157

Kohonen, T., & Honkela, T. (2007). Kohonen Network. *Scholarpedia, 2*(1), 1568. doi:10.4249

Kooperberg, C. (2013). *Polynomial spline routines.* Retrieved from CRAN Project: http://cran.r-project.org/web/packages/polspline/index.html

Korn, S. (2011). *The Opportunity for Predictive Analytics in Finance.* San Diego: HPC Wire. Retrieved 2014, from http://www.hpcwire.com/2011/04/21/the_opportunity_for_pr

edictive_analytics_in_finance/

Kovahi, R., & Provost, F. (1998). Glossary of terms. *Machine Learning, 30*, 271–274.

Kuncheva, L., Rodríguez, J., Plumpton, C., Linden, D., & Johnston, S. (2010). Random subspace ensembles for fMRI classification. *IEEE Transactions on Medical Imaging, 29*(2), 531–542. Retrieved from http://pages.bangor.ac.uk/~mas00a/papers/lkjrcpdlsjtmi10.pdf

Lawson, C. L., & Hanson, R. J. (1995). *Solving Least Squares Problems.* Philadelphia: Society for Industrial and Applied Mathematics.

Lee, Y., Lin, Y., & Wahba, G. (2001). Multicategory Support Vector Machines. *Computing Science and Statistics, 33*. Retrieved from http://www.interfacesymposia.org/I01/I2001Proceedings/YLee /YLee.pdf

Leisch, F., Hornik, K., & Ripley, B. (2013). *Mixture and flexible discriminant analysis, multivariate adaptive regression splines (MARS).* Retrieved from CRAN Project: http://cran.r-project.org/web/packages/mda/index.html

Liaw, A. (2012, October 16). *Documentation for R package randomForest.* Retrieved from The Comprehensive R Archive Network: http://cran.r-project.org/web/packages/randomForest/randomForest.pdf

Lin, C., & More, J. (1999). Newton's Method for Large-scale Bound Constrained Problems. *SIAM Journal on Optimization,, 9*, 1100–1127. Retrieved from http://www-unix.mcs.anl.gov/~more/tron/

Lin, J., Keogh, E., Lonardi, S., & Chiu, B. (2003). A symbolic representation of time series, with implications for streaming algorithms. *Proceedings of the 8th ACM SIGMOD workshop on Research issues in data mining and knowledge discovery.* New York: ACM Pr. doi:10.1145/882082.882086

Lin, Y., & Jeon, Y. (2001). *Random forests and adaptive nearest neighbors.* Technical Report No. 1055, University of Wisconsin. Retrieved from http://citeseerx.ist.psu.edu/viewdoc/summary?doi=10.1.1.153.9168

Lo, V. S. (2002). The True Lift Model. *ACM SIGKDD Explorations Newsletter, 4*(2), 78–86.

Lu, H., Plataniotis, K., & Venetsanopoulos, A. (2011). A Survey of Multilinear Subspace Learning for Tensor Data. *Pattern Recognition, 44*(7), 1540–1551. doi:10.1016/j.patcog.2011.01.004

Łukaszyk, S. (2004). A new concept of probability metric and its applications in approximation of scattered data sets. *Computational Mechanics, 33*, 299-300. Retrieved 2014

MacLennan, J. (2012, September). *Polling and Statistical Models Can't Predict the Future.* Cameron Alverson. Retrieved 2014

Mangasarian, O., & Musicant, D. (1999). Successive Overrelaxation for Support Vector Machines. *IEEE Transactions on Neural Networks, 10*, 1032–1037. Retrieved from ftp://ftp.cs.wisc.edu/math-prog/tech-reports/98-18.ps

Mannila, H. (1996). Data mining: machine learning, statistics, and databases. *Int'l Conf. Scientific and Statistical Database Management.* IEEE Computer Society.

Marascuilo, L. A. (1977). *Nonparametric and distribution-free methods for the social sciences.* Brooks/Cole Publishing Co.

Mark, J., & Goldberg, M. (2001). Multiple Regression Analysis and Mass Assessment: A Review of the Issues. *The Appraisal Journal*, 89–

109.

Markoff, J. (2012, November 23). Scientists See Promise in Deep-Learning Programs. *New York Times*. Retrieved from http://www.nytimes.com/2012/11/24/science/scientists-see-advances-in-deep-learning-a-part-of-artificial-intelligence.html?_r=0

Maronna, R., Martin, D., & Yohai, V. Y. (2006). *Robust Statistics: Theory and Methods.* New York: Wiley.

MARS - Multivariate Adaptive Regression Splines . (n.d.). Retrieved from Salford Systems.

McCallum, A., & Nigam, K. (1998). A comparison of event models for Naive Bayes text classification. *AAAI-98 workshop on learning for text categorization* , (p. 752).

McCullagh, P., & Nelder, J. (1989). *Generalized Linear Models* (2nd ed.). Boca Raton: Chapman and Hall/CRC.

McCulloch, W., & Pitts, W. (1943). A Logical Calculus of Ideas Immanent in Nervous Activity. *Bulletin of Mathematical Biophysics, 5*(4), 115–133. doi:10.1007/BF02478259

McDonald, M. (2010). *New Technology Taps 'Predictive Analytics' to Target Travel Recommendations.* Oyster Bay: Travel Market Report. Retrieved 2014, from http://www.travelmarketreport.com/technology?articleID=4259&LP=1,

McKay, L. (2009, August). The New Prescription for Pharma. *Destination CRM*. Retrieved 2014, from http://www.destinationcrm.com/articles/Web-Exclusives/Web-Only-Bonus-Articles/The-New-Prescription-for-Pharma-55774.aspx

Menard, S. (2002). *Applied Logistic Regression* (2nd ed.). SAGE.

Metsis, V., Androutsopoulos, I., & Paliouras, G. (2006). Spam filtering with Naive Bayes—which Naive Bayes? *Third conference on email and anti-spam (CEAS)*, (p. 17).

Meyer, D., Leisch, F., & Hornik, K. (2003). The support vector machine under test. *Neurocomputing, 55*, 169. doi:10.1016/S0925-2312(03)00431-4

Microsoft Decision Trees Algorithm Technical Reference. (2014). Retrieved from Microsoft Technet: http://technet.microsoft.com/en-us/library/cc645868.aspx

Milborrow, S. (2011). *Earth - Multivariate adaptive regression splines* . Retrieved from Orange: http://orange.biolab.si/blog/2011/12/20/earth-multivariate-adaptive-regression-splines/

Milborrow, S. (2011). *Multivariate Adaptive Regression Spline Models*. Retrieved from CRAN Project: http://cran.r-project.org/web/packages/earth/index.html

Milborrow, S. (2014). *Notes on the earth package.* CRAN.org.

Minsky, M., & Papert, S. (1969). *An Introduction to Computational Geometry.* Boston: MIT Press.

Mirkes, E. (2011). *KNN and Potential Energy: applet.* University of Leicester.

Mitchell, T. (1997). *Machine Learning.* New York: McGraw-Hill.

Montgomery, D. C. (2001). *Design and Analysis of Experiments* (5th ed.). New York: Wiley.

Moore, D., & McCabe, G. (2003). *Introduction to the Practice of Statistics* (4e ed.). W H Freeman & Co.

Multivariate Adaptive Regression Splines (MARSplines). (n.d.). Retrieved

from   StatSoft:
http://www.statsoft.com/Textbook/Multivariate-Adaptive-
Regression-Splines

Myers, J. H., & Forgy, E. W. (1963). The Development of Numerical Credit
Evaluation Systems. *J. Amer. Statist. Assoc.*, *49*(12), 799–806.
doi:10.1080/01621459.1963.10500889

NASA. (2003). *NASA - Dryden Flight Research Center - News Room: News
Releases: NASA NEURAL NETWORK PROJECT PASSES
MILESTONE.* Nasa.gov.

Nelder, J., & Wedderburn, R. (1972). Generalized Linear Models. *Journal
of the Royal Statistical Society. Series A (General), 135*(3), 370–
384. doi:10.2307/2344614

Neyman, J. (1937). Outline of a Theory of Statistical Estimation Based on
the Classical Theory of Probability. *Philosophical Transactions of
the Royal Society of London A, 236*, 333–380. Retrieved from
http://www.jstor.org/discover/10.2307/91337

Nieto-Garcia, F., Bush, T., & Keyl, P. (1990). Body mass definitions of
obesity: sensitivity and specificity using self-reported weight and
height. *Epidemiology, 1*(2), 146–152.

Nigrini, M. (2011). *Forensic Analytics: Methods and Techniques for
Forensic Accounting Investigations.* Hoboken, NJ: John Wiley &
Sons Inc.

Nigsch, F., Bender, A., van Buuren, B., Tissen, J., Nigsch, E., & Mitchell, J.
(2006). Melting point prediction employing k-nearest neighbor
algorithms and genetic parameter optimization. *Journal of
Chemical Information and Modeling, 46*(6), 2412–2422.
doi:10.1021/ci060149f

Nikulin, M. (2001). Loss function. In M. Hazewinkel, *Encyclopedia of
Mathematics.* New York: Springer.

NIST. (2012). Section 4.3.1 A Glossary of DOE Terminology. In *NIST/SEMATECH e-Handbook of Statistical Methods.* NIST.org.

NIST. (2012). Section 5.7 A Glossary of DOE Terminology. In *NIST/SEMATECH e-Handbook of Statistical Methods.* NIST.gov. Retrieved from http://www.itl.nist.gov/div898/handbook/

Nyce, C. (2007). *Predictive Analytics White Paper.* Malvern: American Institute for Chartered Property Casualty Underwriters/Insurance Institute of America. Retrieved 2014, from http://www.theinstitutes.org/doc/predictivemodelingwhitepaper.pdf

Palei, S. K., & Das, S. K. (2009). Logistic regression model for prediction of roof fall risks in bord and pillar workings in coal mines: An approach. *Safety Science, 47*, 88. doi:10.1016/j.ssci.2008.01.002

Papagelis, A. D. (2001). Breeding Decision Trees Using Evolutionary Techniques. *Proceedings of the Eighteenth International Conference on Machine Learning*, (pp. 393-400).

Parry, G. (1996, November–December). The characterization of uncertainty in Probabilistic Risk Assessments of complex systems. *Reliability Engineering & System Safety, 54*(2-3), 119–1. Retrieved 2014, from http://www.sciencedirect.com/science/article/pii/S0951832096000695

Pedregosa, F., Varoquaux, G., Gramfort, A., Michel, V., Thirion, B., Grisel, O., . . . Cournapeau, D. (2011). Scikit-learn: Machine Learning in Python. *Journal of Machine Learning Research, 12*, 2825–2830.

Peduzzi, P., Concato, J., Kemper, E., Holford, T., & Feinstein, A. (1996). A simulation study of the number of events per variable in logistic regression analysis. *Journal of Clinical Epidemiology, 49*(12), 1373–9. doi:10.1016/s0895-4356(96)00236-3

Peirce, C. S. (1992). *Reasoning and the Logic of Things, The Cambridge Conference Lectures of 1898.* (K. Ketner, Ed.) Cambridge, MA: Harvard University Press.

Penrose, R. (1955). A generalized inverse for matrices. *Proceedings of the Cambridge Philosophical Society, 51,* 406–413. doi:10.1017/S0305004100030401

Platt, J. (1999). Using Analytic QP and Sparseness to Speed Training of Support Vector Machines. *NIPS'99.* Retrieved from http://research.microsoft.com/en-us/um/people/jplatt/smo-nips.pdf

Platt, J., Cristianini, N., & Shawe-Taylor, J. (2000). Large margin DAGs for multiclass classification. In S. Solla, T. Leen, & K.-R. Müller, *Neural Information Processing Systems* (pp. 547–553). Boston: MIT Press.

Prentice, R., & Pyke, R. (1979). Logistic disease incidence models and case-control studies. *Biometrika, 66*(3), 403-411. doi:10.1093/biomet/66.3.403

Press, W., Teukolsky, S., Vetterling, W., & Flannery, B. (2007). Section 16.5. Support Vector Machines. In *Recipes: The Art of Scientific Computing* (3rd ed.). New York: Cambridge University Press.

Prinzie, A. V. (2008). Random Forests for multiclass classification: Random MultiNomial Logit. *Expert Systems with Applications, 34*(3), 1721–1732. doi:10.1016/j.eswa.2007.01.029

Prinzie, A., & Van den Poel, D. (2008). Random Forests for multiclass classification: Random MultiNomial Logit". *Expert Systems with Applications, 34*(3), 1721–1732.

Quinlan, J. R. (1986). Induction of Decision Trees. *Machine Learning, 1,* 81-106.

Radcliffe, N. J. (2007). Using Control Groups to Target on Predicted Lift:

Building and Assessing Uplift Models. *Direct Marketing Analytics Journal, Direct Marketing Association*, 14-21.

Radcliffe, N. J., & Surry, P. D. (1999). Differential response analysis: Modelling true response by isolating the effect of a single action. In *Proceedings of Credit Scoring and Credit Control VI*. Edinburgh: Credit Research Centre, University of Edinburgh Management School.

Radcliffe, N., & Surry, P. (2011). *Real-World Uplift Modelling with Significance-Based Uplift Trees*. Stochastic Solutions White Paper 2011.

Rao, C. (1973). *Linear statistical inference and its applications* (2nd ed.). New York: John Wiley & Sons.

Ree, M. J., Carretta, T. R., & Earles, J. A. (1998). In top-down decisions, weighting variables does not matter: A consequence of Wilk's theorem. *Organizational Research Methods, 1*(4), 407-420. doi:10.1177/109442819814003

Rennie, J., Lawrence, S., Teevan, J., & Karger, D. (2003). Tackling the Poor Assumptions of Naive Bayes Text Classi. *Proceedings of the Twentieth International Conference on Machine Learning (ICML-2003)*. Washington, DC.

Rennie, J., Shih, L., Teevan, J., & Karger, D. (2003). *Tackling the poor assumptions of Naive Bayes classifiers*. ICML. Retrieved 2014, from http://people.csail.mit.edu/jrennie/papers/icml03-nb.pdf

Rexer, K., Allen, H., & Gearan, P. (2011). 2011 Data Miner Survey Summary. *Procedings of Predictive Analytics World*.

Ridgeway, G. (2007). *Generalized Boosted Models: A guide to the gbm package*. Retrieved from http://cran.r-project.org/web/packages/gbm/gbm.pdf

Riedmiller, M. (2010). *Machine Learning: Multi Layer Perceptrons*.

Albert-Ludwigs-University. Freiburg: AG Maschinelles Lernen. Retrieved 2014, from http://ml.informatik.uni-freiburg.de/_media/teaching/ss10/05_mlps.printer.pdf

Riesenhuber, M., & Poggio, T. (1999). Hierarchical models of object recognition in cortex. *Nature neuroscience*.

Rish, I. (2001). An empirical study of the naive Bayes classifier. *IJCAI 2001 workshop on empirical methods in artificial intelligence, 3*, pp. 41-46.

Robbins, H. (1956). An Empirical Bayes Approach to Statistics. *Proceedings of the Third Berkeley Symposium on Mathematical Statistics and Probability, Volume 1: Contributions to the Theory of Statistics* (pp. 157–163). Berkeley, CA: University of California Press. Retrieved from http://projecteuclid.org/euclid.bsmsp/1200501653

Rochester, N., Holland, J., Habit, L., & Duda, W. (1956). Tests on a cell assembly theory of the action of the brain, using a large digital computer. *IRE Transactions on Information Theory, 2*(3), 80–93. doi:10.1109/TIT.1956.1056810

Rodriguez, J., Kuncheva, L., & Alonso, C. (2006). Rotation forest: A new classifier ensemble method. *IEEE Transactions on Pattern Analysis and Machine Intelligence, 28*(10), 1619-1630.

Rokach, L., & Maimon, O. (2005). Top-down induction of decision trees classifiers-a survey. *IEEE Transactions on Systems, Man, and Cybernetics, Part C, 35*(4), 476–487. doi:10.1109/TSMCC.2004.843247

Rokach, L., & Maimon, O. (2008). *Data mining with decision trees: theory and applications.* World Scientific Pub Co Inc.

Rosenbaum, P. R. (2002). *Observational Studies* (2nd ed.). New York: Springer-Verlag.

Rosenblatt, F. (1958). Perceptron: A Probalistic Model For Information Storage And Organization In The Brain. *Psychological Review, 65*(6), 386–408. doi:10.1037/h0042519

Rousseeuw, P. J., & Leroy, A. M. (2003). *Robust Regression and Outlier Detection.* New York: Wiley.

Rudy, J. (2013). *py-earth* . Retrieved from jcrudy: https://github.com/jcrudy/py-earth/

Rumelhart, D., & McClelland, J. (1986). *Parallel Distributed Processing: Explorations in the Microstructure of Cognition.* Boston: MIT Press.

Russell, I. (1996). *Neural Networks Module.* Retrieved from University of Hartford : http://uhaweb.hartford.edu/compsci/neural-networks-definition.html

Russell, S., & Norvig, P. (2003). *Artificial Intelligence: A Modern Approach* (2nd ed.). Prentice Hall.

Rzepakowski, P., & Jaroszewicz, S. (2010). Decision trees for uplift modeling with single and multiple treatments. *The 10th IEEE International Conference on Data Mining.* Sydney, Australia. doi:10.1109/ICDM.2010.62

Sahu, A., Runger, G., & Apley, D. (2011). Image denoising with a multi-phase kernel principal component approach and an ensemble version. *IEEE Applied Imagery Pattern Recognition Workshop*, (pp. 1-7).

Scheffé, H. (1959). *The Analysis of Variance.* New York: Wiley.

Schiff, M. (2012, March 6). *BI Experts: Why Predictive Analytics Will Continue to Grow.* Renton: The Data Warehouse Institute. Retrieved 2014, from http://tdwi.org/Articles/2012/03/06/Predictive-Analytics-Growth.aspx?Page=1

Schmidhuber, J. (2012). On the eight competitions won by his Deep Learning team 2009–2012. (A. Kurzweil, Interviewer) Retrieved from http://www.kurzweilai.net/how-bio-inspired-deep-learning-keeps-winning-competitions

Seber, G. A., Lee, & J., A. (2003). *Linear Regression Analysis* . New York: Wiley.

Secomandi, N. (2000). Comparing neuro-dynamic programming algorithms for the vehicle routing problem with stochastic demands. *Computers & Operations Research, 27*(11-12), 1201–1225. doi:10.1016/S0305-0548(99)00146-X

Senn, S. (2003). A conversation with John Nelder. *Statistical Science, 18*(1), 118–131. doi:10.1214/ss/1056397489

Shalev-Shwartz, S., Singer, Y., & Srebro, N. (2007). Pegasos: Primal Estimated sub-GrAdient SOlver for SVM. *ICML'07*. Retrieved from http://ttic.uchicago.edu/~shai/papers/ShalevSiSr07.pdf

Shasha, D. (2004). *Performance Discovery in Time Series.* Berlin: Springer.

Shaw, B., & Jebara, T. (2009). Structure preserving embedding. *Proceedings of the 26th Annual International Conference on Machine Learning.* ACM.

Sheskin, D. J. (2011). *Handbook of Parametric and Nonparametric Statistical Procedures.* Boca Raton, FL: CRC Press.

Shinde, A., Sahu, A., Apley, D., & Runger, G. (2014). Preimages for Variation Patterns from Kernel PCA and Bagging. *IIE Transactions, 46*(5).

Sibson, R. (1973). SLINK: an optimally efficient algorithm for the single-link cluster method. *The Computer Journal (British Computer Society), 16*(1), 30–34. doi:doi:10.1093/comjnl/16.1.30

Siegelmann, H., & Sontag, E. (1991). Turing computability with neural nets. *Appl. Math. Lett.,* 4(6), 77-80. doi:10.1016/0893-9659(91)90080-F

Singh, R., & Mukhopadhyay, K. (2011). Survival analysis in clinical trials: Basics and must know areas. *Perspect Clin Res, 2*(4), 145–148. doi:doi:10.4103/2229-3485.86872

Skurichina, M. (2002). Bagging, boosting and the random subspace method for linear classifiers. *Pattern Analysis and Applications, 5*(2), 121–135. doi:10.1007/s100440200011

Snedecor, G., & Cochran, W. (1989). *Statistical Methods* (8th ed.). Iowa State University Press.

Stasinopoulos, M., & Rigby, R. (2007). Generalized additive models for location scale and shape (GAMLSS) in R. *Journal of Statistical Software,* 23(7). Retrieved from http://www.jstatsoft.org/v23/i07

STATISTICA Data Miner . (2012). Retrieved from STATISTICA: http://www.statsoft.com/Products/STATISTICA/Data-Miner

Stevenson, E. (2011, December 16). Tech Beat: Can you pronounce health care predictive analytics? *Times-Standard.* Retrieved 2014, from http://www.times-standard.com/business/ci_19561141

Steyerberg, E. W. (2010). *Clinical Prediction Models.* New York: Springer.

Stigler, S. M. (1986). *The history of statistics : the measurement of uncertainty before 1900.* Cambridge, MA: Belknap Press of Harvard University Press.

Strano, M., & Colosimo, B. (2006). Logistic regression analysis for experimental determination of forming limit diagrams. *International Journal of Machine Tools and Manufacture, 46*(6). doi:10.1016/j.ijmachtools.2005.07.005

507

Strickland, J. (2005). *Random Variate Generation: @Risk Simulation Modeling.* Fort Lee: US ALMC. Retrieved from http://simulation-educators.com/uploads/2/7/7/2/2772366/sim_04.pdf

Strickland, J. (2013). *Introduction toe Crime Analysis and Mapping.* Lulu.com. Retrieved from http://www.lulu.com/shop/jeffrey-strickland/introduction-to-crime-analysis-and-mapping/paperback/product-21628219.html

Strobl, C., Malley, G., & Tutz. (2009). An Introduction to Recursive Partitioning: Rationale, Application and Characteristics of Classification and Regression Trees, Bagging and Random Forests. *Psychological Methods, 14*(4), 323–348. doi:10.1037/a0016973

Stromberg, A. J. (2004). Why write statistical software? The case of robust statistical methods. *Journal of Statistical Software.* Retrieved from http://www.jstatsoft.org/v10/i05/paper

Strukov, D. B., Snider, G. S., Stewart, D. R., & Williams, R. S. (2008). Nature 2008. *453*, 80–83.

Suykens, J. A., & Vandewalle, J. P. (1999). Least squares support vector machine classifiers. *Neural Processing Letters, 9*(3), 293–300.

Tan, J., & Dowe, D. (2004). MML Inference of Decision Graphs with Multi-Way Joins and Dynamic Attributes. Retrieved from http://www.csse.monash.edu.au/~dld/Publications/2003/Tan+Dowe2003_MMLDecisionGraphs.pdf

Tao, D. (2006). Asymmetric bagging and random subspace for support vector machines-based relevance feedback in image retrieval. *IEEE Transactions on Pattern Analysis and Machine Intelligence.*

Terrell, D., & Scott, D. (1992). Variable kernel density estimation. *Annals of Statistics, 20*(3), 1236–1265. doi:10.1214/aos/1176348768

The ADAPTIVEREG Procedure. (n.d.). Retrieved from SAS Support.

The CLUSTER Procedure: Clustering Methods. (n.d.). In *SAS/STAT 9.2 Users Guide*. SAS Institute. Retrieved Retrieved 2014-12-26

The DISTANCE Procedure: Proximity Measures. (n.d.). In *SAS/STAT 9.2 Users Guide*. SAS Institute. Retrieved Retrieved 2014-12-26

The SPLICE dataset: Classification. (2010, October 19). Retrieved from Journal of Machine Learning Research: http://jmlr.org/papers/volume1/meila00a/html/node32.html

Tillmann, A. M. (2015). On the Computational Intractability of Exact and Approximate Dictionary Learning. *IEEE Signal Processing Letters, 22*(1), 45-19.

Tiwaria, A., & Sekhar, A. (2007). Workflow based framework for life science informatics. *Computational Biology and Chemistry, 31*(5-6), 305–319. doi:doi:10.1016/j.compbiolchem.2007.08.009

Tofallis, C. (2008). Least Squares Percentage Regression. *Journal of Modern Applied Statistical Methods, 7*, 526–534. doi:10.2139/ssrn.1406472

Tolosi, L., & Lengauer, T. (2011). Classification with correlated features: unreliability of feature ranking and solutions. *Bioinformatics*. doi:10.1093/bioinformatics/btr300

Toussaint, G. .. (2005). Geometric proximity graphs for improving nearest neighbor methods in instance-based learning and data mining. *International Journal of Computational Geometry and Applications, 15*(2), 101–150. doi:10.1142/S0218195905001622

Tremblay, G. (2004). Optimizing Nearest Neighbour in Random Subspaces using a Multi-Objective Genetic Algorithm. *17th International Conference on Pattern Recognition*, (pp. 208–211).

Tryon, R. C. (1939). *Cluster Analysis: Correlation Profile and Orthometric (factor) Analysis for the Isolation of Unities in Mind and Personality*. Edwards Brothers.

Uplift Modelling FAQ. (2007, September 27). Retrieved from The Scientific   Marketer: http://scientificmarketer.com/2007/09/uplift-modelling-faq.html

Venables, W. N., & Ripley, B. D. (2002). *Modern Applied Statistics with S.* New York: Springer.

Wainer, H., & Thissen, D. (1976). Three steps toward robust regression. *Psychometrika, 41*(1), 9-34. doi:10.1007/BF02291695

Wald, A. (1971). *Statistical decision functions* (2nd ed.). Chelsea Pub Co.

Walsh, B. (2004, April 26). *Markov Chain Monte Carlo and Gibbs Sampling.* Retrieved from Lecture Notes for EEB 581: http://web.mit.edu/~wingated/www/introductions/mcmc-gibbs-intro.pdf

Ward, J. H. (1963). Hierarchical Grouping to Optimize an Objective Function. *Journal of the American Statistical Association, 50*(301), 236–244. doi:doi:10.2307/2282967

Weisberg, S. (2005). *Applied Linear Regression* (3rd ed.). New York: Wiley.

Werbos, P. (1975). Beyond Regression: New Tools for Prediction and Analysis in the Behavioral Sciences.

Wernick, Yang, Brankov, Yourganov, & Strother. (2010, July 4). Machine Learning in Medical Imaging. *EEE Signal Processing Magazine, 27*(4), 25-38.

Wiener, W. (1942). *Extrapolation, Interpolation and Smoothing of Stationary Time Series.* Boston: MIT Press.

Wilkinson, L. (1999). Statistical Methods in Psychology Journals: Guidelines and Explanations. *American Psychologist, 54*(8), 594–604. doi:10.1037/0003-066X.54.8.594

Wilks, S. S. (1938). Weighting systems for linear functions of correlated variables when there is no dependent variable. *Psychometrika, 3*(1), 23-40. doi:10.1007/BF02287917

Willey, G. R. (1953). *Prehistoric Settlement Patterns in the Virú Valley, Peru.* Bureau of American Ethnology.

Witten, I., Frank, E., & Hall, M. (2011). *Data Mining: Practical machine learning tools and techniques* (3rd ed.). San Francisco: Morgan Kaufmann.

Wood, S. (2006). *Generalized Additive Models: An Introduction with R.* London: Chapman & Hall/CRC.

Wu, J., & Chen, E. (2009). "A Novel Nonparametric Regression Ensemble for Rainfall Forecasting Using Particle Swarm Optimization Technique Coupled with Artificial Neural Network. In H. Wang, Y. Shen, T. Huang, & Z. Zeng, *6th International Symposium on Neural Networks, ISNN 2009.* New York: Springer. doi:10.1007/978-3-642-01513-7_6

Wu, T., Lin, C., & Weng, R. (2003). Probability Estimates for Multi-class Classification by Pairwise Coupling. *Advances in Neural Information Processing, 16.* Retrieved from http://books.nips.cc/papers/files/nips16/NIPS2003_0538.pdf

Yang, J. J., Pickett, M. D., Li, X. M., Ohlberg, D. A., Stewart, D. R., & Williams, R. S. (2008). Nat. Nanotechnol. *3*, 429–433.

Yarnold, P. R., & Soltysik, R. C. (2004). *Optimal Data Analysis.* American Psychological Association.

Zeger, S., Liang, K., & Albert, P. (1988). Models for Longitudinal Data: A Generalized Estimating Equation Approach. *Biometrics, 44*(4), 1049–1060. doi:10.2307/2531734

Zhang, e. a. (2013). Agglomerative clustering via maximum incremental path integral. In *Pattern Recognition.*

Zhang, e. a. (October 7–13, 2012). Graph degree linkage: Agglomerative clustering on a directed graph. *12th European Conference on Computer Vision.* Florence, Italy. Retrieved from http://arxiv.org/abs/1208.5092

Zhang, H. (2004). The Optimality of Naive Bayes. *FLAIRS2004 conference.*

Zhong, J. (2009). Predictive Modeling & Today's Growing Data Challnges. *Predictive Analytics World.* San Francisco.

Zhu, Z., Chen, W., Wang, G., Zhu, C., & Chen, Z. (2009). P-packSVM: Parallel Primal grAdient desCent Kernel SVM. *ICDM'09.* Retrieved from http://people.csail.mit.edu/zeyuan/paper/2009-ICDM-Parallel.pdf

Index

CPSIA information can be obtained
at www.ICGtesting.com
Printed in the USA
BVHW081305090222
628402BV00001B/2